U0128843

普通高等教育"十一五"计算机类规划教材

计算机专业英语

Professional English in Computer Field

主编　霍宏涛

参编　王　宇　邵　翀

主审　刘　舒

机械工业出版社

本书是为开设计算机专业英语课程的普通高校和广大有志于自学计算机英语的人员而编写的教材。全书共 15 章，分为两大部分：一部分是传统的计算机科学技术领域，包括计算机系统、操作系统、数据库、数据结构、计算机网络等内容；另一部分是新兴的领域，包括信息安全与技术、地理信息系统、图像处理和电子商务等内容。每章包括两篇正文和两篇阅读材料以及练习。每篇正文后附有单词注解和难句翻译。正文属于精读、精讲的内容。阅读材料主要侧重相应领域的最新发展动态，选文主要来源于近三年的外文期刊和有关网站，目的是开拓学生的专业视野，激发学生的学习和阅读兴趣。本书内容新颖，选文来源宽泛，注重保持选文内容的原汁原味。

　　本书可以作为计算机类专业本科或者专科的专业英语教材，也可以作为信息类专业的选修教材，还可供参加计算机水平考试的考生、IT 行业的工程技术人员学习参考。

图书在版编目（CIP）数据

计算机专业英语/霍宏涛主编 . —北京：机械工业出版社，2007.5
普通高等教育"十一五"计算机类规划教材
ISBN 978-7-111-21424-3

Ⅰ. 计... Ⅱ. 霍... Ⅲ. 电子计算机—英语—高等学校—教材
Ⅳ. H31

中国版本图书馆 CIP 数据核字（2007）第 063311 号

机械工业出版社（北京市百万庄大街 22 号　邮政编码 100037）
策划编辑：刘丽敏　责任编辑：杨　娟　版式设计：冉晓华
封面设计：张　静　责任印制：杨　曦
北京富生印刷厂印刷
2007 年 6 月第 1 版第 1 次印刷
184mm×260mm・20.5 印张・504 千字
标准书号：ISBN 978-7-111-21424-3
定价：29.00 元

前　言

计算机和信息技术的领跑者是以美国为首的英语系国家，所涉及的文献资料都以英语作为载体。因此，英语是 IT 领域的行业性语言，有着其他语言所无法替代的功能。很难想象一个不熟悉英语的人如何从事与计算机相关的工作和学习。而且，计算机科学技术的发展日新月异，这就要求计算机类专业的本科生必须具备熟练阅读有关的英文参考资料，如原版教材、科技期刊、联机文档和设备说明书的能力。因为计算机领域每天都有新的理论、技术、软件诞生，所以计算机专业英语的教材必须做到与时俱进、及时更新。学生通过一个学期的专业英语学习，应该不仅可以基本具备阅读各类英文文献的能力，而且可以及时了解计算机各领域的最新发展动态，并达到拓宽视野的目的。基于此，我们编写了本书。

全书共分 15 章，主要分为两大部分：一部分是传统的计算机科学技术领域，包括计算机系统、操作系统、数据库、数据结构、计算机网络等内容；另一部分是新兴的领域，包括信息安全与技术、地理信息系统、图像处理和电子商务等内容。每章包括两篇正文和两篇阅读材料以及练习。每篇正文后附有单词注解和难句翻译。单词以计算机的技术术语为主，句子则以句法复杂、具有专业英语句子特征的长句为主。两篇正文力求从经典文献（原版教材、科技期刊）中选取与本章主题有关的文章，长度为 1500～2000 词，具有一定的难度。正文通过教师讲授，学生加以复习即可掌握，属于精读、精讲的内容。阅读材料主要侧重于相应领域的最新发展动态，选文主要来源于近三年的外文期刊和有关网站，目的是开拓学生的专业视野、补充学生的专业知识、激发学生的学习和阅读兴趣。

本教材主要具有以下特色：一是内容新。全书 15 章基本做到了每章至少有 1 篇选自近三年的国外期刊和网站的文章。学生在学习掌握经典技术术语、培养英文阅读能力的同时，可以及时掌握最新的技术发展动态，进而为主动追踪有关的技术发展提供语言基础。二是选文来源宽泛。有些专业英语选文侧重于正规外文教材，这样的文章文字严谨，语法、用词规范，但学生学习工作时遇到最多的不是英文教材，而是英文期刊、联机文档和网站信息，这是由本科应用型人才培养的目标所决定的。因此，编者在选文时，既包括教材、期刊，又包括联机文档和 IT 类的技术网站。文章风格迥异，用词、句法都有差别，能够更好地培养学生的阅读能力，增强其适应性。三是尽量保持选文的原汁原味。一些教材在选文时由于篇幅限制等原因，删减较大，破坏了文章的整体性，也不利于学生阅读能力的培养。我们在选文时尽量保持原文的内容，除了格式和插图的调整外，基本上对内容不作改动。学生可以直观感受到自己阅读一篇专业论文所需的时间和内容掌握程度。四是没有全文翻译。编者认为，专业英语课程的主要目的是培养学生的英语阅读能力，而非"翻译"能力。英语阅读能力的目标就是不需翻译而直接消化、理解文章的内容。随着阅读能力的提高，翻译过程必将消失。同时，我们在翻译难句时，也体会到句子的翻译在一定程度上是一个"信息损失"的过程。因此，本书没有将任何一篇文章进行全文翻译，难句翻译也是尽量压缩。目的就是要克服学生的翻译依赖心理，直接消化内容。

本书可以作为计算机类专业本科或者专科的专业英语教材，也可以作为信息类专业的选修教材。讲授课时在 36 学时左右。本书对于计算机专业的学生熟悉、掌握国内外计算机领域的新理论、新技术、新工具具有重要意义，可以帮助学生熟练浏览国外有关的英文网站，阅读有关英文教材、期刊等文献资料。

本书由霍宏涛提出编写大纲，并负责全书的统稿和初审工作。王宇负责第 1～7 章的编写工作，邵翀负责第 8～11 章的编写工作，霍宏涛负责第 12～15 章的编写工作。龚秋平、杨明两位教师也参与了本书的编写工作。刘舒教授在百忙中审阅了本书的全部书稿，并提出了具体的意见和建议，在此表示衷心的感谢。

编　者
2007.6

Contents

Chapter One   The Fundamental of Computers

Unit 1   Computer Types

A computer is a machine that can be programmed to **manipulate** symbols. Its principal characteristics are:

- It responds to a specific set of instructions in a **well-defined** manner.
- It can execute a prerecorded list of instructions (a program).
- It can quickly **store** and **retrieve** large amounts of data.

Therefore computers can perform complex and repetitive procedures quickly, precisely and reliably. Modern computers are electronic and digital. The actual **machinery** (wires, transistors, and circuits) is called hardware; the instructions and data are called software. All **general-purpose computers** require the following hardware components:

- Central processing unit (CPU): The heart of the computer; this is the component that actually executes instructions organized in programs ("software") which tell the computer what to do.
- Memory (fast, expensive, short-term memory): Enables a computer to store, at least temporarily, data, programs, and **intermediate** results.
- Mass storage device (slower, cheaper, long-term memory): Allows a computer to permanently retain large amounts of data and programs between jobs. Common mass storage devices include disk drives and tape drives.
- Input device: Usually a keyboard and mouse; the input device is the **conduit** through which data and instructions enter a computer.
- Output device: A display screen, printer, or other device that lets you see what the computer has accomplished.

In addition to these components, many others make it possible for the basic components to work together efficiently.[1] For example, every computer requires a bus that transmits data from one part of the computer to another.

Computer Sizes and Power

Computers can be generally classified by size and power as follows, though there is considerable **overlap**:

- Personal computer: A small, single-user computer based on a microprocessor.
- Workstation: A powerful, single-user computer. A workstation is like a personal computer, but it has a more powerful microprocessor and, in general, a higher-quality monitor.

- Minicomputer: A multi-user computer capable of supporting up to hundreds of users.
- **Mainframe**: A powerful multi-user computer capable of supporting many hundreds or thousands of users simultaneously.
- Supercomputer: An extremely fast computer that can perform hundreds of millions of instructions per second.

1.1 Supercomputer and Mainframe

Supercomputer is a broad term for one of the fastest computers currently available. Supercomputers are very expensive and are employed for specialized applications that require immense amounts of mathematical calculations. For example, weather forecasting requires a supercomputer. Other uses of supercomputers scientific simulations, (animated) graphics, fluid dynamic calculations, nuclear energy research, electronic design, and analysis of geological data (e. g. in petrochemical prospecting). Perhaps the best known supercomputer manufacturer is Cray Research.

Mainframe was a term originally referring to the cabinet containing the central processor unit.[2] After the emergence of smaller "minicomputer" designs in the early 1970s, the traditional big iron machines were described as "mainframe computers" and eventually just as mainframes. Nowadays a mainframe is a very large and expensive computer capable of supporting hundreds, or even thousands, of users simultaneously. The chief difference between a supercomputer and a mainframe is that a supercomputer channels all its power into executing a few programs as fast as possible, whereas a mainframe uses its power to execute many programs concurrently. In some ways, mainframes are more powerful than supercomputers because they support more simultaneous programs. But supercomputers can execute a single program faster than a mainframe. The distinction between small mainframes and minicomputers is vague, depending really on how the manufacturer wants to market its machines.

1.2 Minicomputer

It is a midsize computer. In the past decade, the distinction between large minicomputers and small mainframes has blurred, however, as has the distinction between small minicomputers and workstations. But in general, a minicomputer is a multiprocessing system capable of supporting from up to 200 users simultaneously.

1.3 Workstation

It is a type of computer used for engineering applications (CAD/CAM), desktop publishing, software development, and other types of applications that require a **moderate** amount of computing power and relatively high quality graphics capabilities. Workstations generally come with a large, high-resolution graphics screen, at large amount of RAM, built-in network support, and a graphical user interface. Most workstations also have a mass storage device such as a disk drive, but a special type of workstation, called a diskless workstation, comes without a disk drive. The most common operating systems for workstations are UNIX and Windows NT. Like personal computers, most workstations are single-user computers. However, workstations are typically linked together to form a local-area network, although they can also be used as stand-alone systems.

1.4　Personal Computer

It can be defined as a small, relatively inexpensive computer designed for an individual user. In price, personal computers range anywhere from a few hundred pounds to over five thousand pounds. All are based on the microprocessor technology that enables manufacturers to put an entire CPU on one chip. Businesses use personal computers for word processing, accounting, desktop publishing, and for running **spreadsheet** and database management applications. At home, the most popular use for personal computers is for playing games and recently for **surfing** the Internet. Personal computers first appeared in the late 1970s. One of the first and most popular personal computers was the Apple II, introduced in 1977 by Apple Computer. During the late 1970s and early 1980s, new models and competing operating systems seemed to appear daily. Then, in 1981, IBM entered the **fray** with its first personal computer, known as the IBM PC. The IBM PC quickly became the personal computer of choice, and most other personal computer manufacturers fell by the wayside. P. C. is short for personal computer or IBM PC. One of the few companies to survive IBM's **onslaught** was Apple Computer, which remains a major player in the personal computer marketplace. Other companies adjusted to IBM's dominance by building IBM **clones**, computers that were internally almost the same as the IBM PC, but that cost less. Because IBM clones used the same microprocessors as IBM PCs, they were capable of running the same software. Over the years, IBM has lost much of its influence in directing the evolution of PCs. Therefore after the release of the first PC by IBM the term PC increasingly came to mean IBM or IBM-compatible personal computers, to the exclusion of other types of personal computers, such as Macintoshes. In recent years, the term PC has become more and more difficult to **pin down.** In general, though, it applies to any personal computer based on an Intel microprocessor, or on an Intel-compatible microprocessor. For nearly every other component, including the operating system, there are several options, all of which fall under the rubric of PC. [3]

Today, the world of personal computers is basically divided between Apple Macintoshes and PCs. The principal characteristics of personal computers are that they are single-user systems and are based on microprocessors. However, although personal computers are designed as single-user systems, it is common to link them together to form a network. In terms of power, there is great variety. At the **high-end**, the distinction between personal computers and workstations has faded. High-end models of the Macintosh and PC offer the same computing power and graphics capability as **low-end** workstations by Sun Microsystems, Hewlett-Packard, and DEC.

Key Words

manipulate	*v.* 操作，控制
well-defined	*adj.* 明确定义的

store	v. 存储
retrieve	v. 获取，获得
machinery	n. 机械装置
general-purpose computer	通用计算机，一般用途的计算机
intermediate	adj. 中间的
conduit	n. 导线管
overlap	n. 重叠
mainframe	n. 大型计算机
moderate	adj. 中等的，适度的
spreadsheet	n. 电子表格程序
surf	v. 浏览（专指上网浏览，和 Internet 连用）
fray	n. 竞争
onslaught	n. 猛攻
clone	n. 克隆，仿制，仿造
pin down	确定，明确
high-end	adj. 高端的
low-end	adj. 低端的

Notes

1. In addition to these components, many others make it possible for the basic components to work together efficiently.

除了这些组成元素之外，还有一些其他的部分使得这些基本的组成元素能够一起有效地工作。

2. Mainframe was a term originally referring to the cabinet containing the central processor unit.

"大型机"这个词最早是指包含中央处理器单元的柜子。

3. For nearly every other component, including the operating system, there are several options, all of which fall under the rubric of PC.

包括操作系统在内的几乎每个组成元素都有多个符合 PC 规定的选项。

Unit 2　The Year 2038 Problem

1.　What's So Special about 2038？

Early UNIX programmers had quite a sense of humor. In their documentation for the tunefs utility, a command-line program that fine-tuned the file system on the machine's hard disk, a note at the end reads "You can tune a file system, but you can't tune a fish". A later generation of UNIX authors, fearful that stuffy, humorless corporate drones would remove this cherished **pun**, added a programmer's comment inside the documentation's source code that read, "Take this out and a UNIX demon will dog your steps until the time _ t's **wrap around**!"[1]

On January 19, 2038, that is precisely what's going to happen.

For the uninitiated, time _ t is a data type used by C and C++ programs to represent dates and times internally. (You, Windows programmers out there might, also recognize it as the basis for the CTime and CTimeSpan classes in MFC.) time _ t is actually just an integer, a whole number, that counts the number of seconds since January 1, 1970 at 12:00 AM Greenwich Mean Time. A time _ t value of 0 would be 12:00:00 AM (exactly midnight) 1-Jan-1970, a time _ t value of 1 would be 12:00:01 AM (one second after midnight) 1-Jan-1970, etc. Since one year lasts for a little over 31,000,000 seconds, the time _ t representation of January 1, 1971 is about 31,000,000, the time _ t representation for January 1, 1972 is about 62,000,000, et cetera.

By the year 2038, the time _ t representation for the current time will be over 2,140,000,000. And that's the problem. A modern 32-bit computer stores a "signed integer" data type, such as time _ t, in 32 bits. The first of these bits is used for the positive/negative sign of the integer, while the remaining 31 bits are used to store the number itself. The highest number these 31 data bits can store works out to exactly 2,147,483,647. A time _ t value of this exact number, 2,147,483,647, represents January 19, 2038, at 7 seconds past 3:14 AM Greenwich Mean Time. So, at 3:14:07 AM GMT on that fateful day, every time _ t used in a 32-bit C or C++ program will reach its upper limit.

One second later, on 19-January-2038 at 3:14:08 AM GMT, disaster strikes.

2. What Will the Time _ t's Do When This Happens?

Signed integers stored in a computer don't behave exactly like an automobile's **odometer.** When a 5-digit odometer reaches 99, 999 miles, and then the driver goes one extra mile, the digits all "turn over" to 00000. But when a signed integer reaches its maximum value and then gets incremented, it wraps around to its lowest possible negative value. This means a 32-bit signed integer, such as a time _ t, set to its maximum value of 2,147,483,647 and then incremented by 1, will become − 2,147,483,648. Note that " − " sign at the beginning of this large number. A time _ t value of − 2, 147, 483, 648 would represent December 13, 1901 at 8:45:52 PM GMT.

So, if all goes normally, 19-January-2038 will suddenly become 13-December-1901 in every time _ t across the globe, and every date calculation based on this figure will go **haywire.** And it gets worse. Most of the support functions that use the time _ t data type cannot handle negative time _ t values at all. They simply fail and return an error code. Now, most "good" C and C++ programmers know that they are supposed to write their programs in such a way that each function call is checked for an error return, so that the program will still behave nicely even when things don't go as planned. But all too often, the simple, basic, everyday functions they call will "almost never" return an error code, so an error condition simply isn't checked for. It would be too tedious to check everywhere; and besides, the extremely rare conditions that result in the function's failure would "hardly ever" happen in the real world.[2] (Programmers: When was the last time you checked the return value from printf or malloc?) When one of the time_t support functions fails, the failure might not even be detected by the program calling it, and more often than not this means the calling program will crash.

3. Will Fixing Year 2000 Bugs Help Fix Year 2038 Bugs?

No. time_t is never, ever at fault in any Year 2000 bug.[3] Year 2000 bugs usually involve one of three things: the user interface, i. e. , what year do you assume if the user types in "00"; a database where only the last two digits are stored, i. e. , what year do you assume if the database entry contains a 00 for its year; and, in rare instances, the use of data items (such as the struct tm data structure's tm_year member in a C or C++ program) which store the number of years since 1900 and can result in displays like "19100" for the year 2000.

Year 2038 bugs, on the other hand, occur when a program reads in a date and carries it around from one part of itself to another.

You see, time_t is a convenient way to handle dates and times inside a C or C++ program. For example, suppose a program reads in two dates, date A and date B, and wants to know which date comes later. A program storing these dates as days, months, and years would first have to compare the years, then compare the months if the years were the same, then compare the days if the months were the same, for a total of 3 comparison operations. A program using time_t's would only have to compare the two time_t values against each other, for a total of 1 comparison operation. Additionally, adding one day to a date is much easier with a time_t than having to add 1 to the day, then see if that puts you past the end of the month, then increase the month and set the day back to 01 if so, then see if that puts you past the end of the year, et cetera. If dates are manipulated often, the advantage of using time_t's quickly becomes obvious. Only after the program is done manipulating its time_t dates, and wants to display them to the user or store them in a database, will they have to be converted back into days, months, and years.

So, even if you were to fix every Year 2000 bug in a program in such a way that users and databases could use years as large as 9999, it wouldn't even brush on any of the Year 2038 bugs **lurking** within the same program.

4. The Problem with Pooh-poohing

Admittedly, some of my colleagues don't feel that this **impending** disaster will strike too many people. They reason that, by the time 2038 rolls around, most programs will be running on 64-bit or even 128-bit computers. In a 64-bit program, a time_t could represent any date and time in the future out to 292,000,000,000 A. D. , which is about 20 times the currently estimated age of the universe.

The problem with this kind of optimism is the same root problem behind most of the Year 2000 concerns that **plagued** the software industry in previous years: **Legacy Code.** Developing a new piece of software is an expensive and time-consuming process. It's much easier to take an existing program that we know works, and code one or two new features into it, than it is to throw the earlier program out and write a new one from **scratch.** This process of enhancing and maintaining "legacy" source code can go on for years, or even decades. The MS-DOS layer still at the heart of Microsoft's Windows 98 and Windows ME was first written in 1981, and even it was a quick "port" (without many changes) of an earlier operating system called CP/M, which was written in the 1970s. Much of the financial software hit by the various Year 2000 bugs had also been used and maintained since the 1970s, when the year 2000 was still thought of as more of a science fiction movie title than an actual impending future. Surely, if this software had been written in the 1990s its Year 2000 Compliance would have been crucial to its authors, and it would have been designed with the year 2000 in mind. But it wasn't.

I should also mention that computer designers can no longer afford to make a "clean break" with the computer architectures of the past. No one wants to buy a new kind of PC if it doesn't run all their old PC's programs. So, just as the new generation of Microsoft Windows operating systems has to be able to run the old 16-bit programs written for Windows 3 or MS-DOS, so any new PC architecture will have to be able to run existing 32-bit programs in some kind of "**backward compatibility**" mode.

Even if every PC in the year 2038 has a 64-bit CPU, there will be a lot of older 32-bit programs running on them. And the larger, more complex, and more important any program is, the better are its chances that it'll be one of these old 32-bit programs. [4]

5. What about Making Time _ t Unsigned in 32-bit Software?

One of the quick-fixes that has been suggested for existing 32-bit software is to re-define time _ t as an unsigned integer instead of a signed integer. An unsigned integer doesn't have to waste one of its bits to store the plus/minus sign for the number it represents. This doubles the range of numbers it can store. Whereas a signed 32-bit integer can only go up to 2,147,483,647, an unsigned 32-bit integer can go all the way up to 4,294,967,295. A time _ t of this magnitude could represent any date and time from 12:00:00 AM 1-Jan-1970 all the way out to 6:28:15 AM 7-Feb-2106, surely giving us more than enough years for 64-bit software to dominate the planet.

It sounds like a good idea at first. We already know that most of the standard time _ t handling functions don't accept negative time _ t values anyway, so why not just make time _ t into a data type that only represents positive numbers?

Well, there's a problem. time _ t isn't just used to store absolute dates and times. It's also used, in many applications, to store differences between two date/time values, i. e. to answer the question of "How much time is there between date A and date B?". (MFC's CTimeSpan class is one notorious example.) In these cases, we do need time _ t to allow negative values. It is entirely possible that date B comes before date A. **Blindly** changing time _ t to an unsigned integer will, in these parts of a program, make the code unusable.

Changing time _ t to an unsigned integer would, in most programs, be robbing Peter to pay Paul. You'd fix one set of bugs (the Year 2038 Problem) only to introduce a whole new set (time differences not being computed properly).

6. Not Very Obvious, Is It?

The greatest danger with the Year 2038 Problem is its invisibility. The more-famous Year 2000 is a big, round number; it only takes a few seconds of thought, even for a **computer-illiterate** person, to imagine what might happen when 1999 turns into 2000. But January 19, 2038 is not nearly as obvious. Software companies will probably not think of trying out a Year 2038 **scenario** before **doomsday** strikes. Of course, there will be some warning ahead of time. Scheduling software, billing programs, personal reminder calendars, and other such pieces of code that set dates in the near future will fail as soon as one of their target dates exceeds 19-Jan-2038, assuming a time _ t is used to store them.

But the healthy paranoia that surrounded the search for Year 2000 bugs will be absent. Most software development departments are managed by people with little or no programming experience. (Dilbert's boss is an extreme case of this, but computer-illiterate software managers are more common than you might think.) It's the managers and their V. P. s that have to think up long-term plans and worst-case scenarios, and insist that their products be tested for them. Testing for dates beyond January 19, 2038 simply might not occur to them. And, perhaps worse, the parts of their software they had to fix for Year 2000 Compliance will be completely different from the parts of their programs that will fail on 19-Jan-2038, so fixing one problem will not fix the other.

Key Words

pun	*n.*	俏皮话
wrap around		回卷（指运算过界后，进位导致的符号位不合理的改变而引起的大数变小、小数变大的行为）
odometer	*n.*	里程表
haywire	*adj.*	混乱的
lurk	*v.*	潜伏
pooh-pooh	*v.*	轻视
impending	*adj.*	即将发生的
plague	*v.*	折磨
legacy code		难以替换的代码
scratch	*n.*	零，什么都没有（这里指一行代码都没有，需要程序员自己写）
backward compatibility		向后兼容
blindly	*adv.*	盲目地
computer-illiterate	*adj.*	计算机盲的，不懂计算机的
scenario	*n.*	方案
doomsday	*n.*	最后的审判日

Notes

1. A later generation of UNIX authors, fearful that stuffy, humorless corporate drones would remove this cherished pun, added a programmer's comment inside the documentation's source code that read, "Take this out and a UNIX demon will dog your steps until the time _ t's wrap around!"

一代后期的 UNIX 作者由于担心那些自命不凡、没有幽默感的企业里的"雄蜂"们会删掉这段他们心爱的俏皮话，于是在源代码文档上加了一段程序员的注释，"删掉它，UNIX demon 将会跟踪你所做的一切，直到 time _ t 函数发生回卷！"

2. It would be too tedious to check everywhere; and besides, the extremely rare conditions that result in the function's failure would "hardly ever" happen in the real world.

每个地方都检查是非常令人厌倦的，并且在现实生活中这种导致函数失败的极端情况是很难发生的。

3. time _ t is never, ever at fault in any Year 2000 bug.

time _ t 从来都不是一个"千年虫"问题。

4. And the larger, more complex, and more important any program is, the better are its chances that that it'll be one of these old 32-bit programs.

并且一个程序越庞大、越复杂、越重要，它越有可能是旧的 32 位的程序。

Reading Material 1　History of Electronic Digital Computers

The start of World War II produced a large need for computer capacity, especially for the military. New weapons were made for which trajectory tables and other essential data were needed. In 1942, John P. Eckert, John W. Mauchly, and their associates at the Moore school of Electrical Engineering of University of Pennsylvania decided to build a high-speed electronic computer to do the job. This machine became known as ENIAC (Electrical Numerical Integrator and Calculator).

The size of ENIAC's numerical "word" was 10 decimal digits, and it could multiply two of these numbers at a rate of 300 per second, by finding the value of each product from a multiplication table stored in its memory. ENIAC was therefore about 1,000 times faster than the previous generation of relay computers.

ENIAC used 18,000 vacuum tubes, about 1,800 square feet of floor space, and consumed about 180,000 watts of electrical power. It had punched card I/O, 1 multiplier, 1 divider/square rooter, and 20 adders using decimal ring counters, which served as adders and also as quick-access (.0002 seconds) read-write register storage. The executable instructions making up a program were embodied in the separate "units" of ENIAC, which were plugged together to form a "route" for the flow of information.

Fascinated by the success of ENIAC, the mathematician John Von Neumann undertook, in 1945, an abstract study of computation that showed that a computer should have a very simple, fixed physical structure, and yet be able to execute any kind of computation by means of a proper programmed control without the need for any change in the unit itself.

Von Neumann contributed a new awareness of how practical, yet fast computers should be organized and built. These ideas, usually referred to as the stored-program technique, became essential for future generations of high-speed digital computers and were universally adopted.

1.　Advances in the 1950s

Early in the 1950s two important engineering discoveries changed the image of the electronic-computer field, from one of fast but unreliable hardware to an image of relatively high reliability and even more capability. These discoveries were the magnetic core memory and the Transistor-Circuit Element. These technical discoveries quickly found their way into new models of digital computers. RAM capacities increased from 8,000 to 64,000 words in commercially available machines by the 1960s, with access times of 2 to 3 MS (Milliseconds). These machines were very expensive to purchase or even to rent and were particularly expensive to operate because of the cost of expanding programming. Such computers were mostly found in large computer centers operated by industry, government, and private laboratories-staffed with many programmers and support personnel. This situation led to modes of operation enabling the sharing of the high potential available.

One such mode is batch processing, in which problems are prepared and then held ready for computation on a relatively cheap storage medium. Magnetic drums, magnetic-disk packs, or magnetic tapes were usually used. When the computer finishes with a problem, it "dumps" the whole problem (program and results) on one of these peripheral storage units and starts on a new problem.

Another mode for fast, powerful machines is called time-sharing. In time-sharing, the computer processes many jobs in such rapid succession that each job runs as if the other jobs did not exist, thus keeping each "customer" satisfied. Such operating modes need elaborate executable programs to attend to the administration of the various tasks.

2. Advances in the 1960s

In the 1960s, efforts to design and develop the fastest possible computer with the greatest capacity reached a turning point with the LARC machine, built for the Livermore Radiation Laboratories of the University of California by the Sperry-Rand Corporation, and the Stretch computer by IBM. The LARC had a base memory of 98,000 words and multiplied in 10 Greek MU seconds. Stretch was made with several degrees of memory having slower access for the ranks of greater capacity, the fastest access time being less then 1 Greek MU second and the total capacity in the vicinity of 100,000,000 words.

CPUs for these uses did not have to be very fast arithmetically and were usually used to access large amounts of records on file, keeping these up to date. By far, the most number of computer systems were sold for the more simple uses, such as hospitals (keeping track of patient records, medications, and treatments given). They were also used in libraries, such as the National Medical Library retrieval system, and in the Chemical Abstracts System, where computer records on file now cover nearly all known chemical compounds.

3. More Recent Advances

The trend during the 1970s was, to some extent, moving away from very powerful, single-purpose computers and toward a larger range of applications for cheaper computer systems. Most continuous-process manufacturing, such as petroleum refining and electrical-power distribution systems, now used computers of smaller capability for controlling and regulating their jobs.

In the 1980s, very large scale integration (VLSI), in which hundreds of thousands of transistors were placed on a single chip, became more and more common. Many companies, some new to the computer field, introduced in the 1970s programmable minicomputers supplied with software packages. The "shrinking" trend continued with the introduction of personal computers (PCs), which are programmable machines small enough and inexpensive enough to be purchased and used by individuals.

Many companies, such as Apple Computer and Radio Shack, introduced very successful PCs in the 1970s, encouraged in part by a fad in computer (video) games. In the 1980s some friction occurred in the crowded PC field, with Apple and IBM keeping strong. In the manufacturing of semiconductor chips, the Intel and Motorola Corporations were very competitive into the 1980s, although Japanese firms were making strong economic advances, especially in the area of memory chips. By the late 1980s, some personal computers were run by microprocessors that, handling 32 bits of data at a time, could process about 4,000,000 instructions per second.

Reading Material 2　Cable vs. DSL

Life is full of hard choices: McDonald's or Burger King? Britney or Christina? Cable modem or DSL? Sometimes your options are indistinguishable (well, except that McDonald's fries are tastier), but in the case of broadband Internet services, one thing is crystal clear: both are vastly superior to slow 56Kbps dial-up connections.

There are about 16 million cable and DSL subscribers in the United States, and that number is steadily rising, according to research firm Instat-MDR. Still, that's only about 20 percent of all domestic Internet surfers. What about the rest of you? Isn't it time you moved into the fast lane?

A broadband connection isn't a miracle cure for sluggish Web surfing, but it isn't half bad. Most Web pages load at least three times faster using DSL or a cable modem than they do over dial-up. Broadband is also much swifter for downloading files, streaming video, or sending big e-mail attachments. If you work from home, need to access files on a company server, regularly move around big chunks of data, or surf the Net more than an hour per day, the time you'll save is easily worth the $40 to $50 cost per month of either service.

DSL and cable modem services are largely concentrated in high-population metro areas, so if you can get one type, you can probably get both. Which should you choose? Is one truly superior? Read on to uncover the reality.

1.　What Is DSL Internet Connection?

DSL uses a sophisticated modulation scheme to pack data onto copper wires. DSL is sometimes referred to as a last-mile technology because it is used only for connections from a telephone switching station to a home or office, not used between switching stations. DSL is also called an always on connection because it uses existing 2-wire copper telephone line connected to the premise and will not tie up your phone as a dial-up connection does. There is no need to dial in to your ISP as DSL is always on. The two main categories of DSL for home subscribers are called ADSL and SDSL.

ADSL: ADSL is the most commonly deployed type of DSL in North America. Short for asymmetric digital subscriber line (ADSL) supports data rates of from 1.5 to 9 Mbps when receiving data (known as the downstream rate) and from 16 to 640 Kbps when sending data (known as the upstream rate). ADSL requires a special ADSL modem.

SDSL: SDSL is still more common in Europe. Short for symmetric digital subscriber line, a technology allows more data to be sent over existing copper telephone lines (POTS). SDSL supports data rates up to 3 Mbps. SDSL works by sending digital pulses in the high-frequency area of telephone wires and can not operate simultaneously with voice connections over the same wires. SDSL requires a special SDSL modem. SDSL is called symmetric because it supports the same data rates for upstream and downstream traffic.

Two other types of DSL technologies are High-data-rate DSL (HDSL) and Very high DSL (VDSL). VDSL offers fast data rates over relatively short distances—the shorter the distance, the faster the connection rate. Collectively, all types of DSL are referred to as xDSL.

2. What Is a Cable Internet Connection?

Through the use of a cable modem you can have a broadband Internet connection that is designed to operate over cable TV lines. Cable Internet works by using TV channel space for data transmission, with certain channels used for downstream transmission, and other channels for upstream transmission. Because the coaxial cable used by cable TV provides much greater bandwidth than telephone lines, a cable modem can be used to achieve extremely fast access to the Web. This, combined with the fact that millions of homes are already wired for cable TV, has made cable Internet service something cable TV companies have really jumped onboard with.

3. Cable vs. DSL: The Speeds

The topic of "Which is better and faster" has been a highly debated topic, and still there doesn't appear to be a clear winner. DSL offers users a choice of speeds ranging from 144 Kbps to 1.5 Mbps. Cable modem download speeds are typically up to 2 times faster than 1.5 Mbps DSL, but the reason there is no clear speed winner is because cable technology is based on shared bandwidth, with many factors influencing a user's download speed. With shared bandwidth the speed fluctuates depending on the number of subscribers on the network. With DSL, the connection is yours and not shared, and you tend to have a more constant speed. This is one reason why cable Internet providers don't often publish speed information. In more rural areas with fewer subscribers, you're bound to have faster download speeds than a subscriber in a metropolitan center. Because cable modem speeds fluctuate, it is difficult to gauge an exact download speed. On the upload stream, however, cable and DSL are closely matched for speed. Both DSL and cable Internet speeds are largely dependant on the service provider and either the distance away from the switching station you are or how many subscribers are in your immediate area.

4. Cable vs. DSL: Home Networking & Security

Both DSL and cable Internet can easily be shared with computers on your home LAN through software (Microsoft Internet Connection Sharing for example) or by using a connection sharing device, such as a router and firewall software. Using a SOHO router is most-often the recommended option as this will also provide you with a much needed firewall protection for your LAN as well. It is important to check with your service provider, however, as sharing your broadband connect may violate your Terms of Service agreement. In many areas, service providers will allow you to connect additional computers to your broadband Internet service for a nominal fee. Because cable is shared connection, you are actually on a LAN with all subscribers in your areas. This would really create security issues only if no security measures are in place, but cable service providers generally provide cable modems with security features in the hardware. Overall the security of these broadband connections are closely matched, with DSL boasting a bit better security—and it is always advisable to consider purchasing additional hardware or software to protect your system, as your service provider may only provide the basics with the installation & set-up of your account.

5. Cable vs. DSL: The Price

The price consumers will pay for DSL or cable Internet services is not standard. It depends on how much competition there is for broadband services, and the area you live in. For example, in some areas it's only been in the past few years that cable Internet has been available. Until then, DSL costs were quite high, but as cable Internet became available the price of DSL went down. With either option you generally will pay a one-time set-up fee. For cable you could expect this fee to be anywhere from $50 to $100, while the cost for DSL installation is a bit more and could run up to $150 for set-up. Once the installation is completed, you will usually pay for your Internet subscription on a monthly basis. Cable, again, is usually a bit cheaper with monthly fees averaging $40 to $50. You can expect to pay about $5 to $10 more a month for DSL service.

If you live in an area where both cable and DSL is offered then you may find yourself being able to nab a better deal on your broadband service. Your local DSL or cable carrier may offer introductory offers such as free installation or offer the Internet service free for a couple months. In addition, you can also check and see if the service provider offer discounts on service bundles. For example, many cable companies offer discounts for "surf and watch" which gives you a price discount if you subscribe to both cable TV and cable Internet from the same provider (also many cable operators now offer VoIP capabilities as part of the mix). If you choose DSL you may qualify for a "surf and talk" bundle plan. If you're not already a broadband subscriber you can save money by checking with local service providers and signing up for your broadband account when you can catch a good deal.

Exercises

Ⅰ. Fill in the following blanks with proper words or phrases:

1. A computer is a machine that can be programmed to _____.

2. The actual machinery (wires, transistors, and circuits) of a computer is called _____; the instructions and data are called _____.

3. A small, single-user computer based on a microprocessor is call _____.

4. _____ is an extremely fast computer that can perform hundreds of millions of instructions per second.

5. Today, the world of personal computers is basically divided between Apple _____ and _____.

6. A modern 32-bit computer stores a _____ data type, such as time _ t, in 32 bits.

7. The maximum number of a 32-bit signed integer is _____.

8. The MS-DOS layer at the heart of Microsoft's Windows 98 and Windows ME was first written

in the year of _____.

    9. In a 64-bit program, a time _ t could represent any date and time in the future out to _____ A. D.

    10. For a 32-bit unsigned integer, the maximum year can be represented is _____.

Ⅱ. Answer the following questions:

1. What are the principal characteristics of a computer?

2. Please list the hardware components of general-purpose computers.

3. Give some different types of computer according to its size and power.

4. Describe the general hardware requirements of a workstation.

5. What will people usually do on a personal computer for business use and home use?

Chapter Two　Computer Architecture

Unit 1　Computer Motherboard

Computer systems, such as desktop computers, laptop computers, work stations, and servers, are information handling systems that are utilized by many individuals and businesses today. These computer systems typically include a system board, or motherboard, secured within a **chassis**, and a **multitude** of different internal components such as memory units, processor units, power systems, a cooling system, and various input/output PCI cards. A computer system may also include one or more built-in **peripheral devices**, including a keyboard, mouse, video display, and both serial and parallel ports. The main board, which is a printed circuit board known as a motherboard, is used to electrically connect these components together. Computers typically contain a **plurality** of integrated circuit packages that are mounted to a printed circuit board commonly referred to as a motherboard. The integrated circuit packages and printed circuit board are typically located within a protective chassis. The motherboard is the base of the computer system. The motherboard is the physical arrangement that contains the system's basic circuitry and components. Motherboards commonly include the basic functional units of a computer such as microprocessor, memory, basic input/output system (BIOS), expansion slots, and interconnecting circuitry. Additional components can be coupled to a motherboard through its expansion slots. Electronic system motherboards are becoming increasingly integrated to support a growing number of features. While a central processing unit (CPU) performs most computer jobs, it is really a motherboard that brings it all together to turn a CPU into a modern personal computer.

A typical motherboard comprises a large printed circuit board having a number of components mounted thereon, including a processor coupled to a host or local bus, a chipset, system memory coupled to a memory bus, and a peripheral component interconnect (PCI) bus. A chipset mounted to the motherboard by the manufacturer provides core logic that operatively links the CPU, the memory modules, and other components of the system. A read only memory (ROM) chip containing the system's startup program (**firmware**) is also mounted to the motherboard. The chipset bridges the PCI bus with the local bus and also bridges the PCI bus to each of an Industry Standard Architecture (ISA) bus and a Small Computer System Interface (SCSI) bus, if present. The chipset may also provide a system memory controller and bridge the memory bus to the local bus (as well as to the PCI bus). In addition, a motherboard typically includes input/output (I/O) connectors, floppy disk and hard disk drive connections, as well as circuitry for controlling any built-in peripheral devices e. g. , hard disk drives, floppy disk drives, and CD ROM drives. A typical motherboard housed within a personal computer comprises one or more layers of printed conductors extending at least partially across the motherboard. The printed conductors surface at localized regions of the motherboard. Those regions allow connection of integrated or discreet devices using various connection techniques, such as plug-and-socket, wire wrap, or solder. Modern motherboard systems further comprise a power saving mode. Typically, a computer motherboard includes many input/output (I/O) ports for connecting to various peripherals, and these I/O ports are arranged on the personal computer. Most personal computers also include a dedicated serial port, a **dedicated** keyboard port, and one or more expansion slots configured to receive expansion cards for **augmenting** the PC's functionality. [1] For example, a network expansion card can be inserted into an expansion slot of a general-purpose PC to provide a port for connecting that PC to a local area network (LAN).

Most personal computers are constructed with a single motherboard that provides connection for CPU and other components in the computer. Generally speaking, a motherboard is manufactured so that it can accommodate dissimilar microprocessors, or microprocessors which respond to differing system bus frequencies or power supply voltages. In a typical computer system, a motherboard is integrated with PCI slots to enable customers to plug different PCI cards into the computer for processing output signals. [2] For this reason, the computer chassis typically includes multiple slot openings covered with **clamps**, which hold the card in place and can be removed before and restored after plugging PCI cards onto the **slots.** This has been the prevailing configuration of computer chassis. The motherboard is typically permanently attached to the chassis and is also connected to other internal components via cables or internal connectors. In many systems, the motherboard generally extends in a plane between the chassis and the remaining internal components of the system. Most motherboards are secured to the chassis by screws. The motherboard is mounted to the chassis of the electronic device via a plurality of screws extending through holes in the board into the chassis. **Screws** are inserted through the openings in the chassis and into the openings that are provided in the motherboard for this purpose. The mounting holes on the motherboard are often surrounded by a grounding pad. The grounding pad is a conductive surface that is used as an electrical ground for the motherboard. To enhance the structural integrity of the computer assembly, the integrated circuit packages are typically soldered to the printed circuit board.

Motherboards and their host computer systems are typically required to meet specified standards for mechanical configuration such that system failures are reduced and component interchangeability is maintained. PC/XT is the original open motherboard standard created by IBM for the first home computer, the IBM-PC. The Baby AT (BAT) was also established by IBM at the **inception** of the IBM personal computer AT (Advanced Technology). The BAT motherboard has the advantage that it is very common, it is easy to insert add-in cards and the design places the central processing unit (CPU) module near the front of the chassis where it is cooled by incoming air. The BAT motherboard has the disadvantage that there is no expansion room for additional I/O connectors out the back of the motherboard. The LPX standard is based on a design by Western Digital, it allows for smaller cases based on the ATX motherboard by arranging the expansion cards in a **riser.** The LPX motherboard has the advantage that it is common. I/O is integrated on the motherboard and easily goes out the back of the chassis and the CPU usually placed near the front of chassis where it is cooled by incoming air. ATX is the evolution of the Baby AT form factor, it is now the most popular form factor available today. A full size ATX board is 12 " wide by 9. 6" deep (305mm × 244mm). This allows many ATX form factor chassis to accept microATX boards as well.

On the motherboard, in addition to the central processing unit (CPU), the chipset and the slots for installing the interface cards, the motherboard further includes the memory module slot to installing memory modules. The motherboard has a plurality of memory slots. Each of the plurality of memory slots has such a structure that a memory module can be inserted thereto or removed therefrom. A user can install his memory modules offered from different manufacturers with different numbers according to specific requirements. Typically, a memory module comprises several memory devices. The memory used in a normal computer such as the synchronous dynamic random access memory (SDRAM) operates to control data access in response to the rising edges of the system clock signals. The double data rate (DDR) dynamic random access memory can operate to control the data access on both the rising and falling edges of the system clocks. The DDR DRAM has advantage of performing at the double access rate in comparison with the conventional DRAM due to the upgraded memory access speed. According to different requirements of users, the amount of the memory module slots for installing memory modules is variable. In each memory module, several memory chips are arranged on a single module substrate.

A motherboard and one or more daughter boards (also referred to as a peripheral card, expansion board, or daughterboard) are used to transfer digital signals between respective assemblies used in a computer or other electronic equipment. The mother and daughter boards may be arranged perpendicular to each other, as in an edge card configuration, depending upon the design of the overall product. Daughter boards are coupled to a motherboard via sockets, to expand the functionality of the motherboard. The daughter boards may contain memory modules, or other expansion units to the motherboard. Generally, one or more card connectors are located on a motherboard, each card connector for receiving a peripheral card. The daughter boards are added to a computer system to enhance that system's capabilities. A peripheral card may provide a network interface, enhanced audio capability, or enhanced graphics. A peripheral card is typically PCI compatible or ISA compatible, such that the peripheral card (and connector) can be coupled to the PCI bus or ISA bus, respectively. The connection between the daughterboards and the motherboards is generally intended to provide for the transmission of power, ground and electrical signals between the daughterboard and the motherboard. [3]

Key Words

chassis	n.	底架
multitude	n.	许多
peripheral devices		外设
plurality	n.	多数
firmware	n.	固件 [储存于只读存储器 (ROM) 中的程序]

dedicated	*adj.* 专用的
augment	*v.* 扩展，增加
clamp	*n.* 夹钳
slot	*n.* 插槽
screw	*n.* 螺钉
inception	*n.* 初期，开端
riser	*n.* 竖板

Notes

1. Most personal computers also include a dedicated serial port, a dedicated keyboard port, and one or more expansion slots configured to receive expansion cards for augmenting the PC's functionality.

很多个人计算机都包括了一个专门的串口、键盘口和一个或者多个用于插接扩展卡来增强 PC 的功能的扩展插槽。

2. In a typical computer system, a motherboard is integrated with PCI slots to enable customers to plug different PCI cards into the computer for processing output signals.

在一个典型的计算机系统中，主板集成了 PCI 插槽，使得客户可以插入不同的 PCI 卡以处理输出信号。

3. The connection between the daughterboards and the motherboards is generally intended to provide for the transmission of power, ground and electrical signals between the daughterboard and the motherboard.

扩展板和主板的连接部分通常用于在扩展板和主板之间传输电能、接地信号和电信号。

Unit 2   Memory Hierarchy in Cache-based Systems

Despite improvements in technology, microprocessors are still much faster than main memory. Memory access time is increasingly the **bottleneck** in overall application performance. As a result, an application might spend a considerable amount of time waiting for data. This not only negatively impacts the overall performance, but the application cannot benefit much from a processor clock-speed upgrade either.

One way to overcome this problem is to insert a small high-speed buffer memory between the processor and main memory. Such a buffer is generally referred to as cache memory, or cache for short.

The application can take advantage of this enhancement by **fetching** data from the cache instead of main memory. Thanks to the shorter access time to the cache, application performance is improved. Of course, there is still traffic between memory and the cache, but it is minimal. This relatively simple concept works out well in practice. The vast majority of applications benefit from caches.

1. Cache Hierarchy

As Figure 2.2.1 shows, the cache is placed between the CPU and the main memory.

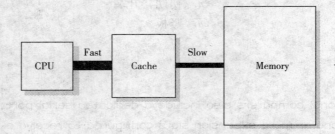

Figure 2.2.1   Example of a cache-based memory system

The system first copies the data needed by the CPU from memory into the cache, and then from the cache into a register in the CPU. Storage of results is in the opposite direction. First the system copies the data into the cache. Depending on the cache architecture details, the data is then immediately copied back to memory (write-through), or deferred (write-back). If an application needs the same data again, data access time is reduced significantly if the data is still in the cache.

To **amortize** the cost of the memory transfer, more than one element is loaded into the cache. The unit of transfer is called a cache block or cache line. Access to a single data element brings an entire line into the cache. The line is guaranteed to contain the element requested.

Related to this is the concept of sub-blocking. With sub-blocking, a cache allocates a line/block with a length that is a multiple of the cache line. The slots within the larger block are then filled with the individual cache lines (or sub-blocks). This design works well if lines are accessed **consecutively**, but is less efficient in case of irregular access patterns, because not all slots within one block may be filled.

So far, we have only applied caches to data transfer. There is, however, no reason why you could not use caches for other purposes—to fetch instructions, for example. Cache Functionality and Organization explores these other purposes in more detail.

Thanks to advances in chip process technology, it is possible to implement multiple levels of cache memory. Some of these levels will be a part of the microprocessor (they are said to be on-chip), whereas other levels may be external to the chip.

To distinguish between these caches, a level notation is used. The higher the level, the farther away the cache is from the CPU. Figure 2.2.2 shows an example. The level 1 (L1) cache is on-chip, whereas the level 2 (L2) cache is external to the microprocessor.

Note that in Figure 2.2.2, and in the remainder of this article, we distinguish between the CPU and microprocessor. CPU refers to the execution part of the processor, whereas microprocessor refers to the entire chip, which includes more than the CPU.

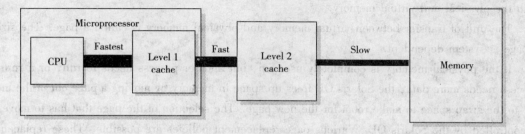

Figure 2. 2. 2   Multiple levels of cache memory

In Figure 2. 2. 2, the size of the cache increases from left to right, but the speed decreases. In other words, the capacity increases, but it takes longer to move the data in and out.

1. 1   Latency and Bandwidth

Latency and bandwidth are two **metrics** associated with caches and memory. Neither of them is **uniform**, but is specific to a particular component of the memory **hierarchy.**

The latency is often expressed in processor cycles or in nanoseconds, whereas bandwidth is usually given in megabytes per second or gigabytes per second.

Although not entirely correct, in practice the latency of a memory component is measured as the time it takes to fetch one unit of transfer (typically a cache line). As the speed of a component depends on its relative location in the hierarchy, the latency is not uniform. As a **rule of thumb**, it is safe to say that latency increases when moving from left to right in Figure 2. 2. 2.

Some of the memory components, the L1 cache for example, may be physically located on the microprocessor. The advantage is that their speed will scale with the processor clock. It is, therefore, meaningful to express the latency of such components in processor clock cycles, instead of nanoseconds. On some microprocessors, the integrated (on-chip) caches do not always run at the speed of the processor. They operate at a clock rate that is an integer **quotient** (1/2, 1/3, and so forth) of the processor clock.

Cache components external to the processor do not usually, or only partially, benefit from a processor clock upgrade. Their latencies are often given in nanoseconds. Main memory latency is almost always expressed in nanoseconds.

Bandwidth is a measure of the speed of a memory component. This number reflects how fast large bulks of data can be moved in and out. Just as with latency, the bandwidth is not uniform.

1. 2   Virtual Memory

Although not considered in detail in this article, virtual memory is mentioned for reasons of completeness and to introduce the TLB cache.

On a virtual memory system, memory extends to disk. Addresses need not fit in physical memory. Certain portions of the data and instructions can be temporarily stored on disk, in the **swap space.** The latter is disk space set aside by the Solaris OE and used as an extension of physical memory. The system administrator decides on the size of the swap space. The Solaris OE manages both the physical and virtual memory.

The unit of transfer between virtual memory and physical memory is called a page. The size of a page is system dependent.

If the physical memory is completely used up, but another process needs to run, or a running process needs more data, the Solaris OE frees up space in memory by moving a page out of the memory to the swap space to make room for the new page. The selection of the page that has to move out is controlled by the Solaris OE. Various page replacement policies are possible. These replacement policies are, however, beyond the scope of this article.

Certain components in the system (the CPU for example) use virtual addresses. These addresses must be mapped into the physical RAM memory. This mapping between a virtual and physical address is relatively expensive. Therefore, these translated addresses (plus some other data structures) are stored in an entry in the so-called **Translation Lookaside Buffer** (TLB). The TLB is a cache and behaves like a cache. For example, to amortize the cost of setting up an entry, you would like to reuse it as often as possible.

The unit of virtual management is a page; one entry in the TLB corresponds to one page.

2. Cache Functionality and Organization

In a modern microprocessor several caches are found. They not only vary in size and functionality, but also their internal organization is typically different across the caches. This section discusses the most important caches, as well as some popular cache organizations.

2.1 Instruction Cache

The instruction cache is used to store instructions. This helps to reduce the cost of going to memory to fetch instructions.

The instruction cache regularly holds several other things, like branch prediction information. In certain cases, this cache can even perform some limited operation (s).[1] The instruction cache on UltraSPARC, for example, also pre-decodes the incoming instruction.

2.2 Data Cache

A data cache is a fast buffer that contains the application data. Before the processor can operate on the data, it must be loaded from memory into the data cache. The element needed is then loaded from the cache line into a register and the instruction using this value can operate on it. The resultant value of the instruction is also stored in a register. The register contents are then stored back into the data cache.[2]

Eventually the cache line that this element is part of is copied back into the main memory.

2.3 TLB Cache

Translating a virtual page address to a valid physical address is rather costly. The TLB is a cache to store these translated addresses.

Each entry in the TLB maps to an entire virtual memory page. The CPU can only operate on data and instructions that are mapped into the TLB. If this mapping is not present, the system has to re-create it, which is a relatively costly operation.

The larger a page, the more effective capacity the TLB has. If an application does not make good use of the TLB, increasing the size of the page can be beneficial for performance, allowing for a bigger part of the address space to be mapped into the TLB. [3]

Some microprocessors, including UltraSPARC, implement two TLBs. One for pages containing instructions (I-TLB) and one for data pages (D-TLB).

2.4   Putting It All Together

Now, all of the ingredients needed to build a generic cache-based system (Figure 2.2.3) have been discussed.

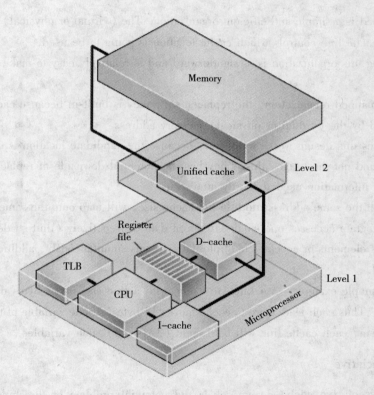

Figure 2.2.3   Generic system architecture

Figure 2.2.3 shows unified cache at level 2. Both instructions and data are stored in this type of cache. It is shown outside of the microprocessor and is therefore called an external cache. This situation is quite typical; the cache at the highest level is often unified and external to the microprocessor.

Note that the cache architecture shown in Figure 2.2.3 is rather generic. Often, you will find other types of caches in a modern microprocessor. The UltraSPARC III Cu microprocessor is a good example of this. As you will see, it has two additional caches that have not been discussed yet.

Figure 2.2.3 clearly demonstrates that, for example, the same cache line can potentially be in multiple caches. In case of a containing cache philosophy, the levels of the cache hierarchy that are further away from the CPU always contain all the data present in the lower levels. The opposite of this design is called non-containing.

3. Cache Organization and Replacement Policies

Caches have a certain organization and a replacement policy. The organization describes in what way the lines are organized within the cache. The replacement policy dictates which line will be removed (evicted) from the cache in case an incoming line must be placed in the cache.

3.1 Direct Mapped

Direct mapped is a simple and efficient organization. The (virtual or physical) memory address of the incoming cache line controls which cache location is going to be used.

Implementing this organization is straightforward and is relatively easy to make it scale with the processor clock.

In a direct mapped organization, the replacement policy is built-in because cache line replacement is controlled by the (virtual or physical) memory address.

In many cases this design works well, but, because the candidate location is controlled by the memory address and not the usage, this policy has the potential downside of replacing a cache line that still contains information needed shortly afterwards.

Any line with the same address **modulo** the cache size, will map onto the same cache location. As long as the program accesses one single stream of data consecutively (unit stride) all is well. If the program skips elements or accesses multiple data streams simultaneously, additional cache refills may be generated.

Consider a simple example—a 4-kilobyte cache with a line size of 32 bytes direct-mapped on virtual addresses. Thus each load/store to cache moves 32 bytes. If one variable of type float takes 4 bytes on our system, each cache line will hold eight ($32/4 = 8$) such variables.

3.2 Fully Associative

The **fully associative cache** design solves the potential problem of thrashing with a direct-mapped cache.[4] The replacement policy is no longer a function of the memory address, but considers usage instead.

With this design, typically the oldest cache line is evicted from the cache. This policy is called least-recently-used (LRU).

The downside of a fully associative design is cost. Additional logic is required to track usage of lines. The larger the cache, the higher the cost. Therefore, it is difficult to scale this technology to very large (data) caches. Luckily, a good alternative exists.

3.3   Set Associative

A **set-associative cache** design uses several direct-mapped caches. Each cache is often referred to as a set. On an incoming request, the cache controller decides which set the line will go into. Within the set, a direct-mapped scheme is used to allocate a slot in the cache.

The name reflects the number of direct-mapped caches. For example, in a 2-way set associative design two direct mapped caches are used.

Another design parameter is the algorithm that selects the set. This could be random, LRU, or any other selection scheme.

Figure 2.2.4 shows a four-way set associative cache.

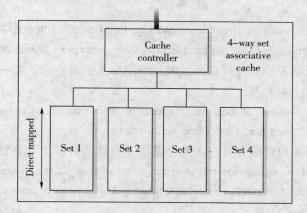

Figure 2.2.4   Four-way set associative design

Note that a set-associative cache tends to reduce the amount of **thrashing.** Thrashing can still occur, however, not only within one set but also between sets.

Thrashing between sets is a function of the algorithm that selects the set; whereas thrashing within one set is related to the (virtual) memory address of the data. Usually, the size of a set is 2n kilobytes (n = 1, 2, ...). If (virtual) addresses of incoming lines in the same set are 2m apart (m > n), thrashing occurs.

Key Words

bottleneck	n.	瓶颈
fetch	v.	取，获得
amortize	v.	分摊，补偿
consecutively	adv.	连续地
latency	n.	延迟
metric	n.	衡量标准
uniform	adj.	不变的，始终如一的
hierarchy	n.	分层结构

rule of thumb	单凭经验的方法
quotient	*n.* 商（数），系数
swap space	交换空间（用作虚拟内存的硬盘部分）
Translation Lookaside Buffer	转换检测缓冲器，转换查找表
modulo	*v.* 以……为模
fully associative cache	全关联缓存
set-associative cache	组关联缓存
thrashing	颠簸（指一个进程的页面经常换入换出）

Notes

1. The instruction cache regularly holds several other things, like branch prediction information. In certain cases, this cache can even perform some limited operation(s).

指令缓存经常保存一些其他的东西，例如程序分支预测信息。在一些特定的例子中，这个缓存甚至可以执行一些有限的操作。

2. The resultant value of the instruction is also stored in a register. The register contents are then stored back into the data cache.

作为指令执行结果的数值也被存入寄存器。寄存器的内容于是存回数据缓存。

3. If an application does not make good use of the TLB, increasing the size of the page can be beneficial for performance, allowing for a bigger part of the address space to be mapped into the TLB.

如果应用程序没有充分利用 TLB，增加页面尺寸可以提高性能，因为它允许更大的地址空间映射到 TLB。

4. The fully associative cache design solves the potential problem of thrashing with a direct-mapped cache.

全关联缓存的设计解决了由于直接映射缓存所导致的潜在的颠簸的问题。

Reading Material 1   Multi-core (computing)

A multi-core microprocessor is one that combines two or more independent processors into a single package, often a single integrated circuit (IC). A dual-core device contains two independent microprocessors. In general, multi-core microprocessors allow a computing device to exhibit some form of thread-level parallelism (TLP) without including multiple microprocessors in separate physical packages. This form of TLP is often known as chip-level multiprocessing.

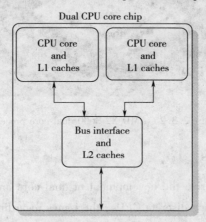

Figure 2.3.1   Dual CPU core chip structure

1. Terminology

There is some discrepancy in the semantics by which the terms "multi-core" and "dual-core" are defined. Most commonly they are used to refer to some sort of central processing unit (CPU), but are sometimes also applied to DSPs and SoCs. Additionally, some use these terms only to refer to multi-core microprocessors that are manufactured on the same integrated circuit die. These persons generally prefer to refer to separate microprocessor dies in the same package by another name, such as "multi-chip module", "double core", or even "twin core". This article uses both the terms "multi-core" and "dual-core" to reference microelectronic CPUs manufactured on the same integrated circuit, unless otherwise noted.

2. Development Motivation

While CMOS manufacturing technology continues to improve, reducing the size of single gates, physical limits of semiconductor-based microelectronics become a major design concern. Some effects of these physical limitations can cause significant heat dissipation and data synchronization problems. The demand for more complex and capable microprocessors causes CPU designers to utilize various methods of increasing performance. Some ILP methods like superscalar pipelining are suitable for many applications, but are inefficient for others that tend to contain difficult-to-predict code. Many applications are better suited to TLP methods, and multiple independent CPUs is one common method used to increase a system's overall TLP. A combination of increased available space due to refined manufacturing processes and the demand for increased TLP is the logic behind the creation of multi-core CPUs.

Figure 2.3.2   AMD X2 3600 dual-core processor

3. Commercial Incentives

Several business motives drive the development of dual-core architectures. Since SMP designs have been long implemented using discrete CPUs, the issues regarding implementing the architecture and supporting it in software are well known. Additionally, utilizing a proven processing core design (e.g. Freescale's e700 core) without architectural changes reduces design risk significantly. Finally, the connotation of the terminology "dual-core" (and other multiples) lends itself to marketing efforts.

Additionally, for general-purpose processors, much of the motivation for multi-core processors comes from the increasing difficulty of improving processor performance by increasing the operating frequency (frequency-scaling). In order to continue delivering regular performance improvements for general-purpose processors, manufacturers such as Intel and AMD have turned to multi-core designs, sacrificing lower manufacturing costs for higher performance in some applications and systems.

Multi-core architectures are being developed, but so are the alternatives. An especially strong contender for established markets is to integrate more peripheral functions into the chip.

3.1 Advantages

Proximity of multiple CPU cores on the same die have the advantage that the cache coherency circuitry can operate at a much higher clock rate than is possible if the signals have to travel off-chip, so combining equivalent CPUs on a single die significantly improves the performance of cache snoop (alternative: Bus snooping) operations. In simpler words, it means that because the signal between different chips has to travel a shorter distance, it does not degenerate as much, which allows more data to be sent at the same period of time—as individual signals can be shorter and do not need to be repeated as often.

Assuming that the die can fit into the package, physically, the multi-core CPU designs require much less Printed Circuit Board (PCB) space than multi-chip SMP designs.

A dual-core processor uses slightly less power than two coupled single-core processors, principally because of the increased power required to drive signals external to the chip and because the smaller silicon process geometry allows the cores to operate at lower voltages; such reduction reduces latency. Furthermore, the cores share some circuitry, like the L2 cache and the interface to the front side bus (FSB).

In terms of competing technologies for the available silicon die area, multi-core design can make use of proven CPU core library designs and produce a product with lower risk of design error than devising a new wider core design. Also, adding more cache suffers from diminishing returns.

3.2   Disadvantages

In addition to operating system (OS) support, adjustments to existing software are required to maximize utilization of the computing resources provided by multi-core processors. Also, the ability of multi-core processors to increase application performance depends on the use of multiple threads within applications. For example, most current (2006) video games will run faster on a 3 GHz single-core processor than on a 2GHz dual-core processor (of the same core architecture), despite the dual-core theoretically having more processing power, because they are incapable of efficiently using more than one core at a time.

Integration of a multi-core chip drives production yields down and they are more difficult to manage thermally than lower-density single-chip designs.

From an architectural point of view, ultimately, single CPU designs may make better use of the silicon surface area than multiprocessing cores, so a development commitment to this architecture may carry the risk of obsolescence.

Raw processing power is not the only constraint on system performance. Two processing cores sharing the same system bus and memory bandwidth limits the real-world performance advantage. If a single core is close to being memory bandwidth limited, going to dual-core might only give 30% to 70% improvement. If memory-bandwidth is not a problem a 90% improvement can be expected. It would be possible for an application that used 2 CPUs to end up running faster on one dual-core if communication between the CPUs was the limiting factor, which would count as more than 100% improvement.

4.   Hardware Trend

- ◆   Multi-core to many-core: from dual-, quad-, eight-core to tens or even hundreds of cores
- ◆   Mixed with simultaneous multithreading or hyperthreading
- ◆   Heterogeneous: special purpose processors cores in additional to general purpose cores for higher efficiency in processing multimedia, recognition and networking
- ◆   Energy-efficiency: focus on performance-per-watt with advanced fine-grain or ultra fine-

grain power management and dynamic voltage and frequency scaling (DVFS)

◆ Hardware-assisted platform virtualization

◆ Memory-on-chip

5. Software Impact

Software benefits from multicore architectures where code can be executed in parallel. Under most common operating systems this requires code to execute in separate threads. Each application running on a system runs in its own thread so multiple applications will benefit from multicore architectures. Each application may also have multiple threads but, in most cases, it must be specifically written to utilize multiple threads. Operating system software also tends to run many threads as a part of its normal operation. Running virtual machines will benefit from adoption of multiple core architectures since each virtual machine runs independently of others and can be executed in parallel.

Most application software is not written to use multiple concurrent threads intensively because of the challenge of doing so. A frequent pattern in multithreaded application design is where a single thread does the intensive work while other threads do much less. For example a virus scan application may create a new thread for the scan process, while the GUI thread waits for commands from the user (e. g. cancel the scan). In such cases, multicore architecture is of little benefit for the application itself due to the single thread doing all heavy lifting and the inability to balance the work evenly across multiple cores. Programming truly multithreaded code often requires complex co-ordination of threads and can easily introduce subtle and difficult to find bugs due to the interleaving of processing on data shared between threads (thread-safety). Debugging such code when it breaks is also much more difficult than single-threaded code. Also there has been a perceived lack of motivation for writing consumer-level threaded applications because of the relative rarity of consumer-level multiprocessor hardware. Although threaded applications incur little additional performance penalty on single-processor machines, the extra overhead of development was difficult to justify due to preponderance of single-processor machines.

As of Fall 2006, with the typical mix of mass-market applications the main benefit to an ordinary user from a multi-core CPU will be improved multitasking performance. In particular, the impact on foreground responsiveness from a CPU-intensive background task (such as running a full system scan with antivirus or other anti-malware utilites) may be reduced.

Given the increasing emphasis on multicore chip design, stemming from the grave thermal and power consumption problems posed by any further significant increase in processor clock speeds, the extent to which software can be multithreaded to take advantage of these new chips is likely to be the single greatest constraint on computer performance in the future. If developers are unable to design software to fully exploit the resources provided by multiple cores, then they will ultimately reach an insurmountable performance ceiling.

Current software titles designed to utilize multi-core technologies include: World of Warcraft, City of Heroes, City of Villains, Maya, Blender3D, Quake 3 & Quake 4, Elder Scrolls: Oblivion (requires editing the .ini file to activate), Falcon 4: Allied Force, 3DS Max, Adobe Photoshop,

Windows XP Professional, Windows 2003, Mac OS X, Linux, Tangosol Coherence, GigaSpaces EAG, numerous Ulead products including MediaStudio Pro 7 & 8 (pro video editor), VideoStudio 10 and 10 Plus (consumer video editor), DVD MovieFactory 5 & 5 Plus (DVD authoring) and PhotoImpact 12 (graphics tool), and many operating systems that are streamlined for server use.

Most video games designed to run on Sony's Playstation 3 are expected to take advantage of its 8-core cell microprocessor. The highly anticipated first-person shooter Resistance: Fall of Man reportedly dedicates a single SPE core of the cell to enemy AI. How other upcoming PS3 title utilize the hardwares multi-core design is unknown.

Parallel programming techniques can benefit from multiple cores directly. Some existing parallel programming models such as OpenMP and MPI can be used on multi-core platforms. Other research efforts have been seen also, like Cray's Chapel, Sun's Fortress, and IBM's X10.

Concurrency acquires a central role in true parallel application. The basic steps in designing parallel applications are:

5.1　Partitioning

The partitioning stage of a design is intended to expose opportunities for parallel execution. Hence, the focus is on defining a large number of small tasks in order to yield what is termed a fine-grained decomposition of a problem.

5.2　Communication

The tasks generated by a partition are intended to execute concurrently but cannot, in general, execute independently. The computation to be performed in one task will typically require data associated with another task. Data must then be transferred between tasks so as to allow computation to proceed. This information flow is specified in the communication phase of a design.

5.3　Agglomeration

In the third stage, we move from the abstract toward the concrete. We revisit decisions made in the partitioning and communication phases with a view to obtaining an algorithm that will execute efficiently on some class of parallel computer. In particular, we consider whether it is useful to combine, or agglomerate, tasks identified by the partitioning phase, so as to provide a smaller number of tasks, each of greater size. We also determine whether it is worthwhile to replicate data and/or computation.

5.4　Mapping

In the fourth and final stage of the parallel algorithm design process, we specify where each task is to execute. This mapping problem does not arise on uniprocessors or on shared-memory computers that provide automatic task scheduling.

On the other hand, on the server side, multicore processors are ideal because they allow many users to connect to a site simultaneously and have independent threads of execution. This allows for web servers and application servers that have much better throughput.

6. Licensing

Another issue is the question of software licensing for multi-core CPUs. Typically enterprise server software is licensed "per processor". In the past a CPU was a processor (and moreover most computers had only one CPU) and there was no ambiguity. Now there is the possibility of counting cores as processors and charging a customer for two licenses when they use a dual-core CPU. However, the trend seems to be counting dual-core chips as a single processor as Microsoft, Intel, and AMD support this view. Oracle counts AMD and Intel dual-core CPUs as a single processor but has other numbers for other types. IBM, HP and Microsoft count a multi-chip module as multiple processors. If multi-chip modules counted as one processor then CPU makers would have an incentive to make large expensive multi-chip modules so their customers saved on software licensing. So it seems that the industry is slowly heading towards counting each die as a processor, no matter how many cores each die has. Intel has released Paxville which is really a multi-chip module but Intel is calling it a dual-core. It is not clear yet how licensing will work for Paxville. This is an unresolved and thorny issue for software companies and customers.

Reading Material 2 I^2C

In consumer electronics, telecommunications and industrial electronics, there are often many similarities between seemingly unrelated designs. For example, nearly every system includes:

- Some intelligent control, usually a single-chip microcontroller;
- General-purpose circuits like LCD drivers, remote I/O ports, RAM, EEPROM, or data converters;
- Application-oriented circuits such as digital tuning and signal processing circuits for radio and video systems, or DTMF generators for telephones with tone dialing.

To exploit these similarities to the benefit of both systems designers and equipment manufacturers, as well as to maximize hardware efficiency and circuit simplicity, Philips developed a simple bi-directional 2-wire bus for efficient inter-IC control. This bus is called the Inter IC or I^2C-bus. At present, Philips' IC range includes more than 150 CMOS and bipolar I^2C-bus compatible types for performing functions in all three of the previously mentioned categories. All I^2C-bus compatible devices incorporate an on-chip interface which allows them to communicate directly with each other via the I^2C-bus. This design concept solves the many interfacing problems encountered when designing digital control circuits.

Here are some of the features of the I^2C-bus:

- Only two bus lines are required; a serial data line (SDA) and a serial clock line (SCL).
- Each device connected to the bus is software addressable by a unique address and simple master/ slave relationships exist at all times; masters can operate as master-transmitters or

as master-receivers.

◆ It's a true multi-master bus including collision detection and arbitration to prevent data corruption if two or more masters simultaneously initiate data transfer.

◆ Serial, 8-bit oriented, bidirectional data transfers can be made at up to 100 kbit/s in the standard mode or up to 400 kbit/s in the fast mode.

◆ On-chip filtering rejects spikes on the bus data line to preserve data integrity.

◆ The number of ICs that can be connected to the same bus is limited only by a maximum bus capacitance of 400 pF.

The I^2C-bus supports any IC fabrication process (NMOS, CMOS, bipolar). Two wires, serial data (SDA) and serial clock (SCL), carry information between the devices connected to the bus. Each device is recognized by a unique address (whether it's a microcontroller, LCD driver, memory or keyboard interface) and can operate as either a transmitter or receiver, depending on the function of the device. Obviously an LCD driver is only a receiver, whereas a memory can both receive and transmit data. In addition to transmitters and receivers, devices can also be considered as masters or slaves when performing data transfers (see Table 2.4.1). A master is the device which initiates a data transfer on the bus and generates the clock signals to permit that transfer. At that time, any device addressed is considered a slave.

Table 2.4.1   Definition of I^2C-bus terminology

Term	Description
Transmitter	The device which sends data to the bus
Receiver	The device which receives data from the bus
Master	The device which initiates a transfer, generates clock signals and terminates a transfer
Slave	The device addressed by a master
Multi-master	More than one master can attempt to control the bus at the same time without corrupting the message
Arbitration	Procedure to ensure that, if more than one master simultaneously tries to control the bus, onle one is allowed to do so and the winning message is not corrupted
Synchronization	Procedure to synchronize the clock signals of two or more devices

The I^2C-bus is a multi-master bus. This means that more than one device capable of controlling the bus can be connected to it. As masters are usually micro-controllers, let's consider the case of a data transfer between two microcontrollers connected to the I^2C-bus (see Figure 2.4.1).

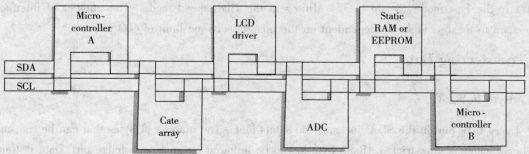

Figure 2.4.1   Example of an I^2C-bus configuration using two microcontrollers

This highlights the master-slave and receiver-transmitter relationships to be found on the I^2C-bus. It should be noted that these relationships are not permanent, but only depend on the direction of data transfer at that time. The transfer of data would proceed as follows:

1) Suppose microcontroller A wants to send information to microcontroller B:

◆ microcontroller A (master), addresses microcontroller B (slave)

◆ microcontroller A (master-transmitter), sends data to microcontroller B (slave-receiver)

◆ microcontroller A terminates the transfer

2) If microcontroller A wants to receive information from microcontroller B:

◆ microcontroller A (master) addresses microcontroller B (slave)

◆ microcontroller A (master-receiver) receives data from microcontroller B (slave-transmitter)

◆ microcontroller A terminates the transfer

Even in this case, the master (microcontroller A) generates the timing and terminates the transfer.

The possibility of connecting more than one microcontroller to the I^2C-bus means that more than one master could try to initiate a data transfer at the same time. To avoid the chaos that might ensue from such an event—an arbitration procedure has been developed. This procedure relies on the wired-AND connection of all I^2C interfaces to the I^2C-bus.

If two or more masters try to put information onto the bus, the first to produce a "one" when the other produces a "zero" will lose the arbitration. The clock signals during arbitration are a synchronized combination of the clocks generated by the masters using the wired-AND connection to the SCL line.

Generation of clock signals on the I^2C-bus is always the responsibility of master devices; each master generates its own clock signals when transferring data on the bus. Bus clock signals from a master can only be altered when they are stretched by a slow-slave device holding-down the clock line, or by another master when arbitration occurs.

Both SDA and SCL are bi-directional lines, connected to a positive supply voltage via a current-source or pull-up resistor. When the bus is free, both lines are HIGH. The output stages of devices connected to the bus must have an open-drain or open-collector to perform the wired-AND function. Data on the I^2C-bus can be transferred at rates of up to 100 kbit/s in the Standard-mode, up to 400 kbit/s in the Fast-mode, or up to 3.4 Mbit/s in the High-speed mode. The number of interfaces connected to the bus is solely dependent on the bus capacitance limit of 400 pF.

1. Transferring Data

1.1 Byte Format

Every byte put on the SDA line must be 8-bits long. The number of bytes that can be transmitted per transfer is unrestricted. Each byte has to be followed by an acknowledge bit. Data is transferred with the most significant bit (MSB) first (see Figure 2.4.2). If a slave can't receive or transmit another complete byte of data until it has performed some other function, for example, servicing an internal interrupt, it can hold the clock line SCL LOW to force the master into a wait state. Data transfer then continues when the slave is ready for another byte of data and releases clock line SCL.

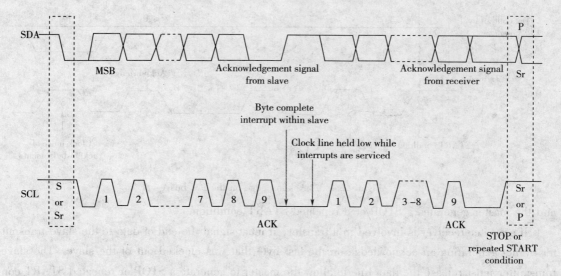

Figure 2.4.2　Data transfer on the I^2C-bus

In some cases, it's permitted to use a different format from the I^2C-bus format (for CBUS compatible devices for example). A message which starts with such an address can be terminated by generation of a STOP condition, even during the transmission of a byte. In this case, no acknowledge is generated.

1.2　Acknowledge

Data transfer with acknowledge is obligatory. The acknowledge-related clock pulse is generated by the master. The transmitter releases the SDA line (HIGH) during the acknowledge clock pulse.

The receiver must pull down the SDA line during the acknowledge clock pulse so that it remains stable LOW during the HIGH period of this clock pulse (see Figure 2.4.3). Of course, set-up and hold times must also be taken into account.

Usually, a receiver which has been addressed is obliged to generate an acknowledge after each byte has been received, except when the message starts with a CBUS address.

When a slave doesn't acknowledge the slave address (for example, it's unable to receive or transmit because it's performing some real-time function), the data line must be left HIGH by the slave. The master can then generate either a STOP condition to abort the transfer, or a repeated START condition to start a new transfer.

If a slave-receiver does acknowledge the slave address but, some time later in the transfer cannot receive any more data bytes, the master must again abort the transfer. This is indicated by the slave generating the not-acknowledge on the first byte to follow. The slave leaves the data line HIGH

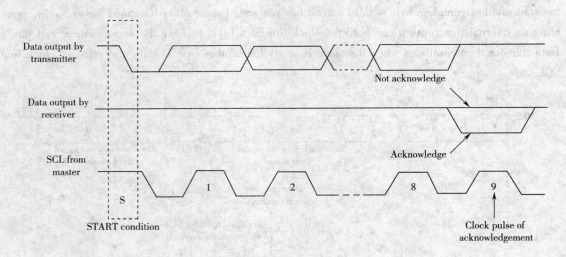

Figure 2. 4. 3　Acknowledge on the I^2C-bus

and the master generates a STOP or a repeated START condition.

If a master-receiver is involved in a transfer, it must signal the end of data to the slave-transmitter by not generating an acknowledge on the last byte that was clocked out of the slave. The slave-transmitter must release the data line to allow the master to generate a STOP or repeated START condition.

2. Arbitration and Clock Generation

2. 1　Synchronization

All masters generate their own clock on the SCL line to transfer messages on the I^2C-bus. Data is only valid during the HIGH period of the clock. A defined clock is therefore needed for the bit-by-bit arbitration procedure to take place.

Clock synchronization is performed using the wired-AND connection of I^2C interfaces to the SCL line. This means that a HIGH to LOW transition on the SCL line will cause the devices concerned to start counting off their LOW period and, once a device clock has gone LOW, it will hold the SCL line in that state until the clock HIGH state is reached (see Figure 2. 4. 4). However, the LOW to HIGH transition of this clock may not change the state of the SCL line if another clock is still within its LOW period. The SCL line will therefore be held LOW by the device with the longest LOW period. Devices with shorter LOW periods enter a HIGH wait-state during this time.

When all devices concerned have counted off their LOW period, the clock line will be released and go HIGH. There will then be no difference between the device clocks and the state of the SCL line, and all the devices will start counting their HIGH periods. The first device to complete its HIGH period will again pull the SCL line LOW.

In this way, a synchronized SCL clock is generated with its LOW period determined by the device with the longest clock LOW period, and its HIGH period determined by the one with the shor-

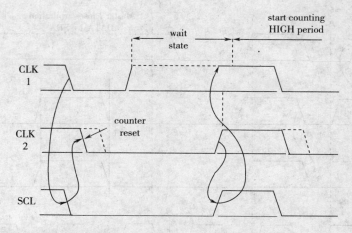

Figure 2.4.4   Clock synchronization during the arbitration procedure

test clock HIGH period.

2.2   Arbitration

A master may start a transfer only if the bus is free. Two or more masters may generate a START condition within the minimum hold time ($t_{HD;STA}$) of the START condition which results in a defined START condition to the bus.

Arbitration takes place on the SDA line, while the SCL line is at the HIGH level, in such a way that the master which transmits a HIGH level, while another master is transmitting a LOW level will switch off its DATA output stage because the level on the bus doesn't correspond to its own level.

Arbitration can continue for many bits. Its first stage is comparison of the address bits. If the masters are each trying to address the same device, arbitration continues with comparison of the data-bits if they are master-transmitter, or acknowledge-bits if they are master-receiver. Because address and data information on the I^2C-bus is determined by the winning master, no information is lost during the arbitration process.

A master that loses the arbitration can generate clock pulses until the end of the byte in which it loses the arbitration.

As an Hs-mode master has a unique 8-bit master code, it will always finish the arbitration during the first byte.

If a master also incorporates a slave function and it loses arbitration during the addressing stage, it's possible that the winning master is trying to address it. The losing master must therefore switch over immediately to its slave mode.

Figure 2.4.5 shows the arbitration procedure for two masters. Of course, more may be involved (depending on how many masters are connected to the bus). The moment there is a difference between the internal data level of the master generating DATA 1 and the actual level on the SDA line, its data output is switched off, which means that a HIGH output level is then connected to the bus.

37

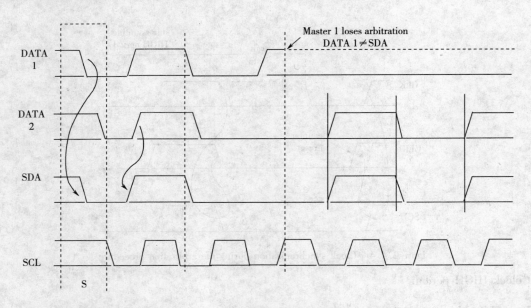

Figure 2.4.5   Arbitration procedure of two masters

This will not affect the data transfer initiated by the winning master.

Since control of the I^2C-bus is decided solely on the address or master code and data sent by competing masters, there is no central master, nor any order of priority on the bus.

Special attention must be paid if, during a serial transfer, the arbitration procedure is still in progress at the moment when a repeated START condition or a STOP condition is transmitted to the I^2C-bus. If it's possible for such a situation to occur, the masters involved must send this repeated START condition or STOP condition at the same position in the format frame. In other words, arbitration isn't allowed between:

◆   A repeated START condition and a data bit;

◆   A STOP condition and a data bit;

◆   A repeated START condition and a STOP condition.

Slaves are not involved in the arbitration procedure.

2.3   Use of the Clock Synchronizing Mechanism as a Handshake

In addition to being used during the arbitration procedure, the clock synchronization mechanism can be used to enable receivers to cope with fast data transfers, on either a byte level or a bit level.

On the byte level, a device may be able to receive bytes of data at a fast rate, but needs more time to store a received byte or prepare another byte to be transmitted. Slaves can then hold the SCL line LOW after reception and acknowledgment of a byte to force the master into a wait state until the slave is ready for the next byte transfer in a type of handshake procedure (see Figure 2.4.2).

On the bit level, a device such as a microcontroller with or without limited hardware for the I^2C-bus, can slow down the bus clock by extending each clock LOW period. The speed of any master is thereby adapted to the internal operating rate of this device.

Exercises

Ⅰ. Fill in the following blanks with proper words or phrases:

1. The _____, which is a printed circuit board, is used to electrically connect many components of a computer together.

2. A _____ chip containing the system's startup program is also mounted to the motherboard.

3. A motherboard typically includes input/output (I/O) connectors, floppy disk and hard disk drive connections, as well as circuitry for controlling any built-in peripheral devices e.g., _____, _____, and _____.

4. _____ is the original open motherboard standard created by IBM for the first home computer, the IBM-PC.

5. _____ can operate to control the data access on both the rising and falling edges of the system clocks.

6. _____ time is increasingly the bottleneck in overall application performance of a computer system.

7. With _____, a cache allocates a line/block with a length that is a multiple of the cache line.

8. For multiple levels of cache memory, the _____ the level, the father away the cache is from the CPU.

9. _____ and _____ are two metrics associated with caches and memory.

10. On a virtual memory system, memory extends to disk. Certain portions of the data and instructions can be temporarily stored on disk, in the _____.

Ⅱ. Answer the following questions:

1. What kinds of components does a computer system include?

2. Please list several common functional units on a motherboard of a computer.

3. Give some examples of buses on a general motherboard.

4. What's the difference between SDRAM and DDR DRAM?

5. What are the motherboard and daughter board used to?

6. How does a simple Cache-Based Memory System work?

7. Under what condition, the swap space will work? How?

8. Please list several types of caches according to its functionality.

9. Briefly describe three different kinds of cache organization.

10. Please draw a figure of 2-level cache memory system with CPU and memory on it; mark the speed of these different levels.

Chapter Three Data Structure

Unit 1 Balanced Tree Data Structures

1. Introduction

Tree structures support various basic dynamic set operations including Search, Predecessor, Successor, Minimum, Maximum, Insert, and Delete in time proportional to the height of the tree. Ideally, a tree will be balanced and the height will be log n where n is the number of nodes in the tree. To ensure that the height of the tree is as small as possible and therefore provide the best running time, a balanced tree structure like a **red-black tree**, or AVL tree must be used.

When working with large sets of data, it is often not possible or desirable to maintain the entire structure in primary storage (RAM). Instead, a relatively small portion of the data structure is maintained in primary storage, and additional data is read from secondary storage as needed. Unfortunately, a magnetic disk, the most common form of secondary storage, is significantly slower than random access memory (RAM). In fact, the system often spends more time retrieving data than actually processing data.

Balanced trees are optimized for situations when part or the entire tree must be maintained in secondary storage such as a magnetic disk. Since disk accesses are expensive (time consuming) operations, a balance tree tries to minimize the number of disk accesses. For example, a balance tree with a height of 2 and a **branching factor** of 1001 can store over one billion keys but requires at most two disk accesses to search for any node. [1]

2. The Structure of Balanced Trees

Unlike a binary-tree, each node of a balanced tree may have a variable number of keys and children. The keys are stored in non-decreasing order. Each key has an associated child that is the root of a subtree containing all nodes with keys less than or equal to the key but greater than the proceeding key. A node also has an additional rightmost child that is the root for a subtree containing all keys greater than any keys in the node.

A balanced tree has a minimum number of allowable children for each node known as the minimization factor. If it is this minimization factor, every node must have at least t – 1 keys. Under certain circumstances, the root node is allowed to violate this property by having fewer than t – 1 keys. [2] Every node may have at most 2t – 1 keys or, equivalently, 2t children.

Since each node tends to have a large branching factor (a large number of children), it is typically necessary to traverse relatively few nodes before locating the desired key. If access to each node requires a disk access, then a balance tree will minimize the number of disk accesses required. The minimization factor is usually chosen so that the total size of each node corresponds to a multiple of the block size of the underlying storage device. This choice simplifies and optimizes disk access. Consequently, a balanced tree is an ideal data structure for situations where all data cannot reside in primary storage and accesses to secondary storage are comparatively expensive (or time consuming).

Height of Balanced Trees

For n greater than or equal to one, the height of an n-key balanced tree T, height h, with a minimum degree t greater than or equal to 2.

$$h <= \log_t \frac{n+1}{2}.$$

The worst case height is O (log n). Since the **"branchiness"** of a balanced tree can be large compared to many other balanced tree structures, the base of the logarithm tends to be large; therefore, the number of nodes visited during a search tends to be smaller than required by other tree structures. Although this does not affect the **asymptotic worst case** height, balanced trees tend to have smaller heights than other trees with the same asymptotic height.

3. Operations on Balanced Trees

The algorithms for the search, create, and insert operations are shown below. Note that these algorithms are **single pass**; in other words, they do not traverse back up the tree. Since balanced trees strive to minimize disk accesses and the nodes are usually stored on disk, this single-pass approach will reduce the number of node visits and thus the number of disk accesses. Simpler double-pass approaches that move back up the tree to fix violations are possible.

Since all nodes are assumed to be stored in secondary storage (disk) rather than primary storage (memory), all references to a given node be proceeded by a read operation denoted by Disk-Read. Similarly, once a node is modified and it is no longer needed, it must be written out to secondary storage with a write operation denoted by Disk-Write. The algorithms below assume that all nodes referenced in parameters have already had a corresponding Disk-Read operation. New nodes are created and assigned storage with the Allocate-Node call. The implementation details of the Disk-Read, Disk-Write, and Allocate-Node functions are operating system and implementation dependent.

3.1   Balanced-Tree-Search (x, k)

```
i < -1
while i <= n[x] and k > key_i[x]
        do i < -i+1
if i <= n[x] and k = key_i[x]
        then return (x, i)
if leaf[x]
```

```
        then return NIL
     else Disk-Read(c_i[x])
        return B-Tree-Search(c_i[x], k)
```

The search operation on a balanced tree is **analogous** to a search on a **binary tree**. Instead of choosing between a left and a right child as in a binary tree, a balanced tree search must make an n-way choice. The correct child is chosen by performing a linear search of the values in the node. After finding the value greater than or equal to the desired value, the child pointer to the immediate left of that value is followed. If all values are less than the desired value, the rightmost child pointer is followed. Of course, the search can be terminated as soon as the desired node is found. Since the running time of the search operation depends upon the height of the tree, balanced-tree-Search is O $(\log_t n)$.

3.2 Balanced-Tree-Create (T)

```
x < - Allocate-Node()
leaf[x] < - TRUE
n[x] < - 0
Disk-Write(x)
root[T] < - x
```

The Balanced-Tree-Create operation creates an empty balanced tree by allocating a new root node that has no keys and is a leaf node. Only the root node is permitted to have these properties; all other nodes must meet the criteria outlined previously. The Balanced-Tree-Create operation runs in time O (1).

3.3 Balanced-Tree-Split-Child (x, i, y)

```
z < - Allocate - Node()
leaf[z] < - leaf[y]
n[z] < - t - 1
for j < - 1 to t - 1
        do key_j[z] < - key_{j+t}[y]
if not leaf[y]
        then for j < - 1 to t
                do c_j[z] < - c_{j+t}[y]
n[y] < - t - 1
for j < - n[x] + 1 downto i + 1
        do c_{j+1}[x] < - c_j[x]
c_{i+1} < - z
for j < - n[x] downto i
        do key_{j+1}[x] < - key_j[x]
key_i[x] < - key_t[y]
```

$n[x] <- n[x] + 1$

Disk-Write(y)

Disk-Write(z)

Disk-Write(x)

If node becomes "too full", it is necessary to perform a split operation. The split operation moves the median key of node x into its parent y where x is the ith child of y. A new node, z, is allocated, and all keys in x right of the median key are moved to z. The keys left of the median key remain in the original node x. The new node, z, becomes the child immediately to the right of the median key that was moved to the parent y, and the original node, x, becomes the child immediately to the left of the median key that was moved into the parent y.

The split operation transforms a full node with $2t - 1$ keys into two nodes with $t - 1$ keys each. Note that one key is moved into the parent node. The Balanced-Tree-Split-Child algorithm will run in time $O (t)$ where t is constant.

3.4 Balanced-Tree-Insert (T, k)

$r < - root[T]$

if $n[r] = 2t - 1$

then $s < - Allocate-Node( )$

$root[T] < - s$

$leaf[s] < - FALSE$

$n[s] < -0$

$c_1 < - r$

Balanced-Tree-Split-Child(s, 1, r)

Balanced-Tree-Insert-Nonfull(s, k)

else Balanced-Tree-Insert-Nonfull(r, k)

3.5 Balanced-Tree-Insert-Nonfull (x, k)

$i < - n[x]$

if $leaf[x]$

then while $i > = 1$ and $k < key_i[x]$

do $key_{i+1}[x] < - key_i[x]$

$i < -i - 1$

$key_{i+1}[x] < - k$

$n[x] < - n[x] + 1$

Disk $- Write(x)$

else while $i > =$ and $k < key_i[x]$

do $i < - i - 1$

$i < - i + 1$

Disk-Read($c_i[x]$)

$$\text{if } n[\,c_i[\,x\,]\,] = 2t - 1$$
$$\text{then Balanced-Tree-Split-Child}(\,x,\,i,\,c_i[\,x\,]\,)$$
$$\text{if } k > key_i[\,x\,]$$
$$\text{then } i < -i + 1$$
$$\text{Balanced-Tree-Insert-Nonfull}(\,c_i[\,x\,],\,k\,)$$

To perform an insertion on a balanced tree, the appropriate node for the key must be located using an algorithm similar to Balanced-Tree-Search. Next, the key must be inserted into the node. If the node is not full prior to the insertion, no special action is required; however, if the node is full, the node must be split to make room for the new key. [3] Since splitting the node results in moving one key to the parent node, the parent node must not be full or another split operation is required. This process may repeat all the way up to the root and may require splitting the root node. This approach requires two passes. The first pass locates the node where the key should be inserted; the second pass performs any required splits on the ancestor nodes.

Since each access to a node may correspond to a costly disk access, it is desirable to avoid the second pass by ensuring that the parent node is never full. To accomplish this, the presented algorithm splits any full nodes encountered while descending the tree. [4] Although this approach may result in unnecessary split operations, it guarantees that the parent never needs to be split and eliminates the need for a second pass up the tree. Since a split runs in linear time, it has little effect on the O ($t \log_t n$) running time of Balanced-Tree-Insert.

Splitting the root node is handled as a special case since a new root must be created to contain the median key of the old root. Observe that a balanced tree will grow from the top.

3.6　Balanced-Tree-Delete

Deletion of a key from a balanced-tree is possible; however, special care must be taken to ensure that the properties of a balanced tree are maintained. Several cases must be considered. If the deletion reduces the number of keys in a node below the minimum degree of the tree, this violation must be corrected by combining several nodes and possibly reducing the height of the tree. If the key has children, the children must be rearranged.

4. Applications

4.1　Databases

A database is a collection of data organized in a fashion that facilitates updating, retrieving, and managing the data. The data can consist of anything, including, but not limited to names, addresses, pictures, and numbers. Databases are commonplace and are used everyday. For example, an airline reservation system might maintain a database of available flights, customers, and tickets issued. A teacher might maintain a database of student names and grades.

Because computers excel at quickly and accurately manipulating, storing, and retrieving data, databases are often maintained electronically using a database management system. Database management systems are essential components of many everyday business operations. Database products like Microsoft SOL Server, Sybase Adaptive Server, IBM DB2, and Oracle serve as a foundation for accounting systems, **inventory** systems, medical recordkeeping systems, airline reservation systems, and countless other important aspects of modern businesses.

It is not uncommon for a database to contain millions of records requiring many gigabytes of storage. For examples, TELSTRA, an Australian telecommunications company, maintains a customer billing database with 51 billion rows (yes, billion) and 4. 2 **terabytes** of data. In order for a database to be useful and usable, it must support the desired operations, such as retrieval and storage, quickly. Because databases cannot typically be maintained entirely in memory, balanced trees are often used to index the data and to provide fast access. For example, searching an unindexed and unsorted database containing n key values will have a worst case running time of O (n); if the same data is indexed with a balanced tree, the same search operation will run in O (log n). To perform a search for a single key on a set of one million keys (1, 000, 000), a linear search will require at most 1, 000, 000 comparisons. If the same data is indexed with a balanced tree of minimum degree 10, 114 comparisons will be required in the worst case. Clearly, indexing large amounts of data can significantly improve search performance. Although other balanced tree structures can be used, a balanced tree also optimizes costly disk accesses that are of concern when dealing with large data sets.

4. 2   Concurrent Access to Balanced-Trees

Databases typically run in multi-user environments where many users can concurrently perform operations on the database. Unfortunately, this common scenario introduces complications. For example, imagine a database storing bank account balances. Now assume that someone attempts to withdraw $40 from an account containing $60. First, the current balance is checked to ensure sufficient funds. After funds are **disbursed**, the balance of the account is reduced. This approach works flawlessly until concurrent transactions are considered. Suppose that another person simultaneously attempts to withdraw $30 from the same account. At the same time the account balance is checked by the first person, the account balance is also retrieved for the second person. Since neither person is requesting more funds than are currently available, both requests are satisfied for a total of $70. After the first person's transaction, $20 should remain ($60 − $40), so the new balance is recorded as $20. Next, the account balance after the second person's transaction, $30 ($60 − $30), is recorded overwriting the $20 balance. Unfortunately, $70 has been disbursed, but the account balance has only been decreased by $30. Clearly, this behavior is undesirable, and special precautions must be taken.

A balanced tree suffers from similar problems in a multi-user environment. If two or more processes are manipulating the same tree, it is possible for the tree to become corrupt and result in data loss or errors.

The simplest solution is to serialize access to the data structure. In other words, if another process is using the tree, all other processes must wait. Although this is feasible in many cases, it can place an unnecessary and costly limit on performance because many operations actually can be performed concurrently without risk. Locking, introduced by Gray and refined by many others, provides a mechanism for controlling concurrent operations on data structures in order to prevent undesirable side effects and to ensure consistency.

Key Words

red-black tree	红黑树（一种平衡树）
branching factor	分支因子
branchiness	*n.* 分支性
asymptotic	*adj.* 趋近
worst case	最差状况
single pass	单遍，单次
analogous	*adj.* 同样功能的
binary tree	二叉树
inventory	*n.* 目录；存货清单
terabyte	*n.* 存储单元（1 Terabyte = 1024 GB）
disburse	*v.* 支付，支出

Notes

1. For example, a b-tree with a height of 2 and a branching factor of 1001 can store over one billion keys but requires at most two disk accesses to search for any node.

例如，一个高度为2、分支因子为1001的树可以储存高达10亿个键，而最多只需要访问磁盘两次就可以访问到任意一个节点。

2. If t is this minimization factor, every node must have at least t-1 keys. Under certain circumstances, the root node is allowed to violate this property by having fewer than t-1 keys.

如果t是最小因子，每个节点都必须有至少t-1个键。在特定的环境下，根节点的键少于t-1并不违反这个属性。

3. If the node is not full prior to the insertion, no special action is required; however, if the node is full, the node must be split to make room for the new key.

如果节点在插入前不满，则不需要作特殊处理。但是，如果节点是满的，为了给新的键提供空间，就需要将节点拆分。

4. Since each access to a node may correspond to a costly disk access, it is desirable to avoid the second pass by ensuring that the parent node is never full. To accomplish this, the presented algorithm splits any full nodes encountered while descending the tree.

由于每一次对节点的存取都可能导致高成本的磁盘存取，因此应该尽量使父节点永不满，以避免第二次访问。为了达到这个目的，以上算法在向下遍历树结构时拆分所有已满的节点。

Unit 2　Quicksort

Quicksort is a well-known **sorting algorithm** developed by C. A. R. Hoare that, on average, makes Θ (n log n) comparisons to sort n items. However, in the worst case, it makes Θ (n^2) comparisons. Typically, quicksort is significantly faster in practice than other Θ (n log n) algorithms, because its inner loop can be efficiently implemented on most architectures, and in most real-world data it is possible to make design choices which minimize the possibility of requiring **quadratic** time. Quicksort is a comparison sort and, in efficient implementations, is not a stable sort.

1. The Algorithm

Quicksort sorts by employing a **divide and conquer strategy** to divide a into two sub-lists. The steps are:

1) Pick an element, called a pivot, from the list.

2) Reorder the list so that all elements which are less than the **pivot** come before the pivot and so that all elements greater than the pivot come after it (equal values can go either way). After this partitioning, the pivot is in its final position. This is called the **partition** operation.

3) Recursively sort the sub-list of lesser elements and the sub-list of greater elements.

The base case of the recursion are lists of size zero or one, which are always sorted. The algorithm always terminates because it puts at least one element in its final place on each iteration (the loop invariant).

In simple **pseudocode**, the algorithm might be expressed as:

function quicksort(q)
    var list less, pivotList, greater
    if length(q) < = 1
        return q
    select a pivot value pivot from q
    for each x **in** q **except** the pivot element
        if x < pivot **then** add x to less
        if x > = pivot **then** add x to greater
    add pivot to pivotList
    return concatenate[quicksort(less), pivotList, quicksort(greater)]

Notice that we only examine elements by comparing them to other elements. This makes quicksort a comparison sort.

1.1 Version with In-place Partition

The disadvantage of the simple version above is that it requires Ω (n) extra storage space, which is as bad as mergesort (see big-O notation for the meaning of Ω). The additional memory allocations required can also drastically impact speed and cache performance in practical implementations. [1] There is a more complicated version which uses an in-place partition algorithm and can achieve O (log n) space use on average for good pivot choices:

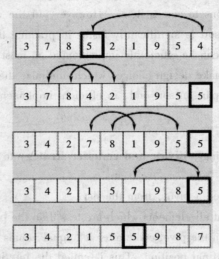

Figure 3.2.1   In-place partition in action on a small list

function partition(array, left, right, pivotIndex)
    pivotValue: = array[pivotIndex]
    swap(array[pivotIndex], array[right])//Move pivot to end
    storeIndex : = left
    for i **from** left **to** right
        if array[i] < = pivotValue
            swap(array[storeIndex], array[i])
            storeIndex: = storeIndex + 1
    swap(array[right], array[storeIndex])//Move pivot to its final place
    return storeIndex

This form of the partition algorithm is not the original form; multiple variations can be found in various textbooks, such as versions not having the storeIndex. However, this form is probably the easiest to understand.

This is the in-place partition algorithm. It partitions the portion of the array between indexes left and right, inclusively, by moving all elements less than or equal to a [pivotIndex] to the beginning of the subarray, leaving all the greater elements following them. In the process it also finds the final position for the pivot element, which it returns. It temporarily moves the pivot element to the end of the subarray, so that it doesn't get in the way. Because it only uses exchanges, the final list has the same elements as the original list. Notice that an element may be exchanged multiple times before reaching its final place.

1. 2   Parallelization

Like mergesort, quicksort can also be easily parallelized due to its divide-and-conquer nature. Individual in-place partition operations are difficult to parallelize, but once divided, different sections of the list can be sorted in parallel. If we have p processors, we can divide a list of n elements into p sublists in $\Theta(n)$ average time, then sort each of these in $O[\ (n/p)\ \log\ (n/p)]$ average time. Ignoring the $O(n)$ preprocessing, this is linear speedup. Given $\Theta(n)$ processors, only $O(n)$ time is required overall.

One advantage of parallel quicksort over other parallel sort algorithms is that no synchronization is required. A new thread is started as soon as a sublist is available for it to work on and it does not communicate with other threads. When all threads complete, the sort is done. [2]

Other more sophisticated parallel sorting algorithms can achieve even better time bounds. For example, in 1991 David Powers described a parallelized quicksort that can operate in $O(\log n)$ time given enough processors by performing partitioning implicitly.

2. Competitive Sorting Algorithms

Quicksort is a space-optimized version of the binary tree sort. Instead of inserting items **sequentially** into an explicit tree, quicksort organizes them concurrently into a tree that is implied by the recursive calls. The algorithms make exactly the same comparisons, but in a different order.

The most direct competitor of quicksort is heapsort. Heapsort is typically somewhat slower than quicksort, but the worst-case running time is always $O(n \log n)$. Quicksort is usually faster, though there remains the chance of worst case performance except in the introsort variant. If it's known in advance that heapsort is going to be necessary, using it directly will be faster than waiting for introsort to switch to it. Heapsort also has the important advantage of using only constant additional space (heapsort is in-place), whereas even the best variant of quicksort uses $\Theta(\log n)$ space. However, heapsort requires efficient random access to be practical.

Quicksort also competes with mergesort, another recursive sort algorithm but with the benefit of worst-case $O(n \log n)$ running time. Mergesort is a stable sort, unlike quicksort and heapsort, and can be easily adapted to operate on linked lists and very large lists stored on slow-to-access media such as disk storage or network attached storage. Although quicksort can be written to operate on linked lists, it will often suffer from poor pivot choices without random access. The main disadvantage of mergesort is that, when operating on arrays, it requires $\Omega(n)$ **auxiliary** space in the best case, whereas the variant of quicksort with in-place partitioning and tail recursion uses only $O(\log n)$ space. (Note that when operating on linked lists, mergesort only requires a small, constant amount of auxiliary storage.)

49

3. Formal Analysis

From the initial description it's not obvious that quicksort takes $O(n \log n)$ time on average. It's not hard to see that the partition operation, which simply loops over the elements of the array once, uses $\Theta(n)$ time. In versions that perform concatenation, this operation is also $\Theta(n)$.

In the best case, each time we perform a partition we divide the list into two nearly equal pieces. This means each recursive call processes a list of half the size. Consequently, we can make only log n **nested calls** before we reach a list of size 1. This means that the depth of the call tree is $O(\log n)$. But no two calls at the same level of the call tree process the same part of the original list; thus, each level of calls needs only $O(n)$ time all together [each call has some constant overhead, but since there are only $O(n)$ calls at each level, this is subsumed in the $O(n)$ factor]. The result is that the algorithm uses only $O(n \log n)$ time.

An alternate approach is to set up a **recurrence** relation for $T(n)$, the time needed to sort a list of size n. Because a single quicksort call involves $O(n)$ work plus two recursive calls on lists of size n/2 in the best case, the relation would be:

$$T(n) = O(n) + 2T(n/2)$$

The master **theorem** tells us that $T(n) = \Theta(n \log n)$.

In fact, it's not necessary to divide the list this precisely; even if each pivot splits the elements with 99% on one side and 1% on the other (or any other fixed fraction), the call depth is still limited to $100 \log n$, so the total running time is still $O(n \log n)$.

In the worst case, however, the two sublists have size 1 and $n-1$, and the call tree becomes a linear chain of n nested calls. The ith call does $O(n-i)$ work, and $\sum_{i=0}^{n} (n-i) = O(n^2)$

The recurrence relation is:

$$T(n) = O(n) + T(1) + T(n-1) = O(n) + T(n-1)$$

This is the same relation as for insertion sort and selection sort, and it solves to $T(n) = \Theta(n^2)$.

3.1 Randomized Quicksort Expected Complexity

Randomized quicksort has the desirable property that it requires only $O(n \log n)$ expected time, regardless of the input. But what makes random pivots a good choice?

Suppose we sort the list and then divide it into four parts. The two parts in the middle will contain the best pivots; each of them is larger than at least 25% of the elements and smaller than at least 25% of the elements. If we could consistently choose an element from these two middle parts, we would only have to split the list at most $2 \log_2 n$ times before reaching lists of size 1, **yielding** an $O(n \log n)$ algorithm.

Unfortunately, a random choice will only choose from these middle parts half the time. The surprising fact is that this is good enough. Imagine that you are **flipping a coin** over and over until you get k heads. Although this could take a long time, on average only 2k flips are required, and the chance that you won't get k heads after 100k flips is **infinitesimally** small. By the same argument, quicksort's recursion will terminate on average at a call depth of only $2(2\log_2 n)$. But if its average call depth is $O(\log n)$, and each level of the call tree processes at most n elements, the total amount of work done on average is the product, $O(n \log n)$.

3.2   Average Complexity

Even if we aren't able to choose pivots randomly, quicksort still requires only $O(n \log n)$ time over all possible **permutations** of its input. Because this average is simply the sum of the times over all permutations of the input divided by n factorial, it's equivalent to choosing a random permutation of the input. When we do this, the pivot choices are essentially random, leading to an algorithm with the same running time as randomized quicksort.

More precisely, the average number of comparisons over all permutations of the input sequence can be estimated accurately by solving the recurrence relation:

$$C(n) = n - 1 + \frac{1}{n} \sum_{i=0}^{n-1} [C(i) + C(n - i - 1)] = 2n\ln n = 1.39n\log_2 n$$

Here, $n-1$ is the number of comparisons the partition uses. Since the pivot is equally likely to fall anywhere in the sorted list order, the sum is averaging over all possible splits.

This means that, on average, quicksort performs only about 39% worse than the ideal number of comparisons, which is its best case. In this sense it is closer to the best case than the worst case. This fast average runtime is another reason for quicksort's practical dominance over other sorting algorithms.

3.3   Space Complexity

The space used by quicksort depends on the version used. The version of quicksort with in-place partitioning uses only constant additional space before making any recursive call. However, if it has made $O(\log n)$ nested recursive calls, it needs to store a constant amount of information from each of them. Since the best case makes at most $O(\log n)$ nested recursive calls, it uses $O(\log n)$ space. The worst case makes $O(n)$ nested recursive calls, and so needs $O(n)$ space.

We are **eliding** a small detail here, however. If we consider sorting arbitrarily large lists, we have to keep in mind that our variables like left and right can no longer be considered to occupy constant space; it takes $O(\log n)$ bits to index into a list of n items. Because we have variables like this in every stack frame, in reality quicksort requires $O(\log^2 n)$ bits of space in the best and average case and $O(n \log n)$ space in the worst case. This isn't too terrible, though, since if the list contains mostly distinct elements, the list itself will also occupy $O(n \log n)$ bits of space.

The **not-in-place** version of quicksort uses $O(n)$ space before it even makes any recursive calls. In the best case its space is still limited to $O(n)$, because each level of the recursion uses half as much space as the last, and

$$\sum_{i=0}^{\infty} \frac{n}{2^i} = 2n$$

Its worst case is dismal, requiring

$$\sum_{i=0}^{n} (n - i + 1) = \Theta(n^2)$$

space, far more than the list itself. If the list elements are not themselves constant size, the problem grows even larger; for example, if most of the list elements are distinct, each would require about $O(\log n)$ bits, leading to a best-case $O(n \log n)$ and worst-case $O(n^2 \log n)$ space requirement.

4. Relationship to Selection

A selection algorithm chooses the kth smallest of a list of numbers; this is an easier problem in general than sorting. One simple but effective selection algorithm works nearly in the same manner as quicksort, except that instead of making recursive calls on both sublists, it only makes a single tail-recursive call on the sublist which contains the desired element. This small change lowers the average complexity to linear or $\Theta(n)$ time, and makes it an in-place algorithm. A variation on this algorithm brings the worst-case time down to $O(n)$ (see selection algorithm for more information).

Conversely, once we know a worst-case $O(n)$ selection algorithm is available, we can use it to find the ideal pivot (the median) at every step of quicksort, producing a **variant** with worst-case $O(n \log n)$ running time. In practical implementations, however, this variant is considerably slower on average.

Key Words

sorting algorithm	排序算法
quadratic	*adj.* 二次的
divide and conquer strategy	分而治之
pivot	*n.* 中心点
partition	*n.* 分割
pseudocode	*n.* 伪码
sequentially	*adv.* 连续地
auxiliary	*adj.* 辅助的
nested call	嵌套调用
recurrence	*n.* 循环，递归
theorem	*n.* 定理
yield	*v.* 产生
flip a coin	*v.* （为作出决定而）掷硬币
infinitesimally	*adv.* 微不足道地
permutation	*n.* 排列
elid	*v.* 修正
not-in-place	不在原来的地方
variant	*n.* 不同版本

Notes

1. The additional memory allocations required can also drastically impact speed and cache performance in practical implementations.

在实现中，所需的额外内存分配也会严重地影响速度和缓存的性能。

2. A new thread is started as soon as a sublist is available for it to work on and it does not communicate with other threads. When all threads complete, the sort is done.

当一个子列表可用时，一个新的线程就会被立即启动去处理它，并且这个线程不会与其他线程交换信息。当所有线程都结束后，排序就完成了。

Reading Material 1　Linked List

In computer science, a linked list is one of the fundamental data structures used in computer programming. It consists of a sequence of nodes, each containing arbitrary data fields and one or two references ("links") pointing to the next and/or previous nodes. A linked list is a self-referential datatype because it contains a pointer or link to another data of the same type. Linked lists permit insertion and removal of nodes at any point in the list in constant time, but do not allow random access. Several different types of linked list exist: singly-linked lists, doubly-linked lists, and circularly-linked lists.

Linked lists can be implemented in most languages. Languages such as Lisp and Scheme have the data structure built in, along with operations to access the linked list. Procedural languages such as C, C++, and Java typically rely on mutable references to create linked lists.

1. Variants

1.1　Linearly-linked List

◆ **Singly-linked List**

The simplest kind of linked list is a singly-linked list (or slist for short), which has one link per node. This link points to the next node in the list, or to a null value or empty list if it is the final node.

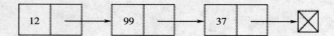

Figure 3.3.1　A singly linked list containing three integer values

◆ **Doubly-linked List**

A more sophisticated kind of linked list is a doubly-linked list or two-way linked list. Each node has two links: one points to the previous node, or points to a null value or empty list if it is the first node; and one points to the next, or points to a null value or empty list if it is the final node.

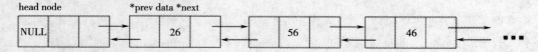

Figure 3.3.2　An example of a doubly linked list

In some very low level languages, Xor-linking offers a way to implement doubly-linked lists using a single word for both links, although the use of this technique is usually discouraged.

1.2　Circularly-linked List

In a circularly-linked list, the first and final nodes are linked together. This can be done for both singly and doubly linked lists. To traverse a circular linked list, you begin at any node and follow the list in either direction until you return to the original node. Viewed another way, circularly-linked lists can be seen as having no beginning or end. This type of list is most useful for managing buffers for data ingest, and in cases where you have one object in a list and wish to see all other objects in the list.

The pointer pointing to the whole list is usually called the end pointer.

◆   **Singly-circularly-linked List**

In a singly-circularly-linked list, each node has one link, similar to an ordinary singly-linked list, except that the next link of the last node points back to the first node. As in a singly-linked list, new nodes can only be efficiently inserted after a node we already have a reference to. For this reason, it's usual to retain a reference to only the last element in a singly-circularly-linked list, as this allows quick insertion at the beginning, and also allows access to the first node through the last node's next pointer.

◆   **Doubly-circularly-linked List**

In a doubly-circularly-linked list, each node has two links, similar to a doubly-linked list, except that the previous link of the first node points to the last node and the next link of the last node points to the first node. As in doubly-linked lists, insertions and removals can be done at any point with access to any nearby node.

1.3   Sentinel Nodes

Linked lists sometimes have a special dummy or sentinel node at the beginning and/or at the end of the list, which is not used to store data. Its purpose is to simplify or speed up some operations, by ensuring that every data node always has a previous and/or next node, and that every list (even one that contains no data elements) always has a "first" and "last" node. Lisp has such a design—the special value nil is used to mark the end of a "proper" singly-linked list, or chain of cons cells as they are called. A list does not have to end in nil, but such a list would be termed "improper".

2.   Applications of Linked Lists

Linked lists are used as a building block for many other data structures, such as stacks, queues and their variations.

The "data" field of a node can be another linked list. By this device, one can construct many linked data structures with lists; this practice originated in the Lisp programming language, where linked lists are a primary (though by no means the only) data structure, and is now a common feature of the functional programming style.

Sometimes, linked lists are used to implement associative arrays, and are in this context called association lists. There is very little good to be said about this use of linked lists; they are easily outperformed by other data structures such as self-balancing binary search trees even on small data sets (see the discussion in associative array). However, sometimes a linked list is dynamically created out of a subset of nodes in such a tree, and used to more efficiently traverse that set.

3. Linked List Operations

When manipulating linked lists in-place, care must be taken to not use values that you have invalidated in previous assignments. This makes algorithms for inserting or deleting linked list nodes somewhat subtle. This section gives pseudocode for adding or removing nodes from singly, doubly, and circularly linked lists in-place. Throughout we will use null to refer to an end-of-list marker or sentinel, which may be implemented in a number of ways.

3.1 Linearly-linked Lists

◆ **Singly-linked Lists**

Our node data structure will have two fields. We also keep a variable firstNode which always points to the first node in the list, or is null for an empty list.

```
record Node{
    data // The data being stored in the node
    next // A reference to the next node; null for last node
}
record List {
    Node firstNode//points to first node of list; null for empty list
}
```

Traversal of a singly-linked list is easy, beginning at the first node and following each next link until we come to the end:

```
node: = list. firstNode
while node not null{
    (do something with node. data)
    node: = node. next
}
```

The following code inserts a node after an existing node in a singly linked list. The diagram shows how it works. Inserting a node before an existing one cannot be done; instead, you have to locate it while keeping track of the previous node.

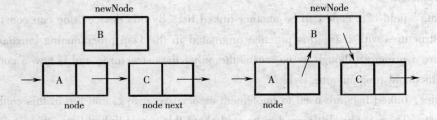

Figure 3.3.3   Insert a node in singly-linked lists

function insertAfter (Node node , Node newNode) {//insert newNode after node
    newNode. next : = node. next
    node. next : = newNode
}

Inserting at the beginning of the list requires a separate function. This requires updating first-Node.

function insertBeginning (List list , Node newNode) {//insert node before current first node
    newNode. next : = list. firstNode
    list. firstNode : = newNode
}

Similarly, we have functions for removing the node after a given node, and for removing a node from the beginning of the list. The diagram demonstrates the former. To find and remove a particular node, one must again keep track of the previous element.

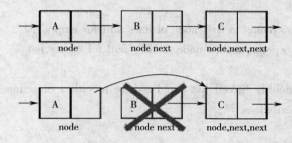

Figure 3. 3. 4   Delete a node in singly-linked lists

function removeAfter (Node node) {//remove node past this one
    obsoleteNode : = node. next
    node. next : = node. next. next
    destroy obsoleteNode
}

function removeBeginning (List list) {//remove first node
    obsoleteNode : = list. firstNode
    list. firstNode : = list. firstNode. next
    //point past deleted node destroy obsoleteNode
}

Notice that removeBeginning sets list. firstNode to null when removing the last node in the list.

The algorithms above can be made simpler if one puts a dummy element at the front of the list. That way, one never needs to insert or remove at the beginning, thus making insertBeginning and removeBeginning unnecessary. Since we can't iterate backwards, efficient "insertBefore" or "removeBefore" operations are not possible.

Appending one linked list to another is also inefficient, because we must traverse the entire first list in order to find its tail, and then append the second list to this. Thus, if two linearly-linked lists are each of length n, list appending has asymptotic time complexity of O (n). In the Lisp family of languages, list appending is provided by the append procedure.

◆ **Doubly-linked Lists**

With doubly-linked lists there are even more pointers to update, but also less information is needed, since we can use backwards pointers to observe preceding elements in the list. This enables new operations, and eliminates special-case functions. We will add a prev field to our nodes, pointing to the previous element, and a lastNode field to our list structure which always points to the last node in the list. Both list. firstNode and list. lastNode are null for an empty list.

> **record** Node {
> 　　data//The data being stored in the node
> 　　next//A reference to the next node; null for last node
> 　　prev//A reference to the previous node; null for first node
> }
>
> **record** List {
> 　　Node firstNode//points to first node of list; null for empty list
> 　　Node lastNode//points to last node of list; null for empty list
> }

Iterating through a doubly linked list can be done in either direction. In fact, direction can change many times, if desired.

> Forwards
> node: = list. firstNode
> **while** node ≠ **null**
> 　　< do something with node. data >
> 　　node: = node. next
> Backwards
> 　node: = list. lastNode
> 　**while** node ≠ **null**
> 　　< do something with node. data >
> 　　node: = node. prev

These symmetric functions add a node either after or before a given node, with the diagram demonstrating after:

3. 2 Circularly-linked Lists

Circularly-linked lists can be either singly or doubly-linked. In a circularly-linked list, all nodes are linked in a continuous circle, without using null. For lists with a front and a back (such as a queue), one stores a reference to the last node in the list. The next node after the last node is the first node. Elements can be added to the back of the list and removed from the front in constant time.

Both types of circularly-linked lists benefit from the ability to traverse the full list beginning at

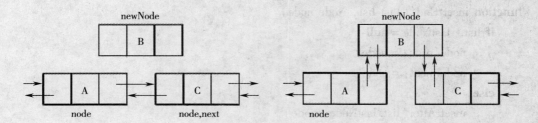

Figure 3. 3. 5   Insert a node in doubly-linked lists

any given node. This often allows us to avoid storing firstNode and lastNode, although if the list may be empty we need a special representation for the empty list, such as a lastNode variable which points to some node in the list or is null if it's empty; we use such a lastNode here. This representation significantly simplifies adding and removing nodes with a non-empty list, but empty lists are then a special case.

◆ **Doubly-circularly-linked Lists**

Assuming that someNode is some node in a non-empty list, this code iterates through that list starting with someNode (any node will do) :

Forwards

node: = someNode

do

> do something with node. value

> node: = node. next

while node ≠ someNode

Backwards

node: = someNode

do

> do something with node. value

> node: = node. prev

while node ≠ someNode

Notice the postponing of the test to the end of the loop. This is important for the case where the list contains only the single node someNode.

This simple function inserts a node into a doubly-linked circularly-linked list after a given element:

function insertAfter (Node node, Node newNode)

newNode. next: = node. next

newNode. prev: = node

node. next. prev: = newNode

node. next: = newNode

To do an "insertBefore", we can simply "insertAfter (node. prev, newNode) ". Inserting an element in a possibly empty list requires a special function：

function insertEnd （List list，Node node）

    if list. lastNode = **null**

        node. prev：= node

        node. next：= node

    else

        insertAfter（list. lastNode，node）

    list. lastNode：= node

To insert at the beginning we simply "insertAfter （list. lastNode, node）". Finally, removing a node must deal with the case where the list empties：

function remove（List list，Node node）

    if node. next = node

        list. lastNode：= **null**

    else

        node. next. prev：= node. prev

        node. prev. next：= node. next

        if node = list. lastNode

            list. lastNode：= node. prev

    destroy node

As in doubly-linked lists, "removeAfter" and "removeBefore" can be implemented with "remove （list, node. prev）" and "remove （list, node. next）".

Reading Material 2　New Algorithms for Maintaining All-pairs Shortest Paths

1. Introduction

Multihop networks, such as the Internet and the Mobile Ad hoc Networks （MANETs）, contain several routers and mobile hosts. The Internet typically employs routing protocols such as the Open Shortest Path Protocol （OSPF） and the Intermediate System-Intermediate System Protocol （IS-IS） and the MANETs employ protocols such as the Fisheye State Routing （FSR）, the Optimized Link State Routing （OLSR）, and the Ad hoc On-Demand Distance Routing （AODV）. In many of these protocols, each router （or a routing device） computes and stores the list of shortest paths from one router to all other routers and hosts in a routing domain. Such networks （graphs） typically contain several routers/switches （nodes） connected by links （edges） with constantly changing costs （weights）, link-ups （edge-insertions） and linkdowns （edge-deletions）. The generic problem of maintaining the shortest path information between all pairs of nodes in a graph, where the edges are inserted/deleted and where the edge-weights constantly increase/decrease, is referred to as the Dynamic All-Pairs Shortest Path Routing Problem (DAPSP). In such a problem, out of the four possible edgeoperations (insertion/deletion and increase/decrease), it can be shown that edge-insertion is equivalent to weight-decrease, and edge-deletion is equivalent to weight-increase.

Like the static solutions of the single source shortest path problem, the well-known static solutions for the all-pairs shortest path problem, like the Floyd Warshall's algorithm or the all-pairs adaptations of Bellman-Ford's algorithm or the Dijkstra's algorithm, which re-compute the shortest paths "from scratch" each time a topology change occurs in the graph, are certainly inefficient in such dynamic practical scenarios.

Over the last few decades, there has been a lot of research done to solve the DAPSP problem. Many other dynamic algorithms were proposed in the literature; however, their worst-case running times were no better than re-computing the all-pairs shortest paths from scratch. Thereafter, a few solutions were proposed whose running times are better than re-computing the shortest paths from scratch. However, those solutions would work only for integer weights. The algorithm proposed by Ausiello and Italiano was applicable for semi-dynamic case (decrease-only) only, and required positive integer weights less than a constant "C". The algorithm's amortized running time per insertion algorithm was O (Cnlogn). Although Henzinger et al. provided a fully-dynamic solution to the all-pairs shortest paths problem, their solution was only for planar graphs with integral values of edge-weights. The running time of their algorithm was O $[n^{4/3} \log (nC)]$ per update operation. The first fully-dynamic solution on general graphs was proposed by King. Her solution too only works with positive integer weights less than C, and the running time of the algorithm was O $[n^{.5} (C\log n)^{1/}]$. Later, Demetrescu and Italiano published two papers containing fully-dynamic algorithms that would perform edge-update operations on general graphs with real-valued edge-weights. If S represents the number of different real values, the amortized running time per update operation for their algorithm was O $[n^{.5} (S\log^3 n)]$. Finally, in 2003, Demetrescu and Italiano proposed a remarkable algorithm that solved the same problem for general digraphs with edge-weights that can assume positive real-values but with substantially improved running time per edge-update operation.

The currently acclaimed fully-dynamic algorithms (mentioned above) are constrained by the following limitations:

1) The existing fully dynamic algorithms process unit changes to the topology (i. e. , edgeinsertion/deletion or weight-increase/decrease) one change at a time, i. e. , sequentially. When there are several such operations occurring in the environment simultaneously, the algorithms are quite inefficient.

2) In environments where the edge-weights change stochastically and continuously, the existing algorithms (mentioned above) would fail to converge to the actual underlying "average" solution.

The problems are worse in large topologies which have a large number of nodes and edges, where a large number of topology changes can occur continuously at all times. In such cases the existing algorithms would fail to determine the shortest path information in a time-critical manner. We will address these problems in our research, and try to design efficient solutions for solving the DAPSP problem.

This paper presents a new algorithm, called APLA, which uses Learning Automata (LA) to generate superior results (when compared to the previous solutions) to the DAPSP problem. In a summary, learning is achieved by interacting with the environment, and processing its responses according to the chosen actions. This is further clarified in the next section.

2. LA and the DAPSP Problem

2.1 Principles of Learning Automata

LA has been used to model biological learning systems and to find the optimal action that is offered by a random environment. Learning is accomplished by actually interacting with the environment and processing its responses to the actions that are chosen, while gradually converging toward an ultimate goal. Learning Automata have found various applications in the past. Two relevant ones are in solving the graph partitioning problem and the capacity assignment problem.

The learning loop, shown in Figure 3.4.1, involves two entities, the Random Environment (RE) and a Learning Automaton. Learning is achieved by the automaton interacting with the environment, and processing the responses it gets to various actions chosen. The intention is that the LA learns the optimal action offered by the environment.

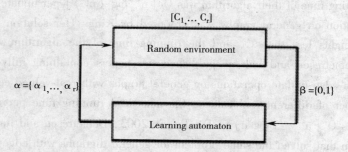

Figure 3.4.1　The Automaton-environment feedback loop

The actual process of learning is represented as a set of interactions between the RE and the LA. The LA is offered a set of actions $\{\alpha_1, \ldots, \alpha_r\}$ by the RE it interacts with, and is limited to choosing only one of these actions at any given time. Once the LA decides on an action α_i, this action will serve as input to the RE. The RE will then respond to the input by either giving a reward, signified by the value "0", or a penalty, signified by the value "1", based on the penalty probability c_i (and reward probability d_i) associated with α_i. This response serves as the input to the automaton. Based upon the response from the RE and the current information it has accumulated so far, the LA decides on its next action and the process repeats. The intention is that the LA learns the optimal action (that is, the action which has the minimum penalty probability), and eventually chooses this action more frequently than any other action.

Variable Structure Stochastic Automata (VSSA) can be described in terms of the time-varying transition and output matrices. They are, however, usually completely defined in terms of action probability updating schemes which are either continuous (operate in the continuous space) or discrete (operate in steps in the space). The action probability vector P (t) of an r-action LA is $[p_1 (t), \ldots, p_r (t)]$ T where, p_i (t) is the probability of choosing action α_i at time "n", and satisfies $0 < = p_i$ (t) $< = 1$.

A VSSA can be formally defined as a quadruple (α, P, β, T), where α, P, β, are described above, and T is the updating scheme. It is a map from P × β to P, and defines the method of updating the action probabilities on receiving an input from the RE. Also they can either be ergodic or absorbing in their Markovian behavior. The updating scheme that is used in our work is called the Linear Reward-Inaction (LRI) Scheme and is described using the equations below:

$p_i(n+1) = 1 - \Sigma_{j \neq i} \lambda_r p_j(n)$ if α_i is chosen and $\beta = 0$

$p_j(n+1) = \lambda r p_j(n)$ if α_i is chosen and $\beta = 0$

$p_j(n+1) = p_j(n)$ if α_i, α_j chosen, and $\beta = 1$

where $\lambda r (0 < \lambda r < 1)$ is the parameter of the scheme.

Typically, λr is chosen to be close to unity. Note that only rewards are processed in this scheme. Therefore, if α_i is chosen and it receives a reward, the probability of choosing this action on the next iteration, p_i (n+1), must be increased. This is accomplished in two steps. First, the probabilities of choosing any other action α_j, for all $j \neq i$, on the next iteration are reduced by setting p_j (n+1) to λr p_j (n) for all $j \neq i$. Next, the probability of choosing α_i on the next iteration, p_i (n+1), is increased by subtracting the sum of all p_j (n+1) for $j \neq i$, from unity.

2. 2 Motivation behind APLA

As mentioned earlier, there are currently inadequate solutions to the DAPSP problem for use in network scenarios when the link-costs are dynamically and stochastically changing. We believe that the reason for this is that the existing models for this problem are inadequate for this setting. We shall attempt to extend the current models by encapsulating the problem within the setting of the field of LA. To achieve this, we have to adequately model the three principal components of any LA system namely, the Automaton, the Environment, and the reward-penalty structure. We now mention how we have this.

The Automata: We propose to station an LA at every node in the network. At every instance, its task is to choose a suitable link from all the outgoing links in that node to all the rest of the nodes in the network. The intention, of course, is that it guesses that this link belongs to the shortest path between any pair of node from that node in the "average" overall network. It accomplishes this by interacting with the Environment (described below). It first chooses an action from its prescribed set of actions. It then requests the Environment for the current random link-cost for the link it has chosen. The system computes the current shortest path by invoking either the RR or the DI algorithms (Demetrescu & Italiano's Algorithm), whence the LA determines whether the choice it made should be rewarded or penalized as described below.

The Environment: The Environment consists of the overall dynamically changing network. In the network, there are multiple link-costs that change continuously and stochastically. These changes are based on a distribution that is unknown to the LA, but assumed to be known to the Environment. In a religious LA-Environment feedback, the Environment also supplies a Reward/Penalty signal to the LA. This feedback is inferred by the system, after it has invoked either RR or DI algorithms.

Reward/Penalty: Based on the action that the LA has chosen (namely, an outgoing-link from a node which the LA stochastically "guesses" to belong to the shortest path between the pair of nodes), and the linkcost that the Environment provides, the updated shortest paths are computed. The effect of this choice is now determined by comparing the cost with the current shortest paths for the "average" network, and the LA thus infers whether the choice should be rewarded or penalized. The automaton then updates the action probabilities using the LRI scheme. The algorithm pursues all the actions that have higher reward estimates than the chosen action. In this manner the cycle continues.

2.3 LA Solution to DAPSP: The APLA Algorithm

The proposed solution to DAPSP, named as APLA algorithm, is described below. There are two variants of the APLA algorithm that we propose: (i) APLA-RR: when APLA uses the algorithm proposed by Ramalingam and Reps, when an link-cost increase/decrease occurs, and (ii) APLA-DI: when APLA uses the algorithm proposed by Demetrescu and Italiano, when an link-cost increase/decrease occurs. Informally, the scheme is as follows:

1) Obtain a snapshot of the given network with each link having a random cost. This cost is based on the random call for a link, where each cost has its own mean and variance. The algorithm maintains an action probability vector, $P(t) = \{p1(t), p(t) \ldots pr(t)\}$, for each node of the network. Initialize the reward estimates vector, $d(t)$, for each node of the network.

2) Run Floyd Warshall's all-pairs static algorithm once to determine the shortest path links on the network's snapshot obtained in the first step.

3) Update the action probability vector of each node such that the outgoing edge from a node that is determined by Step 2 to belong to the shortest path edge between a pair of nodes from that node, has an increased probability than before the update.

4) Randomly choose a node from the current network. For that node, choose a link based on the action probability vector. Request the cost of this link and recalculate the shortest path using either the RR or DI algorithms.

5) Update the action probability vectors such that the edges that belong to the shortest paths between a source-destination pair have a greater likelihood of being selected has increased probability than before the update.

6) Repeat Steps 3-5 above until the algorithm has converged.

3. Example

Let us consider the graph as shown in Figure 3.4.2. In this graph, the weights of the edges are changing randomly in a continuous manner at every time instant. We want to maintain the all-pairs shortest paths in the "average graph" (since the weights of the edges are not constant) using the APLA algorithm. In other words, we want to maintain the shortest paths from A to all the rest of the nodes in the graph, B to all the rest of the nodes in the graph, and so on for all the nodes in the graph.

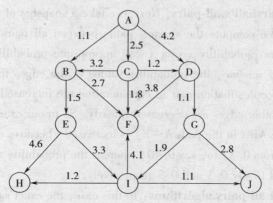

Figure 3.4.2   A hypothetical network with 10 nodes

We maintain a probability vector as shown below in Figure 3.4.3. The columns in the vector represent the source-destination pair, whereas the rows in the vector represent the outgoing links from each of the nodes. At a particular time instant, each of the elements (entries) of the vector represents a probability value corresponding to having an outgoing link from a particular node (listed as rows in the vector) in the source-destination pair (listed in the column). For example, when we consider the node A, and the source destination pair A – F, we want to maintain the probability that each of the outgoing edges from A, i.e., AB, AC, and AD lies in the shortest path between the nodes A and F.

Source_destination pairs(All–pairs of nodes) ⟶

	A–B	A–C	A–E	A–F	⋯	B–A	B–C	B–D	⋯
AB	...	...	...	...	0.3	...	...	...	...
AC					0.3				
AD					0.3				
BE									
BF									
CB									
CD									
:									
:									
:									

Possible outgoing edges from each node ⟶

Figure 3.4.3   Action probability vector. Each of the entries in the vector represents the probability that a particular edge (row indices) lies in the shortest path between a particular source-destination pair (column indices) in a network

Initialization: Let us consider the source destination pair A – F. Initially, from A, any of the outgoing edges AB, AC, or AD have an equally likely probability of being in the shortest path between A and F. So, probability of choosing AB, AC, or AD is initialized to 0.33, 0.33, 0.33 respectively. Similarly, all the other initial entries (probability values) of the probability vector are computed in the above manner.

Applying Floyd-Warshall's all-pairs: Next, we take a snapshot of the network containing different random weights. We compute the shortest paths between all pairs of nodes in the network. Then we update the above probability vector (with appropriate probability values) using the LRI scheme. According to the scheme, the probability values of the edges that lie in the shortest path corresponding to the source destination pair in consideration are increased (rewarded), whereas the probability values of the other edges are decreased linearly. So in our example, the probability value corresponding to the edge AB (in the path A − F) is increased (because edge AB lies in the shortest path between A and F) from 0.33 to, say 0.40, whereas the probability values corresponding to the other edges are decreased to say 0.3 and 0.3 respectively.

Applying RR or DI all-pairs algorithms: In this case, the exact same procedure stated above for Floyd-Warshall is applied. The probability values are updated after applying the RR or DI algorithms.

Exercises

I. Fill in the following blanks with proper words or phrases:

1. For an ideal balanced tree with n nodes in it, the height will be _____.

2. Unlike a binary-tree, each node of a b-tree may have a variable number of _____ and _____.

3. A b-tree has a minimum number of allowable children for each node known as the _____.

4. For n ⩾ 1, the height of an n-key b-tree T with minimum degree of t will be no more than _____.

5. The _____ operation creates an empty b-tree by allocating a new root node that has no keys and is a leaf node.

6. Quicksort sorts by employing a divide and conquer strategy to divide a _____ into two _____.

7. The disadvantage of the simple version above is that it requires _____ extra storage space, which is as bad as mergesort.

8. The version of quicksort with _____ partitioning uses only constant additional space before making any recursive call.

9. Once we know a worst-case O(n) selection algorithm is available, we can use it to find the ideal pivot (the median) at every step of quicksort, producing a _____ with worst-case O(n log n) running time.

II. Answer the following questions:

1. Describe the structure of B-Trees.

2. List several operations on B-Trees.

3. Give the algorithm of B-Tree-Search operation and its time complexity.

4. Why there are two kinds of algorithms for inserting a node into a B-Tree?

5. Give a strategy to avoid the concurrent access to B-trees.

6. Briefly describe the steps of quicksort algorithm.

7. Give the algorithm of quicksort in simple pseudocode.

8. Please describe the disadvantage of the simple version quicksort.

9. What does the space used by quicksort depend on?

Chapter Four Operating System

Unit 1   Operating System Structure

Without its software, a computer is basically a useless **lump** of metal. With its software, a computer can store, process, and retrieve information, find spelling errors in manuscripts, play adventure, and engage in many other valuable activities to earn its keep. Computer software can be roughly divided into two kinds: the system programs, which manage the operation of the computer itself, and the application programs, which solve problems for their users. The most fundamental of all the system programs is the operating system, which controls all the computer's resources and provides the base upon which the application programs can be written.

A modern computer system consists of one or more processors, some main memory (often known as "core memory", even though magnetic cores have not been used in memories of over a decade), clocks, terminals, disks, network interfaces, and other input/output devices. All in all, a complex system. Writing programs that keep track of all these components and use them correctly, let alone optimally, is an extremely difficult job. [1] If every programmer had to be concerned with how disk drives work, and **withal** the dozens of things that could go wrong when reading a disk block, it is unlikely that many programs could be written at all.

Many years ago it became **abundantly** clear that some way had to be found to shield programmers from the complexity of the hardware. The way that has gradually evolved is to put a layer of software on top of the bare hardware, to manage all parts of the system, and present the user with an interface or virtual machine that is easier to understand and program. This layer of software is the operating system.

This situation is shown in Figure 4.1.1. At the bottom is the hardware, which in many cases is itself composed of two or more layers. The lowest layer contains physical devices, consisting of integrated circuit chips, wires, power supplies, **cathode ray tubes**, and similar physical devices. How these are constructed and how they work is the province of the electrical engineer.

Next comes a layer of primitive software that directly controls these devices and provides a cleaner interface to the next layer. This software, called the microprogram, is usually located in read-only memory. It is actually an interpreter, fetching the machine language instructions such as ADD, MOVE, and JUMP, and carrying them out as a series of little steps. To carry out an ADD instruction, for example, the microprogram must determine where the numbers to be added are located, fetch them, add them, and store the result somewhere. The set of instructions that the microprogram interprets defines the machine language, which is not really part of the hard machine at all, but computer manufacturers always describe it in their manuals as such, so many people think of it as being the real "machine". On some machines, the microprogram is implemented in hardware and is not really a distinct.

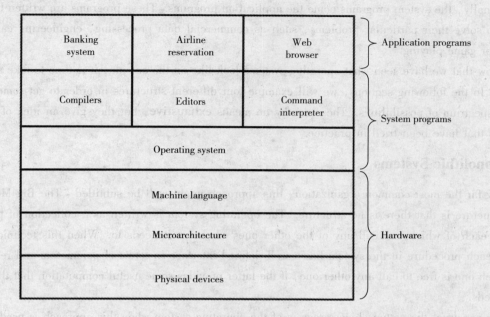

Figure 4. 1. 1   A computer system consists of hardware,
system programs, and application programs

The machine language typically has between 50 and 300 instructions, mostly for moving data around the machine, doing arithmetic and comparing values. In this layer, the input/output devices are controlled by loading values into special device registers. For example, a disk can be commanded to read by loading the values of the disk address, main memory address, byte count, and direction (READ or WRITE) into its registers. In practice, many more parameters are needed and the status returned by the drive after an operation is highly complex. Furthermore, for many I/O devices, timing plays an important role in the programming.

A major function of the operating system is to hide all this complexity and give the programmer a more convenient set of instructions to work with. For example, READ BLOCK FROM FILE is conceptually simpler than having to worry about the details of moving disk heads, waiting for them to settle down, and so on.

On top of the operating system is the rest of the system software. Here we find the command interpreter (**shell**), compilers, editors and similar application-dependent programs. It is important to realize that these programs are definitely not part of the operating system, even though they are typically supplied by the computer manufacturer. This is crucial, but subtle point. The operating system is that portion of the software runs in kernel mode or supervisor mode. It is protected from user tampering by the hardware (ignoring for the moment some of the older microprocessors that do not have hardware protection at all). [2] Compilers and editors run in user mode. If a user does not like a particular compiler, he is free to write his own if he so chooses; he is not free to write his own disk interrupt handler, which is part of the operating system and is normally protected by hardware against attempts by users to modify it.

Finally, the system programs come the application programs. These programs are written by the users to solve their particular problems, such as commercial data processing, engineering calculations, or game playing.

Now that we have seen what operating systems look like on the outside, it is time to take a look inside. In the following sections, we will examine four different structures in order to get some idea of the spectrum of possibilities. These are by no means **exhaustive**, but they give an idea of some designs that have been tried in practice.

1. Monolithic Systems

By far the most common organization, this approach might well be subtitled "The Big Mess". The structure is that there is no structure. The operating system is written as a collection of procedures, each of which can call any of the other ones whenever it needs to. When this technique is used, each procedure in the system has a well-defined interface in terms of parameters and results, and each one is free to call any other one, if the latter provides some useful computation that the former needs.

To construct the actual object program of the operating system when this approach is used, one compiles all the individual procedures, or files containing the procedures, and then binds them all together into a single object file with the linker. In terms of information hiding, there is essentially none—every procedure is visible to every other one.

Even in monolithic systems, however, it is possible to have at least a little structure. The services (system calls) provided by the operating system are requested by putting the parameters in well-defined places, such as in registers or on the stack, and then executing a special **trap instruction** known as kernel call or supervisor call.

This instruction switches the machine from user mode to kernel mode (also known as supervisor mode), and transfers control to the operating system.

The operating system then examines the parameters of the call to determine which system call is to be carried out. Next, the operating system indexes into a table that contains in slot k a pointer to the procedure that carries out system call k. This operation identifies the service procedure, which is then called. Finally, the system call is finished and control is given back to the user program.

This organization suggests a basic structure for the operating system:

1) A main program that invokes the requested service procedure.

2) A set of procedures that carry out the system calls.

3) A set of utility procedures that help the service procedures.

In this model, for each system call there is one service procedure that tasks care of it. The utility procedures do things that are needed by several service procedures, such as fetching data from user programs. This division of the procedures into there layers is shown in Figure 4.1.2.

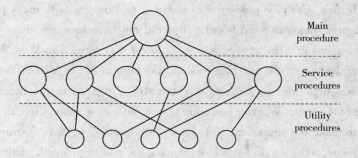

Figure 4.1.2　A simple structuring model for a monolithic system

2. Layered Systems

A generalization of the approach of Figure 4.1.2 is to organize the operating system as a hierarchy of layers, each one constructed upon the one below it. The first system constructed in this way was THE system built at the Technische Hogeschool Eindhoven in the Netherlands. The THE system was a simple batch system for a Dutch computer, the Electrologica X8, which had 32K of 27-bit words.

The system had 6 layers, as shown in Figure 4.1.3. Layer 0 dealt with allocation of the processor, switching between processes when interrupts occurred or timers expired. Above layer 0, the system consisted of sequential processes, each of which could be programmed without having to worry about the fact that multiple processes were running on a single processor. In other words, layer 0 provided that basic multiprogramming of the CPU.

Layered 1 did the memory management. It allocated space for processes in main memory and on a 512K word drum used for holding parts of processes (pages) for which there was no room in main memory. Above layer 1, process did not have to worry about whether they were in memory or on the drum; the layer 1 software took care of making sure pages were brought into memory whenever they were needed.

Layer	Function
5	The operator
4	User programs
3	Input/output management
2	Operator-process communication
1	Memory and drum management
0	Processor allocation and multiprogramming

Figure 4.1.3　Structure of THE operating system

Layer 2 handled communication between each process and the operator **console**. Above this layer each process effectively had its own operator console. Layer 3 took care of managing the I/O devices and buffering the information streams to and from them. Above layer 3 each process could deal with abstract I/O devices with nice properties, instead of real devices with many **peculiarities**. Layer 4 was where the user programs were found. They did not have to worry about process, memory, console, or I/O management. The system operator process was located in layer 5.

A further generalization of the layering concept was present in the MULTICS system. Instead of layers, MULTICS was organized as a series of **concentric rings**, with the inner ones being more privileged than the outer ones. When a procedure in an outer ring wanted to call a procedure in an inner ring, it had to make the equivalent of a system call, that is, a TRAP instruction whose parameters were carefully checked for validity before allowing the call to proceed. Although the entire operating system was part of the address space of each user process in MULTICS, the hardware made it possible to designate individual procedures (memory segments, actually) as protected against reading, writing, or executing.[3]

Whereas the THE layering scheme was really only a design aid, because all the parts of the system were ultimately linked together into a single object program, in MULTICS, the ring mechanism was very much present at run time and enforced by the hardware. The advantage of the ring mechanism is that it can easily be extended to structure user subsystems. For example, a professor could write a program to test and grade student programs and run this program in ring n, with the student program s running in ring n + 1 so that they could not change their grades.

3. Client-server Model

A trend in modern operating systems is to take this idea of moving code up into higher layers even further, and remove as much as possible from the operating systems, leaving a minimal kernel.[4] The usual approach is to implement most of the operating system functions in user processes. To request a service, such as reading a block of a file, a user process (now known as the client process) sends the request to a server process, which then does the work and sends back the answer.

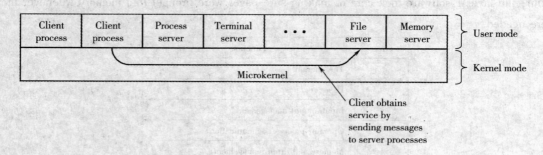

Figure 4.1.4   The client-server model

In this model, shown in Figure 4.1.4, all the kernel does is handle the communication between clients and servers. By splitting the operating system up into parts, each of which only handles one **facet** of the system, such as file service, process service, terminal service, or memory service, each part becomes small and manageable. Furthermore, because all the servers run as user-mode processes, and not in kernel mode, they do not have direct access to the hardware. As a consequence, if a bug in the file server is triggered, the file service may **crash**, but this will not usually bring the whole machine down.

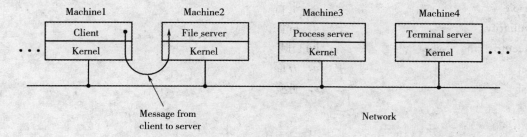

Figure 4. 1. 5   The client-server model in a distributed system

Another advantage of the client-server model is its adaptability to use in distributed system (see Figure 4. 1. 5). If a client communicates with a server by sending it messages, the client need not know whether the message is handled locally in its own machine, or whether it was sent across a network to a server on a remote machine. As far as the client is concerned, the same thing happens in both cases: a request was sent and a reply came back.

The picture painted above of a kernel that handles only the transport of messages from clients to servers and back is not completely realistic. Some operating system functions (such as loading commands into the physical I/O device registers) are difficult, if not impossible, to do from user-space programs. There are two ways of dealing with this problem. One way is to have some critical server processes actually run in kernel mode, with complete access to all the hardware, but still communicate with other processes using the normal message mechanism.

The other way is to build a minimal amount of mechanism into the kernel, but leave the policy decisions up to servers in user space. For example, the kernel might recognize that a message sent to a certain special address means to take the contents of that message and load it into the I/O device registers for some disk, to start a disk read. In this example, the kernel would not even inspect the bytes in the message to see if they were valid or meaningful; it would just blindly copy them into the disk's device registers. The split between mechanism and policy is an important concept; it occurs again and again in operating systems in various contexts.

Key Words

lump	*n*. 块
withal	*adv*. 而且
abundantly	*adv*. 充分地
cathode ray tube	阴极射线管
shell	*n*. 命令行解释器（UNIX 操作系统中的一部分，是使用者与系统的界面）
exhaustive	*adj*. 详尽无遗的

monolithic system	整体式系统
trap instruction	陷阱指令
console	*n.* 平台
peculiarity	*n.* 特性
concentric ring	同心圆
facet	*n.* 方面
crash	*v.* 崩溃

Notes

1. Writing programs that keep track of all these components and use them correctly, let alone optimally, is an extremely difficult job.

写一个能跟踪所有的组成部分、正确地使用他们的程序是一项极其困难的工作，更不用说对其进行优化了。

2. The operating system is that portion of the software that runs in kernel mode or supervisor mode. It is protected from user tampering by the hardware (ignoring for the moment some of the older microprocessors that do not have hardware protection at all).

操作系统是在内核模式或者管理程序模式下运行的软件。硬件保证了它不受用户的影响（除了在一段时期，早期的微处理器没有硬件保护）。

3. Although the entire operating system was part of the address space of each user process in MULTICS, the hardware made it possible to designate individual procedures (memory segments, actually) as protected against reading, writing, or executing.

尽管整个操作系统是 MULTICS 中每个用户线程的地址空间的一部分，硬件通过分配受保护的独立进程（实际上是内存段）来防止读、写或者执行等操作。

4. A trend in modern operating systems is to take this idea of moving code up into higher layers even further, and remove as much as possible from the operating systems, leaving a minimal kernel.

现代操作系统的潮流是通过把尽量多的代码从操作系统中移到更高层来保留一个最小的内核。

Unit 2   Linux

Linux (also known as GNU/Linux) is a Unix-like computer operating system. It is one of the most **prominent** examples of open source development and free software; its underlying source code is available for anyone to use, modify, and redistribute freely.

Initially developed and used primarily by individual **enthusiasts** on personal computers, Linux has since gained the support of corporations such as IBM, Sun Microsystems, Hewlett-Packard, and

Novell, Inc. , and has risen to prominence as an operating system for servers; eight of the ten most reliable internet hosting companies now run Linux on their web servers.

Linux has been more widely **ported** to different computing platforms than any other operating system. It is used in devices ranging from supercomputers to mobile phones, and is gaining popularity in the personal computer market.

1. History

1. 1   Early

In 1983, Richard Stallman founded the GNU Project, with the goal of developing a complete Unix-like operating system composed entirely of free software. By the beginning of the 1990s, GNU had produced or collected most of the necessary components of this system—libraries, compilers, text editors, a UNIX shell—except for the core component, the kernel. The GNU project began developing a kernel, the GNU Hurd, in 1990, based on the Mach microkernel, but the development of this Mach-based design proved difficult and proceeded slowly.

Meanwhile, in 1991, another kernel was begun as a hobby by Finnish University student Linus Torvalds while attending the University of Helsinki. Torvalds originally used Minix on his own computer, a simplified Unix-like system written by Andrew Tanenbaum for teaching operating system design. However, Tanenbaum did not permit others to extend his operating system, leading Torvalds to create a replacement for Minix.

Originally, Torvalds called his kernel "Freax" for "free" and "freak" and with the often-used X in the names of Unix-like systems. The name "Linux" was coined by Ari Lemmke, who administered an FTP server belonging to the Finnish University Network; he invented the name Linux for the directory from which Torvalds' project was first available for download.

At first a computer running Minix was necessary in order to configure and install Linux. Initial versions of Linux also required another operating system to be present in order to boot from a hard disk, but soon there were independent boot loaders such as LILO. The Linux system quickly surpassed Minix in functionality; Torvalds and other early Linux kernel developers adapted their work for the GNU components and user-space programs to create a complete, fully functional, and free (as in freedom) operating system.

Today, Torvalds continues to direct the development of the kernel, while other subsystems such as the GNU components continue to be developed separately. Other groups and companies combine and distribute these components with additional application software in the form of Linux distributions.

1. 2   Linux and the GNU Project

The goal of the GNU project is to produce a Unix-compatible operating system consisting entirely of free software. Most general-purpose Linux distributions rely on GNU libraries and tools.[1] The Free Software Foundation views these Linux distributions as "variants" of the GNU system, and asks that such operating systems be referred to as GNU/Linux or a Linux-based GNU system. While some distributions make a point of using the combined form—notably Debian GNU/Linux—its use outside of the enthusiast community is limited, and Linus Torvalds has said that he finds calling Linux in general GNU/Linux "just ridiculous". The distinction between the Linux kernel and distributions based on it is a source of confusion to many newcomers, and the naming remains controversial.

1.3 SCO Litigation

In March 2003, the SCO Group filed a lawsuit against IBM, claiming that IBM had contributed portions of SCO's copyrighted code to the Linux kernel in violation of IBM's license to use UNIX. Additionally, SCO sent letters to a number of companies warning that their use of Linux without a license from SCO may be **actionable**, and claimed in the press that they would be suing individual Linux users. This controversy has involved lawsuits by SCO against DaimlerChrysler (dismissed in 2004), and AutoZone, and by Red Hat and others against SCO. Furthermore, whether SCO even owns the relevant UNIX copyrights is currently disputed by Novell.

SCO's claims have varied widely. As of 2006, no proof of SCO's claims of copied code in Linux has been provided.

2. Portability

The Linux kernel was originally designed only for Intel 80386 microprocessors, but now supports a wide variety of computer architectures. Linux is one of the most widely ported operating systems, running on a diverse range of systems from the hand-held ARM-based iPAQ to the mainframe IBM System z9. Specialized distributions exist for less mainstream architectures. The ELKS kernel fork can run on Intel 8086 or 286 16-bit microprocessors. Yellow Dog Linux runs on Apple Computer Power-PC architectures and has been ported to the Playstation 3. They are even ports to atypical devices such as iPods and consoles.

3. Copyright, Licensing, and the Linux Trademark

The Linux kernel and most GNU software are licensed under the GNU General Public License version 2. The GPL requires that all distributed source code modifications and derived works also be licensed under the GPL, and is sometimes referred to as a "share and share-alike" or "**copyleft**" license. In 1997, Linus Torvalds stated, "Making Linux GPL'd was definitely the best thing I ever did." Other software may use other licenses; many libraries use the GNU Lesser General Public License (LGPL), a more **permissive** variant of the GPL, and the X Window System uses the MIT License.

After more than ten years, the Free Software Foundation announced that they would be upgrading the GPL to version 3, citing increasing concerns with Intellectual Property laws, especially Software Patents. Linus Torvalds has publicly stated he would not move the Linux kernel to GPL v. 3. Mr. Torvalds opposes in particular certain Digital Rights Management exclusions in the GPL v. 3.

In the United States, the name Linux is a trademark registered to Linus Torvalds. Initially, nobody registered it, but on August 15, 1994, William R. Della Croce, Jr. filed for the trademark Linux, and then demanded **royalties** from Linux distributors. In 1996, Torvalds and some affected organizations sued to have the trademark assigned to Torvalds, and in 1997 the case was settled. The licensing of the trademark is now handled by the Linux Mark Institute. Torvalds has stated that he only trademarked the name to prevent someone else from using it, but was bound in 2005 by United States trademark law to take active measures to enforce the trademark. [2] As a result, the LMI sent out a number of letters to distribution vendors requesting that a fee be paid for the use of the name, and a number of companies have complied.

4. Development

More Than a Gigabuck: Estimating GNU/Linux's Size, a 2001 study of Red Hat Linux 7.1, found that this distribution contained 30 million source lines of code. Using the Constructive Cost Model, the study estimated that this distribution required about eight thousand man-years of development time. According to the study, if all this software had been developed by conventional proprietary means, it would have cost about 1.08 billion dollars (year 2000 U.S. dollars) to develop in the United States.

The majority of the code (71%) was written in the C programming language, but many other languages were used, including C++, Lisp, assembly language, Perl, Fortran, Python and various shell scripting languages. Slightly over half of all lines of code were licensed under the GPL. The Linux kernel was 2.4 million lines of code, or 8% of the total.

In a later study, "Counting Potatoes: The size of Debian 2.2", the same analysis was performed for Debian GNU/Linux version 2.2. This distribution contained over fifty-five million source lines of code, and the study estimated that it would have cost 1.9 billion dollars (year 2000 U.S. dollars) to develop by conventional means.

5. Distributions

Linux is predominantly used as part of a Linux distribution (commonly called a "distro"). These are compiled by individuals, **loose-knit** teams, commercial and volunteer organizations. They commonly include additional systems and application software, an installer system to ease initial system setup, and integrated management of software installation and upgrading. Distributions are created for many different purposes, including computer architecture support, localization to a specific region or language, real-time applications, embedded systems, and many deliberately include only free software. Currently, over three hundred distributions are actively developed, with about a dozen distributions being most popular for general-purpose use.

A typical general-purpose distribution includes the Linux kernel, some GNU libraries and tools, command-line shells, the graphical X Window System and an accompanying desktop environment such as KDE or GNOME, together with thousands of application software packages, from office suites to compilers, text editors, and scientific tools.

6. Desktop Usage

The high level of access granted to Linux's internals has led to Linux users traditionally tending to be more technologically oriented than users of Microsoft Windows and Mac OS, sometimes **reveling** in the tag of "hacker" or "geek". Linux and other free software projects have been frequently criticized for not going far enough to ensure ease of use.

This **stereotype** has begun to be **dispelled** in recent years. Linux may now be used with a user interface that is very similar to those running on other operating systems. However users may have to switch to alternative application software, and there are often fewer "known" software choices (as in the case of computer games) but there exist replacements for all general-purpose software, and general applications like spreadsheets, word processors, and browsers are available for Linux in **profusion**. Additionally, a growing number of proprietary software vendors are supporting Linux, and compatibility layers such as Wine or NdisWrapper allow some Windows application software and drivers to be used on Linux without requiring the vendor to adapt them.

Linux's roots in the UNIX operating system mean that in addition to graphical configuration tools and control panels available for many system settings and services, plain-text configuration files are still commonly used to configure the OS and can readily be made accessible (or not) to users, at the administrator's will.

The Berlin-based organization Relevantive concluded in 2003 that the usability of Linux for a set of desktop-related tasks was "nearly equal to Windows XP". Since then, there have been numerous independent studies and articles which indicate that a modern Linux desktop using either GNOME or KDE is **on par with** Microsoft Windows in a business setting.

7. Enterprise Usage

Linux has historically been used mainly as a server operating system, but its low cost, flexibility, and Unix-like architecture make it suitable for a variety of applications. Linux is the **cornerstone** of the "LAMP" server-software combination (Linux, Apache, MySQL, Perl/PHP/Python) which has achieved popularity among developers, and which is one of the more common platforms for website hosting.

Due to its low cost and its high configurability, Linux is often used in embedded systems such as television **set-top boxes**, mobile phones, and handheld devices. Linux has become a major competitor to the proprietary Symbian OS found in many mobile phones, and it is an alternative to the dominant Windows CE and Palm OS operating systems on **handheld devices**. The popular TiVo digital video recorder uses a customized version of Linux. Several network firewall and router standalone products, including several from Linksys, use Linux internally, using its advanced firewalling and routing capabilities.

Linux is increasingly common as an operating system for supercomputers. For example, in the November 2005 TOP500 list of supercomputers, seven of the top ten supercomputers in the world, including the two fastest, ran Linux. Of the 500 systems, 371 (74.2%) ran Linux.

8. Market Share and Uptake

According to the market research company IDC, 25% of servers and 2.8% of desktop computers ran Linux as of 2004. Proponents and analysts attribute the success of Linux to its security, reliability, low cost, and freedom from vendor **lock-in**. The frictional cost of switching and lack of support for certain hardware and application programs designed for Microsoft Windows, especially games or uncommon business software, have been two important factors inhibiting fast adoption. [3]

The Linux market is rapidly growing and the revenue of servers, desktops, and packaged software running Linux is expected to exceed $35.7 billion by 2008. The actual installed user base may be higher, as most Linux distributions and applications are freely available and redistributable.

The paper "Why Open Source Software/Free Software (OSS/FS)? Look at the Numbers!" identifies many quantitative studies of open source software on topics including market share and reliability, with many studies specifically examining Linux.

9. Installation

The most common method of installing Linux on a personal computer is by booting from a CD-ROM that contains the installation program and installable software. Such a CD can be burned from a downloaded ISO image, purchased alone for a low price, obtained as part of a box set, or in a few cases shipped for free by request. A box set may also include manuals and additional proprietary software. Mini CD images allow Linux to be installed from a disk with a small form factor.

As with servers, personal computers that come with Linux already installed are available from vendors including Hewlett-Packard and Dell, although generally only for their business desktop line.

Alternatives to traditional desktop installation include **thin client** installation and running directly from a Live CD. In a thin client installation, the operating system is loaded and run from a centralized machine over a network connection. In a Live CD setup, the computer boots the entire operating system from CD without first installing it on the computer's hard disk.

On embedded devices, Linux is typically held in the device's firmware and may or may not be consumer-accessible.

10. Programming on Linux

The GNU Compiler Collection (GCC) is the standard compiler family for most Linux systems. Amongst others, GCC provides frontends for C, C++ and Java. Most distributions come installed with interpreters for Perl, Python and other scripting languages, and several now include C# via the Mono project.

There are a number of integrated development environments available including MonoDevelop, KDevelop, Anjuta, NetBeans, and Eclipse while the traditional editors Emacs and Vim remain popular.

The two main widget toolkits used for contemporary GUI programming are Qt and the Gimp Toolkit, known as GTK+.

As well as these free and open source options, there are proprietary compilers and tools available from a range of companies such as Intel, PathScale, Micro Focus COBOL, Franz Inc., and the Portland Group.

11. Support

Technical support is provided by commercial suppliers and by other Linux users, usually in online forums, **IRC**, newsgroups, and mailing lists. Linux User Groups have traditionally been organized to provide support for Linux in specific cities and regions.

The business model of commercial suppliers is generally dependent on charging for support, especially for business users. A number of companies offer a specialized business version of their distribution, which adds proprietary support packages and tools to administer higher numbers of installations or to simplify administrative tasks.

Key Words

prominent	adj.	著名的
enthusiast	n.	爱好者
port	v.	移植
controversial	adj.	有争议的
litigation	n.	诉讼
actionable	adj.	可控告的
portability	n.	可移植性
copyleft	n.	对称版权（是自由软件运动和开放源码运动关于版权思想的核心概念）
permissive	adj.	宽容的
royalty	n.	专利税
loose-knit	adj.	松散的
revel	v.	着迷
stereotype	n.	陈规，陋习
dispel	v.	消除
profusion	n.	丰富
on par with		等同的
cornerstone	n.	基础
set-top box		机顶盒
handheld device		手持设备
lock-in	n.	锁定
thin client		瘦客户端
IRC		Internet Relay Chat 的缩写（是一个多用户、多频道的聊天系统）

Notes

1. The goal of the GNU project is to produce a Unix-compatible operating system consisting entirely of free software. Most general-purpose Linux distributions rely on GNU libraries and tools.

GNU 项目的目标是生成一个完全由免费软件组成的、与 UNIX 兼容的操作系统。绝大多数一般用途的 Linux 的发布依赖 GNU 库和工具。

2. Torvalds has stated that he only trademarked the name to prevent someone else from using it, but was bound in 2005 by United States trademark law to take active measures to enforce the trademark.

Torvalds 声称，他仅仅把名称作为商标登记是为了防止其他人使用，但是在 2005 年，美国商标法认为，他有义务采取主动方式来维护商标权。

3. The frictional cost of switching and lack of support for certain hardware and application programs designed for Microsoft Windows, especially games or uncommon business software, have been two important factors inhibiting fast adoption.

转换过程的磨合消耗以及缺乏对一些特定硬件和专门为 Microsoft Windows 设计的应用程序（尤其是游戏和一些特殊的商业软件）的支持，是导致其无法被迅速采用的两个重要因素。

Reading Material 1   Porting Window CE Operating System to Broadband Enabled STB Devices

1. Introduction

Broadband Internet connection to home becomes one of the fast growing market sectors. The growth is witnessed by the accelerated demands of High-Speed Internet connection. According to Gartner Group prediction there is close to 16 million US households with cable-modem or DSL services in 2001. The projection of the broadband connection via Ethernet or FTTH (Fiber To The Home) will reach 15 million of households by the end of this year 2001 and more than 30 million by 2004 by a report from Multimedia Research Group. This creates very exciting opportunity for the users and service providers (ISPs) to delivery Voice/Data/Video in a unified fashion, which will significantly reshape the Internet, telecom, and entertainment industry. Jupiter reports 30 million US households will have Interactive TV (ITV) capabilities for the next few years. However, seamless integration of the hardware system with well-tailored OS is still yet to be fully addressed. In this paper, we will describe one of our efforts of porting WinCE to Philips broadband enabled set-top box.

This paper is organized as follows: First, we will describe the system architecture and memory map as well as the outlines of the entire porting strategy. In section 3, we briefly describe WinCE OS. In section 4, we provide the information on the development environment and the procedures to configure the environment for building the OS image. We cover the subjects of boot loader, a program stored in FLASH memory to initialize hardware and to bring up the OS kernel functions in section 5.

2. Architecture of the Target Hardware Platform

2.1 Description of the CPU and Media Processor

A STB8300 is powered by a 133-MHz MIPS 3940 RISC core. PR3940 is a high-performance, 32 bits processor core based on the MIPS-II and MIPS-16 instruction set architectures that can increase the code density. It contains built-in memory management unit and cache memory, multiply accumulate unit, and Debug support unit. PR3940 has low power consumption and high performance/cost ration. All those features make it especially suit for embedded controls in consumer electronics applications such as set-top box control processors.

The media processor used in this platform is SAA7240. It is a transport MPEG-2 source decoder designed for application in set-top boxes in a Digital Video Broadcast environment. The device is part of a comprehensive source decoding kit that contains the hardware and software required to receive and decode MPEG-2 transport streams, including descrambling and demultiplexing. It includes a PR3930 core supporting the MIPS16 instruction set and several peripheral interfaces. The SAA7240 is therefore capable of performing all controller tasks in digital television applications.

2. 2 Memory Map

The PR3940 MMU logically expands the physical address space of the CPU by translating addresses composed in a large virtual address space into the physical address space in two ways: static translation and dynamic translation. In the Boot Loader step, we use static translation. When the environment is built, dynamic translation is used.

The entire virtual address space is 4GB. The kernel mode allows access to the entire virtual address space, whereas the user mode is restricted to the lower 2 GB of address space.

The entire memory address space is divided into four memory segments. They are shown as below:

1) kuseg—It is shared by both kernel and users.

2) kseg0—It is cacheable and used for kernel-only execution code.

3) kseg1—It is non-cacheable and used for I/O registers, ROM code and disk buffers.

4) kseg2—It is used for stacks and processor data by the Operating System.

The processor also divides the virtual memory into more small regions and assigns them different functions.

3. Introduction of Windows CE

Windows CE is a portable, real-time, modular operating system that features popular Microsoft programming interfaces and that is supported by tools that enable rapid development of embedded and dedicated systems.

3. 1 Architecture

Windows CE was developed with the purpose of providing a Windows operating system for a variety of hardware. The target systems are diverse, but they have one thing in common: they are designed to be small. Windows CE is a small version of Windows. The difference between it and the series of Windows is that Windows CE is componentized and ROMable. Windows CE can also use a subset of the already familiar Microsoft APIs. This combination has resulted in Windows CE, which can be made to fit to the requirements of any embedded application, while keeping the programmability.

The architecture of Windows CE reflects the hardware the operating system was designed to support. The overall design of Windows CE looks like is shown in the diagram below. The services are grouped in a number of modules, which can be included or excluded when building a Windows CE image for a specific target system.

Windows CE supports a variety of processors: MIPS, ARM, SHx, PowerPC, and x86. It supports main type microprocessors. It is written to be as portable as possible across processors. It contains processor-specific code. Windows CE isolates it in three sections: kernel, OEM Adaptation Layer (OAL), and Boot Loader.

Apart from the OAL and the Kernel in the above diagram, anything can be left out and will in

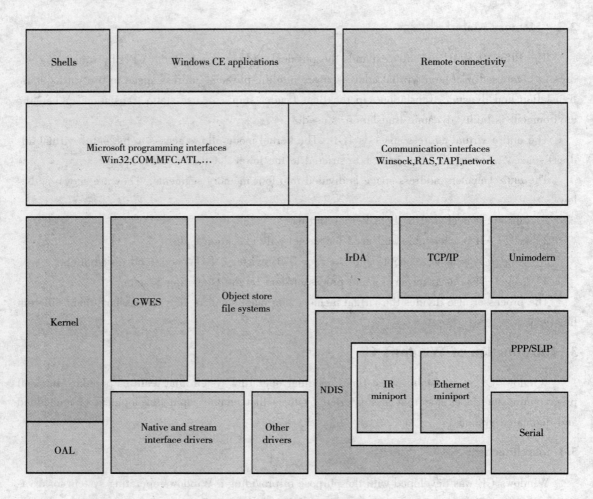

Figure 4. 3. 1   Window CE components

that case not be part of the Windows CE image. If a certain service is needed, only the functions supporting that service are needed.

Kernel contains the core functions of Windows CE: process handling, memory management and interrupt handling. It is designed to be small and fast. It is provided by Microsoft and is chosen by developer based on processor's type and requirement for the system.

OAL contains code specific to a particular platform that is built through the use of a given microprocessor, and it is responsible for abstracting and managing hardware resources of the processor.

Boot Loader is responsible for booting the system by correctly configuring the processor and peripheral chips. Its job is to set the stage for starting the heart of most devices: the system software. It represents the first lines of code to run in any system. So the development of Boot Loader is the first step for this project.

Object Store refers to the three types of persistent storage: file systems, the registry, and property databases. The total size of the object store is limited to 16 MB. Windows CE supports one proprietory file system and up to nine installable file systems. The proprietory file system allows files to be either in RAM or in ROM. If a file is copied to RAM, the file in ROM is hidden behind the RAM-based file.

Graphics, Windowing and Event subsystem (GWES) takes care of any graphics that may be displayed on a Windows CE system. It also handles creation and destruction of windows. The Event subsystem handles the registration and passing on of user events, and custom events. It can't handle events that are generated by the hardware through IRQs.

The Windows CE architecture includes a variety of communications and connectivity options. Communications module in Windows CE contains many standard drivers. Those are described in layers. At the lowest level, Windows CE offers support for serial connections. At the intermediate level, it supports Remote Access Service and Winsock, which use the TCP/IP and PPP/SLIP. At the highest level, it provides FTP and HTTP. Windows CE supports secure communications at all levels.

3.2   Embedded OS Components

An Operating System provides a uniform interface to control the resources of a computer system. The interface consists of a set of system calls, or more commonly, application programming interface (API), which could be used by applications. There are four major categories of interface in a modern OS, including Process Management, Device Input/Output, Memory Management, and File System.

A process is an application that is currently running in the system. In order to use the computing resources more efficiently, multiple processes can run in the time. Actually, an OS swaps each process in and out in a predetermined time interval to give the user an illusion of several processes running simultaneously. The OS is responsible for the process scheduling. However, when multiple processes run at the same time, it is possible for process A to overwrite process B's certain memory location before process A can finishes the job. Hence, the OS must provide synchronization mechanisms to prevent such problem from occurring.

Device I/O software provides controls for hardware components in the system. Most OS provide such controls via four layers of software, Interrupt Handler, Device Driver, Device Independent Software, and User Software. Interrupt Handler invokes Interrupt Service Routine, which is part of the Device Driver. The Device Driver is responsible for all the heavy duty to communicate with the device. The Device Independent Software provides a uniform programming interface for the user programs. While optional, the User Software for the devices provides extra functionally in the form of library object code in the user space.

The size of the physical memory is usually smaller than that of the logical memory. With the features like MMU and TLB available in most CPU, an OS can implement schemes like virtual memory and segmentation to provide user program a much larger flat memory space.

File system provides services to access storage medium, such as Hard Dick Drive (HDD). The storage mediums are formatted with a predefined file system structure, e. g. FAT and NTFS. The OS must provide services to retrieve information from the medium efficiently and quickly.

4. Boot Loader

During development, the boot loader resides on the platform and manages the boot process. The boot loader is used to download code, such as a Windows CE operating system image, from the development workstation to the target device. Once the OS is loaded, the boot loader is used to monitor and debug the target device.

In this project, we write only platform-specific and CPU-specific code modules for the boot loader. These modules initialize the CPU, the serial port and the bi-directional parallel port for the target device. The task of initializing other hardware is in the following stage: OAL development.

The elements of boot loader must be implemented: OEM startup code, Kernel startup code, OEM platform initialization code, Image download code, Parallel port I/O code, and Debug serial I/O code.

The main routines of boot process are init. s and main. c. The first execution code is StartUp routine in init. s. It is used as the primary entry point into the boot loader. In the end of StartUp routine, code jumps to the main routine. In the end of main routine, code jumps into CE Kernel by calling Launch routine implemented in the init. s.

Init. s is used to configure processor that is PNX3940. Main. c is used to configure the basic peripherals for debuging and downloading the boot process: serial port, LED, and parallel port; implement the OEM-specific startup routine that initializes the kernel: KernelRelocate initializes the remainder of the C environment and copies writable data sections into RAM; OEMinitDebugSerial initializes serial port used on this platform for debugging; DownloadImage initializes parallel port used on this platform for downloading image and implementing the download process.

The process of porting the sample boot loader code to the platform is divided into 6 steps.

1) Implement the following code:
◆ The code to start up and initialize the target device: init. s, main. c.
◆ The code to download an OS image to the target device.
◆ The code to read and write data to the parallel port on the target device.
◆ The code to read and write characters to the debug serial port on the target device.

2) Build the boot loader image.

3) Compile and build platform in platform builder.

4) Modify the boot. bib binary image builder file.

5) Create the boot loader binary image file by using romimage. This procedure creates the binary image file named boot. bin.

6) Load and verify the boot loader.

5. OAL

OAL is a collection of functions that may be accessed by the CE operating system to gain access to platform-specific features. The CE kernel calls these functions to obtain access to the capabilities of the platform. OAL forms the connection between the Windows CE kernel and the hardware.

The boot loader is built as a stand-alone image and the OAL functions are included in the kernel image. OAL is the first code to run in the CE kernel. The figure below shows the OAL architecture.

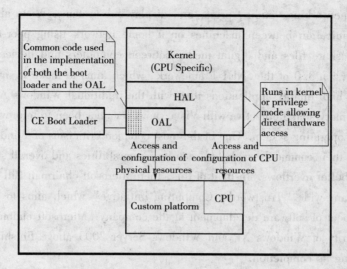

Figure 4. 3. 2   Relation of Windows CE's boot loader, OAL, and the target hardware platform

From this figure, we can find there are an overlap between the OAL and the boot loader. Those codes should be contained in both.

The OAL development process is divided into three phases.

1) Developing a set of OAL functions used to start the CE kernel.

2) Adding remote debugging support and interrupt service routines based on first step.

3) Expanding features to provide module certification.

OAL isolates the hardware with the kernel. It configures the hardware that is not initialized in the boot loader step. After the stage of OAL, hardware in the platform is configured.

Reading Material 2   Windows Vista

Windows Vista is the name of the latest release of Microsoft Windows, a line of graphical operating systems used on personal computers, including home and business desktops, notebook computers, and media centers. Prior to its announcement on July 22, 2005, Vista was known by its codename Longhorn. On November 8, 2006, Windows Vista development was completed and is now in the release to manufacturing stage. Some editions were available to volume license customers, MSDN and TechNet subscribers through November 2006; Microsoft has stated that the scheduled release date for worldwide availability is January 30, 2007. These release dates come more than five years after the release of its predecessor, Windows XP, making it the longest time span between major releases of Windows.

According to Microsoft, Windows Vista contains hundreds of new features; some of the most significant include an updated graphical user interface and visual style dubbed Windows Aero, improved searching features, new multimedia creation tools such as Windows DVD Maker, and completely redesigned networking, audio, print, and display sub-systems. Vista also aims to increase the level of communication between machines on a home network using peer-to-peer technology, making it easier to share files and digital media between computers and devices. For developers, Vista introduces version 3.0 of the .NET Framework, which aims to make it significantly easier for developers to write high-quality applications than with the traditional Windows API.

Microsoft's primary stated objective with Vista, however, has been to improve the state of security in the Windows operating system. One of the most common criticisms of Windows XP and its predecessors has been their commonly exploited security vulnerabilities and overall susceptibility to malware, viruses and buffer overflows. In light of this, then Microsoft chairman Bill Gates announced in early 2002 a company-wide "Trustworthy Computing initiative" which aims to incorporate security work into every aspect of software development at the company. Microsoft claimed that it prioritized improving the security of Windows XP and Windows Server 2003 above finishing Windows Vista, significantly delaying its completion.

During the course of its development, Vista has been the target of a number of negative assessments by various groups. Criticism of Windows Vista has included protracted development time, more restrictive licensing terms, the inclusion of a number of new Digital Rights Management technologies aimed at restricting the copying of protected digital media, and the usability of new features such as User Account Control.

1. Development

Microsoft started work on their plans for "Longhorn" in May 2001, prior to the release of Windows XP. It was originally expected to ship sometime late in 2003 as a minor step between Windows XP (codenamed "Whistler") and "Blackcomb" (now known as Windows "Vienna"). Indeed, Longhorn, Vista's original codename, was an allusion to this plan. While Whistler-Blackcomb is a large ski resort in British Columbia, Longhorn Saloon & Grill is the name of an après bar between the two mountains that Whistler's visitors pass to reach Blackcomb.

Gradually, "Longhorn" assimilated many of the important new features and technologies slated for "Blackcomb", resulting in the release date being pushed back a few times. Many of Microsoft's developers were also re-tasked with improving the security of Windows XP. Faced with ongoing delays and concerns about feature creep, Microsoft announced on August 27, 2004 that it was making significant changes. "Longhorn" development basically started afresh, building on the Windows Server 2003 codebase, and re-incorporating only the features that would be intended for an actual operating system release. Some previously announced features, such as WinFS and NGSCB, were dropped or postponed, and a new software development methodology called the "Security Development Lifecycle" was incorporated in an effort to address concerns with the security of the Windows codebase.

After "Longhorn" was named Windows Vista, an unprecedented beta-test program was started, which involved hundreds of thousands of volunteers and companies. In September 2005, Microsoft started releasing regular Community Technology Previews (CTP) to beta testers. The first of these was distributed among 2005 Microsoft Professional Developers Conference attendees, and was subsequently released to Microsoft Beta testers and Microsoft Developer Network subscribers. The builds that followed incorporated most of the planned features for the final product, as well as a number of changes to the user interface, based largely on feedback from beta testers. Windows Vista was deemed feature-complete with the release of the "February CTP", released on February 22, 2006, and much of the remainder of work between that build and the final release of the product focused on stability, performance, application and driver compatibility, and documentation. Beta 2, released in late May, was the first build to be made available to the general public through Microsoft's Customer Preview Program. It was downloaded by over five million people. Two release candidates followed in September and October, both of which were made available to a large number of users.

While Microsoft had originally hoped to have the operating system available worldwide in time for the 2006 holiday season, it was announced in March 2006 that the release date would be pushed back to January 2007, so as to give the company—and the hardware and software companies which Microsoft depends on for providing device drivers—additional time to prepare. Through much of 2006, analysts and bloggers had speculated that Windows Vista would be delayed further, owing to anti-trust concerns raised by the European Commission and South Korea, and due to a perceived lack of progress with the beta releases. However, with the November 8, 2006 announcement of the completion of Windows Vista, Microsoft's most lengthy operating system development project in the company's history has come to an end.

2. New or Improved Features

2.1 End-user Features

Windows Aero is a new hardware-based graphical user interface, named Windows Aero—an acronym (possibly a backronym) for Authentic, Energetic, Reflective, and Open. The new interface is intended to be cleaner and more aesthetically pleasing than previous Windows, including new transparencies, animations and eye candy.

The new Windows shell is significantly different from Windows XP, offering a new range of organization, navigation, and search capabilities. Windows Explorer's task pane has been removed, integrating the relevant task options into the toolbar. A "Favorite links" pane has been added, enabling one-click access to common directories. The address bar has been replaced with a breadcrumb navigation system. The Start menu has changed as well; it no longer uses ever-expanding boxes when navigating through Programs. Even the word "Start" itself has been removed in favor of a blue Windows Orb.

Windows Search is significantly faster and more thorough search capabilities. Search boxes have been added to the Start menu, Windows Explorer, and several of the applications included with Vista. By default, Instant Search indexes only a small number of folders such as the start menu, the names of files opened, the Documents folder, and the user's E-mail.

Windows Sidebar is a transparent panel anchored to the side of the screen where a user can place Desktop Gadgets, which are small applets designed for a specialized purpose (such as displaying the weather or sports scores). Gadgets can also be placed on other parts of the Desktop, if desired. The technology bears some resemblance to the older Active Channel and Active Desktop technologies introduced with Windows 95 OEM Service Release 2.5, but the gadgets technology is more versatile, and is not integrated with the Internet Explorer browser in the same way as Active Desktop.

Windows Media Player 11 is a major revamp of Microsoft's program for playing and organizing music and video. New features in this version include word wheeling (or "search as you type"), a completely new and highly graphical interface for the media library, photo display and organization, and the ability to share music libraries over a network with other Vista machines, Xbox 360 integration, and support for other Media Center Extenders.

Backup and Restore Center includes a backup and restore application that gives users the ability to schedule periodic backups of files on their computer, as well as recovery from previous backups. Backups are incremental, storing only the changes each time, minimizing the disk usage. It also features CompletePC Backup which backs up an entire computer as an image onto a hard disk or DVD. CompletePC Backup can automatically recreate a machine setup onto new hardware or hard disk in case of any hardware failures.

Windows Mail is a replacement for Outlook Express that includes a completely replaced mail store that improves stability, and enables real-time search. New Junk mail filtering.

Windows Photo Gallery is a photo and movie library management application. WPG can import from digital cameras, tag and rate individual items, adjust colors and exposure, create and display slideshows (with pan and fade effects), and burn slideshows to DVD.

Windows Meeting Space is the replacement for NetMeeting. Users can share applications (or their entire Desktop) with other users on the local network, or over the Internet using peer-to-peer technology.

Windows Media Center, which was previously exclusively bundled as a separate version of Windows XP, known as Windows XP Media Center Edition, will be incorporated into the Home Premium and Ultimate editions of Windows Vista.

Every game included with Windows has been rewritten to take advantage of Vista's new graphics capabilities. New games include Chess Titans, Mahjong Titans and Purble Place. The Games section will also hold links and information to all games on the user's computer. One piece of information that will be shown is the game's ESRB rating.

Previous Versions automatically creates backup copies of files and folders, with daily frequency. Users can also create "shadow copies" by setting a System Protection Point using the System Protection tab in the system control panel. The user can be presented multiple versions of a file throughout a limited history and be allowed to restore, delete, or copy those versions. This feature is available only in the Business, Enterprise, and Ultimate editions of Windows Vista and is inherited from Windows Server 2003.

The Windows Mobility Center is a new control panel that centralizes the most relevant information related to mobile computing (e. g. brightness, sound, battery level / power scheme selection, wireless network, screen orientation, presentation settings, etc.).

Software and security updates have been simplified, now operating solely via a control panel instead of as a web application. Mail's spam filter and Defender's definitions will also be automatically updated via Windows Update.

Windows SideShow, enables the auxiliary displays on newer laptops or on supported Windows Mobile devices. It is meant to be used to display Device gadgets while the computer is on or off.

Speech recognition is fully integrated into Vista. It is an improved version of Microsoft Speech Recognition currently working under Office 2003, with a better interface, a rich and flexible set of commands, and an extensive command-and-control capability to activate the computer by voice. Unlike the Office 2003 version, which works only in Office and WordPad, it works for dictation in multiple applications. In addition, it currently supports several languages: English US and UK, Spanish, French, German, Chinese (Classical and Simplified), and Japanese.

Many new fonts include several designed especially for screen reading, and new high-quality Chinese (Yahei, JhengHei), Japanese (Meiryo) and Korean (Malgun) fonts. See Windows Vista typefaces. ClearType has also been enhanced and enabled by default.

Improved audio controls allow the system-wide volume or volume of individual audio devices and even individual applications to be controlled separately. It introduced new audio functionalities such as Room Correction, Bass Management and Speaker Fill .

System Performance Assessment is a benchmark used by Windows Vista to regulate the system for optimum performance. Games can take advantage of this feature, reading the data produced by this benchmark in order to fine-tune the game details. The benchmark tests CPU, RAM, Graphics acceleration (2D and 3D) and disk access.

2. 2   Core Technologies

Windows Vista is intended to be a technology-based release, to provide a solid base to include advanced technologies, many of which will be related to how the system functions, and hence not readily visible to the user. An example of this is the complete restructuring of the architecture of the audio, print, display, and networking subsystems; while the results of this work will be clearly visible to software developers, end-users will only see what appear to be evolutionary changes in the user interface.

Vista includes technologies such as ReadyBoost and ReadyDrive which employ fast flash memory (located on USB drives and hybrid hard disk drives respectively) to improve system performance by caching commonly-used programs and data. This manifests itself in improved battery life on notebook computers as well, since a hybrid drive can be spun down when not in use. Another new technology called SuperFetch utilizes machine learning techniques to analyze usage patterns in order to allow Windows Vista to make intelligent decisions about what content should be present in system memory at any given time.

As part of the complete redesign of the networking architecture, IPv6 has been fully incorporated into the operating system, and a number of performance improvements have been introduced, such as TCP window scaling. Prior versions of Windows typically needed third-party wireless networking software to work properly; this is no longer the case with Vista, as it includes more comprehensive wireless networking support.

For graphics, Vista introduces a new Windows Display Driver Model, as well as major revision to Direct3D. The new driver model facilitates the new Desktop Window Manager, which provides the tearing-free desktop and special effects that are the cornerstones of Windows Aero. Direct3D 10, developed in conjunction with major display driver manufacturers, is a new architecture with more advanced shader support, and allows the graphics processing unit to render more complex scenes without assistance from the CPU. It features improved load balancing between CPU and GPU and also optimizes data transfer between them.

At the core of the operating system, many improvements have been made to the memory manager, process scheduler, heap manager, and I/O scheduler. A Kernel Transaction Manager has been implemented that gives applications the ability to work with the file system and registry using atomic transaction operations.

2.3 Business Technologies

While much of the focus of Vista's new capabilities has been on the new user interface, security technologies, and improvements to the core operating system, Microsoft is also adding new deployment and maintenance features to make a compelling case for businesses still running Windows NT, 2000, and XP desktops.

Exercises

Ⅰ. Fill in the following blanks with proper words or phrases:

1. Computer software can be roughly divided into two kinds: _____ and _____.

2. The software, called _____, which is usually located in read-only memory, is actually an interpreter, fetching the machine language instructions such as ADD, MOVE, and JUMP, and carrying them out as a series of little steps.

3. The programs, which are written by the users to solve their particular problems, such as commercial data processing, engineering calculations, or game playing, are called _____.

4. A simple structuring model for a monolithic system includes _____, _____ and _____.

5. A trend in modern operating systems is to take this idea of moving code up into higher layers even further, and remove as much as possible from the operating systems, leaving a minimal _____.

6. In 1983, Richard Stallman founded the _____, with the goal of developing a complete Unix-like operating system composed entirely of free software.

7. LILO is an independent _____ for Linux to boot from a hard disk.

8. The _____ and most _____ are licensed under the GNU General Public License version 2.

9. The majority of the code (71%) of Linux system was written in the _____ language.

10. The _____ is the standard compiler family for most Linux systems.

Ⅱ. Answer the following questions:

1. Draw a hierarchical figure of computer system with hardware, system programs, and application programs.

2. For a monolithic system, what should a basic structure of operating system have?

3. For layered systems, list the functions of the six layers.

4. Draw a figure of client-server model in a distributed system.

5. Who started the GNU Project? And what's the goal of GNU Project?

6. What does a typical general-purpose Linux distribution include?

7. Why Linux has achieved popularity among developers?

8. What is GCC on Linux?

Chapter Five   Programming Languages

Unit 1   History of Programming Languages

1. Prehistory

The first programming languages predate the modern computer. From the first, the languages were codes. Herman Hollerith realized that he could encode information on **punch cards** when he observed that railroad train conductors would encode the **appearance** of the ticket holders on the train tickets using the position of punched holes on the tickets. Hollerith then proceeded to encode the 1890 census data on punch cards which he made the same size as the boxes for holding US currency. (The dollar bill was later downsized.)

The first computer codes were specialized for the applications. In the first decades of the twentieth century, numerical calculations were based on **decimal** numbers. Eventually it was realized that logic could be represented with numbers, as well as with words. For example, Alonzo Church was able to express the lambda calculus in a **formulaic** way. The **Turing machine** was an abstraction of the operation of a tape-marking machine, for example, in use at the telephone companies. However, unlike the lambda calculus, Turing's code does not serve well as a basis for higher-level languages — its principal use is in rigorous analyses of algorithmic complexity. [1]

Like many "firsts" in history, the first modern programming language is hard to identify. From the start, the restrictions of the hardware defined the language. Punch cards allowed 80 columns, but some of the columns had to be used for a sorting number on each card. Fortran included some keywords which were the same as English words, such as "IF", "GOTO" (go to) and "CONTINUE". The use of a **magnetic drum** for memory meant that computer programs also had to be interleaved with the rotations of the drum. Thus the programs were more hardware dependent than today.

To some people the answer depends on how much power and human-readability is required before the status of "programming language" is granted. Jacquard looms and Charles Babbage's Difference Engine both had simple, extremely limited languages for describing the actions that these machines should perform. One can even regard the punch holes on a player piano scroll as a limited domain-specific programming language, albeit not designed for human consumption.

2. The 1940s

In the 1940s the first recognizably modern, electrically powered computers were created. The limited speed and memory capacity forced programmers to write hand tuned **assembly language** programs. [2] It was soon discovered that programming in assembly language required a great deal of intellectual effort and was **error-prone.**

In 1948, Konrad Zuse published a paper about his programming language Plankalkül. However, it was not implemented in his time and his original contributions were isolated from other developments.

Some important languages that were developed in this time period include: Plankalkül (Konrad Zuse), ENIAC coding system, 1949-C-10.

3. The 1950s and 1960s

In the 1950s the first three modern programming languages whose descendants are still in widespread use today were designed:

♦   FORTRAN, the "**FOR**mula **TRAN**slator, invented by John W. Backus et al. ;

♦   LISP, the "**LIS**t **P**rocessor", invented by John McCarthy et al. ;

♦   COBOL, the **CO**mmon **B**usiness **O**riented **L**anguage, created by the Short Range Committee, heavily influenced by Grace Hopper.

Another milestone in the late 1950s was the publication, by a committee of American and European computer scientists, of "a new language for algorithms"; the Algol 60 Report (the "**AL-GO**rithmic **L**anguage"). This report consolidated many ideas circulating at the time and featured two key innovations:

♦   The use of **Backus-Naur Form** (**BNF**) for describing the language's syntax. Nearly all subsequent programming languages have used a variant of BNF to describe the **context-free** portion of their syntax.

♦   The introduction of **lexical** scoping for names in arbitrarily nested scopes. [3]

Algol 60 was particularly influential in the design of later languages, some of which soon became more popular. The Burroughs B5000 was designed to be programmed in an extended subset of Algol.

Some important languages that were developed in this time period include: Regional Assembly Language, Autocode, FORTRAN, LISP, ALGOL, COBOL, APL, Simula, BASIC, PL/I.

4. 1967 – 1978: Establishing Fundamental Paradigms

The period from the late 1960s to the late 1970s brought a major flowering of programming languages. Most of the major language paradigms now in use were invented in this period:

♦   **Simula**, invented in the late 1960s by Nygaard and Dahl as a superset of Algol 60, was the first language designed to support object-oriented programming. Smalltalk (mid 1970s) provided a complete ground-up design of an object-oriented language.

♦   **C**, an early systems programming language, was developed by Dennis Ritchie and Ken Thompson at Bell Labs between 1969 and 1973.

♦   **Prolog**, designed in 1972 by Colmerauer, Roussel, and Kowalski, was the first logic programming language.

♦   **ML** built a polymorphic type system (invented by Robin Milner in 1978) on top of Lisp, pioneering statically typed functional programming languages.

Each of these languages spawned an entire family of descendants, and most modern languages count at least one of them in their ancestry.

The 1960s and 1970s also saw considerable debate over the merits of "structured programming", which essentially meant programming without the use of GOTO. This debate was closely related to language design: some languages did not include GOTO, which forced structured programming on the programmer. Although the debate raged hotly at the time, nearly all programmers now agree that, even in languages that provide GOTO, it is bad style to use it except in rare circumstances. As a result, later generations of language designers have found the structured programming debate **tedious** and even bewildering.

Some important languages that were developed in this time period include: Pascal, C, Smalltalk, Prolog, ML, SQL.

5. The 1980s: Consolidation, Modules, Performance

The 1980s were years of relative consolidation. C++ combined object-oriented and systems programming. The United States government standardized Ada, a systems programming language intended for use by **defense contractors**. In Japan and elsewhere, vast sums were spent investigating so-called "fifth generation" languages that incorporated logic programming constructs. The functional languages community moved to standardize ML and Lisp. Rather than inventing new paradigms, all of these movements elaborated upon the ideas invented in the previous decade.

However, one important new trend in language design was an increased focus on programming for large-scale systems through the use of modules, or large-scale organizational units of code. [4] Modula, Ada, and ML all developed notable module systems in the 1980s. Module systems were often wedded to generic programming constructs—generics being, in essence, parameterized modules (see also parametric **polymorphism**).

Although major new paradigms for programming languages did not appear, many researchers expanded on the ideas of prior languages and adapted them to new contexts. For example, the languages of the Argus and Emerald systems adapted object-oriented programming to distributed systems.

The 1980s also brought advances in programming language implementation. The RISC movement in computer architecture **postulated** that hardware should be designed for compilers rather than for human assembly programmers. Aided by processor speed improvements that enabled increasingly aggressive **compilation** techniques, the RISC movement sparked greater interest in compilation technology for high-level languages.

Language technology continued along these lines well into the 1990s. However, the adoption of languages has always been driven by the adoption of new computer systems, and in the mid-1990s one of the most important new systems in computer history suddenly exploded in popularity.

Some important languages that were developed in this time period include: Ada, C++, Eiffel, Perl, FL.

6. The 1990s: the Internet Age

The rapid growth of the Internet in the mid-1990s was the next major historic event in programming languages. By opening up a radically new platform for computer systems, the Internet created an opportunity for new languages to be adopted. In particular, the Java programming language rose to popularity because of its early integration with the Netscape Navigator web browser, and various scripting languages achieved widespread use in developing customized applications for web servers. Neither of these developments represented much fundamental novelty in language design; for example, the design of Java was a more conservative version of ideas explored many years earlier in the Smalltalk community, but the widespread adoption of languages that supported features like **garbage collection** and strong **static typing** was a major change in programming practice. [5]

Some important languages that were developed in this time period include: Haskell, Python, Java, Ruby, PHP, C#.

7. Current Trends

Programming language evolution continues, in both industry and research. Some current directions:

◆ Mechanisms for adding security and reliability verification to the language: **extended static checking**, information flow control, static thread safety.

◆ Alternative mechanisms for **modularity: mixins**, **delegates**, aspects.

◆ Component-oriented software development.

◆ Increased emphasis on distribution and mobility.

◆ Integration with databases, including XML and relational databases.

◆ Open source as a developmental philosophy for languages, including recent languages such as Python, Ruby, and Squeak.

◆ Support for unicode so that source code (program text) is not restricted to those characters contained in the ASCII character set; allowing, for example, use of non-Latin-based scripts or extended **punctuation.**

Key Words

punch card	穿孔卡片
appearance	*n.* 外观
decimal	*adj.* 十进位的
formulaic	*adj.* 公式的
Turing machine	图灵机
magnetic drum	磁鼓
assembly language	汇编语言
error-prone	*adj.* 易于出错的

Backus-Naur Form（BNF）	BNF 范式
context-free	*adj.* 与上下文无关的
lexical	*adj.* 词汇的；语词的
paradigm	*n.* 范例
tedious	*adj.* 冗长乏味的
defense contractors	国防承包商
polymorphism	*n.* 多态性
postulate	*v.* 假设
compilation	*n.* 编译
garbage collection	垃圾回收
static typing	静态验证
extended static checking	延伸静态检查
modularity	*n.* 模块
mixin	*n.* 混合类型
delegate	*n.* 委托
punctuation	*n.* 标点符号

Notes

1. ...its principal use is in rigorous analyses of algorithmic complexity.

……它主要应用在算法复杂的精密分析中。

2. The limited speed and memory capacity forced programmers to write hand tuned assembly language programs.

有限的速度和内存容量迫使程序员手工编写优化了的汇编程序。

3. The introduction of lexical scoping for names in arbitrarily nested scopes.

在任意嵌套中引入了变量名的语义（作用）范围。

4. However, one important new trend in language design was an increased focus on programming for large-scale systems through the use of modules, or large-scale organizational units of code.

然而，语言设计的一个重要的新趋势是应用模块或大型企业级代码单元来开发大型系统已经成为关注的焦点。

5. ... the design of Java was a more conservative version of ideas explored many years earlier in the Smalltalk community, but the widespread adoption of languages that supported features like garbage collection and strong static typing was a major change in programming practice.

……Java 的设计比 Smalltalk 社区在很多年前就已经探索过的想法更保守，但是，对于支持垃圾回收和强静态类型等特性的编程语言的广泛采用是一个在实际编程中的主要变化。

Unit 2   Object-oriented Programming

Object-oriented programming (OOP) is a programming **paradigm** that uses "objects" to design applications and computer programs. It utilizes several techniques from previously established paradigms, including **inheritance**, **modularity**, polymorphism, and **encapsulation**. Even though it originated in the 1960s, OOP was not commonly used in mainstream software application development until the 1990s. Today, many popular programming languages (such as , Java, JavaScript, C#, C ++ , Python, PHP, Ruby and Objective-C) support OOP.

Object-oriented programming's roots reach all the way back to the creation of the Simula programming language in the 1960s, when the **nascent** field of software engineering had begun to discuss the idea of a software crisis. [1] As hardware and software became increasingly complex, how could software quality be maintained? Object-oriented programming in part addresses this problem by strongly emphasizing modularity in software.

Object-oriented programming may be seen as a collection of cooperating objects, as opposed to a traditional view in which a program may be seen as a collection of functions, or simply as a list of instructions to the computer. [2] In OOP, each object is capable of receiving messages, processing data, and sending messages to other objects. Each object can be viewed as an independent little machine with a distinct role or responsibility.

Object-oriented programming is intended to promote greater flexibility and maintainability in programming, and is widely popular in large-scale software engineering. By **virtue** of its strong emphasis on modularity, object oriented code is intended to be simpler to develop and easier to understand later on, lending itself to more direct analysis, coding, and understanding of complex situations and procedures than less modular programming methods.

1. Fundamental Concepts

A survey of nearly 40 years of computing literature by Deborah J. Armstrong identified a number of "quarks," or fundamental concepts, identified in the strong majority of definitions of OOP. They are:

1.1   Class

A class defines the abstract characteristics of a thing, including the thing's characteristics (its **attributes** or **properties**) and the things it can do (its **behaviors** or methods or **features**). For example, the class Dog would consist of traits shared by all dogs, for example breed, fur color, and the ability to bark. Classes provide modularity and structure in an object-oriented computer program. A class should typically be recognizable to a non-programmer familiar with the problem domain, meaning that the characteristics of the class should make sense in context. [3] Also, the code for a class should be relatively self-contained. Collectively, the properties and methods defined by a class are called members.

1.2　Object

A particular instance of a class. The class of Dog defines all possible dogs by listing the characteristics that they can have; the object Lassie is one particular dog, with particular versions of the
characteristics. A Dog has fur; Lassie has brown-and-white fur. In programmer **jargon**, the object
Lassie is an instance of the Dog class. The set of values of the attributes of a particular object is
called its state.

1.3　Method

An object's abilities. Lassie, being a Dog, has the ability to bark. So bark is one of Lassie's
methods. She may have other methods as well, for example, sit or eat. Within the program, using
a method should only affect one particular object; all Dogs can bark, but you need one particular
dog to do the barking.

1.4　Inheritance

In some cases, a class will have "subclasses", more specialized versions of a class. For example, the class Dog might have sub-classes called Collie, Chihuahua, and GoldenRetriever. In this
case, Lassie would be an instance of the Collie subclass. Subclasses inherit attributes and behaviors
from their parent classes, and can introduce their own. Suppose the Dog class defines a method called
bark and a property called furColor. Each of its sub-classes (Collie, Chihuahua, and GoldenRetriever) will inherit these members, meaning that the programmer only needs to write the code for them
once. Each subclass can alter its inherited **traits**. So, for example, the Collie class might specify that
the default furColor for a collie is brown-and-white. The Chihuahua subclass might specify that the
bark method is high-pitched by default. Subclasses can also add new members. The Chihuahua subclass could add a method called tremble. So an individual Chihuahua instance would use a high-
pitched bark from the Chihuahua subclass, which in turn inherited the usual bark from Dog. The Chihuahua object would also have the tremble method, but Lassie would not, because she is a Collie, not
a Chihuahua. In fact, inheritance is an "is-a" relationship: Lassie is a Collie. A Collie is a Dog.
Thus, Lassie inherits the members of both Collies and Dogs. When an object or class inherits its traits
from more than one ancestor class, and neither of these ancestors is an ancestor of the other, then it's
called multiple inheritance. For example, independent classes could define Dogs and Cats, and a Chi-
mera object could be created from these two which inherits all the (multiple) behavior of cats and
dogs. This is not always supported, as it can be hard both to implement and to use well.

1.5　Encapsulation

Conceals the exact details of how a particular class works from objects that use its code or send
messages to it. So, for example, the Dog class has a bark method. The code for the bark method defines exactly how a bark happens (e. g. , by inhale and then exhale, at a particular pitch and volume). Timmy, Lassie's friend, however, does not need to know exactly how she barks. Encapsula-

tion is achieved by specifying which classes may use the members of an object. The result is that each object exposes to any class a certain interface—those members accessible to that class. The reason for encapsulation is to prevent clients of an interface from depending on those parts of the implementation that are likely to change in future, thereby allowing those changes to be made more easily, that is, without changes to clients. For example, an interface can ensure that puppies can only be added to an object of the class Dog by code in that class. Members are often specified as public, protected and private, determining whether they are available to all classes, sub-classes or only the defining class. Some languages go further: Java uses the protected keyword to restrict access also to classes in the same package, C# and VB. NET reserve some members to classes in the same assembly using keywords internal (C#) or Friend (VB. NET), and Eiffel allows one to specify which classes may access any member.

1. 6 Abstraction

Simplifying complex reality by modeling classes appropriate to the problem, and working at the most appropriate level of inheritance for a given aspect of the problem. For example, Lassie the Dog may be treated as a Dog much of the time, a Collie when necessary to access Collie-specific attributes or behaviors, and as an Animal (perhaps the parent class of Dog) when counting Timmy's pets.

1. 7 Polymorphism

Polymorphism is behavior that varies depending on the class in which the behavior is invoked, that is, two or more classes can react differently to the same message. For example, if a Dog is commanded to speak this may elicit a Bark; if a Pig is commanded to speak this may elicit an Oink.

Not all of the above concepts are to be found in all object-based programming languages. In particular, prototype-based programming does not typically use classes. As a result, a significantly different yet analogous terminology is used to define the concepts of object and instance in these languages.

2. History

The concept of objects and instances in computing had its first major breakthrough with the PDP-1 system at MIT which was probably the earliest example of capability based architecture. Another early example was Sketchpad made by Ivan Sutherland in 1963; however, this was an application and not a programming paradigm.

Objects as programming entities were introduced in the 1960s in Simula 67, a programming language designed for making simulations, created by Ole-Johan Dahl and Kristen Nygaard of the Norwegian Computing Center in Oslo. (Reportedly, the story is that they were working on ship simulations, and were confounded by the **combinatorial** explosion of how the different attributes from different ships could affect one another. The idea occurred to group the different types of ships into different classes of objects, each class of objects being responsible for defining its own data and behavior.) Such an approach was a simple **extrapolation** of concepts earlier used in analog programming.

On analog computers, such direct mapping from real-world phenomena/objects to analog phenomena/objects (and conversely), was (and is) called "simulation". Simula not only introduced the **notion** of classes, but also of instances of classes, which is probably the first explicit use of those notions.

The Smalltalk language, which was developed at Xerox PARC in the 1970s, introduced the term object-oriented programming to represent the pervasive use of objects and messages as the basis for computation. Smalltalk creators were influenced by the ideas introduced in Simula 67, but Smalltalk was designed to be a fully dynamic system in which classes could be created and modified dynamically rather than statically as in Simula 67. The ideas in Simula 67 were also used in many other languages, from derivatives of Lisp to Pascal.

Object-oriented programming developed as the dominant programming methodology during the mid-1980s, largely due to the influence of C++, an extension of the C programming language. Its dominance was further **cemented** by the rising popularity of graphical user interfaces, for which object-oriented programming is well-suited. An example of a closely related dynamic GUI library and OOP language can be found in the Cocoa frameworks on Mac OS X, written in Objective C, an object-oriented, dynamic messaging extension to C based on Smalltalk. OOP **toolkits** also enhanced the popularity of "**event-driven programming**" (although this concept is not limited to OOP). Some feel that association with GUIs (real or perceived) was what propelled OOP into the programming mainstream.

OOP also became increasingly popular for developing computer games during the 1990s. As the complexity of games grew, as faster hardware became more widely available and compilers (especially C++) matured, more and more games and their engines were written in OOP languages. Prominent C++ examples include the Doom III engine, Starcraft, Diablo, Warcraft III and World of Warcraft. Since almost all video games feature virtual environments which contain many, often thousands of objects that interact with each other in complex ways, OOP languages are particularly suited for game development.

At ETH Zürich, Niklaus Wirth and his colleagues had also been investigating such topics as data abstraction and modular programming. Modula-2 included both, and their succeeding design, Oberon included a distinctive approach to object orientation, classes, and such. The approach is unlike Smalltalk, and very unlike C++.

Object-oriented features have been added to many existing languages during that time, including Ada, BASIC, Lisp, Fortran, Pascal, and others. Adding these features to languages that were not initially designed for them often led to problems with compatibility and maintainability of code. "Pure" object-oriented languages, on the other hand, lacked features that many programmers had come to depend upon. To bridge this gap, many attempts have been made to create new languages based on object-oriented methods but allowing some procedural features in "safe" ways. Bertrand Meyer's Eiffel was an early and moderately successful language with those goals.

In the past decade Java has emerged in wide use partially because of its similarity to C and to C++, but perhaps more importantly because of its implementation using a **virtual machine** that is intended to run code unchanged on many different platforms. This last feature has made it very attractive to larger development shops with heterogeneous environments. Microsoft's .NET initiative has a similar objective and includes/supports several new languages, or variants of older ones.

More recently, a number of languages have emerged that are primarily object-oriented yet compatible with procedural methodology, such as Python and Ruby. Besides Java, probably the most commercially important recent object-oriented languages are Visual Basic. NET and C# designed for Microsoft's . NET platform.

Just as procedural programming led to refinements of techniques such as structured programming, modern object-oriented software design methods include refinements such as the use of design patterns, design by contract, and modeling languages (such as UML).

Key Words

object-oriented	*adj.* 面向对象的
paradigm	*n.* 范例
inheritance	*n.* 继承
modularity	*n.* 模块性
encasulation	*n.* 封装
nascent	*adj.* 初期的
virtue	*n.* 优点
attribute	*n.* 属性
property	*n.* 属性
behavior	*n.* 行为
feature	*n.* 特征
jargon	*n.* 行话
trait	*n.* 特性
combinatorial	*adj.* 组合的
extrapolation	*n.* 推断
notion	*n.* 概念
cement	*v.* 加强
toolkit	*n.* 工具包，软件包
event-driven programming	事件驱动编程思想
virtual machine	虚拟机

Notes

1. Object-oriented programming's roots reach all the way back to the creation of the Simula programming language in the 1960s, when the nascent field of software engineering had begun to discuss the idea of a software crisis.

面向对象编程的根源可以追溯到 20 世纪 60 年代出现的 Simula 编程语言，当时新生的软件工程界已经开始讨论软件危机了。

2. Object-oriented programming may be seen as a collection of cooperating objects, as opposed to a traditional view in which a program may be seen as a collection of functions, or simply as a list of instructions to the computer.

面向对象的程序可以被看成是一个由相互合作的对象组成的集合，而传统的看法则把程序看成由许多函数组成的集合，或是简单的计算机指令集合。

3. A class should typically be recognizable to a non-programmer familiar with the problem domain, meaning that the characteristics of the class should make sense in context.

一个类对于熟悉问题域的非程序员来说通常应当是可识别的，也就是说，类的特性在上下文中应该是有意义的。

Reading Material 1 Introduction to the C# Language and the . NET Framework

C# is an elegant and type-safe object-oriented language that enables developers to build a wide range of secure and robust applications that run on the . NET Framework. You can use C# to create traditional Windows client applications, XML Web services, distributed components, client-server applications, database applications, and much, much more. Microsoft Visual C# 2005 provides an advanced code editor, convenient user interface designers, integrated debugger, and many other tools to facilitate rapid application development based on version 2. 0 of the C# language and the . NET Framework.

1. C# Language

C# syntax is highly expressive, yet with less than 90 keywords, it is also simple and easy to learn. The curly-brace syntax of C# will be instantly recognizable to anyone familiar with C, C++ or Java. Developers who know any of these languages are typically able to begin working productively in C# within a very short time. C# syntax simplifies many of the complexities of C++ while providing powerful features such as nullable value types, enumerations, delegates, anonymous methods and direct memory access, which are not found in Java. C# also supports generic methods and types, which provide increased type safety and performance, and iterators, which enable implementers of collection classes to define custom iteration behaviors that are simple to use by client code.

As an object-oriented language, C# supports the concepts of encapsulation, inheritance and polymorphism. All variables and methods, including the Main method, the application's entry point, are encapsulated within class definitions. A class may inherit directly from one parent class, but it may implement any number of interfaces. Methods that override virtual methods in a parent class require the override keyword as a way to avoid accidental redefinition. In C#, a struct is like a lightweight class; it is a stack-allocated type that can implement interfaces but does not support inheritance.

In addition to these basic object-oriented principles, C# facilitates the development of software components through several innovative language constructs, including:
- Encapsulated method signatures called delegates, which enable type-safe event notifications.
- Properties, which serve as accessors for private member variables.
- Attributes, which provide declarative metadata about types at run time.
- Inline XML documentation comments.

If you need to interact with other Windows software such as COM objects or native Win32 DLLs, you can do this in C# through a process called "Interop". Interop enables C# programs to do just about anything that a native C++ application can do. C# even supports pointers and the concept of "unsafe" code for those cases in which direct memory access is absolutely critical.

The C# build process is simple compared to C and C++ and more flexible than in Java. There are no separate header files, and no requirement that methods and types be declared in a particular order. A C# source file may define any number of classes, structs, interfaces, and events.

2. .NET Framework Platform Architecture

C# programs run on the .NET Framework, an integral component of Windows that includes a virtual execution system called the common language runtime (CLR) and a unified set of class libraries. The CLR is Microsoft's commercial implementation of the common language infrastructure (CLI), an international standard that is the basis for creating execution and development environments in which languages and libraries work together seamlessly.

Source code written in C# is compiled into an intermediate language (IL) that conforms to the CLI specification. The IL code, along with resources such as bitmaps and strings, is stored on disk in an executable file called an assembly, typically with an extension of .exe or .dll. An assembly contains a manifest that provides information on the assembly's types, version, culture, and security requirements.

When the C# program is executed, the assembly is loaded into the CLR, which might take various actions based on the information in the manifest. Then, if the security requirements are met, the CLR performs just in time (JIT) compilation to convert the IL code into native machine instructions.

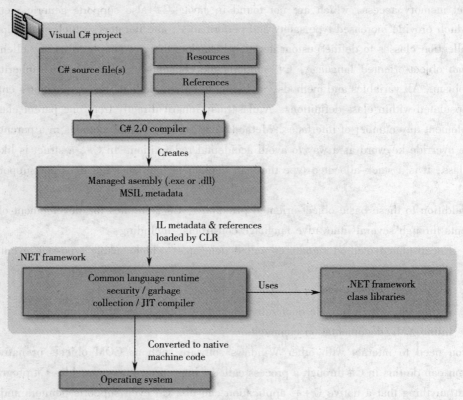

Figure 5. 3. 1   Compile-time and run time relationships

The CLR also provides other services related to automatic garbage collection, exception handling, and resource management. Code that is executed by the CLR is sometimes referred to as "managed code", in contrast to "unmanaged code" which is compiled into native machine language that targets a specific system. The following diagram illustrates the compile-time and run time relationships of C# source code files, the base class libraries, assemblies, and the CLR.

Language interoperability is a key feature of the .NET Framework. Because the IL code produced by the C# compiler conforms to the Common Type Specification (CTS), IL code generated from C# can interact with code that was generated from the .NET versions of Visual Basic, Visual C++, Visual J#, or any of more than 20 other CTS-compliant languages. A single assembly may contain multiple modules written in different .NET languages, and the types can reference each other just as if they were written in the same language.

In addition to the run time services, the .NET Framework also includes an extensive library of over 4000 classes organized into namespaces that provide a wide variety of useful functionality for everything from file input and output to string manipulation to XML parsing, to Windows Forms controls. The typical C# application uses the .NET Framework class library extensively to handle common "plumbing" chores.

Reading Material 2   Introduction to Python

If you do much work on computers, eventually you find that there's some task you'd like to automate. For example, you may wish to perform a search-and-replace over a large number of text files, or rename and rearrange a bunch of photo files in a complicated way. Perhaps you'd like to write a small custom database, or a specialized GUI application, or a simple game.

If you're a professional software developer, you may have to work with several C/C++/Java libraries but find the usual write/compile/test/re-compile cycle is too slow. Perhaps you're writing a test suite for such a library and find writing the testing code a tedious task. Or maybe you've written a program that could use an extension language, and you don't want to design and implement a whole new language for your application.

Python is just the language for you.

You could write a Unix shell script or Windows batch files for some of these tasks, but shell scripts are best at moving around files and changing text data, not well-suited for GUI applications or games. You could write a C/C++/Java program, but it can take a lot of development time to get even a first-draft program. Python is simpler to use, available on Windows, MacOS X, and UNIX operating systems, and will help you get the job done more quickly.

Python is simple to use, but it is a real programming language, offering much more structure and support for large programs than shell scripts or batch files can offer. On the other hand, Python also offers much more error checking than C, and, being a very-high-level language, it has high-level data types built in, such as flexible arrays and dictionaries. Because of its more general data types

Python is applicable to a much larger problem domain than Awk or even Perl, yet many things are at least as easy in Python as in those languages.

If you know anything about programming, you've probably heard the term object-oriented programming, or OOP for short. It's certainly a hot topic, and OOP are three letters every programmer wants on their resume. OOP is basically a shift in the way programmers think about solving problems with computers. It embodies an intuitive way of representing information and actions in a program. It's not the only way to write programs, but for most large projects, it's the way to go.

Python is object-oriented. Languages like C#, Java, and Python are all object-oriented. But Python does them one better. In C# and Java, OOP is not optional. This makes short programs unnecessarily complex, and it requires a bunch of explanation before a new programmer can do anything significant. Python takes a different approach. In Python, using OOP techniques is optional. You have all of OOP's power at your disposal, but you can use it when you need it. Got a short program that doesn't really require OOP? No problem. Got a large project with a team of programmers that demands OOP? That'll work too. Python gives you power and flexibility.

Python allows you to split your program into modules that can be reused in other Python programs. It comes with a large collection of standard modules that you can use as the basis of your programs—or as examples to start learning to program in Python. Some of these modules provide things like file I/O, system calls, sockets, and even interfaces to graphical user interface toolkits like Tk.

Python is an interpreted language, which can save you considerable time during program development because no compilation and linking is necessary. The interpreter can be used interactively, which makes it easy to experiment with features of the language, to write throw-away programs, or to test functions during bottom-up program development. It is also a handy desk calculator.

Python enables programs to be written compactly and readably. Programs written in Python are typically much shorter than equivalent C, C++, or Java programs, for several reasons:

- ◆ the high-level data types allow you to express complex operations in a single statement;
- ◆ statement grouping is done by indentation instead of beginning and ending brackets;
- ◆ no variable or argument declarations are necessary.

Python is extensible: if you know how to program in C it is easy to add a new built-in function or module to the interpreter, either to perform critical operations at maximum speed, or to link Python programs to libraries that may only be available in binary form (such as a vendor-specific graphics library). Once you are really hooked, you can link the Python interpreter into an application written in C and use it as an extension or command language for that application.

Python is free. You can install it on your computer and never pay a penny. But Python's license lets you do much more than that. You can copy or modify Python. You can even resell Python if you want (but don't quit your day job just yet). Embracing open-source ideals like this is part of what makes Python so popular and successful.

Exercises

Ⅰ. Fill in the following blanks with proper words or phrases:

1. The _____ was an abstraction of the operation of a tape-marking machine, for example, in use at the telephone companies.

2. In 1948, Konrad Zuse published a paper about his programming language _____.

3. _____, an early systems programming language, was developed by Dennis Ritchie and Ken Thompson at Bell Labs between 1969 and 1973.

4. The 1960s and 1970s also saw considerable debate over the merits of _____, which essentially meant programming without the use of _____.

5. In the 1980s, one important trend in language design was an increased focus on programming for large-scale systems through the use of _____, or _____ of code.

6. Object-oriented programming (OOP) is a programming paradigm that uses "_____" to design applications and computer programs.

7. _____ is behavior that varies depending on the class in which the behavior is invoked, that is, two or more classes can react differently to the same message.

8. A _____ defines the abstract characteristics of a thing, including the thing's characteristics (its attributes or properties) and the things it can do (its behaviors or methods or features).

Ⅱ. Answer the following questions:

1. Please list at least 5 kinds of programming languages in the 1950s and 1960s.

2. Briefly describe four kinds of major language paradigms now in use in this period between 1967 and 1978.

3. Briefly describe the great changes of programming languages in the 1980s.

4. How does the rapid growth of the Internet in the mid-1990s influence the programming language?

5. Give some directions of programming language evolution nowadays.

6. Briefly describe object-oriented programming (OOP).

7. List several fundamental concepts of OOP.

8. Please introduce the use of encapsulation.

Chapter Six   Database Systems

Unit 1   Introduction to Database Systems

Today, more than any previous time, the success of an enterprise depends on its ability to acquire accurate and timely data about its operations, to manage this data effectively, and to use it to analyze and guide its activities.

The amount of information available to us is **literally** exploding, and the value of data as an organizational asset is widely recognized. Yet without the ability to manage this vast amount of data, and to quickly find the information that is relevant to a given question, as the amount of information increases, it tends to become a distraction and a liability, rather than an asset. This **paradox** drives the need for increasingly powerful and flexible data management systems.

1. What Is a Database

A database is a collection of data items related to some enterprise—for example, the depositor account information in a bank. A database might be stored on cards in a Rolodex or on paper in a file **cabinet**, but we are particular interested in databases stored as bits and bytes in a computer. Such a database can be centralized on one computer or distributed over several, perhaps widely separated geographically.

2. What Is a Database Management System

To make access to them convenient, databases are generally **encapsulated** within a database management system (DBMS). The DBMS supports a high-level language in which the application programmer describes the database access it wishes to perform. Typically, all database access is classified into two broad categories: queries and updates. A query is a request to retrieve data, and an update is a request to insert, delete, or modify existing data items. The most commonly used data access language is the **Structured Query Language** (SQL). Although it is called a query language, updates are also done through SQL. The beauty of SQL lies in its declarative nature: the application programmer need only state what is to be done; the DBMS **figures out** how to do it efficiently. The DBMS interprets each SQL statement and performs the action it describes. The application programmer need not know the details of how the database is stored, need not formulate the algorithm for performing the access, and need not be concerned about many other aspects of managing the database. [1]

3. What Is a Database System

A database system is basically a computerized record-keeping system; in other words, it is a computerized system whose overall purpose is to store information and to allow users to retrieve and update that information on demand. The information in question can be anything that is of significance to the individual or organization concerned—anything, in other words, that is needed to assist in the general process of running the business of that individual or organization. [2]

Figure 6. 1. 1 is a simplified picture of a database system. As the figure shows, such a system involves four major components: data, hardware, software, and users.

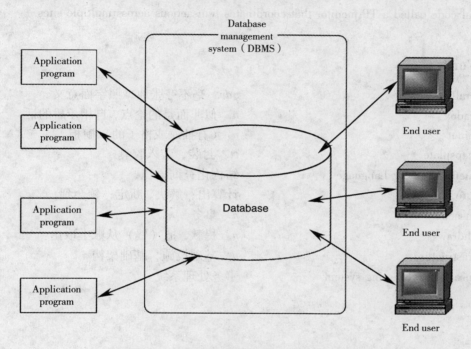

Figure 6. 1. 1   Simplified picture of a database system

4. What Is a Transaction

Databases frequently store information that describes the current state of an enterprise. For example, a bank's database stores the current balance in each depositor's account. When an event happens in the real world that changes the state of the enterprise, a corresponding change must be made to the information stored in the database. With online DBMSs, these changes are made in real time by programs called **transactions**, which execute when the real-world event occurs. For example, when a customer deposits money in a bank (an event in the real world), a deposit transaction is executed. Each transaction must be designed so that it maintains the correctness of the relationship between the database state and the real-world enterprise it is modeling. In addition to changing the state of the database, the transaction itself might initiate some events in the real world. For example, a **withdraw** transaction at an automated teller machine (ATM) initiates the events of dispensing cash, and a transaction that establishes a connection for a telephone call requires the allocation of resources (bandwidth on a long-distance link) in the telephone company's **infrastructure**. [3]

5. What Is a Transaction Processing System

A **transaction processing system** (TPS) includes one or more databases that store the state of an enterprise, the software for managing the transactions that manipulate that state, and the transactions themselves that constitute the application code. In its simplest form the TPS involves a single DBMS that contains the software for managing transactions. More complex systems involve several DBMSs. In this case, transaction management is handled both within the DBMSs and without, by additional code called a TP monitor that coordinates transactions across multiple sites.

Key Words

literally	*adv.* 毫不夸张地，照字面意义
paradox	*n.* 似非而是的论点，自相矛盾的话
cabinet	*n.* （有抽屉或格子的）橱柜
encapsulate	*vt.* 封装，装入胶囊
Structured Query Language	结构化查询语言
figure out	计算出；解决，断定；领会到
transaction	*n.* 事务
withdraw	*n.* 提款，把（钱）从账上取出
infrastructure	*n.* 基础设施，基础架构
transaction processing system	事务处理系统

Notes

1. The application programmer need not know the details of how the database is stored, need not formulate the algorithm for performing the access, and need not be concerned about many other aspects of managing the database.

应用软件程序员不需要知道数据库存储的细节，不需要编制算法进行存取数据，而且不需要关心其他的一些管理数据库的细节问题。

2. The information in question can be anything that is of significance to the individual or organization concerned—anything, in other words, that is needed to assist in the general process of running the business of that individual or organization.

被查询的信息可以是对个人或者组织有意义的任何事物，换句话说，它就是用来协助处理个人或组织的业务运营的。

3. For example, a withdraw transaction at an automated teller machine (ATM) initiates the events of dispensing cash, and a transaction that establishes a connection for a telephone call requires the allocation of resources (bandwidth on a long-distance link)

in the telephone company's infrastructure.

例如，在自动取款机（ATM）上的取款事务发起分配现金事件；建立电话连接的事务需要从电话公司系统中申请分配资源（一个长途连接的带宽）。

Unit 2   Distributed Database

A distributed database is a database in which portions of the database are stored on multiple computers within a network. [1] Users have access to the portion of the database at their location so that they can access the data relevant to their tasks without interfering with the work of others.

A distributed database system consists of a collection of sites, connected together via some kind of communications network, in which:

◆ Each site is a full database system site in its own right, [2] but

◆ The sites have agreed to work together so that a user at any site can access data anywhere in the network exactly as if the data were all stored at the user's own site.

It follows that a "distributed database" is really a kind of virtual database, whose component parts are physically stored in a number of distinct "real" databases at a number of distinct sites (in effect, it is the logical union of those real databases). An example is shown in Figure 6.2.1.

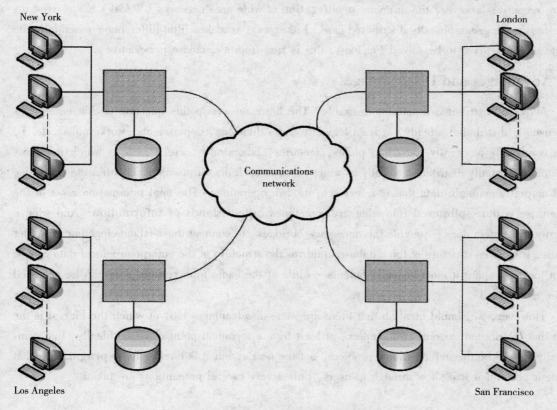

Figure. 6.2.1   A typical distributed database system

Note that, to repeat, each site is a database system site in its own right. In other words, each site has its own local "real" databases, its own local users, its own local **DBMS** and **transaction management software** (including its own local locking, logging, recovery, etc. , software), and its own local data communications manager (DC manager). In particular, a given user can perform operations on data at that user's own local site exactly as if that site did not participate in the distributed system at all (at least, such a capability is an objective). The overall distributed system can thus be regarded as a kind of **partnership** among the individual local DBMSs at the individual local sites; a new software component at each site—logically an extension of the local DBMS—provides the necessary partnership functionality, and it is the combination of these new components together with the existing DBMSs that constitutes what is usually called the **distributed database management system**. [3]

Incidentally, it is common to assume that the component sites are physically dispersed—possibly in fact geographically dispersed also, as suggested by Figure 6. 1. 1—although actually it is sufficient that they be dispersed logically. Two "sites" might even **coexist** on the same physical machine (especially during initial system testing). In fact, the emphasis in distributed systems has shifted back and forth over time; the earliest research tended to assume geographic distribution, but most of the first few commercial installations **involved** local distribution instead, with (e. g.) several "sites" all in the same building and connected together by means of a local area network (LAN). More recently, however, the dramatic **proliferation** of wide area networks (WANs) has revived interested in the geographically distributed case. Either way, it makes little difference—essentially the same problems have to be solved (at least, this is true from a database perspective).

1. Advantages and Disadvantages

Why are distributed databases desirable? The basic answer to this question is that enterprises are usually distributed already, at least logically (into divisions, departments, workgroups, etc.), and very likely physically too (into plants, factories, laboratories, etc.) —from which it follows that data is usually distributed already as well, because each organizational unit within the enterprise will naturally maintain data that is relevant to its own operations. The total information asset of the enterprise is thus **splintered** into what are sometimes called **islands of information**. And what a distributed system does is provide the necessary "bridges" to connect those islands together. In other words, it enables structure of the database to mirror the structure of the enterprise—local data can be kept locally, where it most logically belongs—while at the same time **remote** data can be accessed when necessary.

However, we should mention that there are some disadvantages too, of which the biggest is the fact that distributed systems are complex, at least from a technical point of view. Ideally, that complexity should be the implementer's problem, not the user's, but it is likely—to be **pragmatic**—that some aspects of it will show through to users, unless very careful precautions are taken.

2. Types of Distributed Databases

If data is distributed but all servers run the same DBMS software, we have a **homogeneous** distributed database system. If different sites run under the control of different DBMSs, essentially autonomously, and are connected somehow to enable access to data from multiple sites, we have a **heterogeneous** distributed database system, also referred to as multidatabase system. [4]

The key to building heterogeneous systems is to have well-accepted standards for gateway protocols. A gateway protocol is an API that exposes DBMS functionality to external applications. Examples include ODBC and JDBC. By accessing database servers through gateway protocols, their differences (in capabilities, data formats, etc.) are masked, and the differences between the different servers in a distributed system are bridged to a large degree.

Key Words

DBMS	数据库管理系统
transaction management software	事务管理软件
partnership	*n.* 合作关系，伙伴关系
distributed database management system	分布式数据库管理系统
coexist	*vi.* 共存；并存
involved	*adj.* 有关的；相关的
proliferation	*n.* 发展，增生（现象）
splinter	*v.* 裂成碎片，分裂
island of information	信息孤岛
remote	*adj.* 遥远的
pragmatic	*adj.* 实际的，注重实效的
homogeneous	*adj.* 同构的
heterogeneous	*adj.* 异构的

Notes

1. A distributed database is a database in which portions of the database are stored on multiple computers within a network.

分布式数据库是一个把数据库的各个部分存放于网络上的多个不同计算机的数据库。

2. Each site is a database system site in its own right,...

每个节点是一个自成体系的数据库系统，……

3. The overall distributed system can thus be regarded as a kind of partnership among the individual local DBMSs at the individual local sites; a new software component at each site—logically an extension of the local DBMS—provides the necessary partnership functionality, and it is the combination of these new components together with the

existing DBMSs that constitutes what is usually called the distributed database management system.

整个分布式系统可以被视为由独立的本地节点数据库管理系统组成的一种合作关系；每个节点的新软件组件——逻辑上是本地数据库的延伸——提供了必要的合作功能，这些新组件连同现有数据库系统，通常被称为分布式数据库管理系统（DBMS）。

4. If data is distributed but all servers run the same DBMS software, we have a homogeneous distributed database system. If different sites run under the control of different DBMSs, essentially autonomously, and are connected somehow to enable access to data from multiple sites, we have a heterogeneous distributed database system, also referred to as multidatabase system.

如果数据是分布式的，但是所有的服务器运行相同的数据库管理系统软件，我们称之为同构分布式数据库系统。如果不同的节点分别为不同的数据库管理系统软件所控制，本质上来说是自我管理的，并且通过某种方法连接在一起使得可以访问不同节点的数据，这就是一个异构分布式数据库系统，又称为多数据库系统。

Reading Material 1   SQL Server

Most large-scale databases use the Structured Query Language (SQL) to facilitate user and administrator interactions. This language offers a flexible interface for databases of all shapes and sizes. Microsoft SQL Server is one of the most popular databases.

Microsoft SQL Server is a full-featured relational database management system (RDBMS) that offers a variety of administrative tools to ease the burdens of database development, maintenance and administration. In this article, we'll cover six of the more frequently used tools: Enterprise Manager, Query Analyzer, SQL Profiler, Service Manager, Data Transformation Services and Books Online. Let's take a brief look at each:

Enterprise Manager is the main administrative console for SQL Server installations. It provides you with a graphical "birds-eye" view of all of the SQL Server installations on your network. You can perform high-level administrative functions that affect one or more servers, schedule common maintenance tasks or create and modify the structure of individual databases.

Query Analyzer offers a quick and dirty method for performing queries against any of your SQL Server databases.

It's a great way to quickly pull information out of a database in response to a user request, test queries before implementing them in other applications, create/modify stored procedures and execute administrative tasks.

SQL Profiler provides a window into the inner workings of your database. You can monitor many different event types and observe database performance in real time. SQL Profiler allows you to capture and replay system "traces" that log various activities. It's a great tool for optimizing databases with performance issues or troubleshooting particular problems.

Service Manager is used to control the MS SQL Server (the main SQL Server process), MS-DTC (Microsoft Distributed Transaction Coordinator) and SQL Server Agent processes. An icon for this service normally resides in the system tray of machines running SQL Server. You can use Service Manager to start, stop or pause any one of these services.

Data Transformation Services (DTS) provide an extremely flexible method for importing and exporting data between a Microsoft SQL Server installation and a large variety of other formats. The most commonly used DTS application is the "Import and Export Data" wizard found in the SQL Server program group.

Books Online is an often overlooked resource provided with SQL Server that contains answers to a variety of administrative, development and installation issues. It's a great resource to consult before turning to the Internet or technical support.

In 1988, Microsoft released its first version of SQL Server. During the early 1990s, it began to develop a new version of SQL Server for the NT platform. In 1995, Microsoft released SQL Server 6.0. Since then, SQL Server version 7.0, 2000 and 2005 were released in a decade. SQL Server version 2005 is Microsoft's most significant release of SQL Server to date. We will focus on the discussion of this version in the rest of this article.

SQL Server 2005 is a comprehensive database platform providing enterprise-class data management with integrated business intelligence (BI) tools. The SQL Server 2005 database engine provides more secure, reliable storage for both relational and structured data, enabling you to build and manage highly available, performant data applications that you and your people can use to take your business to the next level.

The SQL Server 2005 data engine lies at the core of this enterprise data management solution. Additionally, SQL Server 2005 combines the best in analysis, reporting, integration, and notification. This enables your team to build and deploy cost-effective BI solutions with which they can drive data into every corner of your business through scorecards, Web services, and mobile devices.

Close integration with Microsoft Visual Studio, the Microsoft Office System, and a suite of new development tools, including the Business Intelligence Development Studio, sets SQL Server 2005 apart. Whether you are a developer, database administrator, information worker, or decision maker, SQL Server 2005 provides innovative solutions that help you gain more value from your data.

SQL Server 2005 provides an integrated data management and analysis solution that can help your staff do the following:

◆ Build, deploy, and manage enterprise applications that are more secure, scalable, and reliable.

◆ Maximize IT productivity by reducing the complexity of developing and supporting database applications.

◆ Share data across multiple platforms, applications, and devices to make it easier to connect internal and external systems.

◆ Control costs without sacrificing performance, availability, scalability, or security.

The following diagram illustrates the core components in SQL Server 2005, showing how SQL Server 2005 is a key part of the Windows Server System in integrating with the Microsoft Windows platform—including the Microsoft Office System and Visual Studio—to offer solutions that deliver da-

Figure 6.3.1   SQL server 2005 core components

ta to every corner of your organization.

Reading Material 2 Oracle Database

An Oracle database is a collection of data treated as a unit. The purpose of a database is to store and retrieve related information. A database server is the key to solving the problems of information management. In general, a server reliably manages a large amount of data in a multiuser environment so that many users can concurrently access the same data. All this is accomplished while delivering high performance. A database server also prevents unauthorized access and provides efficient solutions for failure recovery.

Oracle database is the first database designed for enterprise grid computing, the most flexible and cost effective way to manage information and applications. Enterprise grid computing creates large pools of industry-standard, modular storage and servers. With this architecture, each new system can be rapidly provisioned from the pool of components. There is no need for peak workloads, because capacity can be easily added or reallocated from the resource pools as needed.

This article discusses the oracle database from two points:

◆ Overview of Oracle Application Architecture
◆ Overview of Oracle Information Integration Features

1. Overview of Oracle Application Architecture

In Oracle, there are two common ways to architect a database: client/server or multitier. As internet computing becomes more prevalent in computing environments, many database management systems are moving to a multitier environment.

1. 1 Client/Server Architecture

Multiprocessing uses more than one processor for a set of related jobs. Distributed processing reduces the load on a single processor by allowing different processors to concentrate on a subset of related tasks, thus improving the performance and capabilities of the system as a whole.

An Oracle database system can easily take advantage of distributed processing by using its client/server architecture. In this architecture, the database system is divided into two parts: a front-end or a client, and a back-end or a server.

◆ The Client

The client is a database application that initiates a request for an operation to be performed on the database server. It requests, processes, and presents data managed by the server. The client workstation can be optimized for its job. For example, it might not need large disk capacity, or it might benefit from graphic capabilities.

Often, the client runs on a different computer than the database server, generally on a PC. Many clients can simultaneously run against one server.

◆ The Server

The server runs Oracle software and handles the functions required for concurrent, shared data access. The server receives and processes the SQL and PL/SQL statements that originate from client applications. The computer that manages the server can be optimized for its duties. For example, it can have large disk capacity and fast processors.

1.2 Multitier Architecture

A multitier architecture has the following components:
◆ A client or initiator process that starts an operation.
◆ One or more application servers that perform parts of the operation. An application server provides access to the data for the client and performs some of the query processing, thus removing some of the load from the database server. It can serve as an interface between clients and multiple database servers, including providing an additional level of security.
◆ An end or database server that stores most of the data used in the operation.

This architecture enables use of an application server to do the following:
◆ Validate the credentials of a client, such as a Web browser.
◆ Connect to an Oracle database server.
◆ Perform the requested operation on behalf of the client.

If proxy authentication is being used, then the identity of the client is maintained throughout all tiers of the connection.

2. Overview of Information Integration Features

A distributed environment is a network of disparate systems that seamlessly communicate with each other. Each system in the distributed environment is called a node. The system to which a user is directly connected is called the local system. Any additional systems accessed by this user are called remote systems. A distributed environment allows applications to access and exchange data from the local and remote systems. All the data can be simultaneously accessed and modified.

While a distributed environment enables increased access to a large amount of data across a network, it must also hide the location of the data and the complexity of accessing it across the network.

In order for a company to operate successfully in a distributed environment, it must be able to do the following:
◆ Exchange data between Oracle databases.
◆ Communicate between applications.
◆ Exchange information with customers, partners, and suppliers.
◆ Replicate data between databases.
◆ Communicate with non-Oracle databases.

A homogeneous distributed database system is a network of two or more Oracle databases that reside on one or more computers. Distributed SQL enables applications and users to simultaneously access or modify the data in several databases as easily as they access or modify a single database.

An Oracle distributed database system can be transparent to users, making it appear as though it is a single Oracle database. Companies can use this distributed SQL feature to make all its Oracle databases look like one and thus reduce some of the complexity of the distributed system.

Oracle uses database links to enable users on one database to access objects in a remote database. A local user can access a link to a remote database without having to be a user on the remote database.

Exercises

I. Fill in the following blanks with proper words or phrases:

1. A _____ is a database in which portions of the database are stored on multiple computers within a network.

2. If data is distributed but all servers run the same DBMS software, we call such database system _____.

3. The key to building heterogeneous systems is to have well-accepted standards for _____.

4. Most large-scale databases use the _____ to facilitate user and administrator interactions.

5. _____ offers a quick and dirty method for performing queries against any of your SQL Server databases.

6. _____ provide an extremely flexible method for importing and exporting data between a Microsoft SQL Server installation and a large variety of other formats.

7. The newest version of Microsoft SQL Server is _____.

8. SQL Server 2005 is a comprehensive database platform providing enterprise-class data management with integrated _____ tools.

II. Answer the following questions:

1. What is the distributed database management system?

2. Give some advantages of distributed database system.

3. Give some disadvantages of distributed database system.

4. For a distributed database, why can we say "Each site is a database system site in its own right"?

5. List six of the more frequently used tools of the Microsoft SQL Server.

6. Describe the function of Enterprise Manager on the MS SQL Server.

7. What does the Service Manager do on the MS SQL Server?

8. Give a brief history of Microsoft SQL Server.

9. How can the MS SQL Server 2005 help people on their business?

Chapter Seven   Computer Network

Unit 1   Network Topology

In networking, the term "**topology**" refers to the **layout** of connected devices on a network. This article introduces the standard topologies of computer networking. One can think of a topology as a network's virtual shape or structure. This shape does not necessarily correspond to the actual physical layout of the devices on the network. For example, the computers on a home LAN may be arranged in a circle in a family room, but it would be highly unlikely to find an actual ring topology there.

Network topologies are categorized into the following basic types: bus, ring, star, tree, and mesh. More complex networks can be built as **hybrids** of two or more of the above basic topologies.

1. Bus Topology

A bus topology connects computers along a single or more cable to connect linearly as Figure 7.1.1. A network that uses a bus topology is referred to as a "bus network" which was the original form of **Ethernet** networks. Ethernet 10Base2 (also known as thinnet) is used for bus topology.

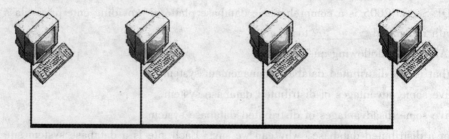

Figure 7.1.1   Bus topology

Bus topology is the cheapest way of connecting computers to form a workgroup or departmental LAN, but it has the disadvantage that a single loose connection or cable break can bring down the entire LAN.

Termination is an important issue in bus networks. The electrical signal from a transmitting computer is free to travel the entire length of the cable. Without the termination, when the signal reaches the end of the wire, it bounces back and travels back up the wire. When a signal echoes back and forth along an unterminated bus, it is called ringing. The terminators absorb the electrical energy and stop the reflections.

Advantages of bus topology:

◆ Bus is easy to use and understand and inexpensive simple network.

◆ It is easy to extend a network by adding cable with a **repeater** that boosts the signal and allows it to travel a longer distance.

Disadvantages of bus topology:

◆ A bus topology becomes slow by heavy network traffic with a lot of computer because networks do not coordinate with each other to reserve times to transmit. [1]

◆ It is difficult to troubleshoot a bus because a cable break or loose connector will cause reflections and bring down the whole network.

2. Star Topology

A star topology links the computers by individual cables to a central unit, usually a hub as in Figure 7.1.2. When a computer or other networking component transmits a signal to the network, the signal travels to the hub. Then, the hub forwards the signal simultaneously to all other components connected to the hub. Ethernet 10BaseT is a network based on the star topology. Star topology is the most popular way to connect computers in a workgroup or departmental network.

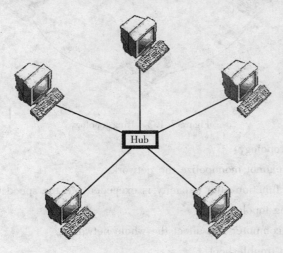

Hub

Figure 7.1.2   Star topology

Advantages of star topology:

◆ The failure of a single computer or cable doesn't bring down the entire network.

◆ The centralized networking equipment can reduce costs in the long run by making network management much easier.

◆ It allows several cable types in same network with a hub that can accommodate multiple cable types.

Disadvantages of star topology:

◆ Failure of the central hub causes the whole network failure.

◆ It is slightly more expensive than using bus topology.

3. Ring Topology

A ring topology connects the computers along a single path whose ends are joined to form a circle as Figure 7. 1. 3. The circle might be logical only but the physical arrangement of the cabling might be similar to star topology, with a hub or concentrator at the center. The ring topology is commonly used in **token ring** networks that the ring of a token ring network is concentrated inside a device called a Multistation Access Unit (MAU) and Fiber Distributed Data Interface (FDDI) networks that the ring in this case is both a physical and logical ring and usually runs around a campus or collection of buildings to form a high-speed **backbone network.**

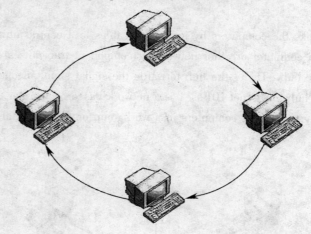

Figure 7. 1. 3   Ring topology

Advantages of ring topology:

◆   One computer cannot monopolize the network.

◆   It continues to function after capacity is exceeded but the speed will be slow.

Disadvantages of ring topology:

◆   Failure of one computer can affect the whole network.

◆   It is difficult to troubleshoot.

◆   Adding and removing computers disrupts the network.

4. Tree Topology

A tree topology combines characteristics of linear bus and star topologies. It consists of groups of star-configured workstations connected to a linear bus backbone cable (See Figure 7. 1. 4). Tree topologies allow for the expansion of an existing network, and enable schools to configure a network to meet their needs.

Advantages of a tree topology:

◆   Point-to-point wiring for individual segments.

◆   Supported by several hardware and software venders.

Disadvantages of a tree topology:

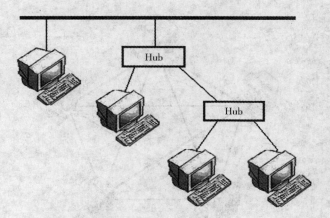

Figure 7. 1. 4   Tree topology

◆   Overall length of each segment is limited by the type of cabling used.

◆   If the backbone line breaks, the entire segment goes down.

◆   More difficult to configure and wire than other topologies.

A consideration in setting up a tree topology using Ethernet protocol is the 5-4-3 rule. One aspect of the Ethernet **protocol** requires that a signal sent out on the network cable reaches every part of the network within a specified length of time. Each concentrator or repeater that a signal goes through adds a small amount of time. [2] This leads to the rule that between any two nodes on the network there can only be a maximum of 5 segments, connected through 4 repeaters/concentrators. In addition, only 3 of the segments may be populated (trunk) segments if they are made of **coaxial** cable. A populated segment is one which has one or more nodes attached to it. In Figure 7. 1. 4, the 5-4-3 rule is adhered to.

This rule does not apply to other network protocols or Ethernet networks where all fiber optic cabling is used.

5. Mesh Topology

In a mesh topology, each computer on network has redundant data paths as showing in Figure 7. 1. 5. The mesh topology provides **fault tolerance**. If a wire, hub, switch, or other component fails, data can travel along an alternate path. A diagram of a mesh network looks like a fishing net. A mesh topology is most often used in large backbone networks in which failure of a single switch or router can result in a large portion of the network going down.

Advantages of mesh topology:

◆   Point-to-point wiring for individual segments.

◆   Provides increased redundancy and reliability as well as ease of troubleshooting.

Disadvantages of mesh topology:

◆   The implementation of mesh topology is expensive than other types of topology.

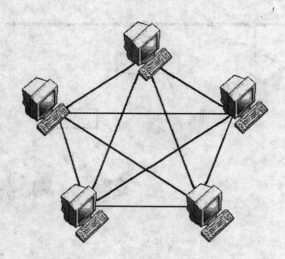

Figure 7. 1. 5   Mesh topology

6. Considerations When Choosing a Topology

◆　Money. A linear bus network may be the least expensive way to install a network; you do not have to purchase **concentrators.**

◆　Length of cable needed. The linear bus network uses shorter lengths of cable.

◆　Future growth. With a star topology, expanding a network is easily done by adding another concentrator.

◆　Cable type. The most common cable in schools is **unshielded twisted pair**, which is most often used with star topologies.

Key Words

topology	*n.*	拓扑结构
layout	*n.*	布局
hybrid	*n.*	混合物
ethernet	*n.*	以太网络
repeater	*n.*	中继器
token ring		令牌环
backbone network		骨干网络
protocol	*n.*	协议
coaxial	*adj.*	同轴的
fault tolerance		误差，错误范围（允许值）
concentrator	*n.*	集线器
unshielded twisted pair		非屏蔽双绞线

Notes

1. A bus topology becomes slow by heavy network traffic with a lot of computer because networks do not coordinate with each other to reserve times to transmit.

当一个总线拓扑结构里有很多的计算机的时候，由于网络无法协调每个计算机以保留传输时间，严重的网络拥塞会导致总线速度变慢。

2. One aspect of the Ethernet protocol requires that a signal sent out on the network cable reaches every part of the network within a specified length of time. Each concentrator or repeater that a signal goes through adds a small amount of time.

以太网协议的一个方面要求一个发送到网络上的信号须在预定的时间内到达网络的每一个角落。信号经过的每个网络集线器或中继器都会增加一个小的延时。

Unit 2　Sliding Window Protocols

In some protocols, **data frames** were transmitted in one direction only. In most practical situations, there is a need for transmitting data in both directions. One way of achieving **full-duplex** data transmission is to have two separate communication channels and use each one for simplex data traffic (in different directions). If this is done, we have two separate physical circuits, each with a "forward" channel (for data) and a "reverse" channel (for **acknowledgements**). In both cases the bandwidth of the reverse channel is almost entirely wasted. In effect, the user is paying for two circuits but using only the capacity of one.

A better idea is to use the same circuit for data in both directions. After all, in protocols 2 and 3 it was already being used to transmit frames both ways, and the reverse channel has the same capacity as the forward channel. In this model the data frames from A to B are intermixed with the acknowledgement frames from A to B. By looking at the kind field in the header of an incoming frame, the receiver can tell whether the frame is data or acknowledgement.

Although interleaving data and control frames on the same circuit is an improvement over having two separate physical circuits, yet another improvement is possible. When a data frame arrives, instead of immediately sending a separate control frame, the receiver restrains itself and waits until the network layer passes it the next packet. [1]The acknowledgement is attached to the outgoing data frame (using the **ack field** in the frame header). In effect, the acknowledgement gets a free ride on the next outgoing data frame. The technique of temporarily delaying outgoing acknowledgements so that they can be hooked onto the next outgoing data frame is known as **piggybacking.**

The principal advantage of using piggybacking over having distinct acknowledgement frames is a better use of the available channel bandwidth. The ack field in the frame header costs only a few bits, whereas a separate frame would need a header, the acknowledgement, and a checksum. In addition, fewer frames sent means fewer "frame arrival" interrupts, and perhaps fewer buffers in the receiver, depending on how the receiver's software is organized. In the next protocol to be examined, the piggyback field costs only 1 bit in the frame header. It rarely costs more than a few bits.

However, piggybacking introduces a complication not present with separate acknowledgements. How long should the **data link layer** wait for a packet onto which to piggyback the acknowledgement? If the data link layer waits longer than the sender's timeout period, the frame will be retransmitted, defeating the whole purpose of having acknowledgements. If the data link layer were an oracle and could foretell the future, it would know when the next network layer packet was going to come in and could decide either to wait for it or send a separate acknowledgement immediately, depending on how long the projected wait was going to be. Of course, the data link layer cannot foretell the future, so it must resort to some ad hoc scheme, such as waiting a fixed number of milliseconds. If a new packet arrives quickly, the acknowledgement is piggybacked onto it; otherwise, if no new packet has arrived by the end of this time period, the data link layer just sends a separate acknowledgement frame.

The protocols are called sliding window protocols. In all sliding window protocols, each **outbound** frame contains a **sequence number**, ranging from 0 up to some maximum. The maximum is usually $2n - 1$ so the sequence number fits exactly in an n-bit field. The stop-and-wait sliding window protocol uses $n = 1$, restricting the sequence numbers to 0 and 1, but more sophisticated versions can use arbitrary n.

The essence of all sliding window protocols is that at any instant of time, the sender maintains a set of sequence numbers corresponding to frames it is permitted to send. These frames are said to fall within the sending window. Similarly, the receiver also maintains a receiving window corresponding to the set of frames it is permitted to accept. The sender's window and the receiver's window need not have the same lower and upper limits or even have the same size. In some protocols they are fixed in size, but in others they can grow or shrink over the course of time as frames are sent and received.

Although these protocols give the data link layer more freedom about the order in which it may send and receive frames, we have definitely not dropped the requirement that the protocol must deliver packets to the destination network layer in the same order they were passed to the data link layer on the sending machine. [2] Nor have we changed the requirement that the physical communication channel is "wire-like" that is, it must deliver all frames in the order sent.

The sequence numbers within the sender's window represent frames that have been sent or can be sent but are as yet not acknowledged. Whenever a new packet arrives from the network layer, it is given the next highest sequence number, and the upper edge of the window is advanced by one. When an acknowledgement comes in, the lower edge is advanced by one. In this way the window continuously maintains a list of unacknowledged frames. Figure 7.2.1 shows an example.

Since frames currently within the sender's window may ultimately be lost or damaged in transit, the sender must keep all these frames in its memory for possible retransmission. Thus, if the maximum window size is n, the sender needs n buffers to hold the unacknowledged frames. If the window ever grows to its maximum size, the sending data link layer must forcibly **shut off** the network layer until another buffer becomes free.

The receiving data link layer's window corresponds to the frames it may accept. Any frame falling outside the window is discarded without comment. When a frame whose sequence number is equal to the lower edge of the window is received, it is passed to the network layer, an acknowledgement is generated, and the window is rotated by one. Unlike the sender's window, the receiver's window always remains at its initial size. Note that a window size of 1 means that the data link layer only accepts frames in order, but for larger windows this is not so. The network layer, in contrast, is always fed data in the proper order, regardless of the data link layer's window size.

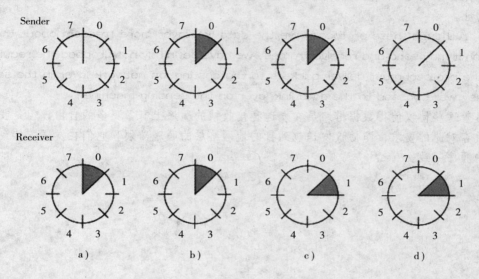

Figure 7.2.1   A sliding window of size 1, with a 3-bit sequence number

a) Initially   b) After the first frame has been sent   c) After the first frame has been received

d) After the first acknowledgement has been received

Figure 7.2.1 shows an example with a maximum window size of 1. Initially, no frames are outstanding, so the lower and upper edges of the sender's window are equal, but as time go on, the situation progresses as shown.

Key Words

data frame	数据帧
full-duplex	*n.* 全双工
acknowledgement	*n.* 确认
ack field	应答域
piggybacking	*n.* 附带传输
data link layer	数据链路层
outbound	*n.* 输出
sequence number	序号
shut off	关闭

Notes

1. When a data frame arrives, instead of immediately sending a separate control frame, the receiver restrains itself and waits until the network layer passes it the next packet.

当数据帧到达时，接收者并不立即发送一个独立的控制帧，而是保留到网络层传来下一个包为止。

2. Although these protocols give the data link layer more freedom about the order in which it may send and receive frames, we have definitely not dropped the requirement that the protocol must deliver packets to the destination network layer in the same order they were passed to the data link layer on the sending machine.

尽管这些协议使得数据链路层在发送和接收帧的顺序上有了更多的自由，但是我们绝对没有放弃对此的要求，即协议发送包到目的地网络层的顺序必须和它们在发送方传到数据链路层的顺序一致。

Reading Material 1   IPv6

1. Introduction

Version 6 of the Internet Protocol (IPv6) has finally arrived in practical form. Although the protocol has been worked on for close to ten years now, official specifications and standards have only recently been finalized, and there are still some aspects of the protocol that are being worked on by the Internet Engineering Task Force (IETF) working groups. The issues that made version 4 of the Internet Protocol (IPv4) inadequate required complex solutions. This has forced designers of the new protocol to work diligently to ensure that the same issues would not be encountered with the new version of the protocol. Members of the Internet community who were responsible for developing the protocol carefully scrutinized each new Request for Comments (RFC) that was developed. For those not familiar with the RFC process, RFCs are documents that detail the protocol specifications so that hardware and software manufacturers will know how to implement the protocol in a standard and agreed-upon manner. Standardization enables each manufacturer and software vendor to follow the same blueprint rather than developing proprietary versions of the protocol. (This was a common problem with earlier networking protocols.) The realization of a new, scalable protocol in which considerable thought has been given to future expansion is a very exciting concept. Never before has the Internet community seen such a magnitude of effort or planning put into the development of a new protocol, and there has certainly never been a protocol more specifically tailored to the growth of the Internet.

2. IPv6 Network Architecture

The Internet has become a victim of its own success. The worldwide success of the Internet has resulted in an explosion of new users and applications, and this growth has placed new demands upon the network infrastructure and upon network administrators. In the early 1990s, the IETF began to design IPv6 with the objective of improving IPv4 to meet these new demands. The areas targeted for improvement included:

- ◆ **Address Space Depletion**: The depletion of IP addresses has been foreseen for many years and many patches and extensions have been added to IPv4 to alleviate and postpone the looming crisis. Among those extensions are variable-length subnet masking (VLSM), Classless Inter-Domain Routing (CIDR), Network Address Translation (NAT), Port Address Translation (PAT), and private address spaces. IPv6 introduces a large unified addressing structure that will make many of these complex extensions obsolete.

- ◆ **Network Performance**: The Internet has outgrown many features in IPv4 that now encumber network performance. Among these features are header checksums, MTU size, and packet fragmentation. IPv6 is streamlined to reduce protocol overhead.

- ◆ **Security**: IPv4 was not designed with security in mind—security was considered the responsibility of higher layers in the Open Systems Interconnect (OSI) model. IPv6 provides integrated security support for encryption and authentication.

◆ **Plug and Play**: Configuring nodes in an IPv4 network has always been complicated. Many configuration tasks are manually intensive and not practical in large networks. A case in point is the renumbering of a network when a new Internet service provider is selected. The growth of mobile computing has also added to the workload of network administrators. IPv6's autoconfiguration facilities take us a step closer to true "Plug and Play" computing.

3. IPv6 Communication Fundamentals

In the following sections, we will examine in further detail how communication occurs between the devices on a network and how IPv6 facilitates that communication. We will examine the communication between hosts of the same subnet as well as host and router between subnets.

3.1　Intra-Subnet Communications

How many of us have cringed at the prospect of connecting our computers or laptops to a network for the first time? A computer must be configured to be able to communicate on a network. Likewise, a network administrator must configure his network devices to facilitate communication between hosts. Nodes at both ends of each network link must have compatible configurations. Many patches have been added to IPv4 to make the configuration process less manually intensive. IPv6 is designed for Plug and Play. Support for autoconfiguration is built into IPv6. We will first examine stateless autoconfiguration and its role in intra-subnet communications. Later, we will discuss stateful autoconfiguration and its role in inter-subnet communications. The keys to understanding intra-subnet communications are the following concepts:

◆ Stateless Autoconfiguration

◆ Link-Local Address

◆ Link-Local Prefix

◆ Interface Identifier

◆ Neighbor Solicitation Message

◆ Neighbor Advertisement Message

◆ Neighbor Cache

Let's imagine a subnet in a dentist's office. The subnet is comprised of a few workstations and printers. It has no routers, no connections to the Internet, and no servers to assist in the configuration process. A host on such a subnet must configure its own IPv6 address with a process known as stateless autoconfiguration.

When a workstation is connected to a port on the subnet, the workstation automatically configures a tentative address, known as the link-local address. This address is formed using the hardware address of the workstation's network interface. The link-local address configured by the workstation is 128 bits long and is comprised of a local-link prefix and the workstation's interface identifier. The local-link prefix is an all-zero network identifier prefaced with the hex digits, FE8. The interface ID, also known as the Media Access Control (MAC) address, resides in a ROM on the interface hardware. Today's MAC addresses are 48 bits long, but new specifications will support 64-bit MAC addresses.

To ensure a unique address, the workstation will send a special Neighbor Solicitation message to the newly configured address and wait one second for a reply. If no Neighbor Advertisement message is returned, the new link-local address is assumed to be unique. (Later, we will see that the Neighbor Solicitation and Neighbor Advertisement messages are also used for other functions that are part of the IPv6 Neighbor Discovery protocol.)

After verifying the uniqueness of the link-local address, the next phase is to query for neighboring routers on the network. In our example of a subnet in a dentist's office, no routers will be found. The workstation is now ready to begin communications with its neighbors.

To communicate with a destination host on the same subnet, the workstation must discover the destination's interface identifier. To do so, the workstation uses the functions provided by the IPv6 Neighbor Discovery protocol. The workstation sends a Neighbor Solicitation message to the destination and the interface identifier is returned in a Neighbor Advertisement message. This interface ID is placed in a header before the IPv6 header and transmitted on the subnet. The workstation then adds an entry to its Neighbor Cache. The entry contains the destination's IPv6 address, its interface identifier, a pointer to packets pending transmission, and a flag indicating whether or not the destination is a router. This cache will be used for future transmissions instead of sending another solicitation message.

The link-local addresses cannot be used for communications outside the local subnet. For inter-subnet communications, site-local addresses or global addresses must be used in conjunction with routers. We will discuss inter-subnet communications in the next section.

3.2 Inter-Subnet Communications

Suppose that in the previous example, our workstation discovered that a router did exist on the subnet. How would the autoconfiguration process differ, and how would the workstation communicate with hosts on different subnets? To discuss inter-subnet communications, we will expound on the stateless autoconfiguration process and introduce the following concepts:

- ◆ Neighbor Discovery
- ◆ Site-Local Address
- ◆ Subnet Identifier
- ◆ Router Solicitation Message
- ◆ Router Advertisement Message
- ◆ Default Router List Cache
- ◆ Destination Cache
- ◆ Prefix List Cache
- ◆ Redirect Message
- ◆ Path MTU Discovery

133

During and after autoconfiguration, the workstation relies heavily on the IPv6 Neighbor Discovery protocol. The Neighbor Discovery protocol allows nodes on the same subnet to discover each other and to find routers for use as the next hop towards a destination on another subnet. The Neighbor Discovery protocol replaces the IPv4 Address Resolution Protocol (ARP), the IPv4 default gateway process, and the IPv4 redirect process.

During the autoconfiguration process, after the workstation generates a unique link-local address, it queries for a router. The workstation sends a Router Solicitation message and a router responds with a Router Advertisement message.

The presence of a router indicates that there may be other subnets connected to the router. Each subnet must have its own subnet identifier, because routing is dependent on unique subnet numbers. Host identifiers are not used for making routing decisions. The workstation address must now have a unique subnet identifier. The link-local address with its zero subnet ID is not sufficient for intersubnet communications.

To support stateless autoconfiguration, the Router Advertisement contains a subnet identifier. Router Advertisements for each router interface contain a different subnet identifier. This identifier will be concatenated with the interface identifier to form the workstation's IPv6 address.

The workstation will discard its tentative link-local address and configure a new address that is known as the site-local address. The site-local address contains a 16-bit subnet ID.

The workstation will use information from the Router Advertisement to update its caches. The subnet ID is added to the workstation's Prefix List cache. This cache will be used to determine if an address is on the workstation's subnet (on-link) or not (off-link). The router's information will be added to the Neighbor cache and Destination cache. If the router can be used as a default router, an entry will be added to the Default Router List cache.

When the workstation is ready to send a packet to a destination host, it queries the Prefix List to determine whether the destination's IPv6 address is onlink or off-link. If the destination host is off-link, the packet will be transmitted to the next hop, which is the router in the Default Router List. The workstation will then update its Destination cache with an entry for the destination host and its next hop address. If the default router selected is not the optimal next hop to the destination, the router will send a Redirect message to the source workstation with the new recommended next hop router for the destination. The workstation will then update its Destination cache with the new next hop for the destination.

The caches are maintained by each IPv6 host and are queried before solicitation messages are transmitted. The caches reduce the number of solicitation and advertisement messages that need to be sent. The caches are periodically purged of expired information, and they are constantly updated.

To facilitate inter-subnet communications, IPv6 provides another useful service, Path MTU Discovery. IPv6 does not allow routers to fragment packets that are too large to be forwarded through the next hop link or interface; only the source node may fragment a packet. Using IPv6's Path MTU Discovery service, a source node can determine the largest packet that may be sent to the destination.

With this information, the source node can appropriately resize its packets prior to transmission.

Site-local addresses can only be used for communications within the site. For communications beyond the site, global addresses must be assigned with a more scalable autoconfiguration procedure.

3.3 Internetwork Communications

In stateless autoconfiguration, each node is responsible for configuring its own address and caches using its interface identifier and information provided by the distributed Neighbor Discovery protocol. In small networks, stateless autoconfiguration is advantageous for its simplicity and ease of use. Its disadvantages include relying on multicast discovery mechanisms, using address space inefficiently, and lacking in security and control over policy and access.

To facilitate communications in larger and more complex internetworks, it may be desirable to manage the autoconfiguration process using a procedure known as stateful autoconfiguration. During our discussion of this process, we will introduce the following concepts:

- Stateful Autoconfiguration
- Dynamic Host Configuration Protocol Version 6 (DHCPv6)
- DHCPv6 Client, Relay, Agent, Server

Stateful autoconfiguration relies on servers to provide the bulk of the configuration information, including the network information required for obtaining an Aggregatable Global Unicast address. These servers are known as Dynamic Host Configuration Protocol version 6 (DHCPv6) servers. From a network administrator's point of view, stateful autoconfiguration is more complex than stateless autoconfiguration because it requires that configuration information be entered into a DHCPv6 database. On the other hand, stateful autoconfiguration provides greater scalability when administering to large networks.

Stateful autoconfiguration can be used simultaneously with stateless autoconfiguration. For example, a node may follow the stateless procedure upon startup to obtain a link-local address. After obtaining the link-local address, it may use stateful autoconfiguration to interact with and obtain additional information from a DHCPv6 server.

To obtain configuration information, a workstation first locates a DHCPv6 server by issuing a DHCP Solicit message or by listening for a DHCPv6 Advertisement. The workstation then issues a unicast DHCPv6 Request. If a DHCPv6 server is not on the local subnet, then a DHCPv6 Relay or Agent will forward the request to a server on behalf of the workstation. The server will respond with a DHCPv6 Reply that contains configuration information for the workstation.

The use of a DHCPv6 service has several advantages:

- Control: The DHCPv6 service controls the distribution and assignment of addresses from a central control point.
- Aggregation: Through the thoughtful distribution of addresses, an addressing hierarchy can be built to ensure address aggregation.
- Renumbering: When a new Internet service provider is chosen to replace the old provider,

new addresses can more easily be distributed with the DHCPv6 service.

◆ Security: A host registration system can be enforced with the DHCPv6 service. This registration system can selectively provide network services to registered hosts and deny access to unregistered hosts.

Reading Material 2   Router

A router is a computer networking device that forwards data packets across a network toward their destinations, through a process known as routing. Routing occurs at Layer 3 [the network layer i. e. Internet Protocol (IP)] of the OSI seven-layer protocol stack.

1. Function

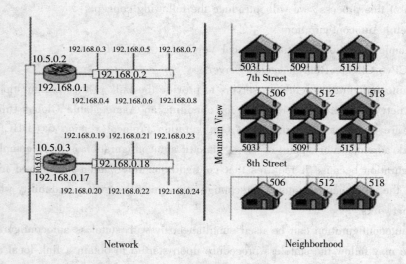

Figure 7. 4. 1   Routers are like intersections whereas switches are like streets

A router acts as a junction between two or more networks to transfer data packets among them. A router is different from a switch. A switch connects devices to form a local area network (LAN).

One easy illustration for the different functions of routers and switches is to think of switches as neighborhood streets, and the router as the intersections with the street signs. Each house on the street has an address within a range on the block. In the same way, a switch connects various devices each with their own IP address on a LAN.

However, the switch knows nothing about IP addresses except its own management address. Routers connect networks together the way that on-ramps or major intersections connect streets to both highways and freeways, etc. The street signs at the intersection (routing table) show which way the packets need to flow.

So for example, a router at home connects the Internet service provider's (ISP) network (usually on an Internet address) together with the LAN in the home 〔typically using a range of private IP addresses, see network address translation (NAT)〕 and a single broadcast domain. The switch connects devices together to form the LAN. Sometimes the switch and the router are combined together in one single package sold as a multiple port router.

In order to route packets, a router communicates with other routers using routing protocols and using this information creates and maintains a routing table. The routing table stores the best routes to certain network destinations, the "routing metrics" associated with those routes, and the path to the next hop router. Routing is most commonly associated with IP, although other less-popular routed protocols are in use.

2. History

The first router was created at Stanford University by a staff researcher named William Yeager in January of 1980. His boss at the time told him that he was the "network guy" and to find a way to connect the computers in the computer science department, medical center and department of electrical engineering. He first wrote a network operating system and routing code to run on a DEC PDP-11/05. He used Alan Snyder's Portable C compiler but it generated too much code so he modified the compiler to improve the code generators. That still wasn't good enough so he wrote an optimizer for PDP-11/05 assembler that reduced the code size further.

3. Types of Routers

In the original era of routing (from the mid-1970s through the 1980s), general-purpose minicomputers served as routers. The ARPAnet (the Internet's predecessor) used what was then called IMPs. Although general-purpose computers can perform routing, modern high-speed routers are highly specialized computers, generally with extra hardware added to accelerate both common routing functions such as packet forwarding and specialized functions such as IPsec encryption.

Other changes also improve reliability, such as using DC power rather than line power (which can be provided from batteries in data centers), and using solid state rather than magnetic storage for program loading. Large modern routers have thus come to resemble telephone switches, with whose technology they are currently converging and may eventually replace. Small routers have become a common household item.

A router that connects clients to the Internet is called an edge router. A router that serves solely to transmit data between other routers, e. g. inside the network of an ISP, is called a core router.

A router is normally used to connect at least two networks, but a special variety of router is the one-armed router, used to route packets in a virtual LAN environment. In the case of a one-armed router, the multiple attachments to different networks are all over the same physical link.

In mobile ad-hoc networks every host performs routing and forwarding by itself, while in wired networks there is usually just one router for a whole broadcast domain.

In recent times many routing functions have been added to LAN switches (a marketing term for high-speed bridges), creating "Layer 2/3 switches" which route traffic at near wire speed.

Routers are also now being implemented as Internet gateways, primarily for small networks like those used in homes and small offices. This application is mainly where the Internet connection is an always-on broadband connection like cable modem or DSL. These are routers in the true sense because they join two networks together—the WAN and the LAN—and have a routing table. Often these small routers support the RIP protocol, although in a home application the routing function does not serve much purpose since there are only two ways to go—the WAN and the LAN. In addition, these routers typically provide DHCP, NAT, DMZ and firewall services. Sometimes these routers can provide content filtering and VPN. Typically they are used in conjunction with either a cable or DSL modem, but that function can also be built-in.

Exercises

Ⅰ. Fill in the following blanks with proper words or phrases:

1. Network topologies are categorized into the following basic types: _____, _____, _____, _____, and _____.

2. A _____ topology connects computers along a single or more cable to connect linearly.

3. Ethernet 10BaseT is a network based on the _____ topology.

4. The ring topology is commonly used in _____ networks that the ring of such network is concentrated inside a device called a Multistation Access Unit (MAU) and Fiber Distributed Data Interface (FDDI) networks.

5. The _____ topology provides fault tolerance.

6. The way of achieving _____ transmission is to have two separate communication channels and use each one for simplex data traffic (in different directions).

7. The technique of temporarily delaying outgoing acknowledgements so that they can be hooked onto the next outgoing data frame is known as _____.

8. In all sliding window protocols, each outbound frame contains a _____, ranging from 0 up to some maximum.

9. For sliding window protocols, the sender must keep _____ in its memory for possible retransmission.

Ⅱ. Answer the following questions:

1. Describe the advantages and disadvantages of bus topology.

2. Describe the advantages and disadvantages of star topology.

3. What is 5-4-3 rule? Why do we need it?

4. List the conditions to choose a topology.

5. Briefly show that how piggybacking works in data transmission.

6. What's the problem that the piggybacking protocol introduces?

7. Describe the essence of all sliding window protocols.

8. Briefly describe how the sliding window protocols work.

Chapter Eight   Internet

Unit 1   A Basic Guide to the Internet

The Internet is a computer network made up of thousands of networks worldwide. No one knows exactly how many computers are connected to the Internet. It is certain, however, that these number in the millions and are growing.

No one is in charge of the Internet. There are organizations which develop technical aspects of this network and set standards for creating applications on it, but no governing body is in control. [1] The Internet backbone, through which Internet traffic flows, is owned by private companies.

All computers on the Internet communicate with one another using the **Transmission Control Protocol/Internet Protocol** suite, **abbreviated** to TCP/IP. Computers on the Internet use the client/server architecture. This means that the remote server machine provides files and services to the user's local client machine. Software can be installed on a client computer to take advantage of the **latest** access technology.

An Internet user has access to a wide variety of services: electronic mail, file transfer, vast information resources, interest group membership, interactive collaboration, multimedia displays, real-time broadcasting, breaking news, shopping opportunities, and much more.

The Internet consists primarily of a variety of access protocols. Many of these protocols feature programs that allow users to search for and retrieve material made available by the protocol.

1. World Wide Web

The World Wide Web (abbreviated as the Web or WWW) is a system of Internet servers that supports **hypertext** to access several Internet protocols on a single interface. Almost every protocol type available on the Internet is accessible on the Web. This includes e-mail, FTP, Telnet, and Usenet News. In addition to these, the World Wide Web has its own protocol: HyperText Transfer Protocol, or HTTP. These protocols will be explained below.

The World Wide Web provides a single interface for accessing all these protocols. This creates a convenient and user-friendly environment. It is not necessary to be conversant in these protocols within separate, command-level environments, as was typical in the early days of the Internet. [2] The Web gathers together these protocols into a single system. Because of this feature, and because of the Web's ability to work with multimedia and advanced programming languages, the Web is the most popular component of the Internet.

The operation of the Web relies primarily on hypertext as its means of information retrieval. HyperText is a document containing words that connect to other documents. These words are called links and are selectable by the user. A single hypertext document can contain links to many documents. In the context of the Web, words or graphics may serve as links to other documents, images, video, and sound. Links may or may not follow a logical path, as each connection is programmed by the creator of the source document. Overall, the Web contains a complex virtual web of connections among a vast number of documents, graphics, videos, and sounds.

Producing hypertext for the Web is accomplished by creating documents with a language called HyperText Markup Language, or HTML. With HTML, tags are placed within the text to accomplish document formatting, visual features such as font size, italics and bold, and the creation of hypertext links. Graphics and multimedia may also be incorporated into an HTML document.

HTML is an evolving language, with new tags being added as each upgrade of the language is developed and released. For example, visual formatting features are now often separated from the HTML document and placed into **Cascading Style Sheets** (CSS). This has several advantages, including the fact that an external style sheet can centrally control the formatting of multiple documents. The **World Wide Web Consortium** (W3C), led by Web founder Tim Berners-Lee, coordinates the efforts of standardizing HTML. The W3C now calls the language XHTML and considers it to be an application of the XML language standard.

The World Wide Web consists of files, called pages or home pages, containing links to documents and resources throughout the Internet.

The Web provides a vast array of experiences including multimedia presentations, real-time collaboration, interactive pages, radio and television broadcasts, and the automatic "push" of information to a client computer or to a **Really Simple Syndicaiton** (RSS) reader. Programming languages such as Java, JavaScript, Visual Basic, Cold Fusion and XML extend the capabilities of the Web. Much information on the Web is served dynamically from content stored in databases. The Web is therefore not a fixed entity, but one that is in a constant state of development and flux.

2. E-mail

Electronic mail, or e-mail, allows computer users locally and worldwide to exchange messages. Each user of e-mail has a mailbox address to which messages are sent. Messages sent through e-mail can arrive within a matter of seconds.

A powerful aspect of e-mail is the option to send electronic files to a person's e-mail address. Non-ASCII files, known as binary files, may be attached to e-mail messages. These files are referred to as **MIME** attachments. MIME stands for Multimedia Internet Mail Extension, and was developed to help e-mail software handle a variety of file types. For example, a document created in Microsoft Word can be attached to an e-mail message and retrieved by the recipient with the appropriate e-mail program. Many e-mail programs offer the ability to read files written in HTML, which is itself a MIME type.

3. Telnet

Telnet is a program that allows you to log into computers on the Internet and use online databases, library catalogs, chat services, and more. There are no graphics in telnet sessions, just text. To telnet to a computer, you must know its address. This can consist of words (locis. loc. gov) or numbers (140. 147. 254. 3). Some services require you to connect to a specific port on the remote computer. In this case, type the port number after the Internet address. Example: telnet nri. reston. va. us 185.

Telnet is available on the World Wide Web. Probably the most common Web-based resources available through Telnet have been library catalogs, though most catalogs have since migrated to the Web. A link to a telnet resource may look like any other link, but it will launch a telnet session to make the connection. A telnet program must be installed on your local computer and configured to your Web browser in order to work.

With the popularity of the Web, Telnet is less frequently used as a means of access to information on the Internet.

4. FTP

FTP stands for File Transfer Protocol. This is both a program and the method used to transfer files between computers. Anonymous FTP is an option that allows users to transfer files from thousands of host computers on the Internet to their personal computer accounts. FTP sites contain books, articles, softwares, games, images, sounds, multimedia, course works, data sets, and more.

If your computer is directly connected to the Internet via an Ethernet cable, you can use one of several PC software programs, such as WS_ FTP for Windows, to conduct a file transfer.

FTP transfers can be performed on the World Wide Web without the need for special software. In this case, the Web browser will suffice. Whenever you download software from a Web site to your local machine, you are using FTP. You can also retrieve FTP files via search engines such as FtpFind, located at http: //www. ftpfind. com/. This option is easiest because you do not need to know FTP program commands.

5. Chat & Instant Messaging

Chat programs allow users on the Internet to communicate with each other by typing in real time. They are sometimes included as a feature of a Web site, where users can log into the "chat room" to exchange comments and information about the topics addressed on the site. Chat may take other, more wide-ranging forms. For example, America Online is well known for sponsoring a number of topical chat rooms.

Internet Relay Chat (IRC) is a service through which participants can communicate to each other on hundreds of channels. These channels are usually based on specific topics. While many topics are **frivolous**, **substantive** conversations are also taking place. To access IRC, you must use an IRC software program.

A variation of chat is the phenomenon of instant messaging. With instant messaging, a user on the Web can contact another user currently logged in and type a conversation. Most famous is America Online's Instant Messenger. ICQ, MSN and Yahoo also offer chat programs. Open Source chat programs include GAIM and Jabber.

Key Words

Transmission Control Protocol	传输控制协议
Internet Protocol	网际协议
abbreviate	v. 缩写
latest	adj. 最新的
hypertext	n. 超文本
Cascading Style Sheet	层叠样式表
World Wide Web Consortium	万维网联盟
Really Simple Syndicaiton	描述新闻频道的语言
MIME	多用途网际邮件扩充协议
frivolous	adj. 无聊的
substantive	adj. 大量的

Notes

1. There are organizations which develop technical aspects of this network and set standards for creating applications on it, but no governing body is in control.

有一些组织参与这一网络技术方面的开发和为网络应用制定标准，但是没有任何一方获得了主导地位。

2. The World Wide Web provides a single interface for accessing all these protocols. This creates a convenient and user-friendly environment. It is not necessary to be conversant in these protocols within separate, command-level environments, as was typical in the early days of the Internet.

万维网提供了一个单一的界面用于访问所有协议，这创造了一个方便、友好的环境，使得人们不再需要精通相互独立的、命令行环境中的协议，而这恰恰是早期因特网的基本要求。

Unit 2   DNS (Domain Name System)

1. Introduction

While DNS is one of the least necessary technologies that make up the Internet as we know it, it is also true that the Internet would never have become as popular as it is today if DNS did not exist. Though this may sound like a bit of a **contradiction**, it is true, none the less.

　　DNS stands for two things: Domain Name Service and Domain Name Servers. One **acronym** defines the protocol; the other defines the machines that provide the service. The job that DNS performs is very simple: it takes the IP addresses that computers connected to the Internet use to communicate with each other and it maps them to hostnames.

　　Human beings tend to have a difficult time remembering long strings of seemingly arbitrary numbers. The way that our brains work, it's difficult to make information like that stick. [1] And that is where DNS comes in. It allows us to substitute words or phrases for those strings of numbers. Words are a lot easier for people to remember than numbers, especially when they can be tied to a specific idea that is linked to the website.

2.　DNS Theory

　　DNS uses a distributed database to maintain its world-wide tree of names.

　　DNS uses a distributed database protocol to delegate control of domain name hierarchies among zones, each managed by a group of name servers. For example, *. cnn. com, where * is anything, is completely the responsibility of CNN (Turner Broadcasting, as they say). CNN is responsible for constructing name servers to handle any domain name ending in cnn. com, referred to as their **Zone of Authority** (ZOA). A zone takes its name from its highest point, so this zone is simply called cnn. com. CNN registers their zone with InterNIC, who loads their name server IP addresses into the root name servers, which makes this information available to the global Internet. CNN can also make subdelegations, like delegating news. cnn. com to their news division. This can be as simple as creating new name server entries with the longer names, but mechanisms exist if the delegee wants to operate an independent name server.

　　Of course, CNN doesn't actually maintain their own name server. Like most people, they let their Internet service provider do it for them. In their case, that means ANSnet, so nis. ans. net is their primary name server, and ns. ans. net their backup name server. How do I know this? I accessed InterNIC's Whois service and retrieved cnn. com's domain information record.

　　So, name servers contain pointers to other name servers that can be used to transverse the entire domain naming **hierarchy**. You may be wondering how Internet hosts find an entry point to this system. Currently, it can be done in three major ways, all of which depend on preloading the IP address of at least one name server. One way is to preconfigure addresses of the root name servers. This method is typically used by Internet service providers on their name servers, typically in the UNIX file /etc. /namedb/named. root. Another way is to preload the address of a name server that supports **recursive queries**, and send any name server lookups to it. This method is common among dial-up Internet subscribers. The user preloads the address of the service provider's name server, which processes all queries and returns the answer to the client. The final method is to automatically configure the address of a recursive name server, perhaps using a **PPP** extension that is not yet widely supported.

Once a host has been configured with initial name server addresses, it can use the DNS protocols to locate the name servers responsible for any part of the DNS naming hierarchy, and retrieve the resource records (RRs) that match DNS names to IP addresses and control Internet mail delivery.

3. Elements of DNS

The DNS has three major components: Domain Name Space and Resource Records, Name Servers, and **Resolvers**.

The Domain Name Space and Resource Records are specifications for a tree structured name space and data associated with the names. Conceptually, each node and leaf of the domain name space tree names a set of information, and query operations are attempts to extract specific types of information from a particular set. A query names the domain name of interest and describes the type of resource information that is desired. For example, the Internet uses some of its domain names to identify hosts; queries for address resources return Internet host addresses.

Name Servers are server programs which hold information about the domain tree's structure and set information. A name server may cache structure or set information about any part of the domain tree, but in general a particular name server has complete information about a subset of the domain space, and pointers to other name servers that can be used to lead to information from any part of the domain tree. Name servers know the parts of the domain tree for which they have complete information; a name server is said to be an AUTHORITY for these parts of the name space. Authoritative information is organized into units called ZONEs, and these zones can be automatically distributed to the name servers which provide redundant service for the data in a zone.

Resolvers are programs that extract information from name servers in response to client requests. Resolvers must be able to access at least one name server and use that name server's information to answer a query directly, or **pursue** the query using **referrals** to other name servers. A resolver will typically be a system routine that is directly accessible to user programs; hence no protocol is necessary between the resolver and the user program.

These three components roughly correspond to the three layers or views of the domain system:

- ◆ From the user's point of view, the domain system is accessed through a simple procedure or OS call to a local resolver. The domain space consists of a single tree and the user can request information from any section of the tree.
- ◆ From the resolver's point of view, the domain system is composed of an unknown number of name servers. Each name server has one or more pieces of the whole domain tree's data, but the resolver views each of these databases as essentially static.
- ◆ From a name server's point of view, the domain system consists of separate sets of local information called zones. The name server has local copies of some of the zones. The name server must periodically refresh its zones from master copies in local files or foreign name servers. The name server must concurrently process queries that arrive from resolvers.

In the interests of performance, implementations may **couple** these functions. For example, a resolver on the same machine as a name server might share a database consisting of the zones managed by the name server and the cache managed by the resolver.

4. The DNS Protocol

The DNS protocol is used to request resource records from name servers.

Part of the confusion associated with the DNS protocol is that it lacks a special name. Thus DNS can refer either to the entire system, or to the protocol that makes it work. This page documents the protocol, which operates in one of two basic modes-lookups or zone transfers.

4. 1 DNS Lookups

Normal resource records lookups are done with UDP. An "intelligent retransmission" is to be used, though one is not specified in the protocol, resulting in a mix of poor strategies with good ones. The protocol itself is stateless; all the information needed is contained in a single message, and having the following format:

Table 8. 2. 1 Message format

Header		Header	
Question	the question for the name server	Authority	RRs pointing toward an authority
Answer	RRs answering the question	Additional	RRs holding additional information

Questions are always Name, Type, Class tuples. For Internet applications, the Class is IN, the Type is a valid RR type, and the Name is a fully-qualified domain name, stored in a standard format. Names can't be **wildcarded**, but Types and Classes can be. In addition, special Types exist to wildcard mail records and to trigger zone transfers. The question is the only section included in a query message; the remaining sections being used for replies.

Answers are RRs that match the Name, Type, Class tuple. If any of the matching records are CNAME pointers leading to other records, the target records should also be included in the answer. There may be multiple answers, since there may be multiple RRs with the same labels.

Authority RRs are type NS records pointing to name servers closer to the target name in the naming hierarchy. This field is completely optional, but clients are encouraged to cache this information if further requests may be made in the same name hierarchy.

Additional RRs are records that the name server believes may be useful to the client. The most common use for this field is to supply A (address) records for the name servers listed in the Authority section.

However, cleverer name servers are feasible. For example, if the question is for an MX record for FreeSoft. org, the answer will currently point to mail. adnc. com. The name server can infer that the client's next request will be an A query for mail. adnc. com, which will be answered by with a CNAME record, the DNS equivalent of a symbolic link, and the target of that link, an A record for gemini. adnc. com. The name server can avoid all this extra traffic by just including the CNAME and A records as additional RRs in the original reply. [2] Not all name servers do this, however. Use the Dig program to watch what really happens.

4.2　Zone Transfers

Sometimes, it is necessary to efficiently transfer the resource records of an entire DNS zone. This is most commonly done by a secondary name server having determined the need to update its database.

The operation of a zone transfer is almost identical to a normal DNS query, except that TCP is used (due to large quantity of reply records) and a special Class exists to trigger a zone transfer. A DNS query with Name = FreeSoft. org, Class = IN, Type = AXFR will trigger a zone transfer for FreeSoft. org. The end of a zone transfer is marked by duplicating the SOA RR that started the zone.

4.3　Lower-level Transport

Either TCP or UDP can be used to transport DNS protocol messages, connecting to server port 53 for either. Ordinary DNS requests can be made with TCP, though convention dictates the use of UDP for normal operation. TCP must be used for zone transfers, however, because of the danger of dropping records with an **unreliable delivery protocol** such as UDP.

Key Words

contradiction	n.	自相矛盾
acronym	n.	首字母缩略字
Zone of Authority		授权域
hierarchy	n.	层级结构
recursive query		递归查询
PPP		点到点协议（Point-to-Point Protocol），位于数据链路层
resolver	n.	解析器
pursue	v.	继续
referral	n.	回应 NS 记录
couple	v.	组合，结合
wildcard	v.	通配　n.　通配符
unreliable delivery protocol		不可靠传送协议（缩写为 UDP，与 TCP 相对应）

Notes

1. Human beings tend to have a difficult time remembering long strings of seemingly arbitrary numbers. The way that our brains work, it's difficult to make information like that stick.

人很难记住由一长串任意的数字组成的字符串。我们大脑的工作方式决定了牢固地记住这些信息是很困难的。

2. The name server can avoid all this extra traffic by just including the CNAME and A records as additional RRs in the original reply.

在最初回复的附加的 RR 域中包括 CNAME 和 A 记录，域名服务器就可以避免这些多余的流量。

Reading Material 1　HTTP Cookies

HTTP cookies, sometimes known as web cookies or just cookies, are parcels of text sent by a server to a web browser and then sent back unchanged by the browser each time it accesses that server. HTTP cookies are used for authenticating, tracking, and maintaining specific information about users, such as site preferences and the contents of their electronic shopping carts. The term "cookie" is derived from "magic cookie", a well-known concept in UNIX computing which inspired both the idea and the name of HTTP cookies.

Cookies have been of concern for Internet privacy, since they can be used for tracking browsing behavior. As a result, they have been subject to legislation in various countries such as the United States and in the European Union. Cookies have also been criticized because the identification of users they provide is not always accurate and because they could potentially be used for network attacks. Some alternatives to cookies exist, but each has its own drawbacks.

Cookies are also subject to a number of misconceptions, mostly based on the erroneous notion that they are computer programs. In fact, cookies are simple pieces of data unable to perform any operation by themselves. In particular, they are neither spyware nor viruses, despite the detection of cookies from certain sites by many anti-spyware products.

Most modern browsers allow users to decide whether to accept cookies, but rejection makes some websites unusable. For example, shopping baskets implemented using cookies do not work if cookies are rejected.

1.　Purpose

Cookies are used by Web servers to differentiate users and to operate in a way that depends on the user. Cookies were invented for realizing a virtual shopping basket: this is a virtual device in which the user can "place" items to purchase, so that users can navigate a site where items are shown, adding or removing items from the shopping basket at any time. Cookies allow for the content of the shopping cart to depend on the user's actions.

Allowing users to log in to a website is another use of cookies. Users typically log in by inserting their credentials into a login page; cookies allow the server to know that the user is already authenticated, and therefore is allowed to access services or perform operations that are restricted to logged-in users.

Several websites also use cookies for personalization based on users' preferences. Sites that require authentication often use this feature, although it is also present on sites not requiring authentication. Personalization includes presentation and functionality. For example, the Wikipedia Web site allows authenticated users to choose the webpage skin they like best; the Google search engine allows users (even non-registered ones) to decide how many search results per page they want to see.

Cookies are also used to track users across a website. Third-party cookies and Web bugs, explained below, also allow for tracking across multiple sites. Tracking within a site is typically done with the aim of producing usage statistics, while tracking across sites is typically used by advertising companies to produce anonymous user profiles, which are then used to target advertising (deciding which advertising image to show) based on the user profile.

2. Realization

Technically, cookies are arbitrary pieces of data chosen by the Web server and sent to the browser. The browser returns them unchanged to the server, introducing a state (memory of previous events) into otherwise stateless HTTP transactions. Without cookies, each retrieval of a Web page or component of a Web page is an isolated event, mostly unrelated to all other views of the pages of the same site. By returning a cookie to a Web server, the browser provides the server a means of connecting the current page view with prior page views. Other than being set by a Web server, cookies can also be set by a script in a language such as JavaScript, if supported and enabled by the Web browser.

Cookie specifications suggest that browsers should support a minimal number of cookies or amount of memory for storing them. In particular, an Internet browser is expected to be able to store at least 300 cookies of 4 kilobytes each, and at least 20 cookies per server or domain.

The cookie setter can specify a deletion date, in which case the cookie will be removed on that date. If the cookie setter does not specify a date, the cookie is removed once the user quits his browser. As a result, specifying a date is a way for making a cookie survive across sessions. For this reason, cookies with an expiration date are called persistent. As an example application, a shopping site can use persistent cookies to store the items users have placed in their basket. In this way, if users quit their browser without making a purchase and return later, they don't have to find the products they previously placed in the shopping cart over again.

3. Misconceptions

Since their introduction on the Internet, misconceptions about cookies have circulated on the Internet and in the media. In 2005, Jupiter Research published the results of a survey, according to which a consistent percentage of respondents believed some of the following claims:

- ◆ Cookies are like worms and viruses in that they can erase data from the user's hard disks;
- ◆ Cookies are a form of spyware in that they can read personal information stored on the user's computer;
- ◆ Cookies generate popups;
- ◆ Cookies are used for spamming;
- ◆ Cookies are only used for advertising.

Cookies are in fact only data, not program code: they cannot erase or read information from the user's computer. However, cookies allow for detecting the Web pages viewed by a user on a given site or set of sites. This information can be collected in a profile of the user. Such profiles are often anonymous, that is, they do not contain personal information of the user (name, address, etc.)

More precisely, they cannot contain personal information unless the user has made it available to some sites. Even if anonymous, these profiles have been the subject of some privacy concerns.

According to the same survey, a large percentage of Internet users do not know how to delete cookies.

Reading Material 2　What Is Web 2.0

The bursting of the dot-com bubble in the fall of 2001 marked a turning point for the web. Many people concluded that the web was overhyped, when in fact bubbles and consequent shakeouts appear to be a common feature of all technological revolutions. Shakeouts typically mark the point at which an ascendant technology is ready to take its place at center stage. The pretenders are given the bum's rush, the real success stories show their strength, and there begins to be an understanding of what separates one from the other.

The concept of "Web 2.0" began with a conference brainstorming session between O'Reilly and MediaLive International. Dale Dougherty, web pioneer and O'Reilly VP, noted that far from having "crashed", the web was more important than ever, with exciting new applications and sites popping up with surprising regularity. What's more, the companies that had survived the collapse seemed to have some things in common. Could it be that the dot-com collapse marked some kind of turning point for the web, such that a call to action such as "Web 2.0" might make sense? We agreed that it did.

This article is an attempt to clarify just what we mean by Web 2.0.

1. The Web as Platform

Like many important concepts, Web 2.0 doesn't have a hard boundary, but rather, a gravitational core. You can visualize Web 2.0 as a set of principles and practices that tie together a veritable solar system of sites that demonstrate some or all of those principles, at a varying distance from that core。

A preliminary set of principles were listed in October 2004. The first of those principles was "The web as platform". Yet that was also a rallying cry of Web 1.0 darling Netscape, which went down in flames after a heated battle with Microsoft. What's more, two of Web 1.0 exemplars, DoubleClick and Akamai, were both pioneers in treating the web as a platform. People don't often think of it as "web services", but in fact, ad serving was the first widely deployed web service, and the first widely deployed "mashup" (to use another term that has gained currency of late). Every banner ad is served as a seamless cooperation between two websites, delivering an integrated page to a reader on yet another computer. Akamai also treats the network as the platform, and at a deeper level of the stack, building a transparent caching and content delivery network that eases bandwidth congestion.

Nonetheless, these pioneers provided useful contrasts because later entrants have taken their solution to the same problem even further, understanding something deeper about the nature of the new platform.

2. Harnessing Collective Intelligence

The central principle behind the success of the giants born in the Web 1. 0 era who have survived to lead the Web 2. 0 era appears to be this, that they have embraced the power of the web to harness collective intelligence.

Hyperlinking is the foundation of the web. As users add new content, and new sites, it is bound in to the structure of the web by other users discovering the content and linking to it. Much as synapses form in the brain, with associations becoming stronger through repetition or intensity, the web of connections grows organically as an output of the collective activity of all web users.

Now, innovative companies that pick up on this insight and perhaps extend it even further, are making their mark on the web.

Wikipedia, an online encyclopedia based on the unlikely notion that an entry can be added by any web user, and edited by any other, is a radical experiment in trust, applying Eric Raymond's dictum (originally coined in the context of open source software) that "with enough eyeballs, all bugs are shallow" to content creation. Wikipedia is already in the top 100 websites, and many think it will be in the top ten before long. This is a profound change in the dynamics of content creation!

Collaborative spam filtering products like Cloudmark aggregate the individual decisions of e-mail users about what is and is not spam, outperforming systems that rely on analysis of the messages themselves.

It is a truism that the greatest internet success stories don't advertise their products. Their adoption is driven by "viral marketing" —that is, recommendations propagating directly from one user to another. You can almost make the case that if a site or product relies on advertising to get the word out, it isn't Web 2. 0.

Even much of the infrastructure of the web—including the Linux, Apache, MySQL, and Perl, PHP, or Python code involved in most web servers—relies on the peer-production methods of open source, in themselves an instance of collective, net-enabled intelligence. There are more than 100, 000 open source software projects listed on SourceForge. net. Anyone can add a project, anyone can download and use the code, and new projects migrate from the edges to the center as a result of users putting them to work, an organic software adoption process relying almost entirely on viral marketing.

3. Blogging and the Wisdom of Crowds

One of the most highly touted features of the Web 2. 0 era is the rise of blogging. Personal home pages have been around since the early days of the web, and the personal diary and daily opinion column around much longer than that, so just what is the fuss all about?

At its most basic, a blog is just a personal home page in diary format. But as Rich Skrenta

151

notes, the chronological organization of a blog "seems like a trivial difference, but it drives an entirely different delivery, advertising and value chain".

One of the things that have made a difference is a technology called RSS. RSS is the most significant advance in the fundamental architecture of the web since early hackers realized that CGI could be used to create database-backed websites. RSS allows someone to link not just to a page, but to subscribe to it, with notification every time that page changes. Skrenta calls this "the incremental web". Others call it the "live web".

Now, of course, "dynamic websites" (i. e. , database-backed sites with dynamically generated content) replaced static web pages well over ten years ago. What dynamic about the live web are not just the pages, but the links. A link to a weblog is expected to point to a perennially changing page, with "permalinks" for any individual entry, and notification for each change. An RSS feed is thus a much stronger link than, say a bookmark or a link to a single page.

RSS also means that the web browser is not the only means of viewing a web page. While some RSS aggregators, such as Bloglines, are web-based, others are desktop clients, and still others allow users of portable devices to subscribe to constantly updated content.

RSS is now being used to push not just notices of new blog entries, but also all kinds of data updates, including stock quotes, weather data, and photo availability. This use is actually a return to one of its roots: RSS was born in 1997 out of the confluence of Dave Winer's "Really Simple Syndication" technology, used to push out blog updates, and Netscape's "Rich Site Summary", which allowed users to create custom Netscape home pages with regularly updated data flows. In the current crop of applications, we see the heritage of both parents.

But RSS is only part of what makes a weblog different from an ordinary web page. Tom Coates remarks on the significance of the permalink:

"It may seem like a trivial piece of functionality now, but it was effectively the device that turned weblogs from an ease-of-publishing phenomenon into a conversational mess of overlapping communities. For the first time it became relatively easy to gesture directly at a highly specific post on someone else's site and talk about it. Discussion emerged. Chat emerged. And—as a result—friendships emerged or became more entrenched. The permalink was the first—and most successful—attempt to build bridges between weblogs. "

In many ways, the combination of RSS and permalinks adds many of the features of NNTP, the Network News Protocol of the Usenet, onto HTTP, the web protocol. The "blogosphere" can be thought of as a new, peer-to-peer equivalent to Usenet and bulletin-boards, the conversational watering holes of the early internet. Not only can people subscribe to each others' sites, and easily link to individual comments on a page, but also, via a mechanism known as trackbacks, they can see when anyone else links to their pages, and can respond, either with reciprocal links, or by adding comments.

Interestingly, two-way links were the goal of early hypertext systems like Xanadu. Hypertext purists have celebrated trackbacks as a step towards two way links. But note that trackbacks are not properly two-way——rather, they are really (potentially) symmetrical one-way links that create the effect of two way links. The difference may seem subtle, but in practice it is enormous. Social networking systems like Friendster, Orkut, and LinkedIn, which require acknowledgment by the recipient in order to establish a connection, lack the same scalability as the web. As noted by Caterina Fake, co-founder of the Flickr photo sharing service, attention is only coincidentally reciprocal. (Flickr thus allows users to set watch lists—any user can subscribe to any other user's photostream via RSS. The object of attention is notified, but does not have to approve the connection.)

If an essential part of Web 2.0 is harnessing collective intelligence, turning the web into a kind of global brain, the blogosphere is the equivalent of constant mental chatter in the forebrain, the voice we hear in all of our heads. It may not reflect the deep structure of the brain, which is often unconscious, but is instead the equivalent of conscious thought. And as a reflection of conscious thought and attention, the blogosphere has begun to have a powerful effect.

First, because search engines use link structure to help predict useful pages, bloggers, as the most prolific and timely linkers, have a disproportionate role in shaping search engine results. Second, because the blogging community is so highly self-referential, bloggers paying attention to other bloggers magnifies their visibility and power. The "echo chamber" that critics decry is also an amplifier.

If it were merely an amplifier, blogging would be uninteresting. But like Wikipedia, blogging harnesses collective intelligence as a kind of filter. What James Suriowecki calls "the wisdom of crowds" comes into play, and much as PageRank produces better results than analysis of any individual document, the collective attention of the blogosphere selects for value.

Exercises

I. Fill in the following blanks with proper words or phrases:

1. The Internet is a _____ made up of thousands of networks worldwide.

2. The _____ is a system of Internet servers that supports hypertext to access several Internet protocols on a single interface.

3. Producing hypertext for the Web is accomplished by creating documents with a language called _____.

4. FTP stands for _____.

5. _____ allow users on the Internet to communicate with each other by typing in real time.

6. DNS stands for two things: _____ and _____.

7. The DNS has three major components _____, _____ and _____.

8. The DNS protocol is used to request resource records from _____.

9. Normal resource records lookups are done with _____.

II. Answer the following questions:

1. List the components of the Internet.

2. What does the Web provide?

3. What's HyperText? Where it can be used?
4. Briefly describe the features of a Telnet program.
5. List several popular instant messenger programs.
6. Why de people introduce DNS into the Internet?
7. Briefly describe the theory of DNS.
8. Briefly describe the functions of three major components of DNS.
9. What kinds of format does a single message of DNS Lookups have?
10. What's the difference between the operation of DNS Zone transfer and DNS query?

Chapter Nine Geographic Information System

Unit 1 GIS Introduction

A **geographic information system** (GIS) is a computer-based tool for mapping and analyzing geographic phenomenon that exist, and events that occur, on Earth. GIS technology integrates common database operations such as query and statistical analysis with the unique visualization and geographic analysis benefits offered by maps.[1] These abilities distinguish GIS from other information systems and make it valuable to a wide range of public and private enterprises for explaining events, predicting outcomes, and planning strategies. Map making and geographic analysis are not new, but a GIS performs these tasks faster and with more sophistication than do traditional manual methods.

Today, GIS is a multi-billion-dollar industry employing hundreds of thousands of people worldwide. GIS is taught in schools, colleges, and universities throughout the world. Professionals and domain specialists in every **discipline** are become increasingly aware of the advantages of using GIS technology for addressing their unique **spatial** problems.

We commonly think of a GIS as a single, well-defined, integrated computer system. However, this is not always the case. A GIS can be made up of a variety of software and hardware tools. The important factor is the level of integration of these tools to provide a smoothly operating, fully functional geographic data processing environment.

Overall, GIS should be viewed as a technology, not simply as a computer system.

In general, a GIS provides facilities for data capture, data management, data manipulation and analysis, and the presentation of results in both graphic and report form, with a particular emphasis upon preserving and utilizing inherent characteristics of spatial data.

The ability to incorporate spatial data, manage it, analyze it, and answer spatial questions is the distinctive characteristic of geographic information systems.[2]

A geographic information system, commonly referred to as a GIS, is an integrated set of hardware and software tools used for the manipulation and management of digital spatial (geographic) and related attribute data.

1. GIS Subsystems

A GIS has four main functional subsystems. These are:

1) Data Input Subsystem

A data input subsystem allows the user to capture, collect, and transform spatial and **thematic data** into digital form. The data inputs are usually derived from a combination of hard copy maps, aerial photographs, **remotely sensed images**, reports, survey documents, etc.

155

2）Data Storage and Retrieval Subsystem

The data storage and retrieval subsystem organizes the data, spatial and attribute, in a form which permits it to be quickly retrieved by the user for analysis, and permits rapid and accurate updates to be made to the database. This component usually involves use of a database management system (DBMS) for maintaining attribute data. Spatial data is usually encoded and maintained in a proprietary file format.

3）Data Manipulation and Analysis Subsystem

The data manipulation and analysis subsystem allows the user to define and execute spatial and attribute procedures to generate derived information. This subsystem is commonly thought of as the heart of a GIS, and usually distinguishes it from other database information systems and **computer-aided drafting**（CAD）systems.

4）Data Output Subsystem

The data output subsystem allows the user to generate graphic displays, normally maps, and tabular reports representing derived information products.

The critical function for a GIS is, by design, the analysis of spatial data.

It is important to understand that the GIS is not a new invention. In fact, geographic information processing has a rich history in a variety of disciplines. In particular, natural resource specialists and environmental scientists have been actively processing geographic data and promoting their techniques since the 1960s.

Today's generic, geographic information system is distinguished from the geo-processing of the past by the use of computer automation to integrate geographic data processing tools in a friendly and comprehensive environment.

The **advent** of sophisticated computer techniques has proliferated the multi-disciplinary application of geo-processing methodologies, and provided data integration capabilities that were logistically impossible before.

2. Components of a GIS

An operational GIS also has a series of components that combine to make the system work. These components are critical to a successful GIS.

1）Hardware

Hardware is the computer system on which a GIS operates. Today, GIS software runs on a wide range of hardware types, from centralized computer servers to desktop computers used in stand-alone or networked configurations.

2）Software

GIS software provides the functions and tools needed to store, analyze, and display geographic information. A review of the key GIS software subsystems is provided above.

3）Data

Perhaps the most important component of a GIS is the data. Geographic data and related tabular data can be collected in-house, compiled to custom specifications and requirements, or occasionally purchased from a commercial data provider. A GIS can integrate spatial data with other existing data resources, often stored in a corporate DBMS. The integration of spatial data (often proprietary to the GIS software), and tabular data stored in a DBMS is a key functionality afforded by GIS.

4) People

GIS technology is of limited value without the people who manage the system and develop plans for applying it to real world problems. GIS users range from technical specialists who design and maintain the system to those who use it to help them perform their everyday work. The identification of GIS specialists versus end users is often critical to the proper implementation of GIS technology.

5) Methods

A successful GIS operates according to a well-designed implementation plan and business rules, which are the models and operating practices unique to each organization. [3] As in all organizations dealing with sophisticated technology, new tools can only be used effectively if they are properly integrated into the entire business strategy and operation. To do this properly requires not only the necessary investments in hardware and software, but also in the retraining and/or hiring of personnel to utilize the new technology in the proper organizational context. Failure to implement your GIS without regard for a proper organizational commitment will result in an unsuccessful system!

3. How Is GIS Data Stored and Used?

A GIS stores information about the features and events in a collection of thematic "layers" or coverage as the following graphic illustrates.

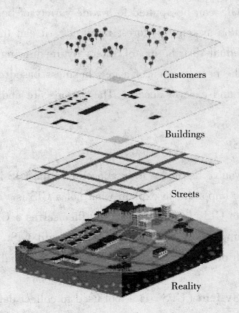

Figure 9. 1. 1   An example of GIS layers

In fact, it is the most distinguishing feature of a GIS to find and display (map) the location of features or events. For example, a traditional computer system may store all information about schools. It will provide the user with a list of all the schools, possibly including addresses, but the user still doesn't know where exactly the schools are. The answer to such a simple questions as: "Are the schools **evenly** distributed across town?" is impossible to give with traditional computer systems. The following example will illustrate this simple functionality. It will show how information alone, without any further analysis, is very useful.

A maintenance crew for light poles is scheduled to replace all light poles in town that are over 50 years old. The crew has a database about the light poles that includes the date of installation. In a traditional database, they could query the database and get a list of the light poles that are over 50 years old. But, where are they? The GIS combines the location and the age information and immediately displays a map that shows the location of all light poles that are over 50 years old. It is much easier now to schedule work for the crew in an efficient manner, because they can quickly develop a route through town to replace the light poles.

Lightpoles and other physical features such as a road, are also called features with an "explicit" geographic location. This means they have a position on the earth that can be measured and described, usually in longitude/latitude, or values from an established grid system. To actually locate an address, or other "implicit" geographic references (i.e. those that don't have a permanent physical location) on a map, a process called **geocoding** is used to assign a specific location code in a longitude/latitude, or other grid system value. They then are linked with an explicit geographic reference. Once all addresses in a GIS are geocoded, all databases that include addresses can be linked and the addresses automatically located.

The functionality of a GIS can be applied to a wide variety of business sectors. It can be used to manage a telecommunication system, or forest resources, it can track the number of voters in a voting precinct and insure equal distribution of voters by re-drawing boundaries when necessary, and it can help determine the best location of a new business based on factors such as income statistics, competitor locations and ease of access. The options are endless and are continually evolving.

4. What is NOT a GIS?

So far in GIS Basics, you've learned a little about just what GIS is, what goes into it, and how it works. In this section it is important to explain what not a GIS is. There are three things that are associated and very related to GIS, but are, NOT, by themselves a GIS.

Below are the three things most commonly confused with GIS. While all three of them are strongly related to GIS, each of them is a separate and distinct spatial tool of its own.

1) GPS

A **Global Positioning System** (GPS) is a tool used to collect data for a GIS. Many people get the terms GIS and GPS confused with each other.

GPS stands for Global Positioning System, which is a system of satellites, ground stations, and receivers that allow you to find your exact location on Earth. By collecting location points you can begin compile datasets that can be used to map whatever data you are collecting.

The U. S. Department of Defense was one of the first to use GPS technology as a **navigation** system. Not long after, biologists, foresters, and transportation departments to name a few, caught on to this revolutionary way of precisely collecting data.

How GPS and GIS relate to one another: The way a GPS works is, by connecting to three or more 24 GPS satellites that orbit 11,000 **nautical miles** above the earth, and are monitored by ground stations located throughout the world.

GPS systems generate geographic reference points in the form of latitude, longitude, and elevation coordinates. Once the data is collected it can be put into a GIS and displayed digitally as it is in the real world.

The technology has advanced greatly over the past ten years. Today boats and many car manufacturers have GPS units mounted so they can track where they are at all times. The increased availability and affordability of handheld GPS units, makes it useful for the average person to use for activities such as backpacking, hunting, and skiing, to name a few.

2) Maps

We're all familiar with maps. They help us locate things, help us get from place to place, and give us a sense of what places are like. They help us see and learn about where we're at, where we've been, where we'd like to go. Maps also provide us with glimpses into the past, of the places and journeys that people before us experienced.

They are a form of visual communication, a way of showing, displaying, or representing the spatial relationships between different places and their features. Like other forms of communication, maps vary greatly in their purpose and style, from a rough diagram you may draw on a napkin for a friend to get to your house, or to a complex city map.

5. GIS Applications

Computerized mapping and spatial analysis have been developed simultaneously in several related fields. The present status would not have been achieved without close interaction between various fields such as utility networks, **cadastral mapping**, **topographic mapping**, thematic **cartography**, image processing, computer science, rural and urban planning, earth science, and geography.

The GIS technology is rapidly becoming a standard tool for management of natural resources. The effective use of large spatial data volumes is dependent upon the existence of an efficient geographic handling and processing system to transform this data into usable information.

The GIS technology is used to assist decision-makers by indicating various alternatives in development and conservation planning and by modeling the potential outcomes of a series of scenarios.[4] It should be noted that any task begins and ends with the real world. Data is collected about the real world. Of necessity, the product is an abstraction; it is not possible (and not desired) to handle every last detail. After the data are analyzed, information is compiled for decision-makers. Based on this information, actions are taken and plans implemented in the real world.

Key Words

Geographic Information System	地理信息系统
discipline	*n.* 学科
spatial	*adj.* 空间的
thematic data	专题数据
remotely sensed image	遥感图像
computer-aided drafting	计算机辅助制图
advent	*n.* 出现
evenly	*adv.* 均匀地
geocoding	*n.* 地理编码
Global Positioning System	全球定位系统
navigation	*n.* 导航
nautical mile	海里
cadastral mapping	地籍测图
topographic map	地形图
cartography	*n.* 制图学

Notes

1. GIS technology integrates common database operations such as query and statistical analysis with the unique visualization and geographic analysis benefits offered by maps.

地理信息系统技术结合了包括查询和统计分析在内的数据库操作与地图提供的特殊的形象化和地理分析的优势。

2. The ability to incorporate spatial data, manage it, analyze it, and answer spatial questions is the distinctive characteristic of geographic information systems.

地理信息系统的特色是具有表示、管理和分析空间数据与处理空间相关问题的能力。

3. A successful GIS operates according to a well-designed implementation plan and business rules, which are the models and operating practices unique to each organization.

一个地理信息系统的成功运行是依靠一个设计良好的实现规划和业务规则。业务规则是依据不同的组织得到的独特的模型和运行习惯。

4. The GIS technology is used to assist decision-makers by indicating various alternatives in development and conservation planning and by modeling the potential outcomes of a series of scenarios.

地理信息系统通过给出不同的发展和保护计划并根据不同情况模拟出可能的结果来帮助决策者。

Unit 2   GIS Data

All themes within a GIS are based on geographically referenced data. The basic data type in a GIS reflects traditional data found on a map. Accordingly, GIS technology utilizes two basic types of data. These are:

◆ **Spatial data**: describes the absolute and relative location of geographic features.

◆ **Attribute data**: describes characteristics of the spatial features. These characteristics can be **quantitative** and/or **qualitative** in nature. Attribute data is often referred to as **tabular data**.

The coordinate location of a forestry stand would be spatial data, while the characteristics of that forestry stand, e. g. cover group, dominant species, crown closure, height, etc., would be attribute data. Other data types, in particular image and multimedia data, are becoming more prevalent with changing technology. Depending on the specific content of the data, image data may be considered either spatial, e. g. photographs, **animation**, movies, etc., or attribute, e. g. sound, descriptions, narrations, etc.

1. Spatial Data Models

Traditionally spatial data has been stored and presented in the form of a map. Three basic types of spatial data models have evolved for storing geographic data digitally. These are referred to as: **Vector**, **Raster**, and Image.

The following diagram reflects the two primary spatial data encoding techniques. These are vec-

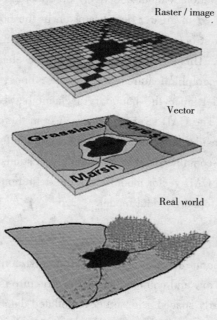

Figure 9. 2. 1   GIS overlay

tor and raster. Image data utilizes techniques very similar to raster data, however typically lacks the internal formats required for analysis and modeling of the data. Images reflect pictures or photographs of the landscape.

1.1　Vector Data Formats

All spatial data models are approaches for storing the spatial location of geographic features in a database. Vector storage implies the use of vectors (directional lines) to represent a geographic feature. Vector data is characterized by the use of sequential points or **vertices** to define a linear segment. Each vertex consists of an X coordinate and a Y coordinate.

Vector lines are often referred to as arcs and consist of a string of vertices terminated by a node. A node is defined as a vertex that starts or ends an arc segment. Point features are defined by one coordinate pair, a vertex. Polygonal features are defined by a set of closed coordinate pairs. In vector representation, the storage of the vertices for each feature is important, as well as the connectivity between features, e. g. the sharing of common vertices where features connect.

Several different vector data models exist, however only two are commonly used in GIS data storage.

The most popular method of retaining spatial relationships among features is to explicitly record adjacency information in what is known as the **topologic** data model. Topology is a mathematical concept that has its basis in the principles of feature adjacency and connectivity.

The topologic data structure is often referred to as an intelligent data structure because spatial relationships between geographic features are easily derived when using them. Primarily for this reason the topologic model is the dominant vector data structure currently used in GIS technology. Many of the complex data analysis functions cannot effectively be undertaken without a topologic vector data structure. Topology is reviewed in greater detail later on in the book.

The secondary vector data structure that is common among GIS software is the computer-aided drafting (CAD) data structure. This structure consists of listing elements, not features, defined by strings of vertices, to define geographic features, e. g. points, lines, or areas. There is considerable redundancy with this data model since the boundary segment between two polygons can be stored twice, once for each feature. [1] The CAD structure emerged from the development of computer graphics systems without specific considerations of processing geographic features. Accordingly, since features, e. g. polygons, are self-contained and independent, questions about the adjacency of features can be difficult to answer. The CAD vector model lacks the definition of spatial relationships between features that is defined by the topologic data model.

1.2　Raster Data Formats

Raster data models incorporate the use of a grid-cell data structure where the geographic area is divided into cells identified by row and column. This data structure is commonly called raster. While the term raster implies a regularly spaced grid, other tessellated data structures do exist in grid based GIS systems. In particular, the **quadtree** data structure has found some acceptance as an alternative

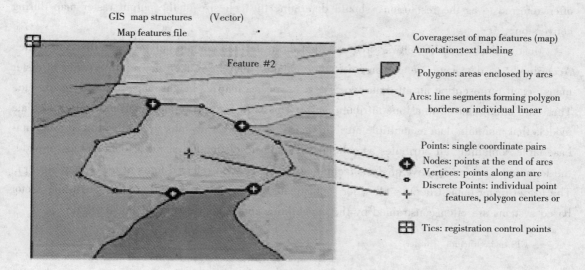

GIS map structures   (Vector)

Map features file

Feature #2

Coverage:set of map features (map)
Annotation:text labeling

Polygons: areas enclosed by arcs

Arcs: line segments forming polygon
borders or individual linear

Points: single coordinate pairs
Nodes: points at the end of arcs
Vertices: points along an arc
Discrete Points: individual point
features, polygon centers or

Tics: registration control points

Figure 9. 2. 2   GIS map structure—Vector systems

raster data model.

The size of cells in a tessellated data structure is selected on the basis of the data accuracy and the **resolution** needed by the user. There is no explicit coding of geographic coordinates required since that is implicit in the layout of the cells. A raster data structure is in fact a **matrix** where any coordinate can be quickly calculated if the origin point is known, and the size of the grid cells is known. Since grid-cells can be handled as two-dimensional arrays in computer encoding many analytical operations are easy to program. This makes **tessellated** data structures a popular choice for many GIS software. Topology is not a relevant concept with tessellated structures since adjacency and connectivity are implicit in the location of a particular cell in the data matrix.

Several tessellated data structures exist, however only two are commonly used in GISs. The most popular cell structure is the regularly spaced matrix or raster structure. This data structure involves a division of spatial data into regularly spaced cells. Each cell is of the same shape and size. Squares are most commonly utilized.

Since geographic data is rarely distinguished by regularly spaced shapes, cells must be classified as to the most common attribute for the cell. The problem of determining the proper resolution for a particular data layer can be a concern. If one selects too coarse a cell size then data may be overly generalized. If one selects too fine a cell size then too many cells may be created resulting in a large data volume, slower processing times, and a more cumbersome data set. [2] As well, one can imply accuracy greater than that of the original data capture process and this may result in some erroneous results during analysis.

As well, since most data is captured in a vector format, e. g. digitizing, data must be converted to the raster data structure. This is called vector-raster conversion. Most GIS software allows the user to define the raster grid (cell) size for vector-raster conversion. It is imperative that the original scale, e. g. accuracy, of the data be known prior to conversion. The accuracy of the data, often referred to as the resolution, should determine the cell size of the output raster map during conversion.

Most raster based GIS software requires that the raster cell contain only a single **discrete** value. Accordingly, a data layer, e. g. forest inventory stands, may be broken down into a series of raster maps, each representing an attribute type, e. g. a species map, a height map, a density map, etc. These are often referred to as one attribute maps. This is in contrast to most conventional vector data models that maintain data as multiple attribute maps, e. g. forest inventory polygons linked to a database table containing all attributes as columns. This basic distinction of raster data storage provides the foundation for quantitative analysis techniques. This is often referred to as raster or map algebra. The use of raster data structures allow for sophisticated mathematical modeling processes while vector based systems are often constrained by the capabilities and language of a relational DBMS.

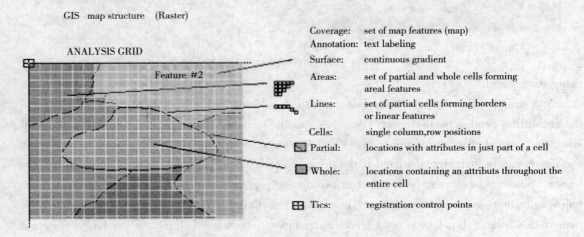

GIS map structure (Raster)

Coverage:	set of map features (map)
Annotation:	text labeling
Surface:	continuous gradient
Areas:	set of partial and whole cells forming areal features
Lines:	set of partial cells forming borders or linear features
Cells:	single column, row positions
Partial:	locations with attributes in just part of a cell
Whole:	locations containing an attributs throughout the entire cell
Tics:	registration control points

Figure 9. 2. 3   GIS map structure—Raster systems

This difference is the major distinguishing factor between vector and raster based GIS software. It is also important to understand that the selection of a particular data structure can provide advantages during the analysis stage. For example, the vector data model does not handle continuous data, e. g. **elevation**, very well while the raster data model is more ideally suited for this type of analysis. Accordingly, the raster structure does not handle linear data analysis, e. g. shortest path, very well while vector systems do. It is important for the user to understand that there are certain advantages and disadvantages to each data model.

The selection of a particular data model, vector or raster, is dependent on the source and type of data, as well as the intended use of the data. Certain analytical procedures require raster data while others are better suited to vector data.

1. 3   Image Data

Image data is most often used to represent graphic or pictorial data. The term image inherently reflects a graphic representation, and in the GIS world, differs significantly from raster data. Most often, image data is used to store **remotely sensed imagery**, e. g. satellite scenes or **orthophotos**, or ancillary graphics such as photographs, scanned plan documents, etc. Image data is typically used in GIS systems as background display data (if the image has been rectified and georeferenced); or as a graphic attribute. Remote sensing software makes use of image data for image classification and processing. Typically, this data must be converted into a raster format (and perhaps vector) to be used analytically with the GIS.

Image data is typically stored in a variety of **de facto** industry standard proprietary formats. These often reflect the most popular image processing systems. Other graphic image formats, such as TIFF, GIF, PCX, etc., are used to store ancillary image data. Most GIS software will read such formats and allow you to display this data.

2. Attribute Data Models

A separate data model is used to store and maintain attribute data for GIS software. These data models may exist internally within the GIS software, or may be reflected in external commercial Database Management Software (DBMS). A variety of different data models exist for the storage and management of attribute data. The most common are Tabular, Hierarchical, Network, Relational, and Object Oriented.

The tabular model is the manner in which most early GIS software packages stored their attribute data. The next three models are those most commonly implemented in database management systems (DBMS). The object oriented is newer but rapidly gaining in popularity for some applications. A brief review of each model is provided.

2.1   Tabular Model

The simple tabular model stores attribute data as sequential data files with fixed formats (or comma delimited for ASCII data), for the location of attribute values in a predefined record structure. This type of data model is outdated in the GIS arena. It lacks any method of checking data integrity, as well as being inefficient with respect to data storage, e. g. limited indexing capability for attributes or records, etc.

2.2   Hierarchical Model

The hierarchical database organizes data in a tree structure. Data is structured downward in a hierarchy of tables. Any level in the hierarchy can have unlimited children, but any child can have only one parent. Hierarchical DBMS have not gained any noticeable acceptance for use within GIS. They are oriented for data sets that are very stable, where primary relationships among the data change infrequently or never at all. Also, the limitation on the number of parents that an element may have is not always conducive to actual geographic phenomenon.

2.3   Network Model

The network database organizes data in a network or plex structure. Any column in a plex structure can be linked to any other. Like a tree structure, a plex structure can be described in terms of parents and children. This model allows for children to have more than one parent.

Network DBMS have not found much more acceptance in GIS than the hierarchical DBMS. They have the same flexibility limitations as hierarchical databases; however, the more powerful structure for representing data relationships allows a more realistic modeling of geographic phenomenon. However, network databases tend to become overly complex too easily. In this regard, it is easy to lose control and understanding of the relationships between elements. [3]

2.4　Relational Model

The relational database organizes data in tables. Each table, is identified by a unique table name, and is organized by rows and columns. Each column within a table also has a unique name. Columns store the values for a specific attribute, e. g. cover group, tree height. Rows represent one record in the table. In a GIS each row is usually linked to a separate spatial feature, e. g. a forestry stand. Accordingly, each row would be comprised of several columns, each column containing a specific value for that geographic feature. The following figure presents a sample table for forest inventory features. This table has 4 rows and 5 columns. The forest stand number would be the label for the spatial feature as well as the primary key for the database table. This serves as the linkage between the spatial definition of the feature and the attribute data for the feature.

Table 9. 2. 1　Sample table for forest inventory features

Unique stand number	Dominant cover group	Avg tree height	Stand site index	Stand age
001	DEC	3	G	100
002	DEC-CON	4	M	80
003	DEC-CON	4	M	60
004	CON	4	G	120

Data is often stored in several tables. Tables can be joined or referenced to each other by common columns (relational fields). Usually the common column is an identification number for a selectedgeographic feature, e. g. a forestry stand polygon number. This identification number acts as the primary key for the table. The ability to join tables through use of a common column is the essenceof the relational model. Such relational joins are usually ad hoc in nature and form the basis of querying in a relational GIS product. Unlike the other previously discussed database types, relationships are implicit in the character of the data as opposed to explicit characteristics of the database set up.

The relational database model is the most widely accepted for managing the attributes of geographic data.

There are many different designs of DBMSs, but in GIS the relational design has been the most useful. In the relational design, data are stored conceptually as a collection of tables. Common fields in different tables are used to link them together. This surprisingly simple design has been so widely used primarily because of its flexibility and very wide deployment in applications both within and without GIS.

In fact, most GIS software provides an internal relational data model, as well as support for commercial **off-the-shelf** (COTS) relational DBMSs. COTS DBMSs are referred to as external DBMSs. This approach supports users with small data sets, where an internal data model is sufficient, and customers with larger data sets who utilize a DBMS for other corporate data storage requirements. With an external DBMS the GIS software can simply connect to the database, and the user can make use of the inherent capabilities of the DBMS. External DBMSs tend to have much more extensive querying and data integrity capabilities than the GIS' internal relational model. The emergence and use of the external DBMS is a trend that has resulted in the **proliferation** of GIS technology into more traditional data processing environments.

The relational DBMS is attractive because of its:

◆ **simplicity** in organization and data modeling;

◆ **flexibility**—data can be manipulated in an ad hoc manner by joining tables;

◆ **efficiency of storage**—by the proper design of data tables redundant data can be minimized;

◆ **non-procedural nature**—queries on a relational database do not need to take into account the internal organization of the data.

The relational DBMS has emerged as the dominant commercial data management tool in GIS implementation and application.

The following diagram illustrates the basic linkage between a vector spatial data (topologic model) and attributes maintained in a relational database file.

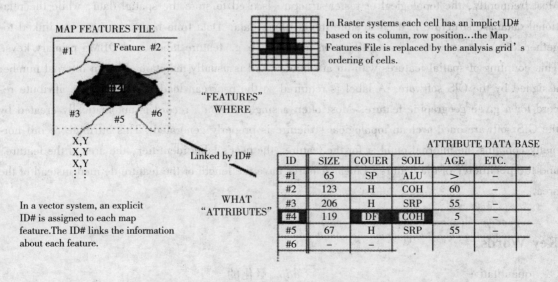

Figure 9. 2. 4   Basic linkages between a vector spatial data (topologic model)
and attributes maintained in a relational database file

2. 5   Object-Oriented Model

The object-oriented database model manages data through objects. An object is a collection of data elements and operations that together are considered a single entity. The object-oriented database is a relatively new model. This approach has the attraction that querying is very natural, as features can be bundled together with attributes at the database administrator's discretion. To date, only a few GIS packages are promoting the use of this attribute data model. However, initial impressions indicate that this approach may hold many operational benefits with respect to geographic data processing. Fulfillment of this promise with a commercial GIS product remains to be seen.

3. Spatial Data Relationships

The nature of spatial data relationships are important to understand within the context of GIS. In particular, the relationship between geographic features is a complex problem in which we are far from understanding in its entirety. This is of concern since the primary role of GIS is the manipulation and analysis of large quantities of spatial data. To date, the accepted theoretical solution is topologically structure spatial data.

It is believed that a topologic data model best reflects the geography of the real world and provides an effective mathematical foundation for encoding spatial relationships, providing a data model for manipulating and analyzing vector based data. [4]

Most GIS software **segregate** spatial and attribute data into separate data management systems. Most frequently, the topological or raster structure is used to store the spatial data, while the relational database structure is used to store the attribute data. Data from both structures are linked together for use through unique identification numbers, e. g. feature labels and DBMS primary keys. This coupling of spatial features with an attribute record is usually maintained by an internal number assigned by the GIS software. A label is required so the user can load the appropriate attribute record for a given geographic feature. Most often a single attribute record is automatically created by the GIS software once a clean topological structure is properly generated. This attribute record normally contains the internal number for the feature, the user's label identifier, the area of the feature, and the **perimeter** of the feature. Linear features have the length of the feature defined instead of the area.

Key Words

quantitative	*adj.*	量化的
qualitative	*adj.*	质化的
tabular data		表格资料
animation	*n.*	动画片

vector	*n.* 矢量
raster	*n.* 栅格
vertex	*n.* 顶点，节点（复数为 vertices）
topologic	*adj.* 拓扑的
quadtree	*n.* 四叉树
resolution	*n.* 分辨率
matrix	*n.* 矩阵
tessellated	*adj.* 棋盘格式的；几何的
discrete	*adj.* 离散的
elevation	*n.* 海拔，高程
remotely sensed imagery	遥感影像
orthophoto	*n.* 正射图片
de facto	*adj.* 事实上的
off-the-shelf	*adj.* 现成的
proliferation	*n.* 扩散
segregate	*v.* 隔离，分开
perimeter	*n.* 边缘

Notes

1. There is considerable redundancy with this data model since the boundary segment between two polygons can be stored twice, once for each feature.

这个数据模型存在相当大的冗余，因为两个多边形的边界部分有可能被存储两次，每次存储对应一个多边形的特征。

2. If one selects too coarse a cell size then data may be overly generalized. If one selects too fine a cell size then too many cells may be created resulting in a large data volume, slower processing times, and a more cumbersome data set.

如果选择的单元尺寸过大，则数据可能会过于泛化。如果选择的单元尺寸过小，则过多的单元会导致数据量过大，处理缓慢，并且产生难以处理的数据集合。

3. However, network databases tend to become overly complex too easily. In this regard, it is easy to lose control and understanding of the relationships between elements.

然而，网络数据库倾向于非常容易地变得过度复杂。这样很容易失控，并且对元素之间的关系产生错误的理解。

4. It is believed that a topologic data model best reflects the geography of the real world and provides an effective mathematical foundation for encoding spatial relationships, providing a data model for manipulating and analyzing vector based data.

拓扑数据模型是一个控制和分析矢量数据的数据模型。它被认为能最好地反映现实世界地理情况，而且为空间关系编码提供有效的数学基础。

Reading Material 1　Application of GIS Techniques in Hong Kong's Population Census

1. Introduction

GIS technology is used in a wide spectrum of official statistics activities nowadays, from data collection, to statistics compilation and data dissemination. The history of applying GIS technology in official statistics work can be traced back to the early 1990s, some 15 years ago, when we disseminated census/by-census results.

In Hong Kong, a population census is conducted every ten years, and a by-census is conducted in between two censuses. While a population census involves the enumeration of everyone in the population, the by-census is a large scale sample enquiry in which only a fraction of the population is sampled for enumeration. The latest population census in Hong Kong was conducted in 2001 and the next by-census will be conducted this year.

With its large scale operation, population census/by-census is an important, and in fact the only source to provide socio-economic and demographic data of the population for small geographical areas, down to street blocks at the lowest level. It is particularly useful when the statistics for a particular geographical area are visualized, say on a map. To get full value of the census/by-census results, a CD-ROM product was produced in collaboration with private company to facilitate the analysis of census results in small geographical areas, for the first time in the early 1990s. It bundled the data, digital maps and GIS software together. Using this product, the residents' profile of a particular area like a housing estate can be visualized on a map, and spatial analysis can be performed using the GIS tools embraced therein. For the government, the information is vital for considering the various kinds of facilities and services needed in the geographic areas concerned, like schools, recreational and transportation facilities and medical services. Businessmen can make use of the information to decide the kind of shops to be set up in the areas, the type of products and services to be sold there, and the prices to be charged. Similar CD-ROM products had been produced in the subsequent census and by-census, namely the 1996 Population By-census and the 01C.

2. Applying GIS in the 01C

Starting with data dissemination, GIS has been gradually engaged in other aspects of official statistics work. GIS techniques were employed to support data collection work for the first time in the 01C through the DMS. This system enables maps to be produced, maintained and updated much more efficiently, and the fieldwork of the census operation to be monitored more effectively. Basically, it contains map layers developed by various parties; for instance, building polygons, road centerlines, facility points, annotations, etc. by the Lands Department, the boundary of Tertiary Planning Units and Street Blocks by the Planning Department and the boundary of segment, building polygons and landmarks, etc. by the Census and Statistics Department (C&SD). It has customized GIS functions which permit the long-term maintenance and updating of map data, the production of maps of various types and scales and the spatial analysis of data to be performed efficiently.

This system had generated some 100,000 location maps to facilitate the enumerators to perform household visits in the 01C. Prior to that, maps were prepared manually in the previous censuses/by-censuses by doing the updating on the large paper maps through manual drawing, identifying the working areas of each fieldworker (i. e. the census enumerator) on the large paper maps, making photocopies of the relevant parts, and then cutting and pasting the areas required to arrive at a reasonably legible/decent map which could be used by the census enumerator. All these are saved with the DMS in place; and most importantly, the efficiency of the project is enhanced. Nowadays we can retrieve a map for a particular enumerator as and when required from the system immediately without the need to search through the paper maps.

3.　Using GIS in 06BC

The DMS, though developed for the 01C, will be used more extensively to support the by-census to be conducted in July/August this year. A few main applications are highlighted below.

3.1　Updating of Sampling Frame

The availability of a complete sampling frame is a pre-requisite for conducting statistical sample surveys. For the purpose of population census/by-census and household surveys, a database containing all addresses in Hong Kong is maintained by the C&SD as the sampling frame. This database is made up of two parts or two registers, namely, the Register of Quarters (RQ) and the Register of Segments (RS). The RQ is a list of addresses of permanent quarters in built-up areas including urban areas, new towns and major developments in the New Territories. Each unit of quarters is identified by a unique address. The RS is a list of area segments in non-built-up areas (in other words, rural/remote areas). Segments are unstructured, and so are the arrangements or positions of the quarters contained in them. Each area segment contains some 8 to 15 quarters and is delineated by some physical or easily identifiable boundaries such as streams, footpaths, lanes and ditches. The use of area segments in non-built up areas is necessary because the quarters in these areas may not have clear addresses and cannot be easily identified.

In the 06BC, a one-tenth sample of the quarters in Hong Kong will be selected from the Frame of Quarters (FOQ) for enumeration. To eliminate coverage errors like omission of quarters, it is absolutely important to ensure that the FOQ is complete and up-to-date. With the implementation of the DMS, GIS techniques have been employed in updating the FOQ. Through overlaying the updated base maps or Digital Orthophotos on a regular basis, information on new buildings, demolished buildings, and other changes can be revealed from the maps and photos, and fed into the FOQ for updating the quarters/buildings records.

3.2　Allocation of Assignments and Itinerary Planning

The census/by-census is a large scale and complex operation and involves a lot of enumerators, from a few thousand for a by-census to over twenty thousand for a full census. Each enumerator has to visit a number of households and interviews all members therein. Determining the number of households and also the particular households to be visited by each enumerator is a very difficult and time-consuming task. In the 06BC, the network analysis tool in GIS is used to tackle this task scientifically. The enumeration effort is estimated based on parameters like walking distance from one location to another to determine the optimal set of assignments (in terms of the number of assignments and also which assignments) for each enumerator; and thus, ensure that each enumerator's set of assignments will be comparable in terms of number of households as well as total walking distance. After the assignments are allocated, the DMS will also plan the itinerary for each enumerator. The assignments given for each enumerator, in the form of an assignment list, will be arranged in an order such that the shortest route (in terms of walking distance) to visit the assignments will be incurred. An enumerator block map, giving an overview of the assignment areas, will also be provided to each enumerator.

3.3 Statistics Compilation

In Hong Kong, there are two basic geographical demarcation systems, namely, the District Council/Constituency Area system for district administration and election purposes, and the Tertiary Planning Unit/Street Block system for town planning purposes. However, it may not be possible to release the statistical data using these two systems directly. First, statistics of an area with very small population cannot be released in order to safeguard the confidentiality of data pertaining to individual persons and households. Second, it is necessary to ensure that the statistics released are precise. Last but not least, the requirements of individual users have to be considered with a view to meeting their needs as far as possible. For those cases where statistics cannot be released using the standard systems, C&SD will have to delineate a set of boundaries for data dissemination purpose.

GIS techniques can help us to perform these jobs efficiently based on the number of residents therein and the spatial locations. For some geographical units (e.g. for those with very few residents), they may have to be grouped with adjacent geographical units into broader groups for data dissemination. The formation of these groups is based on some threshold values of number of residents, types of housing and the spatial locations of these geographical units. In doing the formation, we need to know the orientation of the buildings and group those nearby buildings together so that the small area statistics are meaningful and useful. An example is the formation of building groups in a large estate development "Laguna City" in the eastern part of Kowloon. Blocks 13-15 are grouped together instead of with the other Blocks for data dissemination, taking into account their distinct geographical locations. Such groupings can be done more easily and efficiently with the availability of GIS tools.

3.4 Data Dissemination

A population census/by-census, with its large scale, provides the most detailed statistical database of the population with detailed spatial reference to the locations where people reside. The extent of detail of both the data and the spatial reference renders statistics from population census/by-census most conducive to the utilization of GIS applications. Statistics from population census/by-census have all along been an important fundamental data layer in many GIS applications, both within the private and public sectors, supporting various modeling functions and better informed decision making with a spatial dimension.

Hong Kong has been using GIS technology to support the data dissemination work of population census/by-census since the early 1990s. CD-ROM products containing detailed census/by-census data and digital maps, both produced by C&SD or in collaboration with private companies, allow users to perform spatial analysis using with GIS techniques. Thematic and area maps are produced using GIS technology to disseminate census/by-census results in publications and presentations. Such maps show the spatial distribution of one or more specific themes for standard geographic areas and bring out the content clearly.

4. GIS—a Tool for Wider Application in Statistics Work

Apart from being useful in population census/by-census, GIS is a useful tool for helping researchers and managers better understand problems, interpret data and make decisions involving a spatial dimension. For the general public, it enables them to better understand the community that they live in. Applying GIS techniques to perform spatial analysis on statistical data is certainly a potential area for further development in various kinds of statistical work.

Reading Material 2   Use of ARC/INFO in the National Water-quality Assessment Program—South Platte River Basin Study

1. Introduction

During 1991, the U.S. Geological Survey (USGS) implemented the National Water-Quality Assessment (NAWQA) program. The South Platte River Basin was among the first 20 study units selected for study to help assess the quality of the Nation's water resources. A long-term goal of the national program is to describe the status and trends in the quality of a large part of the Nation's water resources and to provide a sound, scientific understanding of the primary factors (both natural and anthropogenic) affecting the water quality. Sixty study units across the United States make up the national program.

Sixty to seventy percent of the Nation's total water use and population served by public water supplies lie within these study-unit boundaries. A principal design feature of the NAWQA program is the integration of water-quality information at different areal scales. The physical, chemical, and biological water quality conditions within the study unit basin are directly dependent on the environmental setting. GIS has been useful in analyzing and storing the spatial data required to better understand the effects of environmental factors on water quality of the South Platte River Basin.

The purpose of this paper is to present how ARC/INFO has been used to analyze, interpret, store, and present data used in the South Platte River Basin NAWQA study unit and how it has increased efficiency and productivity within the study unit.

2. ARC/INFO Applications

2.1　Surface-water Studies

ARC/INFO was used to accomplish two objectives of the surface-water investigations: (1) to identify, describe, and explain the major factors affecting surface-water quality, and (2) to estimate loads of selected water-quality constituents at key locations along the South Platte River and its tributaries. To accomplish the first objective, detailed land-use coverages were needed, especially along river buffer zones. Using GRID, the cell-based geo processing software of ARC/INFO, information about land use was interpreted from LANDSAT Thematic Mapper ™ image data that were classified using the SPECTRUM software written by Khoral Research Institute (KRI).

Clustered image data were input into SPECTRUM, which classifies the clusters on the basis of spectral reflectance; therefore, the software only classifies land cover. For example, in SPECTRUM, the reflectance of an irrigated alfalfa field in an agricultural area can be the same as an irrigated golf course in an urban area; both the alfalfa field and golf course, therefore, will be classified as the same land-cover unit (that is, irrigated grassland). The same was true for water and shadows; to the satellite, both water and shadows absorb energy and reflect very little back to the satellite sensors. Because information on land use was required, and not land cover, the classification of both the alfalfa field and the golf course as the same unit posed a problem. To overcome this problem and interpret the correct land use from the classified land-cover data, the SPECTRUM image was transferred to GRID.

Broad land-use classification (urban, agriculture, forest, and so on) was interpreted from areal photography, and cells were assigned a value of NODATA (a GRID specific value) to restrict the data set to a single broad class of land use, such as urban areas. The land-cover classes identified in SPECTRUM were used to assign the correct land uses in the urban areas (transportation, commercial, residential, and so on). This process was repeated for the other broad land-use classes to get the final composite grid of land-use classification. To achieve the second objective of estimating loads for water-quality constituents, a flow-routing model was created for a stream network. The lengths of individual reaches and the locations of points of water input to and output from the river were required. To accomplish this, a digital representation of river mileage was needed.

The linear modeling commands within ARC and ARCEDIT, collectively called Dynamic Segmentation, were used to create the mileage system and "superimpose" this model on the line coverage of streams. The mileage systems are continuous for each stream and are independent of the from/to node data structure of the individual arcs. The arcs for the stream coverage were taken from U. S. Geological Survey 1:100,000 Digital Line Graphs (DLGs) and the U. S. Environmental Protection Agency River Reach 3 files. An item named MILES was added to the arc attribute table (AAT) of

174

the stream coverage and calculated in miles from the length, in meters, of each arc. Using the ARCEDIT commands SEL PATH and MAKEROUTE, individual stream mile systems were created for the South Platte River main stem and many of its tributaries. Mileage values for each of the input/output points along the river were obtained using the ARC command ADDROUTEMEASURE. These values were then used as input into a stream-water flow model.

2. 2 Ground-water Studies

One of the objectives of the South Platte River Basin ground-water study was the characterization of the general water-quality conditions of major hydrologic settings in the basin. To avoid bias in the evaluation of the resource, well-sampling sites in the different hydrologic settings were selected randomly using a selection program written in Arc Macro Language (AML) by Scott (1990). This AML requires input polygon coverage of areas of interest. For purposes of this activity, polygon coverage of urban/built-up areas in the mountains that also were underlain by crystalline rock was required. To create this coverage, the ARC command DISSOLVE was used to simplify the number of polygons in both the geology and land-use coverages. The ARC command IDENTITY was then used to merge the two coverages. The ARC command RESELECT was used on the resulting coverage to select polygons, which were classified as both urban/built-up land use and crystalline rock.

Because the selection program requires only the selected polygons, and not the bounding polygon, a problem surfaced with respect to "doughnut hole polygons" that were present in the modified crystalline geology polygon coverage. These doughnut holes were empty interior holes where something other than crystalline rocks (alluvial, sedimentary rocks, and so on) were present during the reselection from the geology coverage. These polygons were not classified as either urban/built-up or crystalline bedrock so no interference occurred with the reselection of the other polygons. Because there was a problem with the doughnut hole polygons not being closed polygons, labels could not be created and the polygons could not be reselected with the ARC RESELECT command; therefore, it was easier to remove the bounding arcs manually in ARCEDIT.

2. 3 Biology Studies

A principal objective of the biology study in the South Platte NAWQA project was to identify biological communities, describe their condition, and relate this information to assessing water quality. Habitat is an example of a factor studied that affects biological communities. Because habitat must be considered in the interpretation of water-quality effects on biological communities, detailed habitat measurements were made.

To assist in tracking changes in channel morphology, the Triangular Irregular Network (TIN) software product of ARC/INFO was used to represent surfaces of stream channels and their flood plains based on surveying data collected in the field. The surveying instrument used, with the use of associated software, created an ASCII coordinate file that was manipulated slightly and input into ARC in the point GENERATE format.

A file containing elevation information for each data point and the user-defined codes used to identify geomorphic features associated with each data point was edited to include INFO commands at the top of the file. ARC was started and the command file executed using a UNIX redirection: arc61 < filename. This process loaded the elevation and code information into the INFO file automatically. The ARC command JOINITEM was then used to join this INFO file to the coverage point attribute table (PAT). Once the elevations were in the PAT, the ARC command CREATETIN was used to create a tin.

The surface was plotted in ARCPLOT by using SURFACEDRAPE commands. The surface was then rotated into different perspectives using the ARCPLOT commands SURFACEOBSERVER and SURFACETARGET to determine the best observation points. Survey data points were color coded (according to what feature they represented) using the ARCPLOT RESELECT command and then plotted on the surface using the ARCPLOT command SUR FACEDRAPE.

For example, edge-of-water points were plotted on the surface in red, points surveyed on islands were plotted in green, points surveyed on gravel bars were plotted in grey, and so on. Other channel geomorphic features such as riffles, pools, and runs were digitized as polygons and also plotted on the surface using SURFACE DRAPE.

2.4　Database Design and Graphics

All of the spatial data and some of the water-quality data required for analyses in the South Platte River Basin study were stored within ARC/INFO. The spatial data were stored in coverages by theme, and the chemical data resided either in coverage attribute files or in related INFO files. Because ARCPLOT map composer can project "on-the-fly", one projection is used for all coverages in the database; therefore, multiple iterations of the coverages (for overlying on base maps of different projections) were not required. Coverages are stored in separate directories by data type and content.

For example, under the top-level directory called GIS are the subdirectories called basecovs (line coverages), ptcovs (point coverages), landuse, dems (U. S. Geological Survey Digital Elevation Models), and dlgs. The ARC relational database structure allowed the efficient storage of both spatial and chemical data for the large number of monitoring sites in the project. Instead of creating separate coverages for many different activities, one large point coverage was created to contain all surface-water sites. These sites were reselected with the use of the ARC RELATE command based on many different criteria, such as which activity the site was used for and any chemical data associated with that site that were stored in related INFO files.

The South Platte River Basin study required "on demand" reports and presentations. To produce these graphics, the ARCPLOT map composer was used. This was efficient because the output was produced in the same application in which the spatial and water-quality data were stored. AMLs were created to produce each figure in map composer, which was edited interactively after the AML finished running. Both the ARCPLOT graphics canvas and a text window running a text-editing program on the AML were displayed simultaneously on the screen. The display of the cursor coordinates on the ARCPLOT canvas was useful for immediate modification of the AML in the text window.

This technique was used to produce a report (Dennehy and others, 1995) in which all of the figures from the GIS, including the cover for the report, were generated in map composer from AMLs and saved as post script files. These postscript files were then imported directly into FrameMaker, merging the graphics with the report text.

Graphics and text from the graphics package CorelDRAW also were imported into ARCPLOT. This made the combined plotting of coverages, text, and nonspatial graphics fairly simple in ARC-PLOT. Color slides also were produced directly from ARCPLOT map composer by correctly specifying the PAGESIZE in the AML to fit the specifications of the imaging camera, usually a 2:3 ratio of height to width. Producing these figures and slides with the use of ARC/INFO eliminated the need to reproduce these figures in other graphics packages.

3. Summary

GIS was used in many aspects of the National Water-Quality Assessment Program's South Platte River Basin study. ARC/INFO was a valuable tool in the South Platte NAWQA study simplifying work tasks, increasing analysis capabilities, and assisting in the production of graphics. The capabilities of ARC/INFO facilitated the studies in many ways. The cell-based processing module GRID was used to produce detailed land-use information from LANDSAT land-cover imagery data in buffer zones along rivers.

Linear modeling with Dynamic Segmentation was used in surface-water studies to produce river mileage for a flow-routing model of transportation of water-quality constituents in the river and its tributaries. In ground-water studies, ARC/INFO overlaying capabilities were used for analyzing different theme coverages, such as geology and land use, to help select well sites in a random manner.

The surface representation capabilities of TIN and ARCPLOT were used in the biology studies to assist in monitoring changes in channel morphology by producing surfaces of stream channels and surrounding flood plains and by producing plots of stream cross sections. In addition to spatial analysis, ARC/INFO was used to manage a large water-quality database and to produce publication-quality graphics. Figures and slides were created directly from the ARC/INFO database, which greatly enhanced productivity. These several applications improved capability to analyze data in a timely manner and distribute it to customers.

Exercises

Ⅰ. Fill in the following blanks with proper words or phrases:

1. Among the four main subsystems of GIS, the _____ allows the user to capture, collect, and transform spatial and thematic data into digital form.

2. Among the four main subsystems of GIS, the _____ allows the user to generate graphic displays, normally maps, and tabular reports representing derived information products.

3. The most important component of a GIS is the _____.

4. GPS stands for _____.

5. GIS stands for _____.

6. Two basic types of data used in GIS technology are _____ and _____.

7. Three basic types of spatial data models have evolved for storing geographic data digitally, which are _____, _____, and _____.

8. _____ Models incorporate the use of a grid-cell data structure where the geographic area is divided into cells identified by row and column.

9. The _____ model is the manner in which most early GIS software packages stored their attribute data.

II. Answer the following questions:

1. What is GIS?

2. List the four main functional subsystems of a GIS.

3. List the main components of a GIS.

4. What's not a GIS? Give some examples.

5. Give some applications of using GIS.

6. Briefly describe the two commonly used vector data models in GIS data storage.

7. What's image data? List some formats of image data.

8. List several common data models for the storage and management of attribute data.

9. Why the relational DBMS is attractive to GIS software?

10. Describe some characters of the object-oriented database model.

Chapter Ten   Information Security

Unit 1   How to Implement Trusted Computing

1. Introduction

Philosophically, one can imagine the security problem two ways: as a perimeter or as a set of secure connections.

1.1   Perimeter Defense

The failure of a perimeter is **starkly** illustrated by the Maginot Line, famous from World War II. The French built a strong, secure wall against potential attack by the Germans, but neglected to make the perimeter complete, leaving out, among other things, an extension into Belgium of the network of trenches, bastions, walls, **redoubts**, mines, barbwire, and lookouts that protected against a frontal assault on France. It was through this break that the Germans passed on their way to Paris.

1.2   Secure Connection

During World War II, an interesting and vital technique practiced by American intelligence relied on secure connection. The technique depended on Navajos, people **indigenous** to the American Southwest, who spoke a doubly-coated dialect of their native language plus symbolic representation (e.g., a platoon was "has-clish-nih", which translates to "mud"; Germany was "besh-be-cha-he", which translates as "iron hat"). They spoke over channels that the Allies understood to be monitored by Axis intelligence, but the trick was that only the sender and receiver could decode the message. [1] Although this technique has been **superseded** by advanced encryption for data protection, it was good enough at the time.

Of the two schemes, secure connection is more desirable theoretically. A perimeter is made up of all kinds of elements thrown together (walls, rivers, wires), and the **interstices** represent potential vulnerabilities. A secure connection can be made between any two elements in a given group of elements that might want to talk to each other. Once such a connection is established, the two parties can chatter away freely without worrying about who might listen in. In the real world of rising reliance on the Internet, which exposes ever increasing amounts of value to potential depredations, the pure secure connection model is unlikely to take hold in the near future. For now, security will be made up of perimeter defenses and a degree of secure, **bilateral** connections.

1. 3　How Is the Industry Addressing Security

Although well established, the perimeter approach continues to suffer from breaches by ever more creative **assailants.** Threats have only increased as connectivity and network complexity have risen. To address this problem, the industry created a **special interest group** (SIG), called the **Trusted Computing Group** (TCG). The TCG's **mandate** was to specify, with input from all sectors of the computing industry, a comprehensive approach to enterprise security based on compatible technology building blocks. Members and nonmembers alike can use these technologies, which take the form of open specifications, **royalty** free to create products. The SIG format has proved to be a highly successful way to introduce new technologies to the entire industry on an open basis. Past successes include the PCI and USB specifications.

The tone of this group was set by IBM, which created the first dedicated security chip in the late 1990s. However, the nature of a universal secure-connection scheme requires that all nodes speak the same language. To gain widespread acceptance, IBM contributed its development work on the chip, now called the **Trusted Platform Module** (TPM), to the group.

The TCG's work is quite far along. The SIG has developed specifications for second-generation TPMs as well as specifications for accompanying software, client PCs, storage devices, mobile phones, servers, and secure network access. Multiple suppliers of the various security elements already have products on the market. TPMs are now built into many notebook computers sold to enterprises, and other implementations of security technology such as servers, network devices, and secure mobile systems are in the works.

2. Elements of a Trusted Solution

The following paragraphs lay out both the existing and planned elements of a complete security solution (Figure 10. 1. 1). The following security technologies have already been specified.

2. 1　The TPM

At the core of the trusted solution is the TPM itself. Currently embodied in a discrete or integrated component, the concept represents the clear superiority of security algorithms executed in hardware. The security itself is still software: keys used to encrypt data for storage or transmission. But the operations themselves are done in a closed hardware environment. nCipher, a security consultancy in Cambridge, England, proved definitively that even very good encryption was vulnerable to attack if it took place in the usual locations (i. e. , in main memory, on the hard drive) because a good sniffer could detect the key by its highly entropic character; that is, a program that could distinguish a good random number from its surroundings could find the key and break the code. Thus, with all operations taking place inside the chip, no location exists where the key can be tested by intruders.

About 20 million TPM chips shipped in 2005, most of them in notebook PCs. By 2010, worldwide shipments of TPM modules in PC client systems will reach more than 250 million. However, as

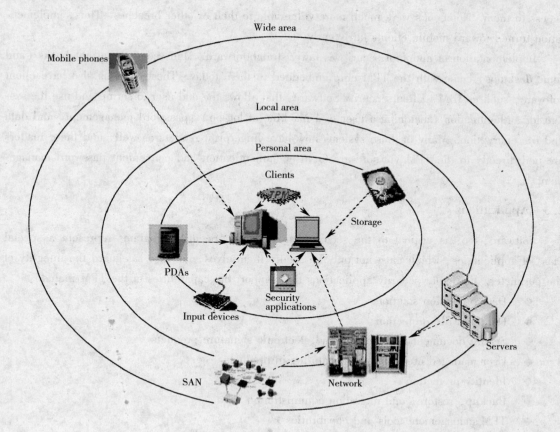

Figure 10. 1. 1 Secure clients in context

categories beyond PCs—e. g. , mobile phones, storage systems, embedded applications, and peripherals—adopt TPMs, the total number of chips shipped could rise dramatically, even exponentially.
Should TPMs become common in phones, for example, annual unit shipments could rise by
hundreds of millions.

2. 2 Endpoints

The first specification for a device into which a TPM could be embedded was the endpoint or
client—the desktop and notebook PCs at the edge of the network. Too long, these endpoints had
been neglected as security efforts were focused on the network and the servers that contain an
organization's most valuable information. But the whole network could be jeopardized by a single
compromised client. An intruder could simply pose as a legitimate user and gain access to whatever
rights and privileges that user had. [2] Thus, one of the first standards set by the TCG was the endpoint
or client security specification for PCs.

Although IBM originally targeted stationary systems (desktops) , it rapidly became apparent
that mobile systems (notebooks) represented a larger vulnerability. Desktop PCs could be locked to
the desk and locked in the building after working hours, and generally only employees had physical

access to them. Notebooks were much more vulnerable to theft or other breaches. Thus, implementation turned toward mobile clients fairly early on.

Implementation of endpoint security is fairly straightforward. Many commercial notebooks (and some desktops) come with the TPM chip embedded in them today. These systems also have client software, such as IBM's Client Security Software, that allows the end user to set up and use the system for authentication (matching a user to a machine at log-on), password management, and data and file encryption. Many of these systems now have fingerprint readers as well, and these readers are tied directly to the TPM via software for user authentication and convenient password management.

2.3 Applications

Software, too, is critical to the security environment. Security programs represent a special class of applications, which must not only be secure themselves, but also safeguard the integrity of the perimeter. Particular security applications that support the capabilities of the TPM include:

- Data protection solutions
- Data and file protection
- Secure document management and electronic signature products
- User managed credentials and auto-log-in products
- Identity protection
- Backup, restore, and migration administration
- TPM management tools and capabilities
- Network protection
- Enhanced email security
- Enhanced Web client authentication

2.4 Trusted Network Connect

Trusted Network Connect (TNC) is a specification that covers the dynamic relationship between clients and servers in the enterprise network. The essence of the TNC specification governs how clients request access to the network, and how a server grants that access. The protocol involves the packaging of a network request with information that positively verifies the user and the hardware as well as the state of the requesting device. [3] A user can be verified by way of a password, fingerprint, or other method, including multi-factor authentication. A device can be verified by an algorithm that interacts with its TPM, producing a unique identity. The state of a device is measured by a number of factors, including whether or not it has up-to-date patches and virus definition files. If a request measurement falls below some threshold set by policy, access can be denied. If the measurement falls within a certain range, the device can be given provisional access, shunted to a quarantine area, and remediate before being let on the network. [4] If the measurement exceeds some threshold, access can be granted with no further delay.

TCG's specification for TNC is available and a number of companies are developing products to support it; some of these products are available now. TNC takes an open architectural approach so that users can mix and match products in their organizations.

3. Planned Elements

The TCG is working specifications for the following security technologies, and products based on these specifications will hit the market in 2006 and 2007.

3. 1   Servers

In some sense, server security has lagged behind that of clients because, the common wisdom goes, servers are behind the perimeter defenses, and anything that gets to them has already been **vetted.** Also, server security protocols can affect performance, and any performance penalty at the server level is unacceptable.

However, servers need to be part of the security story, if for no other reason than that they should not be left vulnerable to a malicious intruder successfully masquerading as a legitimate client. Also, with newer systems, the effect of the performance penalty can be limited. Most servers have multiple processors, many have **dual-threaded processors**, and the latest have **dual-core processors.** These developments mean that security tasks can be executed by a single virtual processor while the rest are occupied with the main task.

TCG has released a specification for secure servers that defines how trusted servers are created, managed, and maintained. Trusted servers can store and protect digital keys, passwords, and certificates to handle:

- ◆ Asset management
- ◆ Configuration management
- ◆ Data migration and backup
- ◆ Distributed trusted computing
- ◆ Document management
- ◆ Financial transactions
- ◆ User and platform authentication

Servers are also integrated to Trusted Network Computing (TNC), TCG's initiative for network access. When the client side asks for access, the server side, after assessing the client's trustworthiness, grants access or not, depending on the policy.

3. 2   Storage

Storage represents a special class of devices with distinctive security issues and technology. For example, even if a PC is password protected, a thief can remove the hard drive and insert it in another PC as a slave device. Unless they are encrypted, all the files can then be opened.

Hard drives can be brought inside the perimeter by equipping them with an unchangeable hardware partition not visible to the operating system. This partition can contain the necessary keys to ensure that the drive is able to talk only to an authorized host over a secure communications link. Drive security applications include:

- ◆ Full-disk encryption
- ◆ Disk-erase enhancement
- ◆ Drive locking
- ◆ **Forensic logging**

In general, buyers purchase storage with the CPU, and so it is fairly easy to determine from documentation whether both main unit and storage subsystem have the required embedded security. TCG is in the process of finalizing an open specification for development of trusted storage for the enterprise. Prototype products have demonstrated that a trusted storage device simply won't work if separated from its authenticated client. In the final specification, TCG will address all types of storage (direct attach, **SAN**, **NAS**).

3.3 Input and Output Devices

Other devices that need to be part of the chain of trust include the input and output devices normally associated with a PC. These devices include the mouse, keyboard, and potentially other devices on the input side, and displays, printers, and other devices on the output side. Data traveling to and from these devices can be intercepted if they are not inside the perimeter. Future devices will have built-in trust elements that interact with host-based TPMs.

3.4 Mobile Phones

Another obvious client platform is the mobile phone. With capabilities increasing such that they could begin to rival PCs, phones have a clear need for security. More value—in the form of both important data and actual financial transactions—is passing through phones. As data devices, phones now have not only a phone number, but a dynamically allocated IP address as well. Phones are becoming nodes on the network, yet to date there has been no organized effort to provide comprehensive security for them.

Just like other clients, phones (and their users) need to be authenticated and their integrity or "digital health" ascertained.

4. How to Approach Trusted Computing

It is not necessary for an organization to implement comprehensive security all at once. Such an effort could be disruptive to the business and is also likely to be outside the budget in any given year. The good thing about TCG-specified products is that they can be layered on over time, each new layer adding a greater degree of security. The IT department can rest assured that the TCG has envisioned the entire solution from scratch and that the last element implemented will work as planned with the first one. Thus, the rollout can be gradual, implemented one step at a time. Already, many TCG-compliant hardware and software products are commercially available.

The job of securing an enterprise can be overwhelming if viewed as a **monolithic** task. However, broken into parts, the undertaking is not so daunting. The order of implementation is important because some things depend on others being in place, and some are more critical than others. We recommend the following steps in the order shown:

- Authentication
- Data protection
- Network **attestation** and platform measurement
- Application protection
- Content protection

4.1 Authentication

This level of security is relatively straightforward. Authentication involves ensuring that a user is who he or she says he or she is, and that the machine requesting access is the machine that user is supposed to be operating. Endpoints (desktops and notebooks) can be definitively authenticated if they are equipped with a TPM and related authentication software. We strongly recommend multi-factor authentication involving at least two factors, typically **biometric** (i. e. , fingerprint) and password.

These days, an increasing number of commercial clients are offered with embedded authentication features, including a TPM chip, security software, and a fingerprint reader right in the bezel. These units can be set up for authentication right out of the box. It is also possible to **retrofit** existing clients with fingerprint or **smart card** readers, but, to be effective, the TPM must be embedded.

Authentication can also be applied at the level of the virtual private network (VPN), such that only an authenticated user-machine combination gains access to a corporate VPN. This capability is useful for mobile executives who must stay in close touch with home base while passing through territory with varying degrees of insecurity. VPN software can be tied to TPM software through the settings interface.

4.2 Data Protection

Once users are clearly identified and married to their machines, the next level, data protection, becomes possible. Data protection takes many forms, but in essence it involves ensuring that user (or customer) data remains inviolate. Protected data cannot be changed without an authorized user's knowledge. It cannot be lost. Unauthorized people cannot access it.

Data protection is more than just a matter of keeping the wrong people out of places they shouldn't be and not having valuable records disappear. Data protection is driven by a host of new legal requirements that protect customer privacy. Organizations that fail to protect their data in the face of these new mandates become subject to legal action and potential severe financial loss. [5]

The newly formed TCG Storage Specification covers secure storage on fixed magnetic media. Critical to data protection will be the secure linking of host CPU and hard drives. Compliant products are designed so that a hard drive cannot be accessed if it is removed from its host. In some cases, the data can be destroyed **deliberately** if a hostile access attempt is made. With the CPU tied to the user, who has to authenticate to log in, the stored data is secure because of the trust link set up between the central unit and the storage device.

Since as much as half the intellectual property of a given organization resides on PC hard drives, **battening down** this particular vulnerability is critical. Data and file encryption are key technologies on which data protection is based.

Today, the flaw of data protection software is that its secret key sits in the registry, whether obfuscated or not. The key can be extracted from the registry with readily available software tools. However, several solutions now on the market use a TPM to protect the private key, a monumental improvement in data protection. [6]

4.3 Network Attestation and Platform Measurement

The TCG has created an open specification, TNC, for network attestation and platform measurement. This level of security can be added onto the platform-level steps laid out in the previous two sections. Essentially, when a client requests network access, it is required to go through a handshaking sequence with the access-granting server, which makes use of data gathered from the client's TPM, the user's authentication method, and a "health check" status composed of information about the status of various client platform measurements. These measurements include the version of the virus scan engine and DAT file, firewall and other settings, and patch status.

Implementation of TNC moves the organization closer to a virtually secure environment in which the perimeter becomes less important, since any two nodes in the system can authenticate to each other and then conduct interchange over a secure link no matter how hostile the environment is.

4.4 Application Protection

In Microsoft's soon-to-be-released operating system, Vista, applications will run under a new model in which users will operate under the least privileged mode possible. This schema will allow applications like Outlook and Office to run in protected areas of the system without the potential threat of invasion by **malefactors.** The code will be protected from intrusion by partitioning the system and having applications run in an area accessible only by a user with high level privileges (i. e., the administrator).

This system is viable because it rests on a foundation of hardware-based security and TCG protocols. The virtual partitioning is hardened by authentication, data protection, and network attestation layers. Thus, the applications are physically secure as well as logically secure.

4.5 Content Protection

Finally, new schema for **digital rights management** (DRM) will be able to operate on top of a highly secure platform. Content owners will be able to release their intellectual property with confidence, knowing that they will be paid for value rendered. Although the TCG has not specified a particular DRM protocol, its security elements are designed to be open and work with whatever DRM software is specified.

186

Because the "root of trust", the machine-level keys, are hidden in the TPM and are used to create a "chain of trust", higher-level keys that are each in turn encrypted with the keys below, many different content protection schemes are possible, each relying on its own key pair. The content owner can rest assured that only the authorized user will be able to open the content because the public and private keys, which are interrelated, are both required to complete the transaction. Content "signed" with a particular user's public key can only be opened with that user's specific private key. Thus, the direct relationship between the owner and user (or buyer and seller) is preserved.

Key Words

perimeter defense	边界防御
starkly	*adv.* 十足地，完全地
redoubt	*n.* 堡垒
indigenous	*adj.* 土著的
supersede	*v.* 取代
interstice	*n.* 空隙
bilateral	*adj.* 双边的
assailant	*n.* 攻击者
special interest group	特别兴趣小组
trusted computing group	可信计算小组
mandate	*n.* 受命进行的工作
royalty	*n.* 专利权税
Trusted Platform Module	可信平台模块
exponentially	*adv.* 以指数方式
vet	*v.* 检查
dual-threaded processor	双线程处理器
dual-core processor	双核处理器
forensic logging	司法记录（日志，可作为证据）
SAN	Storage Area Network 的缩写，存储区域网
NAS	Network Attached Storage 的缩写，网络附加存储
monolithic	*adj.* 整体的
attestation	*n.* 验证
biometric	*n.* 生物测定
retrofit	*v.* 对……作翻新改进
smart card	智能卡
deliberately	*adv.* 故意地
batten down	封住
malefactor	*n.* 坏人
digital rights management	数字版权管理

187

Notes

1. They spoke over channels that the Allies understood to be monitored by Axis intelligence, but the trick was that only the sender and receiver could decode the message.

同盟国知道轴心国间谍监听他们交换信息的通道，但是他们并不担心，因为只有发送者和接受者知道如何解密信息。

2. But the whole network could be jeopardized by a single compromised client. An intruder could simply pose as a legitimate user and gain access to whatever rights and privileges that user had.

但是整个网络可能由于某个有潜在危险的客户而受到威胁。一个侵入者可以简单地伪装成一个合法用户，从而获得该用户的所有权限。

3. The protocol involves the packaging of a network request with information that positively verifies the user and the hardware as well as the state of the requesting device.

这个协议涉及封装一个网络请求，这个网络请求包含的信息可能用于确认用户、硬件以及发送请求的设备的状态。

4. If the measurement falls within a certain range, the device can be given provisional access, shunted to a quarantine area, and remediate before being let on the network.

如果测量结果在一个特定的区间内，该设备可被授予临时的接入权限，转移到一个隔离区，并在准入网络前进行修复。

5. Organizations that fail to protect their data in the face of these new mandates become subject to legal action and potential severe financial loss.

根据这些新的规定，没能保护好数据的组织将面临法律上的制裁（行动）以及潜在的经济上的严重损失。

6. The key can be extracted from the registry with readily available software tools. However, several solutions now on the market use a TPM to protect the private key, a monumental improvement in data protection.

使用现成的软件工具即可以将密钥从注册信息中提取出来。但是，一些流行的方案应用一个 TPM 来保护私钥，这在数据保护方面是个显著的进步。

Unit 2   Computer Virus

A computer virus is a computer program which reproduces. A computer virus is often simply called a virus. The term is commonly used to refer to a range of viruses, but a true virus does not need to be harmful. To distribute itself, a virus needs execution or otherwise be interpreted. Viruses often hide themselves inside other programs to be executed.

A computer virus reproduces by making, possibly evolved, copies of itself in the computer's memory, storage, or over a network. This is similar to, but not exactly the same as the way a biological virus works. It is estimated by some experts that the Mydoom worm infected a quarter-million computers in a single day in January 2004. Another example is the ILOVEYOU virus, which occurred in 2000 and had a similar effect.

There are tens of thousands of viruses operating in the general Internet today, and new ones are discovered every day. While a **generic** explanation of how viruses work is difficult due to the wide variety of infection or spreading patterns, there are broad categories commonly used to describe various types of viruses.

1. Basic Types of Viruses

Virus types are used as a way for people to think about the things that viruses do, but being overly dogmatic about these types can often be confusing.[1] Take these descriptions for the value they bring, but don't assume that they are comprehensive or particularly accurate in terms of describing the potential sorts of viruses that can be encountered.

1.1 Boot Sector Viruses

A boot sector virus affects the boot sector of a hard disk, which is a very crucial part. The boot sector is where all information about the drive is stored, along with a program that makes it up. By inserting its code into the boot sector, a virus guarantees that it loads into memory during every boot sequence. A boot virus does not affect files; instead, it affects the disks that contain them. Perhaps this is the reason for their **downfall.** During the days when programs were carried around on floppies, the boot sector viruses used to spread like wildfire. However, with the CD-ROM revolution, it became impossible to infect pre-written data on a CD, which eventually stopped such viruses from spreading. Though boot viruses still exist, they are rare compared to new-age malicious software. Another reason why they're not so **prevalent** is that operating systems today protect the boot sector, which makes it difficult for them to thrive. Examples of boot viruses are Polyboot. B and AntiEXE.

According to Symantec, Boot sector viruses differ only slightly from Master Boot Record Viruses in their respective effects-both load into memory and stay there (resident viruses), thus infecting any executable launched afterwards. In addition, both types may prevent recent operating systems from booting.

1.2 Multipartite Viruses

Multipartite viruses are a combination of boot sector viruses and file viruses. These viruses come in through infected media and reside in memory. They then move on to the boot sector of the hard drive. From there, the virus infects executable files on the hard drive and spreads across the system. There aren't too many multipartite viruses in existence today, but in their **heyday**, they accounted for some major problems due to their capacity to combine different infection techniques. A well-known multipartite virus is Ywinz.

1.3　Macro Viruses

Macro viruses infect files that are created using certain applications or programs that contain macros. These include Microsoft Office documents such as Word documents, Excel spreadsheets, PowerPoint presentations, Access databases and other similar application files such as Corel Draw, AmiPro etc. Since macro viruses are written in the language of the application and not in that of the operating system, they are known to be platform-independent—they can spread between Windows, Mac and any other system, so long as they are running the required application. With the ever-increasing capabilities of macro languages in applications, and the possibility of infections spreading over networks, these viruses are major threats.

The first macro virus was written for Microsoft Word and was discovered back in August 1995. Today, there are thousands of macro viruses in existence—some examples are Relax, Melissa. A and Bablas.

1.4　Network Viruses

This kind of virus is proficient in quickly spreading across a Local Area Network (LAN) or even over the Internet. Usually, it propagates through shared resources, such as shared drives and folders. Once it infects a new system, it searches for potential targets by searching the network for other vulnerable systems. Once a new vulnerable system is found, the network virus infects the other system, and thus spreads over the network. Some of the most notorious network viruses are Nimda and SQLSlammer.

2.　Methods to Avoid Detection

In order to avoid detection by users, some viruses employ different kinds of **deception.** Some old viruses, especially on the MS-DOS platform, make sure that the "last modified" date of a host file stays the same when the file is infected by the virus. This approach does not fool anti-virus software, however.

Some viruses can infect files without increasing their sizes or damaging the files. They accomplish this by overwriting unused areas of executable files. These are called cavity viruses. For example the CIH virus, or Chernobyl Virus, infects Portable Executable files. Because those files had many empty gaps, the virus, which was 1 KB in length, did not add to the size of the file.

Some viruses try to avoid detection by killing the tasks associated with antivirus software before it can detect them.

As computers and operating systems grow larger and more complex, old hiding techniques need to be updated or replaced.

2.1　Avoiding Bait Files and Other Undesirable Hosts

A virus needs to infect hosts in order to spread further. In some cases, it might be a bad idea to infect a host program. For example, many anti-virus programs perform an integrity check of their own code. Infecting such programs will therefore increase the **likelihood** that the virus is detected. For this reason, some viruses are programmed not to infect programs that are known to be part of anti-virus software. Another type of hosts that viruses sometimes avoid is bait files. Bait files (or goat files) are files that are specially created by anti-virus software, or by anti-virus professionals themselves, to be infected by a virus. These files can be created for various reasons, all of which are related to the detection of the virus:

◆ Anti-virus professionals can use bait files to take a sample of a virus (i. e. a copy of a program file that is infected by the virus). It is more practical to store and exchange a small, infected bait file, than to exchange a large application program that has been infected by the virus.

◆ Anti-virus professionals can use bait files to study the behavior of a virus and evaluate detection methods. This is especially useful when the virus is polymorphic. In this case, the virus can be made to infect a large number of bait files. The infected files can be used to test whether a virus scanner detects all versions of the virus.

◆ Some anti-virus software employs bait files that are accessed regularly. When these files are modified, the anti-virus software warns the user that a virus is probably active on the system.

Since bait files are used to detect the virus, or to make detection possible, a virus can benefit from not infecting them. Viruses typically do this by avoiding suspicious programs, such as small program files or programs that contain certain patterns of "garbage instructions". [2]

A related strategy to make baiting difficult is **sparse** infection. Sometimes, sparse infectors do not infect a host file that would be a suitable candidate for infection in other circumstances. For example, a virus can decide on a random basis whether to infect a file or not, or a virus can only infect host files on particular days of the week.

2.2   Stealth

Some viruses try to trick anti-virus software by intercepting its requests to the operating system. A virus can hide itself by intercepting the anti-virus software's request to read the file and passing the request to the virus, instead of the OS. The virus can then return an uninfected version of the file to the anti-virus software, so that it seems that the file is "clean". Modern anti-virus software employs various techniques to counter stealth mechanisms of viruses. The only completely reliable method to avoid stealth is to boot from a medium that is known to be clean.

2.3   Self-modification

Most modern anti-virus programs try to find virus-patterns inside ordinary programs by scanning them for so-called virus signatures. A signature is a characteristic byte-pattern that is part of a certain virus or family of viruses. If a virus scanner finds such a pattern in a file, it notifies the user that the file is infected. The user can then delete, or (in some cases) "clean" or "**heal**" the infected file. Some viruses employ techniques that make detection by means of signatures difficult or impossible. These viruses modify their code on each infection. That is, each infected file contains a different variant of the virus.

2.3.1 Simple Self-modifications

In the past, some viruses modified themselves only in simple ways. For example, they regularly exchanged subroutines in their code for others that would perform the same action—for example, $2+2$ could be swapped for $1+3$. This poses no problems to a somewhat advanced virus scanner.

2.3.2 Encryption with a Variable Key

A more advanced method is the use of simple encryption to **encipher** the virus. In this case, the virus consists of a small decrypting module and an encrypted copy of the virus code. If the virus is encrypted with a different key for each infected file, the only part of the virus that remains constant is the decrypting module, which would (for example) be appended to the end. In this case, a virus scanner cannot directly detect the virus using signatures, but it can still detect the decrypting module, which still makes indirect detection of the virus possible.

Mostly, the decryption techniques that these viruses employ are simple and mostly done by just XORing each byte with a randomized key that was saved by the parent virus. The use of XOR-operations has the additional advantage that the encryption and decryption routine are the same (a XOR $b=c$, c XOR $b=a$.)

2.3.3 Polymorphic Code

Polymorphic code was the first technique that posed a serious threat to virus scanners. Just like regular encrypted viruses, a polymorphic virus infects files with an encrypted copy of itself, which is decoded by a decryption module. In the case of polymorphic viruses however, this decryption module is also modified on each infection. A well-written polymorphic virus therefore has no parts that stay the same on each infection, making it impossible to detect directly using signatures. Anti-virus software can detect it by decrypting the viruses using an emulator, or by statistical pattern analysis of the encrypted virus body. To enable polymorphic code, the virus has to have a polymorphic engine (also called mutating engine or **mutation** engine) somewhere in its encrypted body. See polymorphic code for technical detail on how such engines operate.

Some viruses employ polymorphic code in a way that **constrains** the mutation rate of the virus significantly. For example, a virus can be programmed to mutate only slightly over time, or it can be programmed to **refrain** from mutating when it infects a file on a computer that already contains copies of the virus. The advantage of using such slow polymorphic code is that it makes it more difficult for anti-virus professionals to obtain representative samples of the virus, because bait files that are infected in one run will typically contain identical or similar samples of the virus. This will make it more likely that the detection by the virus scanner will be unreliable, and that some instances of the virus may be able to avoid detection.

2.3.4 Metamorphic Code

To avoid being detected by emulation, some viruses rewrite themselves completely each time they are to infect new executables. Viruses that use this technique are said to be metamorphic. To enable metamorphism, a metamorphic engine is needed. A metamorphic virus is usually very large and complex. For example, W32/Simile consisted of over 14,000 lines of assembly language code, 90% of its part of the metamorphic engine.

3. Vulnerability and Countermeasures

3.1　The Vulnerability of Operating Systems to Viruses

Another analogy to biological viruses: just as genetic diversity in a population decreases the chance of a single disease wiping out a population, the diversity of software systems on a network similarly limits the destructive potential of viruses.

This became a particular concern in the 1990s, when Microsoft gained market dominance in desktop operating systems and office suites. The users of Microsoft software (especially networking software such as Microsoft Outlook and Internet Explorer) are especially vulnerable to the spread of viruses. Microsoft software is targeted by virus writers due to their desktop dominance, and is often criticized for including many errors and holes for virus writers to exploit. Integrated applications, applications with scripting languages with access to the file system (for example Visual Basic Script (VBS), and applications with networking features) are also particularly vulnerable.

Although Windows is by far the most popular operating system for virus writers, some viruses also exist on other platforms. Any operating system that allows third-party programs to run can theoretically run viruses. Some operating systems are less secure than others. Unix-based OSs (and NTFS-aware applications on Windows NT based platforms) only allow their users to run executables within their protected space in their own directories.

As of 2006, there are relatively few security exploits targeting Mac OS X (a Unix-based operating system); the known vulnerabilities fall under the classifications of worms and Trojans. The number of viruses for the older Apple operating systems, known as Mac OS Classic, varies greatly from source to source, with Apple stating that there are only four known viruses, and independent sources stating there are as many as 63 viruses. It is safe to say that Macs are less likely to be exploited due to their secure Unix base, and because a Mac-specific virus could only infect a small proportion of computers (making the effort less desirable), virus vulnerability between Macs and Windows was/is a chief **catalyst** of the platform wars between Apple Computer and Microsoft.

Windows and Unix have similar scripting abilities, but while Unix natively blocks normal users from having access to make changes to the operating system environment, Windows does not.[3] In 1997, when a virus for Linux was released—known as "Bliss" —leading antivirus vendors issued warnings that Unix-like systems could fall prey to viruses just like Windows. The Bliss virus may be considered characteristic of viruses—as opposed to worms—on Unix systems. Bliss requires that the user run it explicitly and it can only infect programs that the user has the access to modify. Unlike Windows users, most Unix users do not log in as an administrator user except to install or configure software; as a result, even if a user ran the virus, it could not harm their operating system. The Bliss virus never became widespread, and remains **chiefly** a research curiosity. Its creator later posted the source code to Usenet, allowing researchers to see how it worked.

3. 2　The Role of Software Development

Because software is often designed with security features to prevent unauthorized use of system resources, many viruses must exploit software bugs in a system or application to spread. Software development strategies that produce large numbers of bugs will generally also produce potential exploits.

3. 3　Anti-virus Software and Other Preventative Countermeasures

There are two common methods that an anti-virus software application uses to detect viruses. The first, and by far the most common method of virus detection is using a list of virus signature definitions. The disadvantage of this detection method is that users are only protected from viruses that pre-date their last virus definition update. The second method is to use a **heuristic** algorithm to find viruses based on common behaviors. This method has the ability to detect viruses that anti-virus security firms have yet to create a signature for.

Many users install anti-virus software that can detect and eliminate known viruses after the computer downloads or runs the executable. They work by examining the content heuristics of the computer's memory (its RAM, and boot sectors) and the files stored on fixed or removable drives (hard drives, floppy drives), and comparing those files against a database of known virus "signatures". Some anti-virus programs are able to scan opened files in addition to sent and received e-mails "on the fly" in a similar manner. This practice is known as "on-access scanning". Anti-virus software does not change the underlying capability of host software to transmit viruses. There have been attempts to do this but adoption of such anti-virus solutions can void the warranty for the host software. Users must therefore update their software regularly to patch security holes. Anti-virus software also needs to be regularly updated in order to gain knowledge about the latest threats.

One may also prevent the damage done by viruses by making regular backups of data (and the operating systems) on different media, that are either kept unconnected to the system (most of the time), read-only or not accessible for other reasons, such as using different file systems. This way, if data is lost through a virus, one can start again using the backup (which should preferably be recent). If a backup session on optical media like CD and DVD is closed, it becomes read-only and can no longer be affected by a virus. Likewise, an Operating System on a live CD can be used to start the computer if the installed operating systems become unusable. Another method is to use different operating systems on different file systems. A virus is not likely to affect both. Data backups can also be put on different file systems. For example, Linux requires specific software to write to NTFS partitions, so if one does not install such software and uses a separate installation of MS Windows to make the backups on an NTFS partition (and preferably only for that reason), the backup should remain safe from any Linux viruses. Likewise, MS Windows can not read file systems like ext3, so if one normally uses MS Windows, the backups can be made on an ext3 partition using a Linux installation.

Key Words

generic	*adj.*	一般的，泛泛的
dogmatic	*adj.*	教条的
downfall	*n.*	没落
prevalent	*adj.*	流行的
heyday	*n.*	全盛期
deception	*n.*	诡计，欺骗
likelihood	*n.*	可能性
sparse	*adj.*	稀少的
heal	*v.*	治愈
encipher	*v.*	译成密码
polymorphic	*adj.*	多形态的
mutation	*n.*	突变
constrain	*v.*	束缚
refrain	*v.*	抑制
catalyst	*n.*	催化剂
chiefly	*adv.*	主要地
heuristic	*adj.*	启发式的，探索的

Notes

1. Virus types are used as a way for people to think about the things that viruses do, but being overly dogmatic about these types can often be confusing.

人们根据病毒的类型来分辨病毒的行为，但是如果过于拘泥于这些类型，往往就会产生迷惑。

2. Since bait files are used to detect the virus, or to make detection possible, a virus can benefit from not infecting them. Viruses typically do this by avoiding suspicious programs, such as small program files or programs that contain certain patterns of "garbage instructions".

因为诱饵文件被用来发现病毒或使发现病毒成为可能，一个病毒可以通过不感染诱饵文件而躲过侦测。病毒通常通过避开可疑程序的方式来做到这一点，比如，小程序文件或含有典型"垃圾代码"模式的程序。

3. Windows and Unix have similar scripting abilities, but while Unix natively blocks normal users from having access to make changes to the operating system environment, Windows does not.

Windows 和 Unix 使用类似的脚本功能，然而，Unix 会本能地阻止一般用户修改操作系统环境，而 Windows 不会作此限制。

Reading Material 1   A National Cyberspace Security Response System

In the 1950s and 1960s, our Nation became vulnerable to attacks from aircraft and missiles for the first time. The federal government responded by creating a national system to: monitor our airspace with radar to detect unusual activity, analyze and warn of possible attacks, coordinate our fighter aircraft defenses during an attack, and restore our Nation after an attack through civil defense programs.

Today, the Nation's critical assets could be attacked through cyberspace. The United States now requires a different kind of national response system in order to detect potentially damaging activity in cyberspace, to analyze exploits and warn potential victims, to coordinate incident responses, and to restore essential services that have been damaged.

The fact that the vast majority of cyberspace is neither owned nor operated by any single group—public or private—presents a challenge for creating a National Cyberspace Security Response System. There is no synoptic or holistic view of cyberspace. Therefore, there is no panoramic vantage point from which we can see attacks coming or spreading. Information that indicates an attack has occurred (worms, viruses, denial-of-service attacks) accumulates through many different organizations. However, there is no organized mechanism for reviewing these indicators and determining their implications.

To mitigate the impact of cyber attacks, information about them must disseminate widely and quickly. Analytical and incident response capabilities that exist in numerous organizations could be coordinated to determine how to best defend against an attack, mitigate effects, and restore service.

Establishing a proper administrative mechanism for the National Cyberspace Security Response System presents another challenge. Unlike the U. S. airspace-monitoring program during the Cold War, individuals who operate the systems that enable and protect cyberspace usually are not federal employees. Thus, the National Cyberspace Security Response System must operate from a less formal, collaborative network of governmental and nongovernmental organizations.

DHS is responsible for developing the National Cyberspace Security Response System, which includes:

- ◆ Providing crisis management support in response to threats to, or attacks on, critical information systems; and
- ◆ Coordinating with other agencies of the federal government to provide specific warning information, and advice about appropriate protective measures and countermeasures, to state and local government agencies and authorities, the private sector, other entities, and the public.

DHS will lead and synchronize efforts for the National Cyberspace Security Response System as part of its overall information sharing and crisis coordination mandate; however, the system itself will consist of many organizations from both government and private sectors. The authorizing legislation for the Department of Homeland Security also created the position of a privacy officer to ensure that any mechanisms associated with the National Cyberspace Security Response System appropriately balance its mission with civil liberty and privacy concerns. This officer will consult regularly with privacy advocates, industry experts, and the public at large to ensure broad input and consideration of privacy issues so that we achieve solutions that protect privacy while enhancing security.

Among the system components outlined below are existing federal programs and new federal initiatives pending budget-review consideration, as well as initiatives recommended for our partners.

1. Establish Public-private Architecture for Responding to National-level Cyber Incidents

Establishing the National Cyberspace Security Response System will not require an expensive or bureaucratic federal program. In many cases the system will augment the capabilities of several important federal entities with existing cyberspace security responsibilities, which are now part of DHS. The synergy that results from integrating the resources of the National Communications System, the National Infrastructure Protection Center's analysis and warning functions, the Federal Computer Incident Response Center, the Office of Energy Assurance, and the Critical Infrastructure Assurance Office under the purview of the Under Secretary for Information Analysis and Infrastructure Protection will help build the necessary foundation for the National Cyberspace Security Response System.

The Nation's private-sector networks are increasingly targeted, and they will therefore likely be the first organizations to detect attacks with potential national significance. Thus, ISACs will play an increasingly important role in the National Cyberspace Security Response System and the overall missions of homeland security. ISACs possess unique operational insight into their industries' core functions and will help provide the necessary analysis to support national efforts.

Typically, an ISAC is an industry-led mechanism for gathering, analyzing, sanitizing, and disseminating sector-specific security information and articulating and promulgating best practices. ISACs are designed by the various sectors to meet their respective needs and financed through their memberships. DHS will work closely with ISACs as appropriate to ensure that they receive timely and actionable threat and vulnerability data and to coordinate voluntary contingency planning efforts. The federal government encourages the private sector to continue to establish ISACs and, further, to enhance the analytical capabilities of existing ISACs.

1. 1   Analysis

Provide for the Development of Tactical and Strategic Analysis of Cyber Attacks and Vulnerability Assessments

Analysis is the first step toward gaining important insight about a cyber incident, including the nature of attack, the information it compromised, and the extent of damage it caused. Analysis can also provide an indication of the intruder's possible intentions, the potential tools he used, and the vulnerabilities he exploited. There are three closely related, but discrete, categories of analysis related to cyberspace:

Tactical analysis examines factors associated with incidents under investigation or specific, identified vulnerabilities to generate indications and warnings. Examples of tactical analysis include: examining the delivery mechanism of a computer virus to develop and issue immediate guidance on ways to prevent or mitigate damage; and studying a specific computer intrusion, or set of intrusions, to determine the perpetrator, his motive, and his method of attack.

Strategic analysis looks beyond specific incidents to consider broader sets of incidents or implications that may indicate threats of potential national importance. For example, strategic analyses may identify long-term trends related to threat and vulnerability that could be used to provide advanced warnings of increasing risks, such as emerging attack methods. Strategic analysis also provides policymakers with information they can use to anticipate and prepare for attacks, thereby diminishing the damage they cause. Strategic analysis also provides a foundation to identify patterns that can support indications and warnings.

Vulnerability assessments are detailed reviews of cyber systems and their physical components to identify and study their weaknesses. Vulnerability assessments are an integral part of the intelligence cycle for cyberspace security. These assessments enable planners to predict the consequences of possible cyber attacks against specific facilities or sectors of the economy or government. These projections then allow infrastructure owners and operators to strengthen their defenses against various types of threat.

DHS will foster the development of strong analytic capabilities in each of these areas. It should seek partnership and assistance from the private sector, including the ISACs, in developing these capabilities.

1.2 Warning

1.2.1 Encourage the Development of a Private Sector Capability to Share a Synoptic View of the Health of Cyberspace

The lack of a synoptic view of the Internet frustrates efforts to develop Internet threat analysis and indication and warning capabilities. The effects of a cyber attack on one sector have the potential to cascade across several other sectors, thereby producing significant consequences that could rapidly overwhelm the capabilities of many private companies and state and local governments. DHS's integration of several key federal cybersecurity operations centers creates a focal point for the federal government to manage cybersecurity emergencies in its own systems, and, if requested, facilitate crisis management in non-federal critical infrastructure systems.

Separately, industry is encouraged to develop a mechanism—whether virtual or physical—that could enable the sharing of aggregated information on Internet health to improve analysis, warning, response, and recovery. To the extent permitted by law, this voluntary coordination of activities among nongovernmental entities could enable different network operators and Internet backbone providers to analyze and exchange data about attacks. Such coordination could prevent exploits from escalating and causing damage or disruption of vital systems.

DHS will create a single point-of-contact for the federal government's interaction with industry and other partners for 24×7 functions, including cyberspace analysis, warning, information sharing, major incident response, and national-level recovery efforts. Private sector organizations, which have major contributions for those functions, are encouraged to coordinate activities, as permitted by law, in order to provide a synoptic view of the health of cyberspace on a 24×7 basis.

1.2.2　Expand the Cyber Warning and Information Network to Support DHS's Role in Coordinating Crisis Management for Cyberspace

Hours and minutes can make a difference between a major disruption and a manageable incident. Improving national capabilities for warning requires a secure infrastructure to provide assured communications between critical asset owners and operators and their service providers. The Cyber Warning and Information Network (CWIN) will provide an out-of-band private and secure communications network for government and industry, with the purpose of sharing cyber alert and warning information. The network will include voice conferencing and data collaboration.

While the first phase was implemented between the federal government cyber watch centers, CWIN participants will ultimately include other critical government and industry partners, such as ISACs that deal with cyber threats on a daily basis. As other entities expand in this area, membership will increase as well. Key to CWIN membership is the ability to share sensitive cyber threat information in a secure, protected, and trusted environment.

As outlined in the 2003 budget, the federal government will complete the installation of CWIN to key government cybersecurity-related network operation centers, to disseminate analysis and warning information and perform crisis coordination. The federal government will also explore linking the ISACs to CWIN.

1.3　National Incident Management

Enhancing analytical capabilities within DHS, the private sector ISACs, and expanding CWIN will contribute to the improvement of national cyber incident management. However, incident management within the federal government will still require coordination with organizations other than those being transferred to DHS. For example, the Departments of Justice, Defense, and Commerce all have roles to perform in response to incidents in cyberspace. Within the White House a number of offices have responsibilities, including the Office of Science and Technology Policy, which is responsible for executing emergency telecommunications authorities, the National Security Council, which coordinates all matters related to national security and international cooperation, and the Office of Management and Budget.

In addition, national incident management capabilities will also integrate state chief information officers as well as international entities, as appropriate.

1.4　Response and Recovery

1.4.1　Create Processes to Coordinate the Voluntary Development of National Public-Private Continuity and Contingency Plans

Among the lessons learned from security reviews following the events of September 11, 2001, was that federal agencies had vastly inconsistent, and in most cases incomplete, contingency capabilities for their communications and other systems. Contingency planning is a key element of cybersecurity. Without adequate contingency planning and training, agencies may not be able to effectively handle disruptions in service and ensure business continuity. OMB, through the Federal Information Security Management Act requirements and with assistance from the inspectors general, is holding agencies accountable for developing continuity plans.

1.4.2　Exercise Cybersecurity Continuity Plans in Federal Cyber Systems

DHS has the responsibility for providing crisis management support in response to threats to, or attacks on, critical information systems for other government agencies, state and local governments and, upon request, the private sector. In order to establish a baseline understanding of federal readiness, DHS will explore exercises for the civilian agencies similar to the Defense Department "Eligible Receiver" exercises that test cybersecurity preparedness.

To test civilian agencies' security preparedness and contingency planning, DHS will use exercises to evaluate the impact of cyber attacks on governmentwide processes. Weaknesses discovered will be included in agency corrective action plans and submitted to OMB. DHS also will explore such exercises as a way to test the coordination of public and private incident management, response and recovery capabilities.

◆　Encourage increased cyber risk management and business continuity

There are a number of measures that nongovernmental entities can employ to manage the risk posed by cyberspace and plan for business continuity. Risk management is a discipline that involves risk assessment, risk prevention, risk mitigation, risk transfer, and risk retention.

There is no special technology that can make an enterprise completely secure. No matter how much money companies spend on cybersecurity, they may not be able to prevent disruptions caused by organized attackers. Some businesses whose products or services directly or indirectly impact the economy or the health, welfare or safety of the public have begun to use cyber risk insurance programs as a means of transferring risk and providing for business continuity.

An important way to reduce an organization's exposure to cyber-related losses, as well as to help protect companies from operational and financial impairment, is to ensure that adequate contingency plans are developed and tested.

Corporations are encouraged to regularly review and exercise IT continuity plans and to consider diversity in IT service providers as a way of mitigating risk.

◆　Promote public-private contingency planning for cybersecurity

It may not be possible to prevent a wide-range of cyber attacks. For those attacks that do occur, the Nation needs an integrated public-private plan for responding to significant outages or disruptions in cyberspace. Some organizations have plans for how they will recover their cyber network and capabilities in the event of a major outage or catastrophe. However, there is no mechanism for coordinating such plans across an entire infrastructure or at a national level.

The legislation establishing DHS also provides a trusted mechanism for private industry to develop contingency planning by using the voluntary preparedness planning provisions that were established in the Defense Production Act of 1950, as amended.

Infrastructure sectors are encouraged to establish mutual assistance programs for cybersecurity emergencies. DOJ and the Federal Trade Commission should work with the sectors to address barriers to such cooperation, as appropriate. In addition, DHS's Information Analysis and Infrastructure Protection Directorate will coordinate the development and regular update of voluntary, joint government-industry cybersecurity contingency plans, including a plan for recovering Internet functions.

2. Information Sharing

2.1　Improve and Enhance Public-Private Information Sharing about Cyber Attacks, Threats, and Vulnerabilities

Successfully developing capabilities for analysis, indications, and warnings require a voluntary public-private information sharing effort. The voluntary sharing of information about such incidents or attacks is vital to cybersecurity. Real or perceived legal obstacles make some organizations hesitant to share information about cyber incidents with the government or with each other. First, some fear that shared data that is confidential, proprietary, or potentially embarrassing could become subject to public examination when shared with the government. Second, concerns about competitive advantage may impede information sharing between companies within an industry. Finally, in some cases, the mechanisms are simply not yet in place to allow efficient sharing of information.

The legislation establishing DHS provides several specific mechanisms intended to improve two-way information sharing. First, the legislation encourages industry to share information with DHS by ensuring that such voluntarily provided data about threats and vulnerabilities will not be disclosed in a manner that could damage the submitter. Second, the legislation requires that the federal government share information and analysis with the private sector as appropriate and consistent with the need to protect classified and other sensitive national security information.

As required by law, DHS, in consultation with appropriate federal agencies, will establish uniform procedures for the receipt, care, and storage by federal agencies of critical infrastructure information that is voluntarily submitted to the government.

The procedures will address how the department will:

◆ Acknowledge the receipt of voluntarily submitted critical infrastructure information;

◆ Maintain the information as voluntarily submitted critical infrastructure information;

◆ Establish protocols for the care and storage of such information; and

◆ Create methods for protecting the confidentiality of the submitting entity while still allowing the information to be used in the issuance of notices and warnings for protection of the critical infrastructure.

DHS will raise awareness about the removal of impediments to information sharing about cybersecurity and infrastructure vulnerabilities between the public and private sectors. The department will also establish an infrastructure protection program office to manage the information flow, including the development of protocols for how to care for "voluntarily submitted critical infrastructure information".

2. 2 Encourage Broader Information Sharing on Cybersecurity

Nongovernmental organizations with significant computing resources are encouraged to take active roles in information sharing organizations. Corporations, colleges, and universities can play important roles in detecting and reporting cyber attacks, exploits, or vulnerabilities.

In particular, both corporations and institutions of higher learning can gain from increased sharing on cyberspace security issues. Programs such as ISACs, FBI Infragard, or the United States Secret Service electronic crimes task forces can also benefit the respective participants. Because institutions of higher learning have vast computer resources that can be used as launch pads for attacks, colleges and universities are encouraged to consider establishing an on-call point-of-contact to Internet service providers (ISPs) and law enforcement officials.

Corporations are encouraged to consider active involvement in industrywide programs to share information on IT security, including the potential benefits of joining an appropriate ISAC. Colleges and universities are encouraged to consider establishing: (1) one or more ISACs to deal with cyber attacks and vulnerabilities; and, (2) an on-call point-of-contact, to Internet service providers and law enforcement officials in the event that the school's IT systems are discovered to be launching cyber attacks.

Reading Material 2　　Carnivorous

You may have heard about Carnivore, a controversial program developed by the U. S. Federal Bureau of Investigation (FBI) to give the agency access to the online/e-mail activities of suspected criminals. For many, it is eerily reminiscent of George Orwell's book "1984". Although Carnivore was abandoned by the FBI in favor of commercially available eavesdropping software by January 2005, the program that once promised to renew the FBI's specific influence in the world of computer-communications monitoring is nonetheless intriguing in its structure and application.

What exactly was Carnivore? Where did it come from? How did it work? What was its purpose? In this article, you will learn the answers to these questions and more.

1. Carnivorous Evolution

Carnivore was the third generation of online-detection software used by the FBI. While information about the first version has never been disclosed, many believe that it was actually a readily available commercial program called Etherpeek.

In 1997, the FBI deployed the second generation program, Omnivore. According to information released by the FBI, Omnivore was designed to look through e-mail traffic travelling over a specific Internet service provider (ISP) and capture the e-mail from a targeted source, saving it to a tape-backup drive or printing it in real-time. Omnivore was retired in late 1999 in favor of a more comprehensive system, the DragonWare Suite, which allowed the FBI to reconstruct e-mail messages, downloaded files or even Web pages.

DragonWare Suite contained three parts:

♦ Carnivore—A Windows NT/2000-based system that captures the information

♦ Packeteer—No official information released, but presumably an application for reassembling packets into cohesive messages or Web pages

♦ Coolminer—No official information released, but presumably an application for extrapolating and analyzing data found in the messages

As you can see, officials never released much information about the DragonWare Suite, nothing about Packeteer and Coolminer and very little detailed information about Carnivore. But we do know that Carnivore was basically a packet sniffer, a technology that is quite common and has been around for a while.

2. Packet Sniffing

Computer network administrators have used packet sniffers for years to monitor their networks and perform diagnostic tests or troubleshoot problems. Essentially, a packet sniffer is a program that can see all of the information passing over the network it is connected to. As data streams back and forth on the network, the program looks at, or "sniffs", each packet.

Normally, a computer only looks at packets addressed to it and ignores the rest of the traffic on the network. When a packet sniffer is set up on a computer, the sniffer's network interface is set to promiscuous mode. This means that it is looking at everything that comes through. The amount of traffic largely depends on the location of the computer in the network. A client system out on an isolated branch of the network sees only a small segment of the network traffic, while the main domain server sees almost all of it.

A packet sniffer can usually be set up in one of two ways:

♦ Unfiltered—Captures all of the packets

♦ Filtered—Captures only those packets containing specific data elements

Packets that contain targeted data are copied as they pass through. The program stores the copies in memory or on a hard drive, depending on the program's configuration. These copies can then be analyzed carefully for specific information or patterns.

When you connect to the Internet, you are joining a network maintained by your ISP. The ISP's network communicates with other networks maintained by other ISPs to form the foundation of the Internet. A packet sniffer located at one of the servers of your ISP would potentially be able to monitor all of your online activities, such as:

♦ Which Web sites you visit

♦ What you look at on the site

♦ Whom you send e-mail to

♦ What's in the e-mail you send

♦ What you download from a site

♦ What streaming events you use, such as audio, video and Internet telephony

203

◆ Who visits your site (if you have a Web site)

In fact, many ISPs use packet sniffers as diagnostic tools. Also, a lot of ISPs maintain copies of data, such as e-mail, as part of their back-up systems. Carnivore and its sister programs were a controversial step forward for the FBI, but they were not new technology.

3. The Process

Now that you know a bit about what Carnivore was, let's take a look at how it worked:

1) The FBI has a reasonable suspicion that someone is engaged in criminal activities and requests a court order to view the suspect's online activity.

2) A court grants the request for a full content-wiretap of e-mail traffic only and issues an order. A term used in telephone surveillance, "content-wiretap" means that everything in the packet can be captured and used. The other type of wiretap is a trap-and-trace, which means that the FBI can only capture the destination information, such as the e-mail account of a message being sent out or the Web-site address that the suspect is visiting. A reverse form of trap-and-trace, called pen-register, tracks where e-mail to the suspect is coming from or where visits to a suspect's Web site originate.

3) The FBI contacts the suspect's ISP and requests a copy of the back-up files of the suspect's activity.

4) The ISP does not maintain customer-activity data as part of its back-up.

5) The FBI sets up a Carnivore computer at the ISP to monitor the suspect's activity. The computer consists of:

◆ A Pentium III Windows NT/2000 system with 128 megabytes (MB) of RAM

◆ A commercial communications software application

◆ A custom C++ application that works in conjunction with the commercial program above to provide the packet sniffing and filtering

◆ A type of physical lockout system that requires a special passcode to access the computer (This keeps anyone but the FBI from physically accessing the Carnivore system.)

◆ A network isolation device that makes the Carnivore system invisible to anything else on the network (This prevents anyone from hacking into the system from another computer.)

◆ A 2-gigabyte (GB) Iomega Jaz drive for storing the captured data (The Jaz drive uses 2-GB removable cartridges that can be swapped out as easily as a floppy disk.)

6) The FBI configures the Carnivore software with the IP address of the suspect so that Carnivore will only capture packets from this particular location. It ignores all other packets.

7) Carnivore copies all of the packets from the suspect's system without impeding the flow of the network traffic.

8) Once the copies are made, they go through a filter that only keeps the e-mail packets. The program determines what the packets contain based on the protocol of the packet. For example, all e-mail packets use the Simple Mail Transfer Protocol (SMTP).

9) The e-mail packets are saved to the Jaz cartridge.

10) Once every day or two, an FBI agent visits the ISP and swaps out the Jaz cartridge. The agent takes the retrieved cartridge and puts it in a container that is dated and sealed. If the seal is broken, the person breaking it must sign, date and reseal it—otherwise, the cartridge can be considered "compromised".

11) The surveillance cannot continue for more than a month without an extension from the court. Once complete, the FBI removes the system from the ISP.

12) The captured data is processed using Packeteer and Coolminer.

13) If the results provide enough evidence, the FBI can use them as part of a case against the suspect.

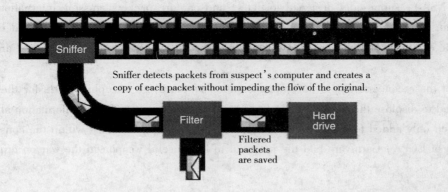

Figure 10.4.1   The example above shows how the system identified which packets to store

4. Prey of the Carnivore

The FBI planned to use Carnivore for specific reasons. Particularly, the agency would request a court order to use Carnivore when a person was suspected of:

- ◆ Terrorism
- ◆ Child pornography/exploitation
- ◆ Espionage
- ◆ Information warfare
- ◆ Fraud

There are some key issues that caused a great deal of concern from various sources.

Privacy—Many folks viewed Carnivore as a severe violation of privacy. While the potential for abuse is certainly there, the Electronic Communications Privacy Act (ECPA) provides legal protection of privacy for all types of electronic communication. Any type of electronics surveillance requires a court order and must show probable cause that the suspect is engaged in criminal activities. Therefore, use of Carnivore in any way that did not adhere to ECPA was illegal and could be considered unconstitutional.

Regulation—There was a widespread belief that Carnivore was a huge system that could allow the U. S. government to seize control of the Internet and regulate its use. To do this would have required an amazing infrastructure—the FBI would have needed to place Carnivore systems at every

ISP, including private, commercial and educational. While it is theoretically possible to do so for all of the ISPs operating in the United States, there is still no way to regulate those operating outside of U. S. jurisdiction. Any such move would have also faced serious opposition from every direction.

Free speech—Some people think that Carnivore monitored all of the content flowing through an ISP, looking for certain keywords such as "bomb" or "assassination". Any packet sniffer can be set to look for certain patterns of characters or data. Without probable cause, though, the FBI had no justification to monitor your online activity and would have been in severe violation of ECPA and your constitutional right to free speech if it did so.

Echelon—This is a secret network rumored to be under development by the National Security Agency (NSA), supposedly designed to detect and capture packets crossing international borders that contain certain keywords, such as "bomb" or "assassination". There is no solid evidence to support the existence of Echelon. Many people confused this rumored system with the Carnivore system.

All of these concerns made the implementation of Carnivore an uphill battle for the FBI. The FBI refused to disclose the source code and certain other pieces of technical information about Carnivore, which only added to people's concerns. But, as long as it was used within the constraints and guidelines of ECPA, Carnivore had the potential to be a useful weapon in the war on crime.

Exercises

Ⅰ. Fill in the following blanks with proper words or phrases:

1. IBM contributed its development work on the chip, now called the _____, to the Trusted Computing Group, for addressing security.

2. If the desktops can be considered as stationary systems, then notebooks will be taken as _____.

3. _____ represent a special class of applications, which must not only be secure themselves, but also safeguard the integrity of the perimeter.

4. _____ is a specification that covers the dynamic relationship between clients and servers in the enterprise network.

5. A _____ is a computer program which reproduces.

6. Some viruses can infect files without increasing their sizes or damaging the files. They overwrite unused areas of executable files. These are called _____.

7. Many users install _____ software that can detect and eliminate known viruses after the computer downloads or runs the executable.

Ⅱ. Answer the following questions:

1. What kinds of particular security applications does the TPM include?

2. What can a trusted server do?

3. List several drive security applications.

4. Give some applications on trusted mobile devices.

5. What is the computer virus?
6. List the basic types of viruses.
7. Introduce the two common methods that an anti-virus software application uses to detect viruses.
8. What will people usually do to avoid computer virus?

Chapter Eleven   Information Security Technologies

Unit 1   Intrusion Detection Systems and Intrusion Response Mechanism

1. Introduction

Intrusion detection systems (IDSs) are security tools that are used to detect traces of malicious activities which are targeted against networks and their resources. IDSs supply a gap of other security measures like Network Firewalls and become an indispensable component in network security area.

James Anderson introduced the concept of intrusion detection in his paper in 1980. Since then intrusion detection systems have been studied and developed for 24 years, but they are still on the stage of development. Many parts of the system are not perfect and need improvement. The criticism of the weakness of present IDSs focuses on the following two points.

Firstly both the false positive rate and false negative rate of IDSs are not acceptable sometimes. Some IDSs could send thousands of false alerts each day, which make administrators of systems know nothing to deal with them. At present, there is rarely an IDS which can combine misuse detection, **anomaly** detection and DOS detection together and is able to find not only known attacks and DOS attacks but also unknown attacks.

Second point is that the response capability of IDSs is weak. After detect attacks, most IDSs do nothing except sending alerts. The analysis and responses of these attacks are the job that administrators have to do manually.

There are many solutions for the first problem, such as using new detection algorithms, improvement of old algorithms, fusion of multiple classifiers and extending detection range of systems etc. [1] The solution for second problem is to develop automatic response system, which is the content we discuss in this paper.

2. Intrusion Responses

Intrusion responses are a series actions and countermeasures when an intrusion is detected. These actions and measures can prevent further attacks or restore the system to a normal state. [2] The actions may come from human or come from computers. Although **intrusion response systems** (IRSs) are tightly coupled with intrusion detection systems and as important as these in defending against threats, not much research effort has been put into their study. Current intrusion response systems can be categorized as notification systems, manual response systems, or automatic response systems. Today the majority of intrusion systems remain a notification system that notifies the administrator that an intrusion has occurred or is occurring. Notification or alert to the administrator could be either by displaying a pop-up window, generating an e-mail, pager or mobile phone message. How the administrator responds to the attack depends on its knowledge and ability. Manual response system allows administrator to manually launch countermeasures against a detected intrusion by choosing from a predetermined set of response programs. This capacity is more useful than notification only but it still needs human to make choice of the programs. In contrast to the two approaches above, automatic response systems could choose countermeasures themselves and respond to an attack immediately without human intervention.

2.1   Why Automatic Intrusion Response

The reasons for development of automatic intrusion response systems (AIRSs) are follows:

First, no matter notification systems or manual response systems, there is a delay between detection of a possible intrusion and response to that intrusion. This delay (or called time window) can range from seconds to hours or even days (e. g. during weekends or holidays). The longer this time window, the higher success rate an intrusion, the more damage to the attacked system. According to research by Cohen, the success rate of an intruder rises with time it can work undisturbed. This interesting study shows that if a skilled attacker can perform an intrusion with an 80% success rate if he is given 10 hours before any response is taken. If the delay is 20 hours, the attacker will succeed by a 95% rate. At 30 hours the attacker almost never fails. In addition, during this time window attacker could easily do what they want, for example, they may delete the records on the system log and install an **orifice** program on the system, which cause a lot of difficulties for tracing the intrusion, analyzing the event. Therefore this time window is very important to both intruders and defenders. The shortest time window among the three types of responses belongs to automatic response system.

The second reason is that both notification system and manual response system need administrators to make further analysis of intrusion alerts. Then administrators have to make a decision to choose appropriate response measures according to the analysis of alerts and the condition of attacked system. If the decision is right depends on the knowledge and experience of the administrator. To finish this task, the administrator should be an expert on network theory, information security and operation systems. Even when an intrusion is detected, it is impossible to take effective and timely responses without such experts there. An automatic response system is such an expert who automatically analyzes intrusion alerts and generates defensive and corrective actions by consideration of related factors.

Anyway, if an IDS can only detect intrusions without effective and timely responses, it is useless in the protection of computers resource. For the reason, someone even claimed that IDSs will be washed out markets. In June 11, 2003, Richard Stiennon presented a report whose topic is "Intrusion Detection Is Dead—Long Live Intrusion Prevention". In practice, an Intrusion Prevention System (IPS) is a new kind of security tools based on IDS and still uses the detection engine of IDSs.

The one of the biggest differences between IPSs and IDSs is that IPSs usually have automatic intrusion response mechanisms. In a word, automatic intrusion responses are very important for both of IPSs and IDSs.

2.2 The Key Factor of Development of Automatic Intrusion Response System

Since automatic intrusion responses are so important, what is the biggest problem in the development of AIRSs? Or in other word, what is the key factor of developing AIRSs? The answer is the development of decision-making mechanisms which make decisions, according to the condition of intrusion attacks and attacked systems, to determine the response plan and countermeasures.

Most current AIRSs' decision-making mechanism use simple decision tables to determine how to response in the case of identified attacks. This decision table only associates a particular attack with a particular response. This kind of decision-making mechanism is static and inherently inflexible because it only takes the type of attack into account. In fact, this decision-making of choosing appropriate responses is a very complex process which is not just influenced by only one factor (e. g. the type of attacks) but by many factors. For example, when an attacker launches same intrusion to both of a server and a workstation in a network, the response measures for the attacked server and the attacked workstation should not be same. The response measures are expected to have minimum impact on the service of the server (e. g. DNS). So for servers on networks, serious responses measures, such as shutting down machine, should be avoided as far as possible. However, when choosing responses for a workstation, it dose not need to give much consideration on the severity of response because the workstation has little influence on other parts of the network. Again, it is meaningless to take these responses, such as terminating attack session or blocking the data packets from an attacker's IP address, after the attacker has finished his job and logged off from the attacked network.

The decision-making process of AIRSs is so complex that it is very difficult or impossible to find a quantitative mathematical model to describe it.

Key Words

intrusion detection system		入侵检测系统
anomaly	n.	异常
intrusion response system		入侵反应系统
orifice	n.	漏洞

Notes

1. There are many solutions for the first problem, such as using new detection algorithms, improvement of old algorithms, fusion of multiple classifiers and extending detection range of systems etc.

第一个问题有很多种解决方案，比如使用新的检测算法、改进已有的算法、融合多种分类器并扩展检测范围等。

2. Intrusion responses are a series actions and countermeasures when an intrusion is detected. These actions and measures can prevent further attacks or restore the system to a normal state.

入侵响应是当检测到入侵后采取的一系列的行动和对策，这些行动和对策可以防止进一步的攻击或者将系统恢复到正常状态。

Unit 2　An Introduction to Information Security

1. Information Security and Cryptographic Systems

"**Information Security**" is rapidly becoming a "buzz-word" of the 1990s. Governments, commercial businesses, and individuals are all storing information in electronic form. This medium allows a number of advantages over previous physical storage: storage is more compact, transfer is almost instantaneous, and accessing via databases is facilitated. The ability to use information more efficiently has resulted in a rapid increase in the value of information. Businesses in a number of commercial arenas today recognize information as their most valuable asset.

However, with the electronic revolution, information faces new and potentially more damaging security threats. Unlike information printed on paper, information in electronic form can potentially be stolen from a remote location. It is much easier to intercept and alter electronic communication than its paper-based predecessors.

1. 1　What Is Information Security?

Simply put, information security describes all measures taken to prevent unauthorized use of electronic data—whether this unauthorized use takes the form of disclosure, alteration, substitution, or destruction of the data concerned. [1]

Only today are the full requirements of securely maintaining electronic information being understood. Information Security is classified as the provision of the following three services:

◆ **Confidentiality**: **concealment** of data from unauthorized parties.

◆ **Integrity**: assurance that data is genuine.

◆ **Availability**: the system still functions efficiently after security provisions are in place.

A number of measures have been proposed to provide these services, and no single measure can ensure complete security. Of the various measures proposed, the use of cryptographic systems offers the highest level of security together with maximum flexibility. Broadly speaking, a cryptographic system transforms electronic data to a modified form. The owner of the information is now assured of its security in this modified form. Depending on the security services required, the assurance may be that the data cannot be altered without detection, or it may be that the data is unintelligible to all but authorized parties. The list of assurances that can be provided goes on and on.

Cryptographic systems are controlled by the use of a key to determine the transformation performed. The key itself also takes the form of an electronic string. Of course, transforming data using a cryptographic system is not the only concern of information security. The owner of the cryptographic key must continue to ensure the security of the information by guarding the key itself. Security of the key, assignment of liability and responsibility for the key, and **audit** of access to the key are all ongoing issues that must be addressed.

That said, there is no doubt that a cryptographic system, correctly managed and implemented, offers the highest security level for electronic information available today.

1.2 What Services Do Cryptographic Systems Provide?

Cryptographic systems (or cryptosystems) potentially provide all three objectives of information security: confidentiality, integrity, and availability. In order to clarify and demonstrate how cryptosystems are employed, confidentiality and integrity are further sub-classified into five services that can be thought of as the building blocks of a secure system:

- ◆ **Confidentiality**: concealment of data from all but authorized parties.
- ◆ **User Authentication**: ensuring that the parties involved in a real-time transaction are who they say they are.
- ◆ **Data Origin Authentication**: assurance of the source of a message.
- ◆ **Data Integrity**: ensuring the data has not been modified by unauthorized parties.
- ◆ **Non-repudiation**: the binding of an entity to a transaction in which it participates, so that the transaction cannot later be **repudiated.** That is, the receiver of a transaction is able to demonstrate to a neutral third party that the claimed sender did indeed send the transaction. [2]

The manner in which a cryptosystem is typically used to provide each service in turn is outlined in Section 3. "Real-world" applications are rarely straightforward, so a typical implementation will require that various services provided by a cryptosystem be combined to provide a variety of services simultaneously. [3]

While this whitepaper focuses on the security services of confidentiality and integrity, availability is an issue which remains crucial when implementing security. This is particularly true in the commercial arena. For example, an extremely secure electronic payment system is virtually useless if it is not able to operate fast enough to handle consumers' needs, or if it restricts the volume of trade so that merchants are forced to turn customers away. Thus when addressing the issues of information security, a business does not only face the question "What security services do I need a cryptosystem to provide?", but also "Which cryptosystem will best ensure that I can continue to use my information as efficiently as possible?"

So, while this whitepaper focuses on the services of confidentiality and integrity, bear in mind that availability will be crucial in many applications. When employing a cryptosystem, this availability translates into the speed of operation of the cryptosystem, its reliability, and its ease of use.

2. Types of Cryptographic Systems

Historically cryptographic systems have provided only confidentiality. Preparing a message for a secure, private transfer involves the process of encryption. Encryption transforms data in user or machine readable form, called the **plaintext**, to an illegible version, called the **ciphertext.** The conversion of plaintext to ciphertext is controlled by an electronic key k. The key is simply a binary string which determines the effect of the encryption function. The reverse process of transforming the ciphertext back into plaintext is called decryption, and is controlled by a related key l.

There are two broad classes of cryptosystems, known as **symmetric-key cryptosystems** and **public-key cryptosystems.** The relationship between k and l differentiates the two.

In a symmetric-key cryptosystem, the same key is used for both encryption and decryption. Figure 11. 2. 1 illustrates the mechanical analogy of a symmetric-key cryptosystem. Since the keys are the same, two users wishing to communicate in confidence must agree and maintain a common secret key. Each entity must trust the other not to **divulge** the key. In applications where a limited number of users exist, symmetric-key cryptography is effective. However, in large networks with users distributed over a wide area, key distribution becomes a problem. Each individual in a network should have a distinct key to communicate with each other person. To set this up, a tremendous number of keys must be established and stored securely. For example, a system with 1, 000 users would require approximately 500, 000 keys to be exchanged and maintained securely. Exchanging and managing such a large number of keys is at best an arduous task and at worst impossible.

Symmetric-key cryptosystems have been used to provide confidentiality for thousands of years. One of the first recorded systems was used by Julius Caesar. Known as the Caesar Cipher, it involves shifting the letters of the alphabet a predetermined number of characters. The number of character shifts is the encryption key, and, of course, shifting back the same number of characters reverses this process to decrypt. Today, symmetric-key cryptosystems are controlled by keys that are based on complex mathematical algorithms.

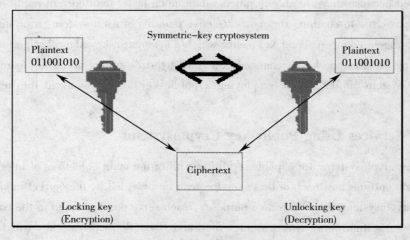

Figure 11. 2. 1   Symmetric-key cryptosystem

On the other hand, public-key cryptosystems are a contemporary technology, introduced as recently as 1976 by two Stanford researchers, Whitfield Diffie and Martin Hellman. In a public-key cryptosystem, the abilities to perform encryption and decryption are separated. The encryption rule employs a public key E (that is k = E), while the decryption rule requires a different (but mathematically related) private key D (that is l = D). Knowledge of the public key allows encryption of plaintext but does not allow decryption of the ciphertext. If a person selects and publishes their public key, then everyone can use that one public key to encrypt messages for that person. The private key is kept secret so that only the intended individual can decrypt the ciphertext. In a network of 1,000 users, there is only a need for one public key and one private key for each user. This requires a total of 2,000 keys instead of the 500,000 keys required for a symmetric-key cryptosystem. Figure 11.2.2 shows the mechanical analogy of a public-key cryptosystem.

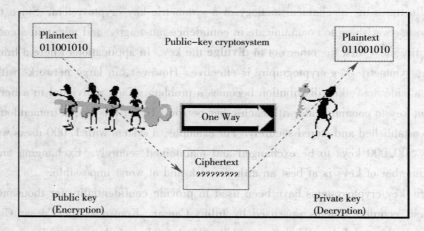

Figure 11.2.2　Public-key cryptosystem

At first sight, it may appear that public-key systems are functionally superior to symmetric-key techniques and that there is little need to consider the latter. However, symmetric-key systems are still widely used because they are able to process data much faster than current public-key schemes. A common approach is to combine the most attractive features of each system: a public-key scheme is used to exchange a common secret key, after which a symmetric-key algorithm performs bulk data encryption using the common key exchanged. Such a "hybrid" system offers the extra speed that a symmetric-key system affords, while employing a public-key system to avoid the key distribution problem.

3. Security Services Using Public-key Cryptosystems

Public-key cryptosystems are capable of fulfilling all of the main objectives of information security. This section outlines how each of these services can be provided by the correct implementation of a public-key cryptosystem. For illustrative purposes, each service is discussed in the context of a hypothetical communication between two users, Alice and Bob. Bob's private key will be denoted by D_{bob} and his public key by E_{bob}. The adversary, trying to subvert secure communication, is Eve.

3.1　Public-key Encryption Confidentiality

Suppose Alice wishes to send a secret message to Bob. During system set-up, Bob makes E_{bob}, his public key, available to all users by publishing it in a public directory, the electronic equivalent of a phone book. To communicate message M to Bob, Alice first looks up E_{bob} in the public directory. Alice then encrypts M by performing the public-key transformation using E_{bob}, to transform M into ciphertext C. This process is denoted by:

$$C = E_{bob}\ (M)$$

to show that C is the result of transforming M using E_{bob}. Finally Alice sends C to Bob. Bob retrieves M by transforming C using D_{bob}.

Alice and Bob are now assured that no-one else can decipher C, since only Bob knows his private key D_{bob}. Therefore Bob alone can compute:

$$M = D_{bob}\ (C)$$

and recover M from C. Thus the service of confidentiality is provided by performing public-key encryption in this way. Figure 11.2.3 illustrates the procedure Alice and Bob undergo during public-key encryption.

Notice, however, that anyone could have encrypted any message and sent it to Bob. While the message is confidential, there is no assurance that the message came from Alice. A method for achieving the extra service of data origin authentication is described in the next section.

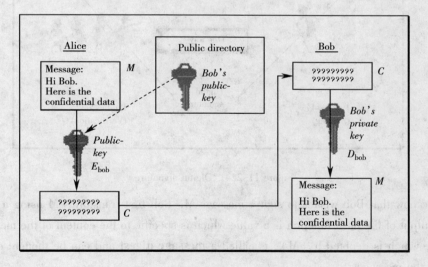

Figure 11.2.3　Public-key encryption

3.2　Digital Signatures

As the name suggests, digital signatures are the electronic equivalent of traditional handwritten signatures. Handwritten signatures provide security services because each individual has distinct handwriting, making their signature hard to forge. If electronic signatures were formed in the same

215

way as written signatures, by simply appending a fixed string to each message that Bob wants to sign, then security would easily be compromised. To forge Bob's signature, all Eve would need is one previous copy of Bob's signature. She could then append it to any message she chooses, and claim that the message has been signed by Bob. This problem arises because, unlike an individual's handwriting, electronic information is easy to duplicate.

To avoid compromise in this way, digital signatures are performed in a more complex manner using a public-key cryptosystem. The essential difference between the use of a public-key cryptosystem for signing and its use for encrypting is that the order in which the keys are used is reversed. [4] In data encryption, first Alice applied E_{bob} to M, then Bob decrypted using D_{bob}. In digital signatures, first Bob applies D_{bob} to compute his signature, then Alice checks, or verifies, the signature using E_{bob}.

Figure 11.2.4 illustrates this "reversal" of the application of the private key and public key. The details of forming a digital signature are more complex, but keep in mind that it is this change that fundamentally determines the whole process.

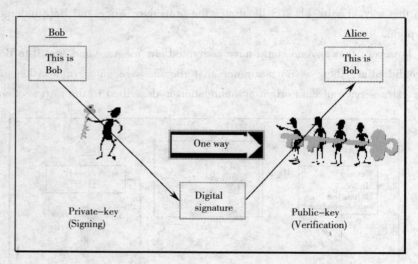

Figure 11.2.4　Digital signature

Suppose now that Bob wishes to sign a message M. Bob first transforms M using a **hash function.** The output of the hash function is a value which is specific to the content of the message itself. This output, which is denoted h (M), is called a **message digest** and can be thought of as a "fingerprint" of the message.

Bob signs M by transforming h (M) using D_{bob}, to obtain:

$$S = D_{bob} (h (M))$$

Here S rather than C denotes the output of the transformation in order to distinguish that S forms part of the signature process as opposed to the encryption process. Bob now sends M and S to Alice as his signature on M.

If Alice wants to verify Bob's signature on M, she first retrieves E_{bob}. Then she recomputes the message digest, h (M), from M using the publicly available hash function. Finally Alice transforms S using E_{bob} and compares the result with h (M). If Alice finds that:

$$E_{bob} (S) = h (M)$$

then she accepts Bob's signature as valid. On the other hand, if:

$$E_{bob} (S) \neq h (M)$$

Alice concludes that S is not Bob's signature for message and that M has been modified. Figure 11.2.5 shows Alice and Bob carrying out this process.

Why does this signature process provide the services of data origin authentication, data integrity, and non-repudiation? First of all, Alice is assured that only Bob could have computed the signature, since only Bob knows D_{bob}, and therefore only Bob could have transformed h (M) to S. Thus data origin authentication is provided. Secondly, once Bob has signed M, the message cannot be altered, since changing M would change h (M), so that S would no longer represent a valid signature on the new message. Thus data integrity is upheld. Finally, non-repudiation is provided because once Bob has signed a message, he cannot later deny signing it. All Alice has to do to be assured of non-repudiation is save Bob's signature on M so that if Bob later denies signing M, the pair of M and S will demonstrate that he is lying.

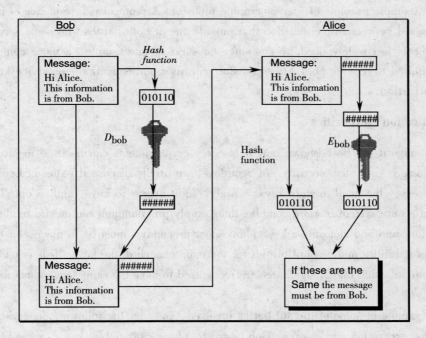

Figure 11.2.5   Digital signature with hash function

3.3   Signed Challenges

In the previous subsection, it was shown how digital signatures use a public-key cryptosystem to provide data origin authentication. The goal of this subsection is to show how the digital signature process can be modified to provide user authentication.

What is the difficulty with providing user authentication? Consider the following scenario. Alice wants user authentication to assure her that she is involved in a real-time communication with Bob. Suppose Bob attempted to provide this assurance by simply signing the message "this is Bob". Certainly Alice is assured that the message originated from Bob at some stage, because, as seen in the last subsection, digital signatures provide data origin authentication. The problem comes with the phrase "real-time". Once Bob has signed "this is Bob", Eve can save this signature and use it to authenticate herself as Bob at any later time.

So a simple digital signature alone does not provide Alice with user authentication. To attain this service, the interaction between Alice and Bob is modified as follows. When Alice enters a real-time communication with Bob and desires user authentication, she first generates an unpredictable random number, R_{alice}, and sends it to Bob. R_{alice} is called a **challenge** in this context. Now, instead of signing just "this is Bob", Bob signs "this is Bob, and you just sent me R_{alice}". Provided this signature is valid, and the signed value R_{alice} is the same as the challenge Alice generated, then Alice is assured that she is communicating with Bob in "real-time". Thus the combination of a digital signature together with the unpredictability of Alice's random challenge provides user authentication.

This is a simple example of a cryptographic protocol. A protocol is a sequence of messages and responses passed between Alice and Bob that provide one or both parties with some service. Cryptographic protocols are widely used by computer networks. For example, a more complex protocol would be required to provide both Alice and Bob with user authentication—a service known as **mutual authentication.**

3. 4　Certification Authorities

By this stage it has been shown how public-key cryptosystems can be used to provide the five "building blocks" for system security. In Section 1, we briefly discussed issues of key management for cryptosystems—the need to store keys securely, audit access to keys, and so on. Therefore implementing a secure system is more complex than simply programming routines to implement a public-key cryptosystem and choosing a key. Many other procedures must be in place, for example, the assignment of liabilities and responsibilities for the maintenance of the keys. This is particularly true in applications in which digital signatures are recognized to have the same legal status as handwritten signatures.

As an example of some of the **subtleties** involved, consider the following scenario. During the procedures for encryption and signing, Bob began by placing his public key in some kind of "electronic phone book" so that the other users could later retrieve it. In fact, the set-up of this "phone book" is crucial to security. Suppose that Eve is also able to place a public key of her choice into this public directory, claiming that the key belongs to Bob. When Alice now encrypts confidential information and sends it to Bob, Eve intercepts the ciphertext and decrypts the information herself. [5] So confidentiality is not upheld. This demonstrates that all users need to have confidence that the public keys they retrieve are authentic and belong to the specified user.

This requirement amounts to the need for some information binding Bob to his public key. This binding is usually provided by a **certificate.** Certificates are issued by a **Certification Authority** (CA). A Certification Authority is a third party trusted by all users.

A CA creates, distributes, **revokes**, and generally manages certificates. To generate Bob's certificate, the CA checks Bob's identity and that E_{bob} really is Bob's public key. The CA then signs with its own private key, D_{CA}, a message comprised of Bob's identification (information such as name, address, and e-mail address), Bob's public key and any other useful information, such as expiration date of the certificate and user privileges.

Now, when Alice wants to obtain Bob's public key, she retrieves Bob's certificate from a public directory, and verifies the CA's signature on the certificate itself. Provided this signature verifies correctly, she has assurance from the trusted CA that E_{bob} really is Bob's public key. Alice can now go ahead and use Bob's public key to encrypt confidential information to send to Bob or to verify Bob's signatures, protected by the assurance of the certificate.

Of course, each user must obtain an authentic copy of the CA's public key, but since this only requires the distribution of one key, it is practical to carry out this distribution by hand, possibly at the same time as each user certifies their own public key in person with the CA.

Provided subtleties such as this are correctly addressed, public-key cryptosystems can ensure the integrity of large computing networks and allow businesses to **reap** the benefits of the coming electronic era, protected from the heightened threats and security concerns of such an environment.

Key Words

information security	信息安全
confidentiality	*n.* 机密性
concealment	*n.* 隐藏
audit	*n.* 审计
authentication	*n.* 验证
repudiate	*v.* 否认
plaintext	*n.* 明文
ciphertext	*n.* 加密文本
symmetric-key cryptosystem	对称密码体制
public-key cryptosystem	公钥密码体制
divulge	*v.* 泄露
hash function	散列函数
message digest	信息摘要
challenge	*n.* 挑战
mutual authentication	双向认证
subtlety	*n.* 微妙之处，精华
certificate	*n.* 证书

Certification Authority	证书颁发机构
revoke	*v.* 撤销
reap	*v.* 获得

Notes

1. Simply put, information security describes all measures taken to prevent unauthorized use of electronic data—whether this unauthorized use takes the form of disclosure, alteration, substitution, or destruction of the data concerned.

简而言之，信息安全描述了所有用于防止未经授权使用电子数据的方法。无论这个未授权所采用的是公开、修改、替代还是破坏相关数据的形式。

2. That is, the receiver of a transaction is able to demonstrate to a neutral third party that the claimed sender did indeed send the transaction.

也就是说，事务的接收方能够向中立的第三方证明发送方的确发送了事务。

3. "Real-world" applications are rarely straightforward, so a typical implementation will require that various services provided by a cryptosystem be combined to provide a variety of services simultaneously.

由于实际生活的应用很少是简单的，所以一个典型的实现通常需要密码系统同时提供多种服务。

4. The essential difference between the use of a public-key cryptosystem for signing and its use for encrypting is that the order in which the keys are used is reversed.

使用公钥加密技术进行签名和加密的根本区别在于使用密钥的顺序是相反的。

5. Suppose that Eve is also able to place a public key of her choice into this public directory, claiming that the key belongs to Bob. When Alice now encrypts confidential information and sends it to Bob, Eve intercepts the ciphertext and decrypts the information herself.

假设 Eve 也可以将自己选的公钥放入这个公共号码簿，并且声明这个密钥是 Bob 的。当 Alice 将经过加密的保密信息发给 Bob 时，Eve 可以截取加密文本并自己解密信息。

Reading Material 1　Introduction to Firewall

Today, more than 100 firewall providers advertise their ware. Unfortunately, many of these so-called "firewalls" aren't really doing as much as you'd think.

To really understand how to protect networks, we need to first understand what a firewall is made up of. With this knowledge, we can intelligently decide if we are building the firewall that serves our needs.

Notice that I still refer to it as "building" a firewall. Most of us do not build our own firewalls anymore. Perhaps a few still do, but that's no longer necessary with today's technology. We must, however, still choose the right combination of products that will successfully protect our networks.

Not all firewalls are created equal. And not all firewalls are doing the job you may think they're created to do.

A firewall should really be doing more than simply filtering and blocking particular network traffic. A good firewall should, at the minimum, provide adequate security for its organization. However, most firewall manufacturers seem to forget that good security includes: reliability, performance and management.

By management, I mean providing intelligent information about the network and firewalls. Most firewalls today are being set up and forgotten. They're abandoned without routine maintenances, penetration tests and auditing.

1. Generation One—Packet-filtering Generation

The two major types of "Generation One" firewalls are: Hardware-based Access Control List (ACL) routers and Software-based, packet-filtering firewalls. There is also the combination of the two in both hardware and software platforms.

Both essentially evolved from general-purpose routers and computer Operating Systems (mostly UNIX) in the early days of Internet networking.

Overtime, both router and Operating System manufacturers were adding more and more capabilities to their products to function as firewalls.

Generally speaking, these firewalls perform two main actions:

◆ **Network Address Translation** (NAT): A method used to hide the network's architecture inside of the firewall, blocked from the outside world, and to conserve routable Internet Protocol (IP) addresses.

◆ **Packet-filtering**: A method by which network traffic is selectively restricted or allowed through based on the firewall's security policy. This policy can depend on packet types (protocols and port addresses), sources and/or destination. Different methods of packet filtering have developed over the years. But surprisingly enough, 90 percent or more of today's firewalls are still only performing these two main actions.

This generation of firewalls provides little or no protection to the application layer. For example, an FTP service can go through HTTP (a web service) with most of today's firewalls, and there is nothing that most packet-filtering firewalls can do about it.

Another case in point: today's firewalls for the most part cannot protect an SMTP service from being attacked by using a Telnet service. But a Telnet service may be blocked at its default port by the same firewall protecting an SMTP service.

In summary, packet-filtering firewalls, while providing basic protection to the internal network, is ill-fit to protect Internet applications.

2. Generation Two—Application Proxy Generation

In the last several years, we are seeing the emergence of a new type of firewall that still uses both NAT and packet-filtering methods at the lower layers of the Open System Interconnection (OSI) model. The only difference is what's called the Application Proxy method, which handles the issues facing Generation One firewalls at the highest layer of the OSI model.

Table 11. 3. 1   Today's firewall solution matrix

Protocols applications	OSI model layer	OSI model description	Firewall generation
DNS, FTP, HTTP, etc.	7	Application	Application proxy
	6	Presentation	
	5	Session	
TCP / UDP	4	Transport	Packet filter
IP	3	Network	Packet filter
	2	Data link	
	1	Physical	

Application Proxy Firewall—In an application proxy firewall, all packets are stopped at the firewall or proxy server (a special type of firewall usually built for certain applications only). The packets are then checked for their sources and destination addresses, type of protocols and port numbers, sometimes even the contents of the payloads and commands. If the packets pass the inspection, they are reconstructed and sent out to their destinations. Again, there are several different implementations of this method. Since all original packets are destroyed before being forwarded to their destinations, Generation Two firewalls prevent attacks based on the weaknesses of the TCP/IP protocols, which were never designed with security in mind. Moreover, this method allows the firewall to perform deep inspection that the packet-filtering method cannot.

Unfortunately, not all application proxy firewalls implement 100 percent of the application proxy as I described it above for each protocol and application. Most only work for popular applications like HTTP, SMTP, etcetera. Even with well-known ones like HTTP, Generation Two firewalls don't always cover all applications that could tunnel through. One reason for this is that so many applications are being developed using HTTP. HTTP is being used to deliver much more than the ordinary web site content. It's also being used to deliver radio and video content, as well as VPN tunnels, peer-to-peer file exchange, music swapping and other applications that may not be desirable for an organization's network.

Another issue is that not all traffic is clear text, on which the firewall can conduct deep inspection. So then, how do firewalls inspect what is inside encrypted HTTP traffic? The answer is that 99.99 percent of today's firewalls can't. How do firewalls know if a secure shell (SSH) session is doing what it's supposed to do? They don't. Routinely, other services are being tunneled through SSH through these firewalls.

So then, couldn't one conclude that a network is only as secure as the SSH and HTTP authentications? The simple answer is yes. As I like to say, a firewall is only as secure as its weakest links.

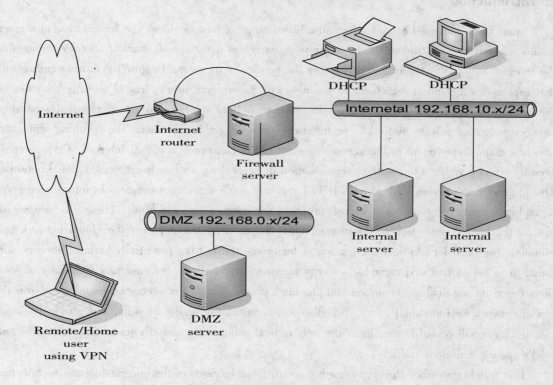

Figure 11.3.1　Firewall architecture

3. Firewall Architecture Design

A typical firewall consists of three or more interfaces, consisting of the: Outside (Connected to Internet), DMZ (Connected to Service Network) and Inside (Connected to Internal Network).

The DMZ (De-Militarized Zone) is a term that stems from the military, describing a buffer zone between two enemies. The purpose of having a DMZ is to separate the public's services from internal services. If DMZ is compromised, internal resources are remain protected.

Remember: you must always assume that the attackers will get through at some point. By setting up the DMZ, we provide less of an attacking surface, which could allow attackers to try. The services hosted in DMZ are typically DNS, Web (HTTP), FTP and SMTP servers.

From a firewall policy point of view, it's not good enough to think about preventing attackers from outside of the firewall, or even from DMZ networks. A firewall design should consider attacks from inside of the firewall. Even further, a good defense should assume that the attacker is already inside of the firewall.

Reading Material 2   Internet Security Architecture

1. Introduction

Apart from increased connectivity and a broad range of new services, the Internet has also given technically advanced intruders the opportunity to carry out a variety of attacks, thereby threatening the integrity of its infrastructure and violating the privacy of its users. Despite the current enthusiasm that supersedes the initial reluctance of business and government users, fear of security breaches on the Internet is forcing most organizations to resort to radical solutions based on physical separation between protected private networks—or intranets—and the public Internet. The resulting segmentation is a major impediment to the accomplishment of the concept of a global Internet. Cryptographic security offers a viable alternative to segmentation by preserving a strongly connected global network. The Internet Engineering Task Force (IETF) recently made significant progress in introducing cryptographic security mechanisms at various layers of the Internet Protocol Suite. These mechanisms allow for the logical protection of information units during their transfer over the global network and eliminate the need for physical segregation of legitimate traffic from potentially harmful network portions. It is hoped that cryptographic security measures will balance the ease and simplicity of solutions based on physical segmentation and provide a practical means of secure communication over the global network for individual users. Nonetheless, segmentation using firewalls and physically separate intranets will probably remain as the only radical solution for globally protecting enterprise networks against malicious traffic.

This article describes the cryptographic security mechanisms of the current Internet architecture in the area of network infrastructure, including Internet and transport layer protocols, routing, directory, and network management functions. Figure 11.4.1 presents the new security components and existing components enhanced with new security features with respect to the layers of the Internet architecture. Section II presents the security architecture for the Internet Protocol, including a detailed description of the two security protocols, IP Authentication Header and IP Encapsulating Payload, a summary of secure hashing techniques adopted by this architecture, and the concept of security associations. The interplay between security protocols and their relationship to security associations are illustrated in a set of typical scenarios pulling together the basic components of the architecture. Section III describes the transport layer security protocol and its basic components: the record layer that provides basic security services for the applications and the handshake protocol which assures key exchange and the negotiation of the security functions used by the record layer. Section IV presents current proposals for key management in the Internet infrastructure. The Internet Security Association and Key Management Protocol and its companion Oakley key exchange protocol are the proposals most likely to become formal standards.

Furthermore, secure data transfer on behalf of users and applications relies on the security of the network control and management protocols that maintain the global connectivity and availability of the network. Among these protocols, the Domain Name System of Internet enjoys the most complete set of security enhancements as presented in section V, whereas the other two major functions of the network infrastructure totally lack or only partially enjoy a comprehensive security design.

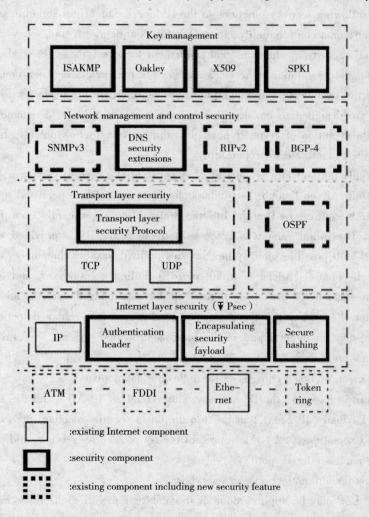

Figure 11.4.1   Cryptographic security components of the Internet infrastructure

2. IP Security

The security architecture of the Internet Protocol known as IP Security (IPsec) is the most advanced effort in the standardization of Internet security. As the common vehicle for various higher layer protocols, the Internet Protocol (IP) is vulnerable to several attacks threatening either the security of the application payload carried by higher layer protocols like the Transmission Control Protocol (TCP) or the behavior of the network itself through the subversion of network control protocols like the Internet Control Message Protocol (ICMP) or the Border Gateway Protocol (BGP). IPsec covers both the new generation of IP (IPv6) and the current version of IP (IPv4) thanks to the retrofitting of IPv6 security mechanisms into IPv4. IPsec can be used to protect an IP layer path between a pair of end-systems or hosts, between a pair of intermediate-systems—called security gateways, or between a host and a security gateway. A security gateway provides the packet forwarding function at the IP layer and thus can be a router, a firewall or a host with IP forwarding capability. IPsec provides the following security functions in the IP layer: data origin authentication, data integrity, replay detection, data confidentiality, limited traffic confidentiality and access control. In addition to the individual security mechanisms that implement these services, IPsec also provides management facilities for the negotiation of services and service parameters between communicating parties, as well as for the exchange of cryptographic keys required by the basic security mechanisms. IPsec mechanisms are designed to be algorithm-independent, in order to accommodate changes in the event of possible evolution of cryptographic algorithms. Nevertheless default algorithms are defined for each service to facilitate interoperability.

IPsec was initially defined in a set of RFCs. A substantially revised version was published in a series of Internet drafts. Even though the fundamental features of IPsec persisted over the revision, the current IPsec architecture based on the Internet drafts differs significantly from the initial version in several respects. The initial version of IPsec as defined by the RFCs provided a framework that would be completed with possible security mechanisms defined in other documents whereas the current version is a self-contained piece of architecture including a framework and a set of security transforms. Thus message fields previously defined in accompanying documents are now part of the base specification for IPsec. For example, security mechanisms like replay detection, message sequence integrity are now an integral part of the base specification and not a security transform defined in other documents.

The current version of IPsec consists of the following components:
- Two security protocols: the IP Authentication Header (IP AH) and the IP Encapsulating Security Payload (IP ESP) that provide the basic security mechanisms within IP;
- Security associations (SA) that represent the set of security services and parameters negotiated on each secure IP path;
- Algorithms for authentication and encryption.

IP AH and IP ESP may be applied alone or in combination with each other. Each protocol can operate in one of two modes: transport mode or tunnel mode. In transport mode, the security mechanisms of the protocol are applied only to the upper layer data and the information pertaining to IP layer operation as contained in the IP header is left unprotected. In tunnel mode, both the upper layer protocol data and the IP header of the IP packet are protected or "tunneled" through encapsulation.

A crucial function closely related to the above mentioned IPsec components is the automatic management of cryptographic keying material and SAs. The Internet Security Association and Key Management Protocol that provides such automatic management functions to security components at the IP layer and above is described in section IV.

3. Transport Layer Security

The main security activity in the area of transport layer is the Transport Layer Security (TLS) Protocol specification based on the Secure Sockets Layer (SSL) Protocol developed by Netscape Communications Corporation. Even though TLS is not part of the IPsec architecture, the goal of the TLS effort is to harmonize the TLS Protocol specification with respect to the common key management architecture used by IPsec.

The TLS Protocol operates above a reliable transport protocol like TCP and provides the following security services: peer entity authentication, data confidentiality, data integrity, key generation and distribution, and security parameter negotiation.

The TLS Protocol consists of two layers: the TLS Record Protocol and the TLS Handshake Protocol. The TLS Record Protocol provides basic connection security for various higher layer protocols through encapsulation. One such protocol is the TLS Handshake Protocol that allows the peer entities located at both ends of the secure channel to authenticate one another, to negotiate encryption algorithms and to exchange secret session keys for encryption. Once a transport connection is authenticated and a secret shared key is established with the TLS Handshake Protocol, data exchanged by application protocols can be protected with cryptographic methods by the TLS Record Layer using the keying materiel derived from the shared secret.

4. Key Management

Key management is the automated facility that provides communicating parties with symmetric keys required for security services such as authentication, data integrity, and confidentiality. Key management is viewed as a natural component of the basic security architecture in Internet. The two IPsec protocols are tightly coupled with key management via the Security Association (SA) concept. Key management is also considered a complementary mechanism for TLS, routing protocols such as RIP and OSPF, and application protocols. Even though the Internet Architecture Board (IAB) has not yet agreed on key management architecture among several existing alternatives, the current work in this area is likely to converge toward a combination of two protocols: the Internet Security Association and Key Management Protocol (ISAKMP), and Oakley key exchange protocol.

ISAKMP is the framework for key exchange and negotiation of SAs. ISAKMP is designed to be key exchange independent and can support several key exchange protocols. Oakley describes a series of key exchange methods based on the Diffie-Hellman method that is compatible with the framework defined by ISAKMP. The other alternative key exchange method, that is, key distribution based on a key server like in Kerberos, is not supported within the current ISAKMP framework.

Furthermore many Internet protocols rely on public key encryption but the current key management initiative based on ISAKMP and Oakley does not address the management of public keys. Various efforts currently aim at providing a public key infrastructure with different models. The Internet X. 509 Public Key Infrastructure work defines public key certificates and certificate management protocols based on the X. 509v3 standard. This standard is tightly coupled with the X. 500 naming scheme in that each X. 509v3 certificate binds a public key with a name expressed in the X. 500 format. Lack of support for X. 500 names in the Internet community probably has been the main obstacle to the acceptance of the corresponding public key management work. Conversely, an alternative solution using Internet names is provided by the Domain Name System Security Extensions effort, as described in section V. Recently, a new direction in public key management was opened in suggesting a simple public key infrastructure based on the idea that the public key itself can be used as the name of the user, thus avoiding the requirement for an additional naming scheme.

5. Domain Name System Security Extensions

The Domain Name System (DNS) provides host names to IP address mapping. The DNS is organized into a hierarchy of servers each having the responsibility of a particular portion of the DNS database. Current DNS protocols completely lack security mechanisms. A variety of threats on the DNS protocols exist that mainly take advantage of the lack of authentication and data integrity. By exploiting the absence of client authentication or by eavesdropping with bulk data transfers between DNS servers, intruders may cause the leakage of information on the topology of private enterprise networks. The impersonation of DNS servers can cause traffic or mail subversion by injecting bogus addressing information.

Current work in the IETF security working groups defines extensions to DNS aiming at the addition of security mechanisms in three areas:

◆ Data origin authentication in order to prevent the tampering with the data stored in the DNS servers,

◆ Transaction authentication to eliminate the possibility of server and client impersonation and data modification during DNS transactions,

◆ Public key certification using DNS as a public key certificate repository.

The DNS extensions do not cover confidentiality, denial of service or any form of access control for DNS requests. In order to assure interoperability between the current DNS protocol and future extensions, the extensions do not require any protocol change other than the support of optional data types to store security information in the basic DNS data structures called "resource records" or RR (Table 11. 4. 1). DNS security extensions introduce two new RR types: the KEY RR and the signature or SIG RR.

Table 11. 4. 1　DNS resource record

Resource domain name (Name)	
Type	Class
Time-to-live	Length
Resource data (IP address)	

The SIG RR is the basic building block through which data origin and transaction authentication is assured. A SIG RR stores the value of a signature that covers one or many resource records as identified by the "Type covered" sub-field in the Resource Data field of the SIG RR. In addition, the Resource Data field of the SIG RR holds the name of the party that issued the signature, the signature time and its expiration date. The Key footprint sub-field contains an algorithm dependent short value for the rapid verification of the public key that can possibly be used for the verification of the signature. This can consist of the hash or some selected octets of the public key. Although various signature algorithms can be used, RSA encryption of the MD5 hash is incorporated as the default signature mechanism.

Data origin authentication can be provided using a SIG RR including a signature that covers one or many DNS RRs. Through the verification of that signature with the DNS public key, recipients can be assured of the origin of the name to address mapping and thwart impersonation attacks.

The KEY RR stores the public key of a party identified by the Resource Domain Name field. A DNS public key certificate consists of a KEY RR containing the public key and the name followed by a SIG RR that includes the signature covering the KEY RR. In the case of a SIG RR that is part of a public key certificate, the signature should be computed using the private key associated with the logical portion of the DNS database named "zone". The concept of a DNS zone is akin to the role of a Certification Authority (CA) in X. 509. A DNS public key certificate thus provides a strong binding between a name and a public key based on a trusted zone authority.

DNS servers do not necessarily bear the role of a CA or zone authority with respect to public key certification. Thus the zone private key and the private key of each DNS server managing the corresponding portion of the DNS database are different. Public key signatures stored in the DNS database must therefore be computed off-line using the zone private key that is not stored in the DNS servers. Moreover current DNS extensions do not include the certification chain concept whereby, each public key can be verified using an ordered list of certificates each delivered by a different CA positioned on a path or chain from the local CA through the root CA. In order to validate a public key certificate using such a chain, the certificate that is signed by the first CA of the chain is verified using the public key of the first CA. The latter public key is in turn signed by the next CA in the chain. The next step of the certificate chain validation consists of verifying this signature using the public key of the next CA. The public key of each CA is thus verified using the certificate delivered by the next CA on the chain until the root CA is reached. The public key of the root CA is self validated since its value is well known by all parties using the certification system.

DNS transaction authentication is provided by a SIG RR that covers the request or response message. In an authenticated response message, the signature covers both the response and the corresponding request that triggered the former. Unlike the signature that is part of the public key certificates, the signature for authenticating DNS responses is computed by the DNS server that issues the response using the server's private key.

Exercises

Ⅰ. Fill in the following blanks with proper words or phrases：

1. IDS stands for _____.

2. _____ are a series actions and countermeasures when an intrusion is detected.

3. AIRS stands for _____.

4. Current intrusion response systems can be categorized as _____, _____, or _____.

5. Cryptographic systems (or cryptosystems) potentially provide all three objectives of information security： _____, _____, and _____.

6. In a cryptographic system, _____ assurance that the parties involved in a real-time transaction are who they say they are.

7. There are two broad classes of cryptosystems, known as _____ cryptosystems and _____ cryptosystems.

8. In a cryptographic system, certificates are issued by a _____, which is a third party trusted by all users.

Ⅱ. Answer the following questions：

1. What's intrusion detection system?

2. Briefly describe the two points of the weakness of present IDSs.

3. What are the reasons of developing automatic intrusion response systems?

4. What is the key factor of developing AIRSs?

5. What is information security?

6. What's the difference between the use of a public-key cryptosystem for signing and its use for encrypting?

7. List some algorithms of Public-Key Cryptosystems.

8. List some algorithms of Symmetric-Key Cryptosystems.

9. Describe the theory of digital signatures.

Chapter Twelve   Digital Image Processing

Unit 1   A Basic Introduction to Image Processing

Digital image processing—the manipulation of images by computer—is a relatively recent development in terms of human's ancient fascination with visual stimuli. The inherent subjective appeal of **pictorial** displays attracts perhaps a disproportionate amount of attention from scientist and **lay person** alike. It is a broad umbrella under which fall diverse aspects of optics, electronics, mathematics, photography, and computer technology. [1]This article is intended as an introductory look at image processing (not machine vision). We will look at how color is represented within an image, how images are stored, what resolution means, as well as the most **rudimentary** statistical analysis of an image.

1. Color Representation

A quick look at how color is represented on a computer. The two most commonly used representations are 8-bit greyscale and 24-bit color. 8-bit greyscale contains 256 shades of grey ($2^8 = 256$) with 0 normally denoting black and 255 denoting white, with other values representing intermediate shades of grey. 24-bit color is simply stored as 3-bytes denoting the red, green and blue components of the color, as in Figure 12.1.1.

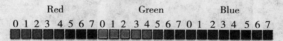

Figure 12.1.1   Red, green and blue components of the 24-bit color

It is worth mentioned that color can be stored in a variety of other ways, each of which have their own advantages and disadvantages: HSI (**Hue, Saturation, Intensity**), CMY (**Cyan, Magenta**, Yellow), Normalized RG, CIE, YIQ and a lot more.

2. Image Representation

Now that we understand how colors are stored, what about whole images? Simply put, images are stored as collections of **pixels** ("pixel" is in fact short for "picture element"), each of which is assigned a color. As an example, the left wing of this Su-47 has been **blown up** so you can see how the individual colors interact to create the star.

How much information can you convey in an image this way? This depends on the resolution at which the image is sampled. Sampling occurs when you scan an image, or take a picture with a digital camera. As with everything digital, the information provided has to be converted into discrete in-

Figure 12.1.2　An example of image representation

formation, so the scanner/digital camera samples as much information as it can and converts it into a digital signal. [2] With digital cameras, this is represented by the size of the **CCD** sensor (normally measured in **megapixels**). The greater the number of pixels the CCD contains, the larger the resolution, the more information is sampled. As an example, look at these three pictures.

Figure 12.1.3　An example of different resolution images

The **leftmost** image is a picture of a friend of mine, sampled at 60x145. The middle image is simply a blow-up of her head, retaining the resolution. The **rightmost** image is her head sampled from a higher-resolution picture. Note the dramatic increase in information from the increased sampling.

Of course, in image processing and machine vision, while increased resolution allows for greater detail and more information to work with, it comes at the price of memory and computing speed. For example, the small left-hand image above occupies 26 kilobytes of memory (uncompressed), whereas the original image occupies over 9 megabytes (uncompressed).

3. Histograms

A **histogram** is one of the simplest methods of analyzing an image. An image histogram maintains a count of the frequency for a given color level. The gray-level histogram is a function showing, for each gray level, the number of pixels in the image that have that gray level. [3] The **abscissa** is gray level and the ordinate is frequency of occurrence (number of pixels). When graphed, a histogram can provide a good representation of the color spread of the image. Histograms can also be used to equalize the image, as well as providing a large number of statistics about it. Here is an example of a histogram for the greyscale version of the Su-47 shown above. Note how the majority of the colors seem to lie between about 80 and 120.

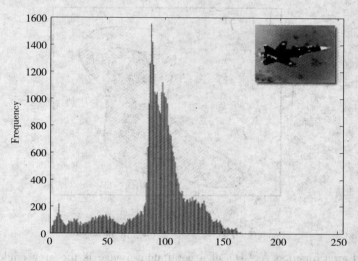

Figure 12. 1. 4   An example of histogram

Extending histograms to RGB images is just as simple: with a separate plot for each color, or a composite plot like the one shown below.

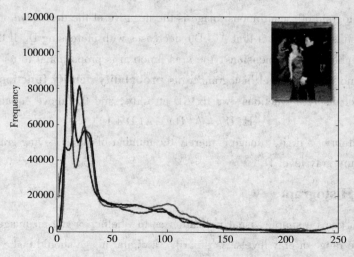

Figure 12. 1. 5   An example of RGB image's histogram

There is another way to define the gray-level histogram, and the following exercise yields insight into the usefulness of this function. Suppose we have a **continuous image**, defined by the function D (x, y), that varies smoothly from high gray level at the center to low gray level at the borders.

We can select some gray level D_1 and define a set of contour lines connecting all points in the image with value D_1. The resulting contour lines form **closed curves** that surround regions in which the gray level is greater than or equal to D_1.

Figure 12. 1. 6 shows an image containing one contour line at the gray level D_1. A second contour line has been drawn at a higher gray level D_2. A_1 is the area of the region inside the first contour line, and similarly, A_2 is the area inside the second line.

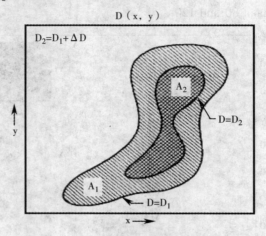

Figure 12. 1. 6   Contour lines in an image

The threshold area function A (D) of a continuous image is the area enclosed by all contour lines of gray level D. Now the histogram may be defined as

$$H(D) = \lim_{\Delta D \to 0} \frac{A(D) - A(D + \Delta D)}{\Delta D} = -\frac{d}{dD}A(D)$$

Thus, the histogram of a continuous image is the negative of the derivative of its area functions. The minus sign results from the fact that A (D) decreases with increasing D. If the image is considered a random variable of two dimensions, the area function is proportional to its **cumulative distribution function** and the gray level histogram to its **probability density function.**

For the case of discrete functions, we fix ΔD at unity, and the above equation becomes

$$H(D) = A(D) - A(D + 1)$$

The area function of a digital image is merely the number of pixels having gray level greater than or equal to D for any gray level D.

4. Uses of the Histogram

The histogram gives a simple visual indication as to whether or not an image is properly scaled within the available range of gray levels. Ordinarily, a digital image should make use of all or almost all of the available gray levels. Failure to do so increases the effective **quantizing interval**. Once the image has been digitized to fewer than 256 gray levels, the lost information can not be restored without redigitizing.

Likewise, if the image has a greater brightness range than the digitizer is set to handle, then the gray levels will be clipped at 0 and/or 255, producing **spikes** at one or both ends of the histogram. It is a good practice routinely to review the histogram when digitizing. A quick check of the histogram can bring digitizing problems into the open before much time has been wasted.

5. The Terminology of Digital Image Processing

While most people have a notion of what an image is, a precise definition is **elusive**. Among the definitions of the word in several of Webster's dictionaries are the following: "A representation, likeness, or imitation of an object or thing,... a vivid or graphic description,... something introduced to represent something else." Thus, in a general sense, an image is a representation of something else. An image contains descriptive information about the object it represents. A photograph displays this information in a manner that allows the viewer to visualize the subject itself. Notice that under this relatively broad definition of image fall many "representations" that are not perceivable by the eye.[4]

The word digital relates to calculation by numerical methods or by discrete units. If we now define a digital image to be a numerical representation of an object (which may itself be an image), the pixels are the discrete units, and the quantized (integer) gray scale supplies the numerical component.

Processing is the act of subjecting something to a process. A process is a series of actions or operations leading to a desired result. Thus, a series of actions is performed upon an object to alter its form in a desired manner. An example is a car wash, wherein automobiles are processed to change them from dirty to clean.

Now we can define digital image processing as subjecting a numerical representation of an object to a series of operations in order to obtain a desired result.

Key Words

pictorial	*adj.* 形象化的，生动的
lay person	非专业人士，门外汉
rudimentary	*adj.* 基本的，初步的
hue	*n.* 色调
saturation	*n.* 饱和度
intensity	*n.* 亮度
cyan	*n.* 青绿色
magenta	*n.* 品红色
pixel	*n.* 像素
blow up	放大
megapixel	*n.* 百万像素
leftmost	*adj.* 最左边的
rightmost	*adj.* 最右边的

CCD	charged coupled device 的缩写，电荷耦合器件
histogram	*n.* 直方图
abscissa	*n.* 横坐标
continuous image	连续图像
closed curve	闭合曲线
cumulative distribution function	累积分布函数
probability density function	概率密度函数
quantizing interval	量化间隔
spike	*n.* 毛刺
elusive	*adj.* 难以精确定义的

Notes

1. The inherent subjective appeal of pictorial displays attracts perhaps a disproportionate amount of attention from scientist and lay person alike. It is a broad umbrella under which fall diverse aspects of optics, electronics, mathematics, photography, and computer technology.

人与生俱来的主观上对生动展示的喜爱吸引了从科学家到非专业人士不同的关注，这个广泛的领域包括光学、电子学、数学、摄影和计算机技术。

2. Sampling occurs when you scan an image, or take a picture with a digital camera. As with everything digital, the information provided has to be converted into discrete information, so the scanner/digital camera samples as much information as it can and converts it into a digital signal.

当扫描图像或者用数码相机照相时，采样就发生了。和所有的数字化一样，提供的信息必须转化成离散信息，这样扫描仪和数码相机就可以尽量多地获得信息，并且转化成数字信号。

3. The gray-level histogram is a function showing, for each gray level, the number of pixels in the image that have that gray level.

灰度直方图是一个函数，表明在图像中每个灰度级所拥有的像素的数量。

4. Notice that under this relatively broad definition of image fall many "representations" that are not perceivable by the eye.

请注意，按照图像的相对广义的定义，许多"表示"是眼睛不可感知的。

Unit 2　Adult Image Detection Using
Statistical Model and Neutral Network

1. Introduction

Images are an essential part of today's World Wide Web. The statistics of more than 4 million

HTML web pages reveal that 70.1% of web pages contain images and that on average there are about 18.8 images per HTML web page. On the other hand, images are also contributing to harmful (e.g. **pornographic**) or even illegal (e.g. **paedophilic**) Internet content. So effective filtering of images is important in an Internet filtering solution.

To block adult content some representative companies as Net Nanny and SurfWatch operate by maintaining lists of URL's and newsgroups and require constant manual updating. Abundant literature is available, but the Internet is very rapidly evolving, not only quantitatively. Each day, 3 million pages are appearing on the Web. Detection based on image content analysis has the advantage to process equally all the images without the need for frequent updating, so will produce more effective filtering.[1]

By taking advantage of the fact that there is a strong **correlation** between images with large patches of skin and adult images we have to develop a skin detector. Skin color offers an effective and efficient way to detect the adult image content. There is already some work on this track.

The WIPE system developed by Wang, Li, Wiederhold and Firschein uses a manually-specified color histogram model as a pre-filter in an analysis pipeline. Input images whose average **probability** of skin is low are accepted as non-offensive. Images that contain considerable skin pass on to a final stage of analysis where they are classified using wavelet features. The algorithm uses a combination of daubechies wavelets, normalized central moments, and color histograms to provide **semantically**-meaningful feature vector matching.

Forysth's research group has designed and implemented an algorithm to screen images of naked people. Their algorithms involve a skin filter and human figure grouper. The skin color model used by Fleck, Forsyth and Bregler consists of a manually specified region in a logopponent color space. Detected regions of skin pixels form the input to a geometric filter based on skeletal structure. As indicated in their paper, 52.2% sensitivity and 96.6% specificity have been obtained for a test set of 138 images with naked people and 1401 assorted **benign** images. However, it takes about 6 minutes on a workstation for the figure grouper in their algorithm to process a suspect image passed by the skin filter. Most of the people in the images used in the experimental protocol are Caucasians and a small number of images are Blacks or Asians.

Jones and Rehg propose techniques for skin color detection by estimating the distribution of skin and non-skin color in the color space using labeled training data. To detect adult images, some simple features are extracted. The discrimination performance based solely on skin is rather good for such simple features.

Bosson et al. propose a pornography detection system which is integrated in a commercial system. This system is also based on skin detection. They compared the generalized linear model, the k-nearest neighbor classifier, the multi-layer perception (MLP) classifier and the support vector machine and found that the MLP gives the best classification performance.[2]

Our approach is as follows. The first main step is skin detection. We build a model with Maximum **Entropy** Modeling (MaxEnt) for the skin distribution. This model imposes constraints on color gradients of neighboring pixels. Parameter estimation as well as optimization cannot be tackled without approximations. With Bethe tree approximation parameter estimation is eradicated and the Belief Propagation (BP) algorithm permits to obtain exact and fast solution for skin probabilities at pixel locations. This model is referred to as TFOM for Tree First Order Model. The output of skin detection is a grayscale skin map with the gray levels being proportional to the skin probabilities. The second main step is pattern recognition. Two fit ellipses are calculated from the skin map—the Global Fit Ellipse and the Local Fit Ellipse. We calculate several simple features from the skin map and fit ellipses which form a pattern. A MLP classifier is trained on 5,084 patterns from the training set. In the test phase, the MLP classifier takes a quick decision on the input pattern in one pass.

The rest of this paper is organized as follows: in section 2 we present the skin detection module. Section 3 is devoted to **feature extraction** and **pattern recognition**. In section 4, some experimental results are presented. Section 5 concludes this paper.

2. Skin Detection

MaxEnt is a method for inferring models from a data set. It works as follows: (1) choose relevant features; (2) compute their histograms on the training set; (3) write down the maximum entropy model within the ones that have the feature histograms as observed on the training set; (4) estimate the parameters of the model; (5) use the model for classification. This plan has been successfully completed for several tasks related to **speech recognition** and language processing. In these applications the underlying graph of the model is a line graph or even a tree but in all cases it has no loops. When working with images, the graph is the **pixel lattice**. It has indeed many loops.

In another paper we adapt this **methodology** to skin detection as follows: in (1) we specialize in colors for two adjacent pixels given "skinness". We choose RGB color space in our approach. In practice we know that the choice of color space is not critical given a histogram-based representation of the color distribution and enough training data. [3] In (2) we compute the histogram of these features in the Compaq manually segmented database. Models for (3) are then easily obtained. In (4) we use the Bethe tree approximation. It consists in approximating locally the pixel lattice by a tree. The parameters of the MaxEnt models are then expressed analytically as functions of the histograms of the features. This is a particularity of our features. In (5) we pursue the approximation in (4): we use the BP algorithm, which is exact in tree graph but only approximative in loopy graphs.

Vezhnevets et al. recently compared some most widely used skin detection techniques and conclude that the proposed MaxEnt model gives the best performance in terms of pixel classification rates. The output of skin detection is a grayscale skin map with the gray levels being proportional to the skin probabilities. We show the output of the skin detection in Figure. 12.2.1, where on the left is the original color image, on the right the corresponding skin map.

3. Adult Image Detection

3.1 Feature Extraction

There are **propositions** for high-level features based on grouping of skin regions that might dis-

Figure 12.2.1   Left: original color image Right: the corresponding skin map

tinguish adult images from those not, but here we have a requirement to process the images speedily, so we are interested to try simpler features.

We first **binarize** the skin map by simple thresholding. We then implement **morphological** open/close operations to remove noise and connect broken regions. Small skin regions are considered insignificant and discarded. Many of our features are based on the fit ellipses calculated on the skin map, since they could meet our requirement for simplicity and capture some important shape information. We observed from experiments that for approaches based on skin detection, portraits have a tendence to be detected as adult images since generally portraits expose plenty of skin as adult ones.[4] The fit ellipses will hopefully at least help discriminate portraits from adult images. We will calculate two fit ellispes for each skin map—the Global Fit Ellipse (GFE) and the Local Fit Ellipse (LFE). The GFE is computed on the whole skin map, while the LFE only on the largest skin region in the skin map.

We extract 9 features from the skin map and fit ellipses. The first 3 are global: (1) average skin probability of the whole image, (2) average skin probability inside the GFE and (3) number of skin regions in the image. The other 6 features computed on the largest skin region of the input image are (1) distance from the **centroid** of the largest skin region to the center of the image, (2) angle of the major axis of the LFE from the horizontal axis, (3) ratio of the minor axis to the major axis of the LFE, (4) ratio of the area of the LFE to that of the image, (5) average skin probability inside the LFE, (6) average skin probability outside the LFE. No effort was done to find the correlation between features.

3.2   Pattern Recognition

The feature extraction steps described in the previous subsection produce a **feature vector** for each image. The task is then to find the decision rule on this feature vector that optimally separates adult images from those not. Evidence from other papers shows that the MLP classifier offers a statistically significant performance over several other approaches such as the generalized linear model, the k-nearest neighbor classifier and the support vector machine.

Our MLP classifier is a semilinear **feedforward** net with one hidden layer. This net outputs a number between 0 and 1, with 1 for adult image and 0 not. The learning procedure starts off with a random set of weight values. For each training pattern p, the net evaluates the output o_p in a feedforward manner. To decrease the error between the output o_p and the true target t_p, the net calculates the corrections of the weight values using the **back propagation** procedure. This procedure is repeated for all the patterns in the training set to yield the resulting corrections for all the weights for that one **iteration**. In a successful learning exercise, the system error will decrease with the number of iterations, and the procedure will converge to a stable set of weights, which will exhibit only small **fluctuations** in value as further learning is attempted. [5]In the test phase, for each test pattern, the net calculates the output in one pass. We then set a threshold T, $0 < T < 1$, to get the binary decision.

4. Experiments

All experiments are made using the following protocol. The database contains 10,168 photographs, which are imported from the Compaq database and the Poesia database. It is split into two equal parts randomly, with 1,297 adult photographs and 3,787 other photographs in each part. One part is used as the training set while the other one, the test set is left aside for the ROC curve computation. The rate is calculated by varying the threshold T. Figure 12.2.2 shows the resulting ROC curve. The elapsed time is about 1.51×10^{-5} second/pixel, i. e., about 1 second for a 256×256 image. Compared with another algorithm, which takes about 6 minutes on a workstation for the figure grouper in their algorithm to process a suspect image passed by the skin filter, our algorithm is more practical.

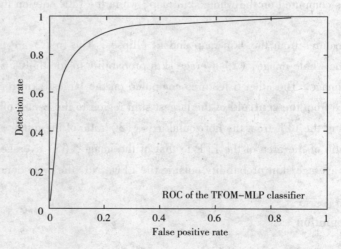

Figure 12.2.2   ROC curve of the TFOM-MLP adult image detection

There are some false alarms worth a look as shown in Figure 12.2.3. The toy dog is detected adult since it takes a skinlike color and the average skin probabilities inside the GFE and the LFE are very high. The portrait is declared adult since it exposes a lot of skin and even the hair and the clothes take skin-like colors. We believe skin detection based solely on color information of one image cannot do much more, so maybe some other sorts of information are needed to improve the adult image detection performance. For example, some kind of face detector could be implemented to improve the results. Moreover, adult images in web pages tend to appear together, and are surrounded by text, which could be an important clue for the adult content detector.

5. Summary and Conclusions

This work is aimed at filtering adult images appear in Internet. The first step of our approach is skin detection. Maximum entropy modeling is used to model the distribution of skinness from the input image. We build a First Order Model that introduces constraints on color gradients of neighboring pixels. We then use Bethe tree approximation to eradicate parameter estimation. It is then called TFOM for Tree First Order Model in this paper. The Belief Propagation algorithm could be further implemented to accelerate the processing. The output of skin detection is a grayscale skin map with the gray levels being proportional to the skin probabilities. We use the fit ellipses to catch the characteristics of skin distribution. Two ellipses are calculated for each skin map—the Global Fit Ellipse (GFE) and the Local Fit Ellipse (LFE). A set of 9 simple features are then computed from the skin map and fit ellipses. A multi-layer **perceptron** classifier is trained for these features. It is a semilinear feedforward net with backpropagation. We have done plenty of experiments. A ROC curve computed from 5,084 test images shows stimulating performance for such simple features. To improve the results one can use a face detector. Moreover, adult images tend to appear together and are surrounded by text in web pages, which could improve the performance of adult image detection.

$O_p = 0.899044$ $O_p = 0.938251$

Figure 12.2.3   First row: original images. Second row: the corresponding skin maps. Third row: the corresponding outputs of the MLP. These results show a toy dog and a portrait detected as adult, which is false.

Key Words

pornographic	*adj.* 色情图像
paedophilic	*adj.* 恋童癖的
correlation	*n.* 关联
probability	*n.* 概率
semantically	*adv.* 语义地
benign	*adj.* 良性的
entropy	*n.* 熵
feature extraction	特征提取
pattern recognition	模式识别
speech recognition	语音识别
pixel lattice	*n.* 像素栅格
methodology	*n.* 方法论
proposition	*n.* 提议，命题，设想
binarize	*v.* 二值化
morphological	*adj.* 形态的
centroid	*n.* 中心
feature vector	特征向量
feedforward	*n.* 前馈
back propagation	反向传播
iteration	*n.* 循环
fluctuation	*n.* 波动
perceptron	*n.* 感知器

Notes

1. Detection based on image content analysis has the advantage to process equally all the images without the need for frequent updating, so will produce more effective filtering.

基于内容分析的图像检测具有如下优势：即同等地处理所有图像，而不需要经常对列表进行更新，因此过滤的效率会更高。

2. They compared the generalized linear model, the k-nearest neighbor classifier, the multi-layer perception (MLP) classifier and the support vector machine and found that the MLP gives the best classification performance.

他们比较了归一化线性模型、k 邻近法分类、多层感知分类（MLP）和支持向量机，发现 MLP 具有最好的分类性能。

3. In practice we know that the choice of color space is not critical given a histogram-based representation of the color distribution and enough training data.

在实践中，如果考虑到色彩分布的直方图表示和足够的训练数据，那么色彩空间的选择就不是一个关键问题。

4. We observed from experiments that for approaches based on skin detection, portraits have a tendence to be detected as adult images since generally portraits expose plenty of skin as adult ones.

通过基于皮肤检测的实验，我们观察到，肖像容易被视作成人图像，因为一般情况下肖像暴露出大量的皮肤区域，这一点与成人图像类似。

5. In a successful learning exercise, the system error will decrease with the number of iterations, and the procedure will converge to a stable set of weights, which will exhibit only small fluctuations in value as further learning is attempted.

在一次成功的学习训练中，系统误差会随着循环次数不断降低，并且这个训练过程将会得到一个稳定的权值集合，这个集合在未来的学习训练过程中只会显示出小的波动。

Reading Material 1　An Introduction to Machine Vision

Machine vision is an incredibly difficult task—a task that seems relatively trivial to humans is infinitely complex for computers to perform. This essay should provide a simple introduction to computer vision, and the sort of obstacles that have to be overcome.

1.　Data Size

We will be looking at the following picture throughout the essay. We will be making a few changes though—we will say that the picture is an 8-bit 640×480 images (not the 200×150 24-bit image it actually is) since this is the "standard" size and color-depth of a computer image.

Figure 12.3.1　The original example image

Why is this important? Well, the first consideration/problem of vision systems is the sheer size of the data it has to deal with. Doing the math, we have 640×480 pixels to begin with $(307, 200)$. This is multiplied by three to account for the red, green and blue (RGB) data $(921, 600)$. So, with just one image we are looking at 900K of data!

So, if we are looking at video of this resolution we would be dealing with 23Mb/sec (or 27Mb/sec in the US) of information! The solution to this is fairly obvious—we just cannot deal with this sort of resolution at this speed at this color-depth! Most vision systems will work with greyscale video with a resolution of 200×150. This greatly reduces the data rate—from 23Mb/sec to 0. 72Mb/sec! Most modern day computer can manage this sort of rate very easily.

Of course, receiving the data is the smallest problem that vision systems face—it is processing it that takes the time. So how can we simplify the data down further? I'll present two simple methods—edge detection and prototyping.

2.　Edge Detection

Most vision systems will be determining where and what something is, and for the most part, by detecting the edges of the various shapes in the image should be sufficient to help us on our way. Let us look at two edge detections of our picture.

The left picture is generated by Adobe Photoshop's "Edge Detection" filter, and the right pic-

Figure 12. 3. 2   An example of edge detection

ture is generated by Generation5's ED256 program. You can see that both programs picked out the same features, although Photoshop has done a better job of accentuating more prominent features.

The process of edge detection is surprisingly simple. You merely look for large changes in intensity between the pixel you are studying and the surrounding pixels. This is achieved by using a filter matrix. The two most common edge detection matrices are called the Laplacian and Laplacian Approximation matrices. I'll use the Laplacian matrix here since the number are all integers. The Laplacian matrix looks like this:

$$
\begin{array}{ccc}
1 & 1 & 1 \\
1 & -8 & 1 \\
1 & 1 & 1
\end{array}
$$

Now, let us imagine we are looking at a pixel that is in a region bordering a black-to-white block. So the pixel and its surrounding 8 neighbours would have the following values:

$$
\begin{array}{ccc}
255 & 255 & 255 \\
255 & 255 & 255 \\
0 & 0 & 0
\end{array}
$$

Where 255 is white and 0 is black. We then multiply the corresponding values with each other:

$$
\begin{array}{ccc}
255 & 255 & 255 \\
255 & -2040 & 255 \\
0 & 0 & 0
\end{array}
$$

We then add all of the values together and take the absolute value—giving us the value of 765. Now, if this value is above our threshold (normally around $20 - 30$, so this is way above the threshold!) then we say that point denotes an edge. Try the above calculation with a matrix that consists of only 255. Experiment with the ED256 program which allows you to play with either the Laplacian or Laplacian Approxmation matrices, even create your own.

3. Prototyping

Prototyping came about through a data classification technique called competitive learning. Competition learning is employed throughout different fields in AI, especially in neural networks or more specifically self-organizing networks. Competitive learning is meant to create x-number of prototypes given a data set. These prototypes are meant to be approximations of groups of data within the dataset.

Somebody thought it would be neat to apply this sort of technique to an image to see if there are data patterns within an image. Obviously it is different for every image, but on the whole, areas of the image can be classified very well using this technique. Here a more specific overview of the algorithm:

4. Prototyping Algorithm

1) Take x samples of the image (x is a high number like 1,000). In our case, these samples would consist of small region of the image (perhaps 15×15 pixels).

2) Create y number of prototypes (y is normally a smaller number like 9). Again, these prototypes would consist of 15×15 groups of pixels.

3) Initialize these prototypes to random values (noisy images).

4) Cycle through our samples, and try and find the prototype that is closest to the sample. Now, alter our prototype to be a little closer to the sample. This is normally done by a weighted average. ED256 brings the chosen prototype 10% closer to the sample.

5) Do this many times—around 5,000. You will find that the prototypes now actually represent groups of pixels that are predominate in the image.

6) Now, you can create a simpler image only made up of y colors by classifying each pixel according to the prototype it is closest too.

Here is our picture in greyscale and another that has been fed through the prototyping algorithm built into ED256. We use greyscale to make prototyping a lot simpler. I have also enlarged the prototypes and their corresponding colors to help you visualize the process.

Figure 12.3.3　Prototyping algorithm demonstration

Notice how the green corresponds to pixels that have predominantly white surroundings, most are red because they are similar to the "brick" prototype. For very dark areas (look at the far right window frame) they are classified as dark red.

For another example, look at this picture of a F-22 Raptor. Notice how the red corresponds to the edges on the right wing (and the left too for the some reason!) and the dark green for the left trailing edges/intakes and right vertical tail. Dark blue is for horizontal edges, purple for the dark aircraft body and black for the land.

Figure 12.3.4   Another demonstration of prototyping algorithm

5. Conclusion

How do these techniques really help machine vision systems? It all boils down to simplifying the data that the computer has to deal with. Less data, the more time can be spent extrapolating features. The trade-off is between data size and retaining the features within the image. For example, with the prototyping example, we would have no trouble spotting the buildings in the picture, but the tree and the car are a lot harder to differentiate. The same applies with a computer.

In general, edge detection helps when you need to fit a model to a picture—for example, spotting people in a scene. Prototyping helps to classify images, by detecting their prominent features. Prototyping has a lot of uses since it can "spot" traits of an image that humans do not.

Reading Material 2   An Overview of JPEG-2000

1. Introduction

As digital imagery becomes more commonplace and of higher quality, there is the need to manipulate more and more data. Thus, image compression must not only reduce the necessary storage and bandwidth requirements, but also allow extraction for editing, processing, and targeting particular devices and applications. The JPEG-2000 image compression system has a rate-distortion advantage over the original JPEG. More importantly, it also allows extraction of different resolutions, pixel fidelities, regions of interest, components, and more, all from a single compressed bitstream. This allows an application to manipulate or transmit only the essential information for any target device from any JPEG-2000 compressed source image. JPEG-2000 has a long list of features, a subset of which are:

◆ State-of-the-art low bit-rate compression performance

- ◆ Progressive transmission by quality, resolution, component, or spatial locality
- ◆ Lossy and lossless compression (with lossless decompression available naturally through all types of progression)
- ◆ Random (spatial) access to the bitstream
- ◆ Pan and zoom (with decompression of only a subset of the compressed data)
- ◆ Compressed domain processing (e. g. , rotation and cropping)
- ◆ Region of interest coding by progression
- ◆ Limited memory implementations.

The JPEG-2000 project was motivated by Ricoh's submission of the CREW algorithm to an earlier standardization effort for lossless and near-lossless compression (now known as JPEG-LS). Although LOCO-I was ultimately selected as the basis for JPEG-LS, it was recognized that CREW provided a rich set of features worthy of a new standardization effort. Based on a proposal authored largely by Martin Boliek, JPEG-2000 was approved as a new work item in 1996, and Boliek was named as the project editor. Also in 1996, Dr. Daniel Lee of Hewlett-Packard was named as the Convener of ISO/IEC JTC1/SC29/WG1 (the Working Group charged with the development of JPEG- 2000, hereinafter referred to as simply WG1).

2. The JPEG-2000 Development Process

A Call for Technical Contributions was issued in March 1997, requesting compression technologies be submitted to an evaluation during the November 1997 WG1 meeting in Sydney, Australia. Further, WG1 released a CD-ROM containing 40 test images to be processed and submitted for evaluation. For the evaluations, it was stipulated that compressed bitstreams and decompressed imagery be submitted for six different bitrates [ranging from 0. 0625 to 2. 0 bits per pixel (bpp)] and for lossless encoding. Eastman Kodak computed quantitative metrics for all images and bit rates, and conducted a subjective evaluation of 18 of the images (of various modalities) at three bitrates in Sydney using evaluators from among the WG1 meeting attendees. The imagery from 24 algorithms was evaluated by ranking the perceived image quality of hard-copy prints.

Although the performance of the top third of the submitted algorithms were statistically close in the Sydney evaluation, the wavelet/trellis coded quantization (WTCQ) algorithm, submitted by SAIC and the University of Arizona (SAIC/UA), ranked first overall in both the subjective and objective evaluations. In the subjective evaluation, WTCQ ranked first (averaged over the entire set of evaluated imagery) at 0. 25 and 0. 125 bpp, and second at 0. 0625 bpp. In terms of RMS error averaged over all images, WTCQ ranked first at each of the six bitrates. Based on these results, WTCQ was selected as the reference JPEG-2000 algorithm at the conclusion of the meeting. It was further decided that a series of "core experiments" would be conducted to evaluate WTCQ and other techniques in terms of the JPEG-2000 desired features and in terms of algorithm complexity.

Results from the first round of core experiments were presented at the March 1998 WG1 meeting in Geneva. Based on these experiments, it was decided to create a JPEG-2000 "Verification Model" (VM) which would lead to a reference implementation of JPEG-2000. The VM would be the software in which future rounds of core experiments would be conducted, and the VM would be updated after each JPEG-2000 meeting based on the results of core experiments. SAIC was appointed to develop and maintain the VM software with Michael Marcellin as the head of the VM Ad Hoc Group. Eric Majani (Canon-France) and Charis Christopoulos (Ericsson-Sweden) were also named as co-editors of the standard at that time. Results from round 1 core experiments were selected to modify WTCQ into the first release of the VM (VM 0).

3.   JPEG-2000 Coding Engine

3.1   Tiles and Component Transforms

In what follows, we provide a description of the JPEG-2000 coding engine. Our goal is to illuminate the key concepts at a sufficient level to impart a fundamental understanding of the algorithm without dwelling too much on details. In the standard, an image can consist of multiple components (e.g., RGB) each possibly subsampled by a different factor. Conceptually, the first algorithmic step is to divide the image into rectangular, non-overlapping tiles on a regular grid. Arbitrary tile sizes are allowed, up to and including the entire image (i.e., no tiles). Components with different subsampling factors are tiled with respect to a high resolution grid, which ensures spatial consistency of the resulting tile-components. Each tile of a component must be of the same size, with the exception of tiles around the border (all four sides) of the image.

When encoding an image having multiple components such as RGB, a point-wise decorrelating transform may be applied across the components. Two transforms are defined in Part I of the standard: 1) the YCrCb transform commonly used with original JPEG images, and 2) the Reversible Component Transform (RCT) which provides similar decorrelation, but allows lossless reconstruction of all components. After this transform all components are treated independently (although different quantization is possible with each component, as well as joint rate allocation across components). For the sake of simplicity, we now describe the JPEG-2000 algorithm with respect to a single tile of a single component (e.g., gray level) image.

3.2   Partitions, Transforms, and Quantization

Given a tile, an L-level dyadic (pyramidal) wavelet transform is performed using either the (9, 7) floating point wavelet, or the (5, 3) integer wavelet. Progression is possible with either wavelet but the (5, 3) must be used if it is desired to progress to a lossless representation. Although we describe the algorithm here in terms of processing on an entire tile, more memory efficient implementations are possible using sliding window or block-based transform techniques.

From an L-level transform it is natural to reconstruct images at L + 1 different "sizes," or "resolutions." We refer to the lowest frequency subband (LFS) as resolution 0, and the original image as resolution L. The LFS is also referred to as the resolutionlevel 0 subband. The three subbands needed to augment resolution j into resolution j + 1 are referred to collectively as "resolution-level j + 1" subbands.

After transformation, all wavelet coefficients are subjected to uniform scalar quantization employing a fixed dead-zone about the origin. This is accomplished by dividing the magnitude of each coefficient by a quantization step size and rounding down. One quantization step size is allowed per subband. These step sizes can be chosen in a way to achieve a given level of "quality" (as in many implementations of JPEG), or perhaps in some iterative fashion, to achieve a fixed rate. The default behavior of the VM is to quantize each coefficient rather finely, and rely on subsequent truncation of embedded bitstreams to achieve precise rate control. The standard places no requirement on the method used to select quantization step sizes. When the integer wavelet transform is employed, the quantization step size is essentially set to 1.0 (i. e., no quantization). In this case, precise rate control (or even fixed quality) is achieved through truncation of embedded bitstreams.

After quantization, each subband is subjected to a "packet partition." This packet partition divides each subband into regular non-overlapping rectangles. Three spatially consistent rectangles (one from each subband at a given resolution level) comprise a packet partition location. The packet partition provides a medium-grain level of spatial locality in the bitstream for the purpose of memory efficient implementations, streaming, and (spatial) random access to the bitstream, at a finer granularity than that provided by tiles. Finally, code-blocks are obtained by dividing each packet partition location into regular non-overlapping rectangles. The code-blocks are then the fundamental entities for the purpose of entropy coding.

To recap, an image is divided into tiles and each tile is transformed. The subbands (of a tile) are divided into packet partition locations. Finally, each packet partition location is divided into code-blocks. This situation is illustrated in Figure 12. 4. 1. This figure depicts a packet partition of

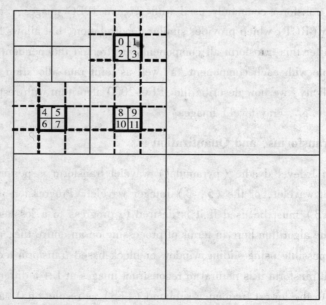

Figure 12. 4. 1 Twelve code-blocks of one packet partition location at
resolution level 2 of a 3-level dyadic wavelet transform.
The packet partition location is emphasized by heavy lines.

the subbands at resolution level 2 (of a 3-level dyadic wavelet transform of one tile). Also shown is the division of one packet partition location into twelve code-blocks.

3.3 Block Coding

Entropy coding is performed independently on each code-block. This coding is carried out as context-dependent, binary, arithmetic coding of bitplanes. Consider a quantized code-block to be an array of integers in sign-magnitude representation, then consider a sequence of binary arrays with one bit from each coefficient. The first such array contains the most significant bit (MSB) of all the magnitudes. The second array contains the next MSB of all the magnitudes, continuing in this fashion until the final array which consists of the least significant bits of all the magnitudes. These binary arrays are referred to as bitplanes.

The number of bitplanes in a given code-block (starting from the MSB) which are identically zero is signaled as side information, as described later. So, starting from the first bitplane having at least a single 1, each bitplane is encoded in three passes (referred to as sub-bitplanes). The scan pattern followed for the coding of bitplanes, within each code-block (in all subbands), is shown in Figure 12.4.2. This scan pattern is basically a column-wise raster within stripes of height four. At the end of each stripe, scanning continues at the beginning (top-left) of the next stripe, until an entire bitplane (of a codeblock) has been scanned.

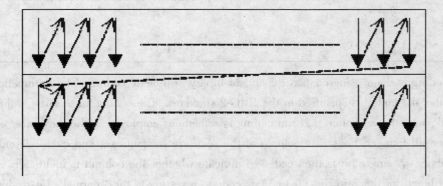

Figure 12.4.2 Scan pattern for bitplane coding

The prescribed scan is followed in each of the three coding passes. The decision as to which pass a given bit is coded in is made based on the "significance" of that bit's location and the significance of neighboring locations. A location is considered significant if a 1 has been coded for that location (quantized coefficient) in the current or previous bitplanes.

The first pass in a new bitplane is called the significance propagation pass. A bit is coded in this pass if its location is not significant, but at least one of its eight-connected neighbors is significant. If a bit is coded in this pass, and the value of that bit is 1, its location is marked as significant for the purpose of coding subsequent bits in the current and subsequent bitplanes. Also, the sign bit is coded immediately after the 1 bit just coded. The second pass is the magnitude refinement pass. In this pass, all bits from locations that became significant in a previous bitplane are coded. The third and final pass is the clean-up pass, which takes care of any bits not coded in the first two passes.

Table 12.4.1 shows an example of the coding order for the quantized coefficients of one 4-sample column in the scan. This example assumes all neighbors not included in the table are identically zero, and indicates in which pass each bit is coded. As mentioned above, the sign bit is coded after the initial 1 bit and is indicated in the table by the + or − sign. Note that the very first pass in a new block is always a clean-up pass because there can be no predicted significant, or refinement bits.

Table 12.4.1　Example of sub-bitplane coding order

Coding pass	Coefficient value			
	10	1	3	−7
Clean-up	1 +	0	0	0
Significance		0		
Refinement	0			
Clean-up			0	1 −
Significance		0	1 +	
Refinement	1			1
Clean-up				
Significance		1 +		
Refinement	0		1	1
Clean-up				

All coding is done using context dependent binary arithmetic coding. The arithmetic coder employed is the MQ-coder as specified in the JBIG-2 standard. The coding for the first and third passes is identical, with the exception that run coding is sometimes employed in the third pass. Run coding occurs when all four locations in a column of the scan are insignificant and each has only insignificant neighbors. A single bit is then coded to indicate whether the column is identically zero or not. If not, the length of the zero run (0 to 3) is coded, reverting to the "normal" bit-by-bit coding for the location immediately following the 1 that terminated the zero run. The sign and magnitude refinement bits are also coded using contexts designed specifically for that purpose.

For brevity, the computation to determine each context is not included here. However, unlike JBIG or JBIG-2 which use thousands of contexts, JPEG-2000 uses no more than nine contexts to code any given type of bit (i.e., significance, refinement, etc.).

This allows extremely rapid probability adaptation and decreases the cost of independently coded segments. Before leaving this section, we mention a few issues regarding the arithmetic coding. The context models are always reinitialized at the beginning of each code-block.

Similarly, the arithmetic codeword is always terminated at the end of each code-block (i.e., once, at the end of the last sub-bitplane). The best performance is obtained when these are the only reinitializations/terminations. It is allowable however, to reset/terminate at the beginning/end of every sub-bitplane within a code-block. This frequent reset/termination, plus optionally restricting context formation to include data from only the current and previous "scan-stripes" is sufficient to enable parallel encoding of all sub-bitplanes within a code-block (of course, parallel encoding of the code-blocks themselves is always possible). Reset/termination strategies can also impact the error resilience of the decoder. Finally, "selective arithmetic coder bypass" can be used to significantly reduce the number of symbols arithmetically coded. In this mode, the third coding pass of every bitplane employs arithmetic coding, as before. However, after the fourth bitplane is coded, the first and second passes are included as raw (uncompressed) data. For natural imagery, all of these modifications produce a surprisingly small loss in compression efficiency. For other imagery types (graphics, compound documents, etc.) significant losses can be observed.

3.4　Packets and Layers

The compressed bitstreams associated with some number of sub-bitplanes from each code-block in a packet partition location are collected together to form the body of a "packet." The body of a packet is preceded by a packet header. The packet header contains: block inclusion information for each block in the packet (some blocks will have no coded data in any given packet); the number of completely zero bitplanes for each block; the number of sub-bitplanes included for each code-block; and the number of bytes used to store the coded sub-bitplanes of each block. It should be noted that the header information is coded in an efficient and embedded manner itself. The data contained in a packet header supplements data obtained from previous packet headers (within the same packet partition location) in a way to just enable decoding of the current packet. A discussion of this process is beyond the scope of this paper.

Figure 12.4.3 depicts one packet for the packet partition location illustrated in Figure 12.4.1. Note that each of the twelve code-blocks can contribute a different number of subbitplanes (possibly zero) to the packet, and empty packet bodies are allowed.

Packet Header	n_0 sub-bitplanse form code-block 0	n_1 sub-bitplanse form code-block 1	--------------	n_{11} sub-bitplanse form code-block 11

Figure 12.4.3　The composition of one packet for the packet partition location of Figure 12.4.1

A packet can be interpreted as one quality increment for one resolution level at one spatial location (packet partition locations correspond roughly to spatial locations). A "layer" is then a collection of packets: one from each packet partition location of each resolution level. A layer then can be interpreted as one quality increment for the entire image at full resolution.

As noted above, there is no restriction on the number of sub-bitplanes contributed by each code-block to a given packet (layer). Thus, an encoder can format packets for a variety of purposes. For instance, consider the case when progression and the features provided by the packet partition are not of interest. The packet partitions can be set larger than the subbands (turned off), and all sub-bitplanes from all blocks can be included in a single packet per resolution layer. This provides the most efficient compression performance, as the packet header information is minimized under this scenario.

On the other hand, if progression by quality (embedding) is desired, a very small number of sub-bitplanes can be included in each packet. The current VM supports a generic scalable setting which includes approximately 50 layers. In this case, on average, less than 1 sub-bitplane per code-block contribute to each packet. The strategy employed by the VM (many others are possible) to form packets in the 50 layer case is based on rate distortion theory. Each packet is constructed to include all sub-bitplanes with (estimated) rate-distortion slope above a given threshold. This threshold is adjusted to achieve the desired size (bit-rate) for the aggregate of all packets within the layer under construction. This provides very fine-grained quality (rate) progression at the expense of some additional overhead due to the (numerous) packet headers. Nevertheless, the VM provides state-of-the-art compression performance even with 50 layers.

Exercises

Ⅰ. Fill in the following blanks with proper words or phrases:

1. The two most commonly used representations are 8-bit greyscale and _____. 8-bit greyscale contains 256 shades of grey ($2^8 = 256$) with 0 normally denoting _____ and 255 denoting _____, with other values representing _____ of grey.

2. Simply put, images are stored as collections of _____, each of which is assigned a color.

3. Of course, in image processing and machine vision, while increased _____ allows for greater detail and more information to work with, it comes at the price of _____ and _____.

4. If the image is considered a random variable of two dimensions, the area function is proportional to its _____ and the gray level _____ to its probability density function.

5. Now we can define _____ as subjecting a numerical representation of an object to a series of operations in order to obtain a desired result.

6. We first binarize the skin map by simple _____. We then implement morphological open/close operations to remove noise and connect _____. Small skin regions are considered insignificant and discarded.

7. We believe skin detection based solely on _____ of one image cannot do much more, so maybe some other sorts of information is needed to improve the _____ detection performance.

8. The output of skin detection is a grayscale skin map with the _____ being proportional to the skin probabilities.

9. Moreover, adult images tend to appear together and are surrounded by _____ in web pages, which could improve the performance of _____.

Ⅱ. Answer the following questions:

1. What is the basic element of an image?

2. Briefly describe the relationship between the image resolution and its storage space and com-

puting speed.

3. Describe the difference between the histogram of a gray image and of a RGB color image.

4. Which part of an image could provide an effective way to detect the adult image content?

5. Describe the function of the Global Fit Ellipse (GFE) and the Local Fit Ellipse (LFE) in the second essay.

6. In your opinion, besides the color information, which features of an image could improve the efficiency of adult image detection?

7. Please give a brief summary of the adult image detection procedure.

Chapter Thirteen   Management Information System

Unit 1   Data Warehouse

A **data warehouse** is a computer system designed for **archiving** and analyzing an organization's historical data, such as sales, salaries, or other information from day-to-day operations. Normally, an organization copies information from its operational systems (such as sales and human resources) to the data warehouse on a regular schedule, such as every night or every weekend; after that, management can perform complex queries and analysis (such as data mining) on the information without slowing down the operational systems.

1. Definition

A data warehouse is the main repository of the organization's historical data, or its corporate memory. For example, an organization would use the information that's stored in its data warehouse to find out what day of the week they sold the most widgets in May 1992, or how employee sick leave the week before Christmas differed between California and Quebec from 2001 to 2005. In other words, the data warehouse contains the raw material for management's decision support system.

While operational systems are optimized for simplicity and speed of modification (online transaction processing, or OLTP) through heavy use of database **normalization** and an **entity-relationship model**, the data warehouse is optimized for reporting and analysis (online analytical processing, or OLAP). Frequently data in data warehouses is heavily **denormalized**, summarized and/or stored in a dimension-based model but this is not always required to achieve acceptable query response times.

More formally, Bill Inmon (one of the earliest and most influential practitioners) defined a data warehouse as follows:

- ◆ Subject-oriented, meaning that the data in the database is organized so that all the data elements relating to the same real-world event or object are linked together;
- ◆ Time-variant, meaning that the changes to the data in the database are tracked and recorded so that reports can be produced showing changes over time;
- ◆ Non-volatile, meaning that data in the database is never over-written or deleted, but retained for future reporting;
- ◆ Integrated, meaning that the database contains data from most or all of an organization's operational applications, and that this data is made consistent.

2. History of Data Warehousing

Data warehouses became a distinct type of computer database during the late 1980s and early 1990s. They developed to meet a growing demand for management information and analysis that could not be met by operational systems. Operational systems were unable to meet this need for a range of reasons:

- ◆ The processing load of reporting reduced the response time of the operational systems,
- ◆ The database designs of operational systems were not optimized for information analysis and reporting,
- ◆ Most organizations had more than one operational system, so company-wide reporting could not be supported from a single system, and
- ◆ Development of reports in operational systems often required writing specific computer programs which was slow and expensive.

As a result, separate computer databases began to be built that were specifically designed to support management information and analysis purposes. These data warehouses were able to bring in data from a range of different data sources, such as mainframe computers, minicomputers, as well as personal computers and office automation software such as spreadsheet, and integrate this information in a single place. [1] This capability, coupled with user-friendly reporting tools and freedom from operational impacts, has led to a growth of this type of computer system.

As technology improved (lower cost for more performance) and user requirements increased (faster data load cycle times and more features), data warehouses have evolved through several fundamental stages:

- ◆ Offline Operational Databases—Data warehouses in this initial stage are developed by simply copying the database of an operational system to an off-line server where the processing load of reporting does not impact on the operational system's performance.
- ◆ Offline Data Warehouse—Data warehouses in this stage of evolution are updated on a regular time cycle (usually daily, weekly or monthly) from the operational systems and the data is stored in an integrated reporting-oriented data structure.
- ◆ Real Time Data Warehouse—Data warehouses at this stage are updated on a transaction or event basis, every time an operational system performs a transaction (e. g. an order or a delivery or a booking etc.).
- ◆ Integrated Data Warehouse—Data warehouses at this stage are used to generate activity or transactions that are passed back into the operational systems for use in the daily activity of the organization. [2]

3. Components of a Data Warehouse

The primary components of the majority of data warehouses are shown in the attached diagram and described in more detail below.

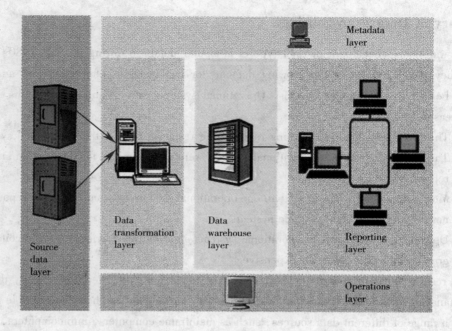

Figure 13. 1. 1   Primary components of data warehouse

3. 1   Data Sources

Data sources refer to any electronic repository of information that contains data of interest for management use or analytics. This definition covers mainframe databases (e. g. IBM DB2), client-server databases (e. g. Oracle database, Microsoft SQL Server, etc.), PC databases (e. g. Microsoft Access), spreadsheets (e. g. Microsoft Excel) and any other electronic store of data. Data needs to be passed from these systems to the data warehouse either on a transaction-by-transaction basis for real-time data warehouses or on a regular cycle (e. g. daily or weekly) for offline data warehouses.

3. 2   Data Transformation Layer

The data transformation layer is the subsystem concerned with extraction of data from the data sources, transformation from the source format and structure into the target (data warehouse) format and structure, and loading into the data warehouse.

3. 3   Data Warehouse Layer

The data warehouse is normally a relational database. It must be organized to hold information in a structure that best supports not only query and reporting, but also advanced analysis techniques, like data mining. Most data warehouses hold information for at least 1 year and sometimes can reach half century, depending on the business/operations data retention requirement. As a result these databases can become very large.

3. 4　Reporting Layer

The data in the data warehouse must be available to the organization's staff if the data warehouse is to be useful. There are a very large number of software applications that perform this function, or reporting can be custom-developed. Examples of types of reporting tools include:

♦ **Business intelligence tools**: These are software applications that simplify the process of development and production of business reports based on data warehouse data.

♦ **Executive information systems**: These are software applications that are used to display complex business metrics and information in a graphical way to allow rapid understanding.

♦ **OLAP tools**: OLAP tools form data into logical multi-dimensional structures and allow users to select which dimensions to view data by.

♦ **Data mining**: Data mining tools are software that allows users to perform detailed mathematical and statistical calculations on detailed data warehouse data to detect trends, identify patterns and analyze data.

3. 5　Metadata Layer

Metadata, or "data about data", is used not only to inform operators and users of the data warehouse about its status and the information held within the data warehouse, but also as a means of integration of incoming data and a tool to update and refine the underlying DW model.

Examples of data warehouse metadata include table and column names, their detailed descriptions, their connection to business meaningful names, the most recent data load date, the business meaning of a data item and the number of users that are logged in currently.

3. 6　Operations Layer

Data warehouse operations are comprised of the processes of loading, manipulating and extracting data from the data warehouse. Operations also cover user management, security, capacity management and related functions

3. 7　Optional Components

In addition, the following components exist in some data warehouses:

1) **Dependent data marts**: A dependent **data mart** is a physical database (either on the same hardware as the data warehouse or on a separate hardware platform) that receives all its information from the data warehouse. The purpose of a data mart is to provide a sub-set of the data warehouse's data for a specific purpose or to a specific sub-group of the organization. A data mart is exactly like a data warehouse technically, but it serves a different business purpose: it either holds information for only part of a company (such as a division), or it holds a small selection of information for the entire company (to support extra analysis without slowing down the main system). In either case, however, it is not the organization's official repository, the way a data warehouse is.

2) **Logical data marts**: A logical data mart is a filtered view of the main data warehouse but

does not physically exist as a separate data copy. This approach to data marts delivers the same benefits but has the additional advantages of not requiring additional (costly) disk space and it is always as current with data as the main data warehouse. The downside is that Logical Data Marts can have slower response times than physicalized ones.

3) **Operational data store**: An ODS is an integrated database of operational data. Its sources include legacy systems, and it contains current or near-term data. An ODS may contain 30 to 60 days of information, while a data warehouse typically contains years of data. ODSs are used in some data warehouse architectures to provide near-real-time reporting capability in the event that the Data Warehouse's loading time or architecture prevents it from being able to provide near-real-time reporting capability.

4. Advantages of Using Data Warehouse

There are many advantages to using a data warehouse, some of them are:

- ◆ Enhances end-user access to a wide variety of data.
- ◆ Business decision makers can obtain various kinds of trend reports e. g. the item with the most sales in a particular area / country for the last two years. This may be helpful for future investments in a particular item.
- ◆ Increases data consistency.
- ◆ Increases productivity and decreases computing costs.
- ◆ Is able to combine data from different sources, in one place.
- ◆ It provides an infrastructure with the capability to support changes to data and to replicate the changed data back into the operational systems.

Key Words

data warehouse	数据仓库
archive	v. 收集归档
normalization	n. 规范化
entity-relationship model	实体联系模型，又称为 ER 模型
denormalize	v. 反规范化
metadata	n. 元数据
data mart	数据集市

Notes

1. These data warehouses were able to bring in data from a range of different data sources, such as mainframe computers, minicomputers, as well as personal computers and office automation software such as spreadsheet, and integrate this information in a single place.

这些数据仓库可以从一定范围的数据源（例如大型计算机、微型计算机以及个人计算机和办公自动化软件，如电子表格）中获取数据，并将这些信息集中在一起。

2. Data warehouses at this stage are used to generate activity or transactions that are passed back into the operational systems for use in the daily activity of the organization.

在此时期，数据仓库被用来生成动作或事务并传递回业务系统中，用于企业的日常工作中。

Unit 2　Data Mining

Data mining consists of finding interesting trends or patterns in large datasets, in order to guide decision about future activities. There is a general expectation that data mining tools should be able to identify these patterns in the data with minimal user input. The patterns identified by such tools can give a data analyst useful and unexpected insights that can be more carefully investigated subsequently, perhaps using other decision support tools.

1. What Is Data Mining?

Data mining differs from and complements other business intelligence products—query and reporting, Online Analytical Processing (OLAP), and statistical tools. Query and reporting, OLAP, and statistical tools are good at allowing the user to **drill down** and understand what has happened in the past. With these tools, if you know what you are looking for, have a good analytical tool, are a good analyst, and have a lot of time, you should be able to eventually find the information you seek. Data mining is used to discover hidden patterns and relationships in your data in order to help you make better business decisions. [1]

Data mining is related to the subarea of statistics called exploratory data analysis, which has similar goals and relies on statistical measures. It is also closely related to the subareas of artificial intelligence called **knowledge discovery** and **machine learning**. The important distinguishing characteristic of data mining is that the volume of data is very large; although ideas from these related areas of study are applicable to data mining problems, **scalability** with respect to data size is an important new criterion. An algorithm is scalable if the running time grows (linearly) in proportion to the dataset size, given the available system resources (e. g. , amount of main memory and disk). Old algorithms must be adapted or new algorithms must be developed to ensure scalability.

Finding useful trends in databsets is a rather loose definition of data mining: In a certain sense, all database queries can be thought of as doing just this. Indeed, we have a continuum of analysis and exploration tools with SQL queries at one end, OLAP queries in the middle, and data mining techniques at the other end. SQL queries are constructed using **relational algebra** (with some extensions); OLAP provides higher-level querying idioms based on the multidimensional data model; and data mining provides the most abstract analysis operations. We can think of different data mining tasks as complex "queries" specified at a high level, with a few parameters that are user-definable, and for which specialized algorithms are implemented.

In the real world, data mining is much more than simply applying one of these algorithms. Data is often noisy or incomplete and unless this is understood and corrected for, it is likely that many interesting patterns will be missed and the reliability of detected patterns will be low. [2] Further, the analyst must decide what kinds of mining algorithms are called for, apply them to a well-chosen subset of data samples and variables (i. e. **tuples** and attributes), digest the results, apply other decision support and mining tools and iterate the process.

2. The Data Mining Process

To be effective in data mining, successful data analysts generally following a four step process:

Problem definition: This is the most important step and is where the domain expert decides the specifics of translating an abstract business objective e. g. "How can I sell more of my product to customers?" into a more **tangible** and useful data mining problem statement e. g. "Which customers are most likely to purchase product A?" To build a predictive model that predicts who is most likely to buy product A, we first must have data that describes the customers who have purchased product A in the past. Then we can begin to prepare the data for mining.

Data gathering and preparation: In this step, we take a closer look at our available data and determine what additional data we will need to address our business problem. We often begin by working with a reasonable sample of the data, e. g., hundred of records (rare, except in some life sciences cases) to many thousands or millions of cases (more typical for business-to-consumer cases). Some processing of the data to transform, for example, a "Date _ of _ Birth" field into "AGE" and to derive fields such as "Number _ of _ times _ Amount _ Exceeds _ 100" is performed to attempt the "tease the hidden information closer to the surface of the data" for easier mining.

Model building and evaluation: Once steps 1 and 2 have been properly completed, this step is where the data mining algorithms sift through the data to find patterns and to build predictive models. Generally, a data analyst will build several models and change mining parameters in an attempt to build the best or most useful models.

Knowledge deployment: Once data mining has found a useful model that adequately models the data, you want to distribute the new insights and predictions to others—managers, call center representatives, and executives. Data mining algorithms eliminate any need to move (rewrite) the models to the data in the database or to extract huge volumes of unscored records for scoring using a predictive model that resides outside of the database. Business intelligence applications built on data mining enabled platform automatically extract new information from your data and distribute it to where and when it is needed most.

Data mining is a huge subject in its own right, and it is clearly not possible to go into very much detail here. We therefore content ourselves by concluding with a brief description of how data mining techniques might apply to an extended version of suppliers and parts. First (in the absence of other resources for the information), we might use neural induction to classify suppliers by their

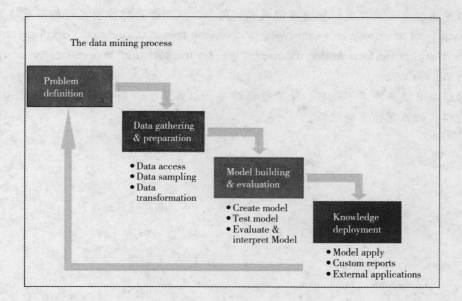

Figure 13. 2. 1   Data mining process

specialty (e. g. , fasteners vs. engine parts), and value prediction to predict which suppliers are most likely to be able to supply which parts. We might then use demographic clustering to associate shipping charges with geographic location, thereby assigning suppliers to shipping regions. Association discovery might then be used to discover that certain parts are generally obtained together in a single shipment; sequential pattern discovery to discover that shipments of fasteners are generally followed by shipments of engine parts; and similar time sequence discovery to discover that there are seasonal quantity changes in shipments of certain parts (some of those changes occurring in the fall and some in the spring).

Key Words

drill down	抽取，提取
knowledge discovery	知识发现
machine learning	机器学习
scalability	*n.* 扩展性，伸缩性
relational algebra	关系代数
tuple	*n.* 元组
tangible	*adj.* 实际的，有形的

Notes

1. Data mining is used to discover hidden patterns and relationships in your data in order to help you make better business decisions.

数据挖掘被用来发现数据中隐藏的模式和关系，从而帮助你作出更好的商业决策。

2. Data is often noisy or incomplete and unless this is understood and corrected for, it is likely that many interesting patterns will be missed and the reliability of detected patterns will be low.

数据经常有噪声或者不完整，除非被理解并加以修正，否则很多有用的模式会被遗漏，所发现的模式的可靠性也会很低。

Reading Material 1   Oracle Data Mining

Oracle Data Mining is powerful data mining software embedded in the Oracle Database that enables you to discover new insights hidden in your data. Oracle Data Mining helps businesses to target their best customers, find and prevent fraud, discover the most influential attributes that affect Key Performance Indicators (KPIs), and find valuable new information hidden in the data. Oracle Data Mining helps technical professionals find patterns in their data, identify key attributes, discover new clusters and associations, and uncover valuable insights.

With Oracle Data Mining, everything occurs in the Oracle Database—in a single, secure, scalable, platform for business intelligence. Oracle Data Mining represents a breakthrough in business intelligence. Oracle Data Mining moves the analytical functions into the database—with the data. Traditional alternatives force you to extract the data out of the database to separate, unsecured and costly dedicated statistical, analytical or mining servers.

Oracle Data Mining enables companies to:

◆ **KNOW MORE**—leverage your data and discover valuable new information and insights that were previously hidden.

◆ **DO MORE**—build applications that automate the extraction and dissemination of new information and insights.

◆ **SPEND LESS**—Oracle Data Mining is significantly less expensive compared to traditional approaches and, as a component of your investment in Oracle technology, significantly reduces your total cost of ownership.

Oracle Data Mining enables you to go beyond standard query and reporting tools and Online Analytical Processing (OLAP). Query and reporting and OLAP tools can tell you who are your top customers, what products have sold the most, and where you are incurring the highest costs. Oracle Data Mining helps you go beyond a manual search and query for information approach towards a new methodology where data mining automatically digs through your massive amounts of data to help you predict, understand, and develop new insights.

In today's competitive marketplace, companies must manage their most valuable assets—their data and the valuable information that lies hidden within it.

Moreover, they must exploit their data. If they don't, their competitors will beat them using new insights, discoveries, and strategies developed by extracting more information from their data. That's where Oracle Data Mining can help. Data mining can sift through massive amounts of data and find new information—valuable insights that can help you find patterns, make predictions, and discover new, previously hidden information.

With Oracle Data Mining, you can implement strategies to:

◆ Develop profiles of targeted, e. g. high value, customers;

◆ Anticipate and prevent customer attrition;

◆ Acquire new customers and identify the most profitable customers;

◆ Identify promising cross-sell opportunities;

◆ Detect noncompliant and fraudulent activities;

◆ Discover new clusters or segments;

◆ Find association relationships of co-occurring items and/or events;

◆ Mine unstructured data, that is, text.

Traditional business intelligence (BI) tools such as reports, interactive query and reporting only report on what has happened in the past. They report on historical sales figures, quantities, and "current status" values. Online Analytical Processing (OLAP) provides rapid drill-down for fast, more detailed information, roll ups, forecasting and trend analysis but usually only for averages, sums, trends, and group-by aggregates. None of these approaches can provide the deeper insights and views to the future like data mining. Data Mining sifts deeper into your data to discover information—patterns, factors, clusters, profiles, and predictions—that remain "hidden" in the data.

Oracle Data Mining uses machine-learning techniques developed in the last decade and doesn't suffer from the same limitations that traditional business intelligence (BI) tools do. Oracle Data Mining goes deep into the data and finds patterns from the data. Oracle Data Mining uses machine-learning algorithms to automatically sift through each record and attribute to uncover patterns and information that may have been hidden. Data mining goes beyond traditional business intelligence tools and analyzes the details of the past, for example, whether an individual purchased item "A". Data mining builds models and uses the models as predictors of the details in the future, for example, the likelihood that a customer will purchase "A" in the future. Data mining is good at providing detailed insights and making individual predictions, such as "Who is likely to buy a mutual fund in the next six months and why?"

Oracle Data Mining (ODM) allows you discover new insights, segments and associations, make more accurate predictions, find the variables that most influence your business, detect anomalies, and in general, extract more information from your data. For example, by analyzing the profiles of your best customers, ODM enables you to build data mining models and integrated applications to identify customers who are likely to become your best customers in the future. These customers may not represent your most valuable customers today, but may match profiles of your current best customers. Moreover, with ODM you can do more and transform a predictive model into a regular production application that distributes lists of your most promising customers to your sales force every Monday morning. Knowing the "strategic value" of your customers—which are likely to become profitable customers in the future and which are not, or predicting which customers are likely to churn or likely to respond to a marketing offer—and integrating this information into your operations is the key to proactively managing your business.

1. Overview of Oracle Data Mining's Algorithms

Oracle Data Mining allows companies to extract hidden information using a wide range of state-of-the-art algorithms. Data mining algorithms are machine-learning techniques for analyzing data for specific categories of problems. Different algorithms are good at different types of analysis. Oracle

Data Mining supports supervised learning techniques (classification, regression, and prediction problems), unsupervised learning techniques (clustering, associations, and feature selection problems), attribute importance techniques (find the key variables), text mining, and has a special algorithm for life sciences sequence searching and alignment problems.

Oracle Data Mining provides four supervised learning algorithms: Naïve Bayes (NB), Decision Trees, Adaptive Bayes Networks (ABN), and Support Vector Machines for Classifications and Predictions. For unsupervised learning, Oracle Data Mining provides five algorithms: Enhanced k-Means Clustering and Orthogonal Partitioning Clustering for finding naturally occurring groupings in the data, Anomaly Detection for finding rare or suspicious events, Association Rules for finding patterns of co-occurring events, and Nonnegative Matrix Factorization (NMF) for feature creation and reducing the number of attributes. Oracle Data Mining provides the Minimum Description Length (MDL) algorithm for Attribute Importance problems to identify the attributes most influential on a dependent field or attribute. Lastly, Oracle Data Mining includes the BLAST (Basic Local Alignment Search Technique) for searching genomic and proteomic data to find sequences that most closely match a specified sequence. Collectively, Oracle Data Mining's algorithms can address a broad range of business, technical, and scientific data mining problems.

2. Oracle Data Mining (ODM) Product

Oracle Data Mining (ODM), an option to Oracle Database 10g Enterprise Edition, enables companies to extract information efficiently from the very largest databases and build integrated business intelligence applications. Data analysts can find patterns and insights hidden in their data. Application developers can quickly automate the extraction and distribution of new business intelligence—predictions, patterns and discoveries—throughout the organization.

ODM supports functionality in Oracle Database 10g for the following data mining problems: classification, prediction, regression, clustering, associations, attribute importance, feature extraction and sequence similarity searches and analysis (BLAST). All model-building, scoring, and metadata management operations are accessed via the Oracle Data Mining Client and either a PL/SQL or Java-based API and occur entirely within the relational database.

With ODM, data mining and scoring functions reside natively in the Oracle Database—the data and data mining activities never leave the database. ODM embeds classification and regression, associations, and clustering models, attribute importance, feature selection, text mining, and sequence matching and alignment algorithms in the Oracle Database. ODM model building and model scoring functions are accessible through both Java and PL/SQL application programmer interfaces (APIs) and the Oracle Data Miner graphical user interface (GUI). The combination of Oracle Data Miner's GUI and ODM's PL/SQL and Java ODM APIs enable Oracle to provide an infrastructure for data analysts and application developers to integrate data mining seamlessly with database applications.

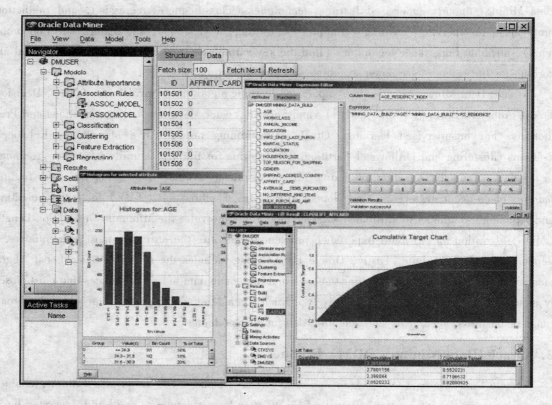

Figure 13. 3. 1   Oracle Data Mining client view

Reading Material 2   Steps Involved in Building a Data Warehouse

The goal of a data warehouse is to provide your company with an easy and quick look at its historical data. Advanced OLAP (on-line analytical processing) tools let DW users generate reports at a click of a mouse and look at the company's performance from various angles. How much data you need to examine depends on the nature of your business.

Suppose you have a manufacturing plant that produces thousands of parts per hour. The type of information you might be interested in includes the number of defects per hour or per day. Although you might want to examine the number of defective parts this year against the same number five years ago, such a ratio probably wouldn't provide the best picture of the company's performance. On the other hand, if you're in a car rental business, you might want to examine the number of customers this month against the same number six months ago. If you need to analyze the purchasing trends for customers with various demographic backgrounds, you might wish to examine data collected for a number of years. In short, if you need to make use of the data residing in some or all of your systems, you need to build a data warehouse.

1. Building a Data Warehouse

In general, building any data warehouse consists of the following steps:

1) Extracting the transactional data from the data sources into a staging area;

2) Transforming the transactional data;

3) Loading the transformed data into a dimensional database;

4) Building pre-calculated summary values to speed up report generation;

5) Building (or purchasing) a front-end reporting tool.

2. Extracting Transactional Data

A large part of building a DW is pulling data from various data sources and placing it in a central storage area. In fact, this can be the most difficult step to accomplish due to the reasons mentioned earlier: Most people who worked on the systems in place have moved on to other jobs. Even if they haven't left the company, you still have a lot of work to do: You need to figure out which database system to use for your staging area and how to pull data from various sources into that area.

Fortunately for many small to mid-size companies, Microsoft has come up with an excellent tool for data extraction. Data Transformation Services (DTS), which is part of Microsoft SQL Server 7. 0 and 2000, allows you to import and export data from any OLE DB or ODBC-compliant database as long as you have an appropriate provider. This tool is available at no extra cost when you purchase Microsoft SQL Server. The sad reality is that you won't always have an OLE DB or ODBC-compliant data source to work with, however. If not, you're bound to make a considerable investment of time and effort in writing a custom program that transfers data from the original source into the staging database.

3. Transforming Transactional Data

An equally important and challenging step after extracting is transforming and relating the data extracted from multiple sources. As I said earlier, your source systems were most likely built by many different IT professionals. Let's face it. Each person sees the world through their own eyes, so each solution is at least a bit different from the others. The data model of your mainframe system might be very different from the model of the client-server system.

Most companies have their data spread out in a number of various database management systems: MS Access, MS SQL Server, Oracle, Sybase, and so on. Many companies will also have much of their data in flat files, spreadsheets, mail systems and other types of data stores. When building a data warehouse, you need to relate data from all of these sources and build some type of a staging area that can handle data extracted from any of these source systems. After all the data is in the staging area, you have to massage it and give it a common shape. Prior to massaging data, you need to figure out a way to relate tables and columns of one system to the tables and columns coming from the other systems.

4. Creating a Dimensional Model

The third step in building a data warehouse is coming up with a dimensional model. Most modern transactional systems are built using the relational model. The relational database is highly normalized; when designing such a system, you try to get rid of repeating columns and make all columns dependent on the primary key of each table. The relational systems perform well in the On-Line Transaction Processing (OLTP) environment. On the other hand, they perform rather poorly in the reporting (and especially DW) environment, in which joining multiple huge tables just is not the best idea.

The relational format is not very efficient when it comes to building reports with summary and aggregate values. The dimensional approach, on the other hand, provides a way to improve query performance without affecting data integrity. However, the query performance improvement comes with a storage space penalty; a dimensional database will generally take up much more space than its relational counterpart. These days, storage space is fairly inexpensive, and most companies can afford large hard disks with a minimal effort.

The dimensional model consists of the fact and dimension tables. The fact tables consist of foreign keys to each dimension table, as well as measures. The measures are a factual representation of how well (or how poorly) your business is doing (for instance, the number of parts produced per hour or the number of cars rented per day). Dimensions, on the other hand, are what your business users expect in the reports—the details about the measures. For example, the time dimension tells the user that 2,000 parts were produced between 7 a.m. and 7 p.m. on the specific day; the plant dimension specifies that these parts were produced by the Northern plant.

Just like any modeling exercise the dimensional modeling is not to be taken lightly. Figuring out the needed dimensions is a matter of discussing the business requirements with your users over and over again. When you first talk to the users they have very minimal requirements: "Just give me those reports that show me how each portion of the company performs." Figuring out what "each portion of the company" means is your job as a DW architect. The company may consist of regions, each of which report to a different vice president of operations. Each region, on the other hand, might consist of areas, which in turn might consist of individual stores. Each store could have several departments. When the DW is complete, splitting the revenue among the regions won't be enough. That's when your users will demand more features and additional drill-down capabilities. Instead of waiting for that to happen, an architect should take proactive measures to get all the necessary requirements ahead of time.

It's also important to realize that not every field you import from each data source may fit into the dimensional model. Indeed, if you have a sequential key on a mainframe system, it won't have much meaning to your business users. Other columns might have had significance ago when the system was built. Since then, the management might have changed its mind about the relevance of such columns. So don't worry if all of the columns you imported are not part of your dimensional model.

5. Loading the Data

After you've built a dimensional model, it's time to populate it with the data in the staging database. This step only sounds trivial. It might involve combining several columns together or splitting one field into several columns. You might have to perform several lookups before calculating certain values for your dimensional model.

Keep in mind that such data transformations can be performed at either of the two stages: while extracting the data from their origins or while loading data into the dimensional model. I wouldn't recommend one way over the other—make a decision depending on the project. If your users need to be sure that they can extract all the data first, wait until all data is extracted prior to transforming it. If the dimensions are known prior to extraction, go on and transform the data while extracting it.

6. Generating Precalculated Summary Values

The next step is generating the precalculated summary values which are commonly referred to as aggregations. This step has been tremendously simplified by SQL Server Analysis Services (or OLAP Services, as it is referred to in SQL Server 7.0). After you have populated your dimensional database, SQL Server Analysis Services does all the aggregate generation work for you. However, remember that depending on the number of dimensions you have in your DW, building aggregations can take a long time. As a rule of thumb, the more dimensions you have, the more time it'll take to build aggregations. However, the size of each dimension also plays a significant role.

Prior to generating aggregations, you need to make an important choice about which dimensional model to use: ROLAP (Relational OLAP), MOLAP (Multidimensional OLAP), or HOLAP (Hybrid OLAP). The ROLAP model builds additional tables for storing the aggregates, but this takes much more storage space than a dimensional database, so be careful! The MOLAP model stores the aggregations as well as the data in multidimensional format, which is far more efficient than ROLAP. The HOLAP approach keeps the data in the relational format, but builds aggregations in multidimensional format, so it's a combination of ROLAP and MOLAP.

Regardless of which dimensional model you choose, ensure that SQL Server has as much memory as possible. Building aggregations is a memory-intensive operation, and the more memory you provide, the less time it will take to build aggregate values.

7. Building (or Purchasing) a Front-End Reporting Tool

After you've built the dimensional database and the aggregations you can decide how sophisticated your reporting tools need to be. If you just need the drill-down capabilities, and your users have Microsoft Office 2000 on their desktops, the Pivot Table Service of Microsoft Excel 2000 will do the job. If the reporting needs are more than what Excel can offer, you'll have to investigate the alternative of building or purchasing a reporting tool. The cost of building a custom reporting (and OLAP) tool will usually outweigh the purchase price of a third-party tool. That is not to say that OLAP tools are cheap (not in the least!).

There are several major vendors on the market that have top-notch analytical tools. In addition to the third-party tools, Microsoft has just released its own tool, Data Analyzer, which can be a cost-effective alternative. Consider purchasing one of these suites before delving into the process of developing your own software because reinventing the wheel is not always beneficial or affordable. Building OLAP tools is not a trivial exercise by any means.

Exercises

Ⅰ. Fill in the following blanks with proper words or phrases:

1. OLTP stands for _____.

2. OLAP stands for _____.

3. Data Mining consists of finding interesting _____ or _____ in large datasets, in order to guide decision about future activities.

4. Data warehouses are updated on a transaction or event basis, every time an operational system performs a transaction, we call it _____ Data warehouses.

5. Data mining process includes four steps: _____, _____, _____, and _____.

6. Data sampling is a sub-process of _____ in data mining process.

Ⅱ. Answer the following questions:

1. Give a brief definition of the term Data Warehouse.

2. List the requirement of data warehouse given by Bill Inmon.

3. What is the Offline Data Warehouse?

4. List the components of a data warehouse.

5. List the advantages of using a data warehouse in business.

6. What is data mining?

7. Give the distinguishing characteristic of data mining.

8. Briefly describe the function of the four steps of data mining process.

Chapter Fourteen   E-Commerce

Unit 1   Electronic Commerce

1. Basic Function of Electronic-Commerce Systems

Electronic commerce is coming of age. Retail on-line buying will be in the billions of dollars in 1998. Electronic sales in a recent quarter are double those of the entire previous year. In some instances, companies create electronic-commerce capabilities out of a fear of falling behind competitors or as a result of the general **momentum** to expand the use of an existing Internet presence. [1] But the primary value **proposition** is the prospect of increased revenue from new markets and creation of new, lower-cost, electronic-distribution channels.

Internet service providers (ISPs) are beginning to launch, or are at least evaluating, electronic-commerce hosting services. These services position the service provider as the outsourcer of the customers' electronic-commerce capabilities, managing the networking and server aspects of the initiative. [2]This allows the ISP's customers to concentrate on their core businesses and expands the relationship of the customer and the ISP. An ISP's ability to offer a rich electronic-commerce environment, on its own or in partnership with an electronic-business provider, will be important in differentiating high-value ISPs from lower-value, access-only ISPs.

1. 1   Customer's Perspective

From a customer's perspective, the purpose of an electronic-commerce system is to enable that customer to locate and purchase a desired good or service over the Internet when the customer is interested in making the purchase. Its function is no more or less than providing a virtual store.

1. 2   Merchant's Perspective

From a merchant's perspective, the key function of an electronic-commerce system is to generate higher revenues than the merchant would achieve without the system. In order for this to happen, the electronic-commerce system must recreate or utilize existing data and business processes. All of the same processes that the merchant must have in place to support an in-store or catalog purchase must also be in place for an electronic purchase: product information, inventory systems, customer service, and transaction capabilities (including credit authorization, tax computation, financial settlement, and shipping).

Additional functions of an electronic-commerce system, related to revenue generation, are to help redefine and enhance an enterprise's brand strength, customer-service capability, and supply-chain effectiveness. An electronic-commerce system is one of the areas of an enterprise's infrastructure that is open to customers via the Web, but it should be linked with other information technology (IT) systems that affect customer service (i. e. , inventory and billing).

1. 3 Basic Components

Provision of this basic system requires Internet access and an access device at the location of the home shopper, a Web-application server and electronic-commerce software (enabling catalog creation and transaction processing), security gateways to limit external access to internal data systems, and integration software to pull data from the appropriate support systems into the commerce environment (see Figure 14. 1. 1).

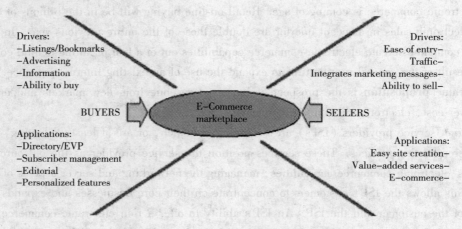

Figure 14. 1. 1　Electronic-commerce model

2. Hosted Electronic-Commerce Services: A Service Provider's Perspective

The benefits to the service provider of hosting electronic-commerce services include the following:

- ◆ hosting revenue for providing connectivity to electronic-commerce services
- ◆ enablement revenue for helping clients develop electronic-commerce offerings (Web sites, catalogs, storefronts) for the customer's hosted offering
- ◆ advertising revenue for aggregating traffic within hosted offerings
- ◆ transaction revenue for enabling on-line commerce

The value to a merchant (the service provider's customer) of an electronic-commerce costing service is that it enables the merchant to focus on its core business processes, leaving the service provider to manage the Internet access, network management, network security, quality of service, and server management. In this scenario, the home shopper still needs Internet access and an access device, but the service provider could provide any or all of the remaining components on behalf of the merchant.

It is important that the service provider provide a hosting infrastructure that can scale and maintain quality of service as the customers' requirements grow. The electronic-commerce platform chosen by the service provider must support a variety of tasks:

- the creation of a standard environment for storefronts and advertising sites
- the provision of a secure transaction environment
- the extraction and communication of orders
- the authorization of credit and clear payments
- the provision of site activity reports
- the provision of billing systems based on customer activity and advertising

In addition, the service provider's customers will look to it for a variety of enablement services: the creation of tools to build storefronts and advertisements; the documentation of the setup and site-building process; and the staging of the environment preliminary to production of the on-line hosting environment. [3]

The customer, the service provider, or a third party could be responsible for the creation and hosting of the customer's Web site, the creation and hosting of the catalog information, and the provision of systems-integration requirements for various information systems.

The service provider must also consider how it will expand its hosting capabilities to enable its customers to obtain the full value possible from an electronic-commerce environment, including links to customer service, inventory, and billing systems (see Figure 14.1.2 and Figure 14.1.3).

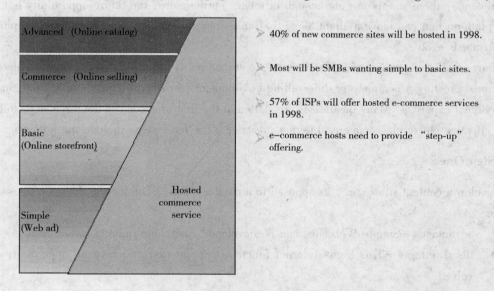

40% of new commerce sites will be hosted in 1998.

Most will be SMBs wanting simple to basic sites.

57% of ISPs will offer hosted e-commerce services in 1998.

e-commerce hosts need to provide "step-up" offering.

Figure 14.1.2   Hosted electronic-commerce model

3. Electronic-commerce Requirements

Enterprises, large or small, tend to develop their Web presence in stages. Once a Web presence is created, then the enterprise wants to use that site to enhance customer service and to produce revenue. It is at the latter stage that electronic-commerce comes into play.

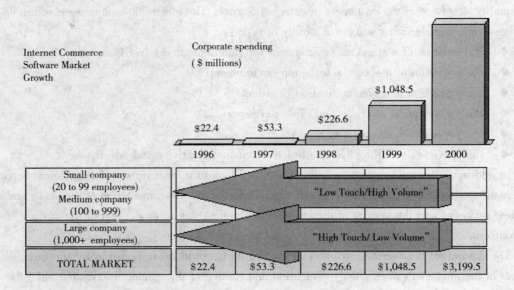

Figure 14. 1. 3   Electronic-commerce hosting strategy

A service provider's hosting customers will go through the same evolution described in the preceding module. It is not enough just to pick off the high-end client who represents the highest per-client revenue; there simply are not enough of them. Furthermore, the future opportunity is to provide a platform that can move a client along the range from low-to high-function as client sophistication and needs evolve.

Many small-and medium-sized businesses are struggling with the high cost of entry to electronic commerce. Creating a complete on-line selling environment can require considerable time, money, and technical expertise. Many businesses are stalled at the first or second of the three steps to building an effective electronic-commerce Internet presence. The three steps include the following.

3.1   Step One

Develop a content site (i. e. , as opposed to a database-driven catalog) and handle transactions off-line.

◆ advantages—Simple Web sites can be developed easily and quickly at low cost.

◆ disadvantages—This limits Internet function to promotion; no revenue opportunity is involved.

3.2   Step Two

Develop an on-line catalog and handle transactions off-line.

◆ advantages—No need for sophisticated technology is involved; the catalog can manage large product assortment.

◆ disadvantages—Catalog building adds expense, without the possibility of reducing expense through on-line transactions.

3.3 Step Three

Develop an on-line catalog and handle transactions on-line.

◆ advantages—This can manage large product assortment and complete sales at lower cost.

◆ disadvantages—Catalog building is expensive, and on-line transaction management requires sophisticated technology.

3.4 The Transaction Server

Service providers must provide a solution for businesses that do not have the budget or technical expertise to progress to Step Three by themselves. The transaction-server aspect of the electronic system enables electronic-directory publishers and ISPs to become full electronic-commerce providers, offering complete outsourcing of electronic transactions and security technology. It can include software for easy site creation, using templates and simple point-click-and-drag method, as well as commerce capability to complete sales for a large set of changing prices and items.

With an electronic commerce-transaction server, service providers can process transactions for multiple sellers from distributed content. Easy-to-use Web site-construction tools help nontechnical businesses create Web sites and catalog pages.

Service providers are likely to configure their offerings in any combination of the following models for their hosted clients on an electronic-commerce platform:

◆ **Single Web site**: The client owns a Web site on a shared Web server and could have a unique uniform resource locator (URL). There are no on-line transactions, but there is e-mail capability.

◆ **Single storefront**: The client owns a single store on a single merchant server at the host. The storefront has unique URL, database, and checkout process.

◆ **Mall**: The customer offers (or client contracts for) multiple storefronts in a mall environment on the same URL and database, with shared registration, shopping cart, checkout, etc.

◆ **Multihome**: Multiple single storefronts reside on one server, but each has its own URL, database, shopping and order forms, etc.

◆ **On-site content and transaction server**: Nondatabase storefronts are hosted in a multihome configuration with back-end transactions handled by a host merchant server. These selling Web sites are created with a buy button feature to enable product and transaction information to be sent to the separate (but same environment) host merchant server.

◆ **Off-site content and on-site transaction server**: Nondatabase storefronts are hosted outside the service provider-hosting environment. Back-end transactions are handled by the remote host-merchant server on the service-provider premises. These selling sites are created with a buy button feature to enable product and transaction information to be sent to the remote host merchant server.

4. Task Categories

For each of the hosted-commerce scenarios described in the previous module, there are certain tasks that accompany the creation and implementation of an electronic presence for a merchant. Some of these tasks could be performed by the merchant, some by the service provider, and some by a third party on behalf of the merchant or service provider.

- ◆ **Site setup and configuration**: planning, system architecture (single-server and distributed), installation, and configuration
- ◆ **Client enablement and support**: store setup, catalog maintenance, store maintenance, order management, shopper management, and reporting
- ◆ **Site administration and operation**: systems management, site maintenance, billing, reporting, and customer service and support
- ◆ **Back-end tasks**: payment processing, tax calculation, and order routing

5. Components of Hosted Electronic-Commerce Systems

Business customers building a transaction server-supported commerce site need a Web site-construction tool that is provided (or a wide variety of popular content-creation tools) to create Internet pages that incorporate the special buy button created by the transaction server-client tools.

5.1 Web-Site Hosting and Publishing

Once the Internet storefront is completed, the site can be published to any server the business customer prefers and the commerce-service provider allows. The commerce-service provider is ready to provide the seller with the on-line transaction functions.

5.2 Transaction Server

The transaction server handles credit-and debit-card transactions (using secure electronic standards technology) on behalf of the merchant and the end customer. It must contain a common payment application programming interface (API) that is used for all payment types and functions: receive, approve, deposit, and refund. The transaction server handles the necessary authorization requests and recording of the transaction and settlement of the transaction information with the merchant, the credit-card company, and the customer. The transaction server manages the payment process, from communicating with the consumer to drafts with the merchant's financial institution. Records of transactions must be maintained to facilitate reconciliation and reporting later. The transaction server should also contain a component to process digital certificates from an organization using certificate-authority software or follow-on security technologies. Multiple merchants can operate on a single transaction server.

6. Security Products and Services

SET, jointly developed by Visa and MasterCard, is the industry standard for secure electronic transactions. As an open multiparty standard protocol for conducting secure bank-card and debit-card payments over the Internet, SET provides message integrity, authentication of all financial data, and encryption of sensitive information.

Registration systems reduce the risk in electronic commerce by establishing trust through authentication and nonrepudiation using SET standards, which in turn drives cost efficiencies and opens new avenues for commerce.

7. Payment Systems

Payment systems require components placed at the end customer's location (home PC, etc.), the merchant's transaction-system location (whether on merchant premises or service provider environment), and the financial institution's location.

Consumers must know that their financial information is confidential; this is accomplished with electronic wallets or credit-card software at the consumer's end point. The consumer's credit information is sent to a transaction server that can accept a variety of electronic payments, just as a physical store can accept credit-or debit-card information. The transaction server also must manage the payment process, from communicating with the consumer to drafts with the financial institution. Financial institutions use gateways to decrypt sensitive information received from the merchant's transaction server about the consumer and manage transaction settlement for the merchant. The transaction server maintains detailed transaction payment information, enabling companies to handle **disputes**, **chargebacks**, or adjustments easily.

Key Words

momentum	n. 潮流；趋势
proposition	n. 命题；建议
dispute	n. 争论，争执
chargeback	n. 退款，返款

Notes

1. In some instances, companies create electronic-commerce capabilities out of a fear of falling behind competitors or as a result of the general momentum to expand the use of an existing Internet presence.

有些公司因为担心落后于竞争对手或是仅仅为了紧跟因特网普及应用的潮流，而具备了开展电子商务的能力。

2. These services position the service provider as the outsourcer of the customers electronic-commerce capabilities, managing the networking and server aspects of the initiative.

这些服务项目将服务商定位于顾客电子商务系统的承包商，主要管理与网络和服务器相关的初步（初始化）工作。

3. In addition, the service provider's customers will look to it for a variety of enablement services: the creation of tools to build storefronts and advertisements; the documentation of the setup and site-building process; and the staging of the environment preliminary to production of the on-line hosting environment.

并且，这些服务商的客户会寻求多种增值服务，比如，创建用于建立店面和广告的工具；站点设置和创建进程的文档归档处理；以及用于将产品正式发布到网络主机上之前所使用的环境。

Unit 2   Taking Payments Online: The 5 Elements of E-Commerce

No longer are Web sites static pages of information. The really successful ones are interactive devices that allow visitors to input data and accomplish tasks. One of the most common tasks that users complete is paying for something online, whether it's a product, a service or a bill. Consumers have gained enough trust in the Internet that putting a credit card number into an online form no longer **conjures up** thoughts of identity theft. This **hypothesis** is backed up by the fact that Internet sales continue to **soar** year after year.

To keep up with the trend, more and more companies are allowing their customers to make payments online. This type of transaction is called e-commerce and it has gained world-wide acceptance. When most people think of e-commerce, they think of a shopping cart. Anyone who has bought products online has experienced an online shopping cart, but there are many other forms of e-commerce. This list includes: paying for invoices online, filling medical prescriptions, making a donation through a Web site, and registering online for a conference. In fact, anytime you pay for something online you are committing an act of e-commerce.

If part of your business strategy includes collecting payments (and what business doesn't), then jumping in on the e-commerce boom is a good idea. You don't have to sell products online, but you should offer your customers a way to pay for your services through your Web site. This method of accepting payments has a few advantages.

◆ **Convenience for your customers**: Customers adapt quickly to things that are easy and chances are they'll pay you faster if you offer an online payment method.

◆ **Convenience for you**: By accepting payments online, you don't have to take a check to the bank and payments are generally deposited quicker.

◆ **Security**: Studies show that putting your credit card into a secure online form is less risky than giving out your card over the phone or in person.

◆ **Your competition is doing it**: Your competitors are probably offering it and it's a good business move to keep up with what the competition is doing.

◆ **It's cool**: E-commerce is a cool thing to offer. It lets your customers know that you're up to speed with technology and are committed to providing them with whatever convenient services this **newfangled** thing called the "Internet" allows.

Accepting payments online can be a daunting process. Many people don't know where to begin. The following section should help just a bit. My intent is to demystify the process, break it down into simple terms and get you on your way to taking advantage of this technology.

Whether you plan on setting up a shopping cart or accepting bill payment online, there are 5 elements that go into employing e-commerce in your business.

1. The Internet Merchant Account

Any business that wants to accept credit cards needs a merchant account. Most brick-and-mortar stores need a Retail Merchant Account. With this type of account, the card is presented at the time of check-out, swiped into a machine and the customer signs the receipt. Completing a financial transaction over the Web comes with a couple of challenges: the customer isn't actually present at the store and neither is their credit card. Because of this scenario, the card can't be physically swiped and the customer can't sign for their purchase. A Retail Merchant Account won't work in this situation, so in comes the Internet Merchant Account.

So how much does an Internet Merchant Account cost and where can you get one? As you probably can guess, the rates are wide ranging. Typically, the Internet Merchant Account will have a per-transaction cost (usually between $.10 and $.25) and you'll also be charged a percentage of the transaction (usually 2% – 3%).[1] Most Internet Merchant Account providers also charge a monthly minimum (usually $25 – $50) or an annual fee (usually $50 – $150) and some charge a one-time set-up fee (usually $50 – $150, but you can get this **waived** if you're really nice).

Internet Merchant Accounts can be obtained from many different sources. Most businesses that already accept credit cards can go through the provider that also handles their Retail Merchant Account. You can also call your bank and ask for one or you can go with an independent organization. Currently, a search for "Internet Merchant Account" on Google returns a little over 19 million results, most of which are providers.

2. The Payment Gateway Account

The Internet Merchant Account won't work without a Payment Gateway. The Payment Gateway provides the interface between your Web site and your merchant account. The Payment Gateway also provides e-mail receipts when orders are placed (both to the customer and to you) and they also ensure that the transaction is secured the entire way. Typically, you'll be able to log into your Payment Gateway Account and view sales reports, charge a credit card or bank account manually or give a refund.

Payment Gateway Accounts also come with a cost. Usually they charge per transaction (typically $.05 – $.25) and sometimes have a monthly minimum depending on your agreement. These charges are in addition to the fees that your merchant provider has.

Payment Gateway providers are less numerous than merchant account providers. Some of the big ones include:

- ◆ Authorize. Net
- ◆ Verisign
- ◆ Linkpoint

3. The Security Certificate (SSL Certificate)

If people are going to give you their credit card or bank account number over the Web, then your Web site has to be secure. A secure Web site not only reduces your liability, but portrays trust to your customers. A Web page itself is secured through an SSL (**secure socket layer**) Certificate. This certificate encrypts any data transmitted through your Web site. It also shows the customer that your Web site is secure by displaying a lock symbol in the browser and changing the **URL** from "http: //" to "https: //".

Security Certificates typically run somewhere between $150 and $300 per year and you can usually get discount pricing if you purchase a certificate for multiple years. Some of the major certificate providers include:

- ◆ Geotrust
- ◆ Verisign
- ◆ Thawte
- ◆ DigiCert

4. The Software

So far we've discussed the Internet Merchant Account, the Payment Gateway Account and the SSL Certificate. These different elements all work together behind the scenes to process and secure e-commerce transactions. What your customer will see when making a purchase online is the software. The software can range from an off-the-shelf shopping cart system to a custom programmed invoice payment form. [2]Included in the software is the actual online form that the customer puts their billing information into. Once the payment is submitted, the software sends the information on its way.

Pricing for any kind of e-commerce software is impossible to pin down. Some off-the-shelf shopping cart systems are free and others cost hundreds of thousands of dollars. Having your software custom programmed by a Web developer is usually more expensive than implementing a system that has already been developed. Generally, you can start with an **off-the-shelf** system and then have it customized to meet your specific requirements.

5. The Expertise

You could try to go it alone, but chances are you're going to want to find an expert that can help you piece all of the elements together. When looking for a consultant, take into consideration experience with e-commerce, references, the success of their clients and capabilities. Also, find someone that you trust and feel that you can develop a healthy working relationship with. After all, if your e-commerce application is successful, you'll be working with this person for a long time.

The cost of an e-commerce consultant is closely tied to the characteristics described above. Experts with more experience and more capabilities generally cost more. Expect to pay somewhere between $75/hour and $200/hour. When looking at your e-commerce endeavor as a whole, I always recommend putting together an overall budget and then finding an expert or development firm that can give you the most value for that budget.[3]

If you're ready to start selling products online or collecting payments online in any way, then you're ready to start taking advantage of an e-commerce system. Large or small, every e-commerce system requires the 5 elements described in this article. Put them all together correctly and you're ready to be an online success.

Key Words

conjure up	想起
hypothesis	*n.* 前提
soar	*v.* 猛增
newfangled	*adj.* 新奇的
waive	*v.* 取消
secure socket layer	SSL 协定（一种加密的通信协定，用在使用者与网络服务器之间）
URL	Uniform Resource Locator，统一资源定位器
off-the-shelf	adj. 现成的

Notes

1. Typically, the Internet Merchant Account will have a per-transaction cost (usually between $.10 and $.25) and you'll also be charged a percentage of the transaction (usually 2% −3%).

一般来说，网络商店账户的每笔业务都会被收取费用（通常在 0.1 美元到 0.25 美元之间），并且还会根据交易额收取一定比例的费用（通常在 2% 到 3% 之间）。

2. The software can range from an off-the-shelf shopping cart system to a custom programmed invoice payment form.

软件系统的范围从可直接购买（无须须制）的购物车系统到可由客户定制的订单付费表格。

3. When looking at your e-commerce endeavor as a whole, I always recommend putting together an overall budget and then finding an expert or development firm that can give you the most value for that budget.

当把电子商务各方面的计划当作一个整体来看时，我总是建议你先制定一个总预算，然后找到一个能用你的预算得到最大收益的专家或是系统开发商。

Reading Material 1   Seven Practical Trends in B2B Marketing

What's the latest thinking in B2B marketing? What techniques and trends are today's best practice B2B marketers using to drive more revenue and demonstrate accountability?

In this article, I'll share seven trends that are changing the practice of B2B marketing. I'll discuss key best practices you should have on your radar, as well as practical tips for how to take advantage of the trend to improve your performance.

1. Embrace Online Channels

The tradeshow must die—at least as a way for B2B companies to drive leads. The same dollars invested in webcasts, online demos, videos, and other online methods are more measurable and more effective. The same is true for other offline marketing methods. E-mail and RSS feeds have lower cost and higher engagement than most direct mail campaigns; mass advertising should be replaced with search engine marketing and online ads; and PR must change to include blogs and SEO optimization.

B2B marketers have been slower than B2C marketers to come around to this change. According to Forrester Research's Q2 2006 Business-To-Business Marketing Effectiveness Survey, 91% of B2B marketers still use trade tradeshows and 77% use print advertising, while only 59% are using search engine marketing. The good news is that Forrester also reports that over 60% of B2B marketers plan to increase spending on search marketing, 50% on webinars, and 40% on e-mail. At the same time, 20% plan to decrease spending on tradeshows and print advertising. As a result of this transformation, eMarketer's B2B Marketing Online report states that online ad spending for B2B companies will grow 24.6% in 2007, versus growth of only 4.4% for offline ad spending.

This is important because as B2B marketers embrace online channels, they will find it is easier to target prospects, build relationships, and measure the bottom-line impact of their activities. Forrester goes on to state that:

"By moving their marketing online, business-to-business (B2B) marketers will evolve from tactical demand generation to strategic ownership of the customer relationship, and they will regain their rightful place as the corporate head of customer experience, knowledge, and influence."

2. Landing Pages, Landing Pages, Landing Pages

The main reason B2B companies' use online advertising is to drive traffic to their website. But that only means they got a prospect to click. Once there, the marketer has just a few seconds to convince that prospect to stick around, read more, and perhaps share some contact information so the company can continue the dialog.

The best way to do this is with a landing page that ties directly to the ad the prospect clicked and makes a compelling offer. This can increase the number of prospects that take the action you want (i. e. convert) by 2X or more, compared with the all-to-common practice of taking the traffic to a home page or generic product information page. B2B marketers can raise conversion rates by another 40% or more by following best-practices. MarketingSherpa's excellent Landing Page Handbook shares some of these tips, including repeating the ad copy in the headline, stripping out site navigation, and reiterating the call to action in multiple places.

3. Test Everything—But Don't Over Test

The best B2B marketers test everything, and almost everything can be tested: offers, copy, headlines, forms, bids, colors, designs, lists, and more. Testing removes any debate about what works and what doesn't; testing lets your customers vote with their actions. Many marketers are surprised to find out that the winner of the test is not the one they would have picked before the test. Landing pages are one of the most valuable things to test. A division of Siemens USA found that testing on the home page improved conversions by 2.3% but testing on the landing page increased conversions by 115%!

Be careful not to overtest. This is especially a problem in the "high value, low volume" world of B2B marketing. A good rule of thumb is that you need at least 15-20 positive actions within a two week period for each item you want to test. (Some may argue you need more for complete statistical confidence, but 15-20 should be enough to make most B2B marketers comfortable.) For example, let's say you have an ad group with a set of keywords that collectively are searched 20,000 times a week. Assuming you get a 2% click-thru rate and a 5% conversion rate, you will get $20,000 \times 2\% \times 2$ weeks = 800 clicks and $800 \times 5\% = 40$ conversions in a two week period. With this volume, you can safely test up to $800/20 = 40$ different versions of your ad copy, and two versions of your landing page.

What this means is that B2B marketers can and should test many versions of their search ad copy and headlines, constantly experimenting to see what works best. Small changes in wording and call to action can make a big difference. At the same time, marketers who work with the lower volumes common to B2B must focus landing page tests on the highest impact pieces, typically the call to action and the form. This also means that high-end testing solutions may be overkill for many B2B marketers.

4. Practice Attention Marketing—and Make It Measurable

Customers today have become adept at tuning out unwanted marketing. Personally, I am in the business of marketing, and yet still I tune out as much marketing as I can. I use TiVo and haven't watched a TV ad in ages, scan right past the ads in my Economist and Entertainment Weekly, automatically recycle any direct mail I receive, and aggressively delete any e-mail I haven't explicitly asked to receive.

There are basically only two ways modern buyers learn about new products, brands, or services:

- ◆ They actively seek something out using a search engine
- ◆ They hear about it through word of mouth from a source they trust

B2B marketers can engage with modern buyers by practicing attention marketing. Here, I'll focus on the technique, commonly called Word of Mouth Marketing. This starts, of course, with having a good product that satisfies a need or want. It then means facilitating conversations between customers, prospects, partners, and influencers. According to the WOMMA (the Word of Mouth Marketing Association) B2B marketers should:

- Identify the members of their community who are most likely to share opinions,
- Seek out how, where, and when they share their opinions,
- Provide methods to make it easier to share opinions,
- Listen to the opinions and respond appropriately to everyone—the supporters, the detractors, and the neutrals.

Of course, don't fall into the trap of investing in community-based techniques without having a plan in place to measure the marketing impact on hard metrics like revenue and growth. This starts with having clear, defined objectives for your program. These can include raising your Net Promoter Score (which ties to growth), creating inbound links to raise organic rankings (which ties to traffic), or enhancing brand awareness (which ties to higher response rates). It can even include capturing customer feedback to influence the product roadmap—just make sure your organization understands marketing's contribution to that process.

5. Help Buyers Research Early in the Sales Cycle

Before the Internet, buyers got most of their information by talking directly with sales reps. As a result, it made sense for sales to engage with the customer early in the buying cycle.

Today, however, buyers use the Internet to research and get smart before they ever want to speak with a representative of your company. By the time they engage with sales, the buyer is more educated than ever before—perhaps even more educated than the sales rep.

In today's world, it is the B2B marketer's job to help educate the buyer in the early stages of the buying cycle. This can help frame the discussion and establish your company's brand as a trusted advisor that understands their problems and knows how to solve them. Doing this well means:

- Leveraging search engine marketing so customers who are seeking your information can find you;
- Creating compelling landing pages for each topic that prospects will want to research.

One final note: Make sure to balance the goal of capturing contact information with the fact that requiring a registration to get to the content can reduce conversions by 75% – 85%, increase bogus registrations, and prevent search engines from finding your content. One way to do this is to give content targeted to prospects early in the sales cycle without requiring registration, reserving registration for more educated buyers who are likely to be further along.

6. Manage Leads—Don't Generate Demand

Forrester recently published research titled "How Mature Is B2B Lead Management?" in which they claim that B2B marketers who shift their focus from "demand generation" to "lead management" are twice as productive.

As Kristin Zhivago points out, one reason for this is because the term "demand generation" implies an outdated mindset where the company is in control of the buying process. In reality, B2B buyers don't "demand" anything—though they do have needs—and few marketers cannot create demand, even with the most clever campaigns.

Even though today's customer controls the buying process, B2B marketers can still guide and assist customers as they move down the marketing funnel.

- ◆ Understand buyers to ensure your solution meets their needs.
- ◆ Help buyers understand that you offer a solution that may meet their needs (this can be a challenge since buyers don't want to be interrupted, so you need to practice attention marketing).
- ◆ Educate buyers about the space and your offerings in it, establishing your brand as a company that understands their problems and knows how to solve them.
- ◆ Understand when the customer has moved through the buying process and is ready to engage with sales.
- ◆ Pass the customer to the right sales channel at the right time. Be ready to recycle the customer back into marketing if necessary.

From the perspective of B2B marketing, these best practices have common names. Helping early-stage buyers find you is Lead Acquisition; educating buyers is Lead Nurturing; understanding when prospects are sales-ready is Lead Scoring; and delivering leads to the right sales channel at the right time is Lead Routing.

Together, Lead Acquisition, Lead Scoring, Lead Nurturing, and Lead Routing make up the discipline of Lead Management. As the Forrester report demonstrates, companies that excel at Lead Management increase the percent of marketing-generated leads that sales acts on, shorten sales cycles, and perhaps most importantly raise the number of marketing-generated leads that result in a sale (from an average of 4% to as high as 10%).

7. Lead Nurturing 101

So you've managed to get a potential customer to register on your landing page. Congratulations! What do you do now?

If you are like many companies, the prospect's information goes into an SFA system like salesforce. com and sales gets alerted about the new lead. The problem is that up to 95% of prospects on your website are not yet ready to talk with a sales representative, according to research by Brian Carroll. They are on your site to research your product and your industry. Some of those prospects may be truly unqualified, but as many of 70% of them will eventually buy a product from you—or your competitors.

So what should you do with those leads?

Giving a non-sales-ready lead to a sales person is a recipe for disaster. Imagine how the first call might go: "Jim, my name is Mike, and I'm your sales rep from Widgets R-Us. I saw you downloaded our whitepaper "10 Ways to Improve Profits through Widget Optimization" and I wanted to know if you have any questions. . . Oh, you haven't read it yet? That's OK. Do you mind if I ask you a few questions? Do you have a budget approved to buy widgets? Are you the decision maker? When do you expect to purchase a Widget solution? Oh, I see, you're just researching right now. OK, I'll call back next month. Bye! "

In this scenario, Mike is trained to ask for BANT criteria (Budget, Authority, Need, and Timing). Except for "Need", these questions are entirely inappropriate at this stage of Jim's buying process (and a little rude if Jim is a gatekeeper but not the final decision maker). As a result, Jim is left with a negative impression of the company.

At the same time, Mike is compensated for driving revenue this quarter, so this lead is useless to him and he's left with the general impression that marketing-generated leads are no good. As a result, he'll be more likely to ignore the next marketing lead he receives—which is why sales ignores up to 80% of all marketing-generated leads. (That's like throwing away 80% of your marketing budget!) Lastly, unless Widget's R-Us has a good process for recycling Jim back into marketing, Jim may never hear from the company again and will end up buying from a competitor.

Fortunately, there is a better way—lead nurturing. Lead nurturing starts by understanding that sales executives don't really care about leads. They want winnable opportunities in their pipeline. They care more about quality (defined as likely to drive revenue this or next quarter) than quantity. The implication is that leads should live in marketing, and that marketing should nurture leads until they are ready to become opportunities. Here is my definition: "Lead nurturing is the process of building a relationship by conducting an informative dialog that helps qualified prospects who are not yet sales-ready, regardless of budget, authority, or timing—and of ensuring a clean hand-off to sales at the right time. "

Research from Forrester demonstrates the ROI of lead nurturing. In particular, companies that excel at lead nurturing:

◆ Decrease the percent of marketing-generated leads that are ignored by sales (from as high as 80% to as low as 25%).

◆ Raise win rates on marketing-generated leads (7% points higher) and reduce "no decisions" (6% lower).

◆ Have more sales representatives that make quota (9% higher) and a shorter ramp up time for new reps (10% decrease).

Additionally, anecdotal evidence suggests that prospects who are nurtured buy more, require less discounting, and have shorter sales cycles than prospects who bought but were not nurtured.

Reading Material 2　　Introduction to How PayPal Works

The simple idea behind PayPal—using encryption software to allow people to make financial transfers between computers— has turned into one of the world's primary methods of online payment.

Despite its occasionally troubled history, including fraud, lawsuits and zealous government regulators, PayPal now boasts more than 100 million accounts worldwide.

PayPal is an online payment service that allows individuals and businesses to transfer funds electronically. You can use it to pay for online auctions, purchase goods and services, or to make donations. You can even use it to send cash to someone.

A basic PayPal account is free. You can send funds to anyone with an e-mail address, whether or not they have a PayPal account. They'll get a message from PayPal about the funds, and then they just have to sign up for their own account.

Funds transferred via PayPal reside in a PayPal account until the holder of the funds retrieves them or spends them. If the user has entered and verified their bank account information, then the funds can be transferred directly into their account.

1. Methods of Withdrawing Funds from a PayPal Account

Signing up for PayPal is quick and doesn't even require you to enter any bank account information, although a checking account or credit card is required to use many of PayPal's features. From the PayPal homepage, just click on the "Sign Up Now" button. At the next page, you'll choose whether you want a personal, business or premier account. If you just plan to use PayPal for the occasional eBay auction or online purchase, a personal account is the right choice. If you intend to use PayPal to accept payments for your own business, then a business or premier account would be more suitable. If you select a personal account, you can upgrade in the future.

From there, you will go to a page that asks for your basic personal information—your name, address, telephone number and e-mail address. You will also be required to enter two security questions in case you lose your password, and you have to enter a randomly generated series of letters and numbers, which help prevent fraud. Once you confirm your account by following instructions you'll receive via e-mail, the sign-up process is done.

Adding a valid, current credit card to your account will allow PayPal to confirm your address (if it matches where you receive your credit card statements). Having a confirmed address shows both buyers and sellers that you are less likely to be a scammer. You can also use your credit card for PayPal's Expanded Use service, which allows you to draw money from the credit card, instead of just from a bank account.

If you want to add funds to your PayPal account from your checking account, or vice versa, you need to enter and verify your bank account with PayPal. When you enter your account number and routing number, PayPal will make two micropayments to that account. These payments are usually about 5 cents. PayPal will then ask you to enter those amounts in order to verify the account (they'll show up on your bank statement). After you enter them, your bank account will be ready for use.

2. PayPal Infrastructure

PayPal doesn't fundamentally change the way merchants interact with banks and credit card companies. It just acts as a middleman. Credit and debit card transactions travel on different networks. When a merchant accepts a charge from a card, the merchant pays an interchange, which is a small fee of about ten cents plus approximately 2 percent. The interchange is made up of a variety of small fees paid to all the different companies that have a part in the transaction—the merchant's bank, the credit card association and the company that issued the card. If someone pays by check, a different network is used, one that costs the merchant less but moves more slowly.

What part does PayPal play in all this? Both buyer and seller deal with PayPal, having already provided their bank account or credit card information. PayPal, in turn, handles all the transactions with various banks and credit card companies, and pays the interchange. They make this back on the fees they charge for receiving money, as well as the interest they collect on money left in PayPal accounts.

PayPal touts their presence as an extra layer as a security feature, because everyone's information, including credit card numbers, bank account numbers and address, stays with PayPal. With other online transactions, that information is transmitted from the buyer to the merchant to the credit card processor.

All the money held in PayPal accounts is placed into one or more bank accounts, where PayPal collects interest. Account holders do not receive any of the interest gained on their money. Some PayPal critics claim that one of the reasons PayPal locks accounts and puts people through a long, frustrating appeal process is so they can keep the funds in the bank longer to collect more interest.

3. PayPal History

Peter Thiel and Max Levchin founded PayPal in 1999 under the name Confinity. The idealistic vision of the company was one of a borderless currency free from governmental controls. However, PayPal's success quickly drew the attention of hackers, scam artists and organized crime groups, who used the service for frauds and money laundering. New security measures stemmed the tide of fraud and customer complaints, but government officials soon stepped in. Regulators and attorney generals in several states, including New York and California, fined PayPal for violations and investigated the company's business practices. Some states, such as Louisiana, banned PayPal from operating in their states altogether. PayPal has since received licenses that allow them to operate in these places.

Despite the initial turmoil, PayPal's market share continued to grow. At first PayPal offered new users $10 to join, plus bonuses for referring friends. The service grew so quickly that it soon became the default online payment service. Buyers wanted to use it since so many merchants accepted it, and merchants accepted it because so many buyers were using it. PayPal owes much of its initial growth to eBay users who used the service to pay for items and accept payments for their online auctions. PayPal even beat eBay at the online payment business, trumping eBay's in-house payment system Billpoint so thoroughly that eBay bought PayPal in 2002. Then it phased out Billpoint and integrated PayPal into its services. Sellers with PayPal accounts can place icons in their auctions and buyers can simply click on a PayPal logo when they win an auction to make an immediate payment.

In early 2002, PayPal held its IPO, opening at $15.41 per share and closing the day's trading above the $20 mark. eBay purchased PayPal that same year for $1.4 billion in stock. Recently, eBay spent another $370 million to buy out another PayPal competitor, VeriSign.

4. PayPal Account Types

The three PayPal account types differ in some important ways. All have access to PayPal's core features, which include:

◆ Send Money
◆ Request Money
◆ Auction Tools
◆ Website Payments
◆ Money Market
◆ Virtual Debit Card
◆ Account Insurance
◆ E-mail Customer Service

Personal accounts give you access to the core features, but that's all. Customer support is mostly via e-mail. There is a phone number available, but it is not toll-free and it sends users to a low-priority line with long wait times. There are no transaction fees for personal accounts, though there are fees for some other features, such as currency exchange. Personal accounts are also subject to volume limits of $500 per month. If you receive more than that, you will need to upgrade to a Premier or Business account (or deny the transfer that would have put you over the limit).

Premier and Business accounts are almost the same. The main difference is that a Business account must be registered with a business or group name, while a Premier account can be registered with a business, group or individual. Business accounts can also be set up for multiple users.

Business and Premier accounts allow access to all of the core features, plus the ability to accept:

◆ Unlimited Credit Card Payments
◆ Payment Receiving Preferences
◆ Subscriptions
◆ ATM/Debit Card
◆ Mass Payments

Business and Premier accounts also get a toll-free customer service number and extended customer service hours.

These extra features come at the cost of transaction fees. Sending money is still free, but 2.9 percent is charged for funds received. Extremely high-volume accounts get a break—after $3,000 has been received in a month, the percentage drops to 2.5 percent. Above $10,000, it goes to 2.2 percent, and money in excess of $100,000 received in a single month is only charged at 1.9 percent. In addition, all transactions in which money is received, regardless of volume, have a $0.30 fee added.

5. Using PayPal: Sending Funds

More than 70 percent of all eBay sellers offer PayPal as a payment option, and a large chunk of PayPal's business still comes from online auctions. However, one of the keys to PayPal's success has been its ability to expand beyond the eBay market. You can use it to send money to a friend, donate to a charity and buy items from online merchants.

If you want to donate to a charity using PayPal, the process is just like sending money to anyone else. You need the charity's e-mail address, or they might have a button on their website that allows you to make a donation directly. The main difference lies in the "Category of Purchase" entry on the PayPal payment page. Technically, this would be a quasi-cash transaction. However, such a transaction could be subject to fees, depending on the source of the money—if you draw your PayPal funds from a credit card, you might be charged cash advance fees. You can just as easily select "Service" as the category, and the donation will work with no problems or fees.

You can use PayPal to purchase goods from non-eBay merchants who have set up a PayPal storefront. Once you've selected your items, go to the Web site's checkout page. You will have the option of selecting a credit card or PayPal to pay for your purchase. Selecting PayPal may send you to a login page for your PayPal account. There you can transfer the appropriate amount to the merchant, who will then complete the sale. Some merchants integrate PayPal into the Web site, meaning that you put your PayPal information directly into their site.

If a Web site only accepts credit cards, you can still use funds in your PayPal account to make a purchase. PayPal users can use the "PayPal Debit Bar" to get a virtual MasterCard number. You can use that card number with any merchant who accepts MasterCard, and the funds will be deducted from the PayPal account. This service is free.

For example, you might want to use your PayPal account to buy something from Amazon. com. However, Amazon doesn't accept PayPal as a payment method. You can activate the Debit Bar from within your PayPal account. Assuming you are carrying enough of a balance in your account to cover the purchase, PayPal will give you a 16-digit number, just like a credit card number. Then you will select MasterCard as your payment method from Amazon's payment page and enter the Debit Bar number.

6. Using PayPal: Receiving Funds

Merchants who want to use PayPal to accept payments have a wide range of options available. For basic payments, such as online auctions or simple Web site sales, the merchant can simply provide buyers with their e-mail address, and buyers can make the appropriate payments to the merchant's PayPal account. eBay sellers can place PayPal buttons on their auctions, and the checkout invoice PayPal sends to auction winners will include a link to pay via PayPal.

PayPal also provides extensive services for online merchants. Prior to services like PayPal, someone who wanted to accept credit card payments online had to set up a merchant account through a credit card company. Creating a Web interface to use this account could be confusing and difficult. PayPal bypasses this problem. Business or Premier PayPal accounts can set up a "Buy Now" button, a PayPal shopping cart, or options for ongoing subscriptions and recurring payments.

A "Buy Now" button allows merchants to paste a small piece of HTML code into their site, creating a button for buyers to click when they want to purchase an item. This takes the buyer to a secure payment page, where they enter their credit card information and shipping address. Once the transaction is complete, the money, minus PayPal's fees, is transferred directly into the merchant's account.

The PayPal shopping cart is more involved, but it has the same result. HTML code for various buttons (add to cart, view cart) is added to lists of items, and the item details are added by the merchant. Buyers can add the items they want to purchase to their cart, and when they check out, they'll go to a secure payment page, just like a Buy It Now page.

PayPal's two main merchant account types, Standard and Pro, offer slightly different packages. With a standard account, when a customer checks out at the shopping cart page, they go to the PayPal site to log in and make the payment. With a Pro account, PayPal processes the transaction in the background—the customer makes the entire sale on the merchant's site. A Pro account has higher percentages on transactions (2.2 to 2.9 percent versus 1.9 to 2.9 percent) and a $20 monthly fee. It also requires knowledge of Web services and APIs (Application Program Interfaces), as well as a minimum of two days for installation.

PayPal also streamlines transactions for merchants who sell to international users. It can convert funds to whatever currency the merchant wants for 2.5 percent.

Exercises

I. Fill in the following blanks with proper words or phrases:

1. ISPs stand for _____.

2. Basic components of an electronic-commerce system includes Internet access, an access device at the location of the home shopper, a _____ server and _____, security gateways, and integration software.

3. With an electronic _____, service providers can process transactions for multiple sellers from distributed content.

4. The model that the client owns a Web site on a shared Web server and could have a unique uniform resource locator (URL) is called _____.

5. The 5 elements of e-commerce are _____, _____, _____, _____, and _____.

6. Usually, a secured Web page in the e-commerce system is secured through an _____ Certificate.

II. Answer the following questions:

1. Briefly describe the purpose of an electronic-commerce system from both the customer's per-

spective and the merchant's perspective.

2. List some benefits that the service provider hosts the electronic-commerce services.

3. Briefly describe the advantages and disadvantages of developing an on-line catalog and handle transactions on-line.

4. List several components of hosted electronic-commerce systems.

5. List some advantages of accepting payments on-line.

6. Explain that an Internet merchant account is needed in an e-commerce system.

7. Give some examples of payment Gateway providers.

8. List some of the major certificate providers.

9. Give an example of making an on-line purchasing. List all possible procedures.

Chapter Fifteen   The Future of
Information Technology

Unit 1   Automated Intrusion Response

The increasing speed of attacks against information technology (IT) systems **highlights** a requirement for comparably timely response. Threats such as **malware** and scripted exploits often allow a timeframe of only a few minutes or even seconds to respond, which effectively eliminates the **feasibility** of manual intervention and highlights a requirement for automated approaches to provide a solution. Here, however, it can be seen that existing security technologies are often insufficient. For example, although **intrusion detection systems** (IDS) can be used to identify potential incidents, they have a tendency to produce high volumes of false alarms and consequently cannot be trusted to issue automated responses for fear of disrupting legitimate activity.

The inability of IDS to directly **tackle** intrusions was the main criticism of a market report released by Gartner in June 2003, which labeled them a "market failure" and predicted their **obsolescence** by 2005. Indeed, more recent years have witnessed an apparent shift in the popularity of the associated security products, with **intrusion prevention systems** (IPS) gaining increasing appeal over IDS solutions. [1] IPS products themselves can actually use similar underlying detection methods to the IDS approach, but differ in that they attempt to **sidestep** the problem of **false-positives** by responding only to attacks that can be detected with high certainty. The confidence that results from this allows the IPS to be placed inline, between the source of an attack and the potential victim, giving it the potential to directly prevent incidents by blocking offending traffic. However, even if this is an important step in the right direction, it still leaves the problem of all the other attacks, which are more difficult to detect, and which are allowed to pass with no response. When viewed in this sense, it becomes apparent that IPS should not be seen as an alternative to IDS, but as another layer of security within a defense-in-depth strategy. As such, this brings back the problem of trusting IDS to make reliable response decisions.

1. Enhancing and Automating the Intrusion Response Process

Existing IDSs do, of course, have some level of automated response capability. The constraint, however, is that these are often limited to passive actions, such as logging and raising alerts to request manual investigation, which do nothing to directly impede the progress of an intruder. To achieve the latter, active responses have been introduced that mainly focus on blocking or terminating offending events. Such response actions might include:

♦   limiting or denying user access;

- blocking network traffic through firewalls and routers;
- terminating network connections.

However, in face of the false alarms, security administrators are naturally **wary** of automating such responses in current IDS. The following comment was typical of those received from an opinion survey conducted among relevant security professionals and related product vendors:

"Proactive measures are a reasonable idea, unless they can be **subverted**. For instance, if you decide to shut down your network connections as a proactive approach, then an intrusion attempt can be used as a denial of service."

As a consequence, it is useful to consider approaches that may be used to mitigate the risk of issuing active responses in false alarm scenarios. The key requirement here is to take into account the possibility of having a false alarm, and attempt to reduce the adverse impacts of automated response. One approach is to concentrate on informing decisions as much as possible, and enabling a responder to issue actions that investigate attacks, collect more evidence, or postpone or delay the attack while investigating, limiting the effects of an attack or a response at the target.[2] So, in addition to automation, two further desirable characteristics can be identified:

- **Flexibility**: The recognition that the type(s) of response that are appropriate will often depend upon the context in which an incident has occurred, such that the same incident will often demand a different response.
- **Intelligence**: The capability to assess the appropriateness of response actions before and after initiating them.

Accepting these requirements leads to the natural question of how they can be achieved, and it is here that the discussion enters the domain of on-going research. However, given that the detection methods in many of today's commercial IDS approaches have their origins in research activities dating back to the 1980s, it is relevant to consider how current research may help to advance commercial incarnations in the future.[3]

2. Establishing the Context of an Incident

In order to choose the most appropriate response action(s), it is relevant to consider the context in which an incident is occurring. For example, a malware infection would require different responses on a standard end-user workstation than it would on a critical database server. In the first case, the priority would be to keep the malicious code from spreading, and hence a suitable response would be to disconnect the host from the network. In the second scenario, however, maintaining the operation of the server would be important, so other response actions might be selected, such as quarantining the malicious code, backing up the database, and temporarily restricting the execution of any processes on the system that are not relevant to database transactions. In this example, the only factor being assessed is the target of the attack. However, it is possible to identify a whole range of factors that may influence the response decision. Some indicative examples are illustrated in Figure 15.1.1, grouped according to whether they are related to the incident or the IDS.

Although the occurrence of an incident obviously remains the trigger for a response, and still re-

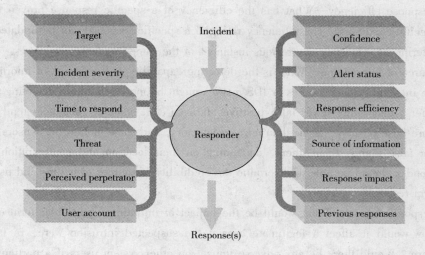

Figure 15. 1. 1   Contextual factors influencing intrusion response

presents the principal influence over what should be done, the assessment of other factors enables the responder to establish the context in which the incident has occurred, and therefore select appropriate responses accordingly. The various factors related to the incident are defined in more detail below.

◆ Target—What system, resource or data appears to be the focus of the attack? What assets are at risk if the incident continues or is able to be repeated? How important is that resource for the continuation of the system's operation?

◆ Incident severity—What impact has the incident already had on the **confidentiality**, integrity, or availability of the system and its data? How strong a response is required at this stage? For example, the detection of a severe incident could warrant the initiation of correspondingly severe responses, in order to protect system resources.

◆ Time to respond—How urgently is a response needed? This factor is mainly influenced by the speed of the attack.

◆ Threat posed by incident—How serious is the threat to the system after the occurrence of the incident? Which attacks are more likely to follow after that incident?

◆ Perceived perpetrator—Does the evidence collected suggest that the perpetrator is an external party or an insider? Is there any history associated with that person/account?

◆ User account—If the attack is being conducted through the suspected compromise of a user account, what privileges are associated with that account?[4] What risk do those privileges pose to the system?

Factors related to the IDS are summarized below.

◆ Confidence—How many monitored characteristics within the system are suggestive of an intrusion having occurred?

◆ Alert status—What is the current status of the IDS, both on the suspect account/process and in the system overall?

◆ Response efficiency—What has the efficiency of a specific response proven to be under specific conditions? The efficiency rating of a specific response can be updated after considering its efficiency in previous instances of the same incident.

◆ Source of information—What is the detecting capability of the source of information about the incident? Some sources or IDS metrics might be more reliable in detecting attacks than others, generating fewer false positive alarms (e. g. anomaly detectors tend to generate more false positive alarms than misuse detectors, and some monitoring sensors produce fewer false alarms than others, depending on their location and configuration). The responder should be able to determine the credibility of sources over time and use this to inform response selection.

◆ Response impact—What would be the impact of initiating a particular form of response? How would it affect a legitimate user if the suspected intrusion were, in fact, a false alarm? Would there be any adverse impact on other system users if a particular response was taken?

◆ Previous responses—If one or more responses have already been issued as a result of the detected incident, and been unsuccessful in countering the intrusion, it would be relevant to consider this before determining the acceptable impact of the next action. The failure of previously issued responses might lead to the selection of more severe response actions.

One advantage of considering such factors is the aforementioned flexibility. In addition, establishing the incident context is also recognized as a means of limiting uncertainty in the response process, and can be a contributor to reducing the potential impacts arising from IDS false alarms.

3. A Framework for Automated Response

Having identified the requirements, it is necessary to consider a means by which they can be achieved. The authors' research has proposed the conceptual framework for a flexible automated intelligent responder (FAIR), based on the concept of a coordinating host handling the monitoring of a number of networked client systems. The core elements are summarized below.

◆ Detection engine—analyses current activity and raises alerts for suspected intrusions. Informs the responder of the intrusion type, along with factors such as the target of the attack, and perceived perpetrator.

◆ Responder—monitors alerts, considering them in conjunction with incident context to take appropriate actions where necessary.

◆ Collector—provides initial activity data to detection engine, and subsequently informs responder about current context on the target system (e. g. applications running, active network connections, processor load).

◆ Intrusion specifications—intrusion specifications contain information about specific types of intrusions and their characteristics, such as incident severity rating, estimates of likely impacts (e. g. in terms of confidentiality, integrity and availability), and the speed with which the attack is likely to evolve.

◆ Profiles—contain data about users, systems and attackers, which can provide additional context for response decisions.

◆ Response actions—details of available response actions, enabling selection of responses with the most appropriate characteristics (e. g. stopping power, intrusiveness).

◆ Response policy—uses expert systems technology to indicate the most desirable characteristics for responses in the current context.

◆ Responder agent—initiates and manages any response actions required on the target (e. g. correcting vulnerabilities, authentication challenges, limiting access rights).

The responder uses information from several sources to determine the context of an attack, which informs the ultimate response decisions.

In terms of bringing such research forward to operational reality, elements of the FAIR architecture have been realized within an initial **proof-of-concept** prototype. This demonstrates many of the core elements of the architecture and its associated assessment of contextual factors leading to the ability to show flexible response decisions being made on the basis of simulated attacks. However, further work is required to incorporate the adaptive learning capability that would enable automated refinements to the response policy based on experience over time. [5] In addition, a comprehensive operational evaluation of the concept would still be required in order to demonstrate the reliability and impact of the system. Nonetheless, the pursuit of such research is clearly warranted by the threats that are posed to systems and the risks of not responding to them in an appropriate and timely manner.

Key Words

highlight	v.	突出
malware	n.	恶意软件（目的在于毁坏或变更操作系统的电脑病毒或软件）
feasibility	n.	可行性，可能性
intrusion detection system		入侵检测系统
tackle	v.	处理
obsolescence	n.	过时
intrusion prevention system		入侵防护系统
sidestep	v.	回避
false-positive	n.	误判率
wary	adj.	机警的，小心的
subvert	v.	推翻
confidentiality	n.	机密性
perpetrator	n.	犯罪者
proof-of-concept	n.	概念验证

Notes

1. Indeed, more recent years have witnessed an apparent shift in the popularity of the associated security products, with intrusion prevention systems (IPS) gaining increasing appeal over IDS solutions.

的确，近些年安全产品的流行已经有了明显的转移，入侵防护系统比入侵检测系统更具有吸引力。

2. One approach is to concentrate on informing decisions as much as possible, and enabling a responder to issue actions that investigate attacks, collect more evidence, or postpone or delay the attack while investigating, limiting the effects of an attack or a response at the target.

一种方法是将精力尽可能地集中在信息决策上，并且使防御者采取攻击调查、证据收集或者在调查的时候推迟或延误攻击行动，这样就可以减少攻击的影响或者目标的反映。

3. However, given that the detection methods in many of today's commercial IDS approaches have their origins in research activities dating back to the 1980s, it is relevant to consider how current research may help to advance commercial incarnations in the future.

然而，目前商业化入侵检测系统的检测方法的研究活动可以追溯到 20 世纪 80 年代，所以可以考虑当前的研究如何在未来帮助提高商业化的产品。

4. If the attack is being conducted through the suspected compromise of a user account, what privileges are associated with that account?

如果攻击通过一个可能有潜在危险的账户进行，那么这个账户的权限是什么呢？

5. However, further work is required to incorporate the adaptive learning capability that would enable automated refinements to the response policy based on experience over time.

然而，未来的工作要求具有能够通过时间积累经验来自动完善响应策略的适应性学习的能力。

Unit 2　Native XML Databases

When **native XML databases** appeared on the heels of the XML 1.0 recommendation, most people weren't sure what to make of them. Were they a replacement for relational databases or a return to **hierarchical databases**? No, said the vendors. They were designed to manage large numbers of XML documents.

Native XML databases are databases designed especially to store XML documents. Like other databases, they support features like transactions, security, multi-user access, programmatic APIs, query languages, and so on. The only difference from other databases is that their internal model is based on XML and not something else, such as the relational model.

Native XML databases are most commonly used to store document-centric documents. The main reason for this is their support of XML query languages, which allow you to ask questions like, "Get me all documents in which the third paragraph after the start of the section contains a bold word," or even just to limit full-text searches to certain portions of a document. Such queries are clearly difficult to ask in a language like SQL. Another reason is that native XML databases preserve things like document order, processing instructions, and comments, and often preserve CDATA sections, entity usage, and so on, while XML-enabled databases do not. [1]

Native XML databases are also commonly used to integrate data. While data integration has historically been performed through federated relational databases, these require all data sources to be mapped to the relational model. This is clearly unworkable for many types of data and the XML data model provides much greater flexibility. Native XML databases also handle **schema** changes more easily than relational databases and can handle schemaless data as well. Both are important considerations when integrating data from sources not under your direct control.

The third major use case for native XML databases is **semi-structured** data, such as is found in the fields of finance and biology, which change so frequently that definitive schemas are often not possible. Because native XML databases do not require schemas (as do relational databases), they can handle this kind of data, although applications often require humans to process it.

The final major use of native XML database is in handling schema evolution. While native XML databases do not provide complete solutions by any means, they do provide more flexibility than relational databases. For example, native XML databases do not require existing data to be **migrated** to a new schema, can handle schema changes for which there is no data migration path, and can store data even if it conforms to an unknown version of a schema.

Other uses of native XML databases include providing data and **metadata** caches for long-running transactions, handling large documents, handling hierarchical data, and acting as a mid-tier data cache.

1. What Is a Native XML Database?

The term "native XML database" first gained prominence in the marketing campaign for Tamino, a native XML database from Software AG. Perhaps due to the success of this campaign, the term came into common usage among companies developing similar products. The **drawback** of this is that, being a marketing term, it has never had a formal technical definition.

One possible definition is that a native XML database is one that:

◆ Defines a (logical) model for an XML document—as opposed to the data in that document—and stores and retrieves documents according to that model. At a minimum, the model must include elements, attributes, PCDATA, and document order. Examples of such models are the XPath data model, the XML Infoset, and the models implied by the **DOM** and the events in SAX 1.0.

◆ Has an XML document as its fundamental unit of (logical) storage, just as a relational database has a row in a table as its fundamental unit of (logical) storage.

◆ Is not required to have any particular underlying physical storage model. For example, it can be built on a relational, hierarchical, or object-oriented database, or use a proprietary storage format such as indexed, compressed files.

The first part of this definition is similar to the definitions of other types of databases, concentrating on the model used by the database. It is worth noting that a given native XML database might store more information than is contained in the model it uses. For example, it might support queries based on the XPath data model but store documents as text. In this case, things like CDATA sections and entity usage are stored in the database but not included in the model.

The second part of the definition states that the fundamental unit of storage in a native XML database is an XML document. While it seems possible that a native XML database could assign this role to document fragments, it is filled by documents in all native XML databases today.

The third part of the definition states that the underlying data storage format is not important. This is true, and is analogous to stating that the physical storage format used by a relational database is unrelated to whether that database is relational.

2. Native XML Database Architectures

The architectures of native XML databases fall into two broad categories: text-based and model-based.

2.1 Text-based Native XML Databases

A text-based native XML database is one that stores XML as text. This might be a file in a file system, a **BLOB** in a relational database, or a proprietary text format.

Common to all text-based native XML databases are indexes, which allow the query engine to easily jump to any point in any XML document. This gives such databases a tremendous speed advantage when retrieving entire documents or document fragments. This is because the database can perform a single index lookup, position the disk head once, and, assuming that the necessary fragment is stored in contiguous bytes on the disk, retrieve the entire document or fragment in a single read.[2] In contrast, reassembling a document from pieces, as is done in a relational database and some model-based native XML databases, requires multiple index lookups and multiple disk reads.

In this sense, a text-based native XML database is similar to a hierarchical database, in that both can outperform a relational database when retrieving and returning data according to a predefined hierarchy. Also like a hierarchical database, text-based native XML databases are likely to encounter performance problems when retrieving and returning data in any other form, such as inverting the hierarchy or portions of it.[3] Whether this will prove to be true is as yet unknown, but the predominance of relational databases, whose use of logical pointers allows all queries of the same complexity to be performed with the same speed, seems to indicate it will be the case.

2.2 Model-based Native XML Databases

The second category of native XML databases is model-based native XML databases. Rather than storing the XML document as text, they build an internal object model from the document and store this model. How the model is stored depends on the database. Some databases store the model in a relational or object-oriented database. For example, storing the DOM in a relational database might result in tables such as Elements, Attributes, PCDATA, Entities, and Entity References. Other databases use a proprietary storage format optimized for their model.

Model-based native XML databases built on other databases are likely to have performance similar to those databases when retrieving documents for the obvious reason that they rely on those systems to retrieve data. However, the design of the database, especially for native XML databases built on top of relational databases, has significant room for variation. For example, a database that used a straight object-relational mapping of the DOM could result in a system that required executing separate SELECT statements to retrieve the children of each node. On the other hand, most such databases optimize their storage models and retrieval software.

Model-based native XML databases that use a proprietary storage format are likely to have performance similar to text-based native XML databases when retrieving data in the order in which it is stored. This is because most such databases use physical pointers between nodes, which should provide performance similar to retrieving text.

Like text-based native XML databases, model-based native XML databases are likely to encounter performance problems when retrieving and returning data in any form other than that in which it is stored, such as when inverting the hierarchy or portions of it. Whether they will be faster or slower than text-based systems is not clear.

3. Features of Native XML Databases

This section briefly discusses a number of the features found in native XML databases. It should help give you an idea of what features are available today and what features to expect in the future.

3. 1   Document Collections

Many native XML databases support the notion of a collection. This plays a role similar to a table in a relational database or a directory in a file system. For example, suppose you are using a native XML database to store sales orders. In this case, you might want to define a sales order collection so that queries over sales orders could be limited to documents in that collection.

As another example, suppose you are storing the manuals for all of a company's products in a native XML database. In this case, you might want to define a hierarchy of collections.

Whether collections can be nested depends on the database.

3. 2   Query Languages

Almost all native XML databases support one or more query languages. The most popular of these are XPath (with extensions for queries over multiple documents) and XQuery, although numerous proprietary query languages are supported as well. When considering a native XML database, you should probably check that the query language supports your needs, as these might range from full-text-style searches to the need to recombine fragments from multiple documents.

In the future, most native XML databases will probably support XQuery from the W3C.

3.3 Updates and Deletes

Native XML databases have a variety of strategies for updating and deleting documents, from simply replacing or deleting the existing document to modifications through a live DOM tree to languages that specify how to modify fragments of a document. Most of these methods are proprietary. However, two somewhat standard languages for updating XML documents have emerged:

- ◆ XUpdate, from the XML: DB Initiative, is an XML-based language. It uses XPath to identify a set of nodes, then specifies whether to insert or delete these nodes, or insert new nodes before or after them. XUpdate has been implemented in a number of native XML databases.

- ◆ A set of extensions to XQuery has been proposed by members of the W3C XQuery working group and Patrick Lehti. Variations on these extensions have been implemented in a number of native XML databases and it seems likely that these will form the basis of the update syntax in XQuery.

In spite of these languages, update abilities are likely to remain fragmented until an update syntax is formally added to XQuery.

3.4 Transactions, Locking, and Concurrency

Virtually all native XML databases support transactions (and presumably support **rollbacks**). However, **locking** is often at the level of entire documents, rather than at the level of individual nodes, so multi-user **concurrency** can be relatively low. Whether this is an issue depends on the application and what constitutes a "document". For example:

- ◆ A document is a chapter of a user's guide and writers edit chapters. Document-level locking is unlikely to cause concurrency problems, as two writers updating the same chapter at the same time is unlikely.

- ◆ A document stores all of the data about a company's sales leads and salespeople enter new sales lead information. Document-level locking is likely to cause concurrency problems, as the chances of two salespeople updating lead information at the same time are fairly high. Fortunately, this can be at least partially solved by creating one sales lead document per prospective customer.

- ◆ A document contains the data used in a workflow, such as a financial contract. Each step of the workflow reads data from the document and adds its own data. For example, one step might perform a credit check and add a credit score to the document. Another step might check for outstanding balances on other contracts with the same customer and add the total outstanding balance. If node-level locking is used, some of these steps may be executed in parallel. If document-level locking is used, they must be executed serially to avoid writing conflicts. This may cause unacceptable delays in high-volume applications.

The problem with node-level locking is implementing it. Locking a node usually requires locking its parent, which in turn requires locking its parent, and so on back to the root, effectively locking the entire document. To see why this is true, consider a transaction that reads a leaf node. If the transaction does not acquire locks on the ancestors of the leaf node, another transaction can delete an ancestor of the leaf node, in turn deleting the leaf node. However, it is also clear that another transaction should be able to update those parts of the document not on the direct path from the root to the leaf node.

A partial solution for this problem is proposed by Stijn Dekeyser, et al. While they do not entirely avoid the problem of locking the ancestors of a target node, they do make these locks more flexible by annotating them with the query defining the path from the locked node to the target node. This allows other transactions to determine whether they conflict with transactions already holding locks. (Because evaluating queries in order to acquire locks is prohibitively expensive, the actual scheme is somewhat more limited than what is described here, but this is the general idea.) In the future, most native XML databases will probably offer node-level locking.

3.5   Round-Tripping

One important feature of native XML databases is that they can round-trip XML documents. That is, you can store an XML document in a native XML database and get the "same" document back again. This is important to document-centric applications, [4]for which things like CDATA sections, entity usage, comments, and processing instructions form an integral part of the document. It is also vital to many legal and medical applications, which are required by law to keep exact copies of documents.

All native XML databases can round-trip documents at the level of elements, attributes, PCDATA, and document order. How much more they can round-trip depends on the database. As a general rule, text-based native XML databases round-trip XML documents exactly, while model-based native XML databases round-trip XML documents at the level of their document model. In the case of particularly minimal document models, this means round-tripping at a level less than canonical XML.

Since the level of round-tripping you need depends entirely on your application, you may have a choice of many native XML databases or be restricted to only a few.

3.6   Remote Data

Some native XML databases can include remote data in documents stored in the database. Usually, this is data retrieved from a relational database with ODBC, OLE DB, or JDBC and modeled using the table-based mapping or an object-relational mapping. Whether the data is live—that is, whether updates to the document in the native XML database are reflected in the remote database—depends on the native XML database. [5]Eventually, most native XML databases will probably support live remote data.

3.7 Indexes

All native XML databases support indexes as a way to increase query speed. There are three types of indexes. Value indexes index text and attribute values and are used to resolve queries such as, "Find all elements or attributes whose value is 'santa Cruz'." Structural indexes index the location of elements and attributes and are used to resolve queries such as, "Find all Address elements." Value and structural indexes are combined to resolve queries such as, "Find all City elements whose value is 'santa Cruz'." Finally, full-text indexes index the individual tokens in text and attribute values and are used to resolve queries such as, "Find all documents that contain the words 'Santa Cruz'," or, in conjunction with structural indexes, "Find all documents that contain the words 'santa Cruz' inside an Address element."

Most native XML databases support both value and structural indexes. Some native XML databases support full-text indexes.

3.8 External Entity Storage

A difficult question when storing XML documents is how to handle external entities. That is, should they be expanded and their value stored with the rest of the document, or should the entity reference be left in place? There is no single answer to this question.

For example, suppose a document includes an external general entity that calls a CGI program for the current weather report. If the document is used as a Web page to give current weather reports, it would be a mistake to expand the entity reference, as the Web page would no longer return live data. On the other hand, if the document were part of a collection of historical weather data, it would be a mistake not to expand the entity reference, as the document would always retrieve the current data rather than containing the historic data. [6]

As another example, consider a product manual that consisted of nothing but references to external entities that point to the chapters of the manual. If some of these chapters were used in other documents, such as manuals for different model of the same product, it would be a mistake to expand these references.

Key Words

native XML database	原生 XML 数据库
hierarchical database	层次数据库
schema	*n.* 模式
semi-structured	*adj.* 半结构化的
migrate	*v.* 移植
metadata	*n.* 元数据
drawback	*n.* 缺点，短处
DOM	文档对象模型（Document Object Model）

BLOB	数据库中的二进制大对象（binary large object）
rollback	*n.* 回滚
locking	*n.* 锁定，封锁
concurrency	*n.* 并行，并发

Notes

1. Another reason is that native XML databases preserve things like document order, processing instructions, and comments, and often preserve CDATA sections, entity usage, and so on, while XML-enabled databases do not.

另一个原因是，native XML 数据库保留了文件顺序、处理指令、注释、CDATA 块以及实体引用等，而支持 XML 的数据库（XML-enabled database）无法做到。

2. This is because the database can perform a single index lookup, position the disk head once, and, assuming that the necessary fragment is stored in contiguous bytes on the disk, retrieve the entire document or fragment in a single read.

这是因为数据库只需进行一次检索和磁头定位，并且假定所需的文件（片段）在磁盘上是连续存储的话，只需一次读盘就可读出整个文件或文件片段。

3. Also like a hierarchical database, text-based native XML databases are likely to encounter performance problems when retrieving and returning data in any other form, such as inverting the hierarchy or portions of it.

和层次结构数据库一样，当以其他形式比如转置层次存取数据时，基于文本的原生 XML 数据库也会遇到效率问题。

4. One important feature of native XML databases is that they can round-trip XML documents. That is, you can store an XML document in a native XML database and get the "same" document back again. This is important to document-centric applications, ...

Native XML 数据库的一个重要特性是它可以为 XML 文档提供"往返车票（round-trip）"。就是说，你可以将 XML 文件存放在原生 XML 数据库中，而且再取回"同样"的文件。这对于以文档为中心的应用程序来说非常重要，……

5. Whether the data is live—that is, whether updates to the document in the native XML database are reflected in the remote database—depends on the native XML database.

Native XML 数据库决定了这些数据是不是新鲜的——即 Native XML 数据库中文档的更新是否在外部数据库中反映出来。

6. On the other hand, if the document were part of a collection of historical weather data, it would be a mistake not to expand the entity reference, as the document would always retrieve the current data rather than containing the historic data.

另一方面，如果文件是气象历史资料的一部分，那么不完全展开它反而是不对的，否则文件总是含有当前的数据而不是历史资料了。

Reading Material 1　3G Technology

1. Standard

3G stands for third-generation wireless technology and networks. 3G is based on an International Telecommunication Union (ITU) initiative for a single global wireless standard called International Mobile Telecommunications-2000 (IMT-2000). This concept of a single standard evolved into a family of five 3G wireless standards. Of those five, the most widely accepted are CDMA2000, WCD-MA (UMTS) and TD-SCDMA.

According to the ITU and IMT-2000, a wireless standard must meet minimum bit-rate requirements to be considered 3G:

- ◆ 2 Mbps in fixed or in-building environments
- ◆ 384 Kbps in pedestrian or urban environments
- ◆ 144 Kbps in wide area mobile environments
- ◆ Variable data rates in large geographic area systems (satellite)

In addition to providing faster bit rates and greater capacity over previous-generation technologies, 3G standards excel by effectively:

- ◆ Delivering mobile data
- ◆ Offering greater network capacity
- ◆ Operating with existing second-generation technologies
- ◆ Enabling rich data applications such as VoIP, video telephony, mobile multimedia, interactive gaming and more

2. History

First generation wireless, or 1G, refers to analog networks introduced in the mid-1980s. Examples include Advanced Mobile Phone Service (AMPS) used in North America and Total Access Communications System (TACS) used in the UK. Most 1G technologies and systems were country or region-specific and thus offered limited coverage.

As mobile communications grew in popularity, networks often became overloaded, resulting in busy signals and dropped calls. The solution was second-generation wireless, or 2G, which emerged in the early 1990s. 2G technologies were digital and offered the much-needed capacity that 1G analog systems did not afford. Several technologies were widely used:

- ◆ TDMA (IS-54 and IS-136)
- ◆ GSM (a TDMA based technology)
- ◆ CDMA IS-95 or cdmaOne (a CDMA based technology)

However, these 2G technologies are incompatible with each other. Thus, mobile service subscribers were still often limited to using their phones in a single country or region.

In an effort to standardize future digital wireless communications and make global roaming with a single handset possible, the ITU established a single standard for wireless networks in 1999. Called IMT-2000, which is commonly referred to today as 3G, the initiative set forth the requirements (mentioned above) for the third generation of wireless networks.

3. Today

Today, WCDMA (Wideband CDMA) and CDMA2000 are by far the dominant standards in terms of current commercial services, operator deployment plans and vendor support.

Launched commercially by wireless operators in 2000, CDMA2000 1X was the world's first operational 3G technology, capable of transmitting data faster than most dial-up services. Today, more than 190 million people enjoy the benefits of CDMA2000 1X, which provides enhanced data capacity compared to all 2G technologies.

Also known as UMTS (Universal Mobile Telecommunications System), WCDMA (Wideband CDMA) is the 3G standard chosen by most GSM/GPRS wireless network operators wanting to evolve their systems to 3G network technology. WCDMA offers enhanced voice and data capacity and peak data rates faster than most dial-up services and average rates consistently greater than GSM/GPRS (Global System for Mobile communications/General Packet Radio Service) and EDGE (Enhanced Data for GSM Evolution). As of February 2006, more than 51 million subscribers were using WCDMA for their mobile voice and data needs.

4. Features and Benefits

3G wireless services enable consumers and professionals to experience excellent voice quality as well as a wide array of compelling data services, including:

- ◆ Mobile Internet connectivity
- ◆ Mobile e-mail
- ◆ Multimedia services, such as digital photos and movies taken by and shared via wireless handsets
- ◆ Wireless application downloading
- ◆ Video-on-demand
- ◆ Real-time multiplayer gaming
- ◆ Enhanced emergency and location-based services
- ◆ Low-latency push-to-talk and push-to-video message services

For consumers, 3G quite simply means a more rewarding wireless experience—high-quality, low-cost voice, and fun and useful data services whenever they want them, whenever they need them and wherever they have mobile phone service.

Enterprises can leverage 3G's advanced data capabilities to gain critical competitive advantages such as increased productivity, streamlined processes, improved customer service and enhanced communications. Workforces can essentially work from anywhere at anytime.

3G technology also benefits the other participants in the wireless value chain. Wireless network operators are able to capitalize on increased voice capacity, greater network efficiency, lower costs per user served, increased ARPU (average revenue per user) and greater service differentiation. Device manufacturers can leverage the enhanced capabilities of 3G networks to sell premium wireless devices in volume. Finally, 3G technology's data capabilities open up an enormous world of opportunity for application developers and content providers.

5. Future

The future of 3G is impressive—in fact, it's already here.

5.1 CDMA2000 1xEV-DO

Launched in 2002, CDMA2000 1xEV-DO is a data-optimized evolution of the CDMA2000 standard, capable of delivering peak forward link data rates of 2.4 Mbps, or rates comparable to wired broadband. By dividing radio spectrum into separate voice and data channels, EV-DO, which uses a 1.25 MHz data channel, improves network efficiency and eliminates the chance that an increase in voice traffic would cause data speeds to drop.

5.2 CDMA2000 1xEV-DO Rev. A

EV-DO Rev. A is a significant evolutionary step in the CDMA2000 1xEV-DO progression. Expected to launch in 2006, EV-DO Rev. A provides a peak forward link data rate of 3.1 Mbps and a peak reverse link rate of 1.8 Mbps.

In addition, EV-DO Rev. A incorporates comprehensive improvements to the airlink that reduce call set up times, decrease transmission delays and enable greater service control. These enhancements, combined with the increased data rates, enable network operators using EV-DO Rev. A to offer richer, more interactive applications and services such as wireline-quality VoIP, low-latency push-to-talk, online gaming, video on demand and video messaging, as well as the ability to upload large data files.

EV-DO Rev. A also features Platinum Multicast. Offering three times more capacity than Gold Multicast, Platinum Multicast provides even greater network efficiency and reduces the cost of rich media content delivery to a large subscriber base when coupled with a content delivery system solution. Platinum Multicast's multi-tone modulation enhancement uses CDMA and OFDM waveforms on the forward link to multimedia handsets, while continuing to use CDMA for forward and reverse links on unicast services.

With its additional speed and capacity, Platinum Multicast enables operators to deliver live content such as breaking news, traffic, sports and weather. Furthermore, it offers operators greater flexibility—depending on network needs, operators can choose to deliver more channels of content or fewer channels of content in higher resolution.

5.3 EV-DO Rev. B

EV-DO Rev. B, a further development on the CDMA2000 roadmap beyond Rev. A, offers multi-channel capabilities, which allow network operators to aggregate multiple 1.25 MHz channels simultaneously and increase data rates dramatically. The first implementation of Rev. B will support up to 9. 3 Mbps on the forward link and 5. 4 Mbps on the reverse link (the standard, at its theoretical limit and aggregating 20 MHz of spectrum, allows up to 75 Mbps on the forward link and 27 Mbps on the reverse link). One of the chief advantages of Rev. B is that it puts the control for scaling bandwidth into the network operators' hands, allowing operators to tailor their systems to the spectrum they have available.

Rev. B's flexibility will enable significant capacity and performance improvements, while protecting CDMA2000 operators' current investments in networks and devices. Furthermore, it will allow more of operators' spectrum to be used for IP-based services, including mobile broadband data, wireline-quality VoIP and multicast traffic in a manner that results in lower operator costs through greater efficiencies.

5. 4　HSDPA/HSUPA

HSDPA (high-speed downlink packet access) is an evolution of WCDMA, optimized for packet-switched data applications. HSDPA provides impressive enhancements over WCDMA on the downlink (also referred to as the forward link) —promising 14. 4 Mbps peak data rates—resulting in a better end-user experience. Subscribers with HSDPA service are able to receive e-mails with large attachments, surf the web or download multimedia or text files faster than ever.

For operators, HSDPA offers a three-to five-fold capacity increase over WCDMA, which translates into significantly more data users and lower cost per bit. In December of 2005, the first HSDPA network was launched in the United States. At the conclusion of January 2006, there were more than 50 other HSDPA networks planned or in deployment and nine announced trials around the world.

HSDPA will be followed by another evolution still in standards development. Just as EV-DO Rev. A greatly improves the uplink of 1xEV-DO, HSUPA (high-speed uplink packet access) extends the benefits of HSDPA to the uplink (also referred to as the reverse link). HSUPA will support up to 5. 76 Mbps peak rates, further improving the end user experience. HSUPA will provide end users with a DSL-like experience and enable lower latency services such as VoIP, multiplayer interactive gaming, push-to-talk and more. The first HSUPA deployments are expected in 2007.

Moving forward, both CDMA2000 and WCDMA will continue to evolve with the goal to increase network capacity, improve data rates and enhance system performance.

Reading Material 2　Voice over IP

1. Introduction

Dating back over 100 years, traditional voice networks and the telephone have become an integral part of modern society. In fact, it is not unusual, even in remote parts of the world, for people to feel that they are entitled to basic telephone service. Obviously, the telephone and the associated networks are a large part of modern communications and technology. However, in recent years, data networks have been growing at a tremendous rate, largely due to the growing Internet. According to some experts, data traffic is predicted to soon exceed traditional voice traffic. As a result, more and more companies have become interested in implementing VoIP. But what exactly is VoIP and how does it work? Also, what are the benefits of VoIP?

2. What Is VoIP?

VoIP, or Voice over IP, is an application that enables data packet networks to transport real time voice traffic. It consists of hardware and software that allows companies and persons to engage in telephone conversations over data networks. According to an article written by techguide.com, "VoIP can be defined as the ability to make telephone calls (i. e. , to do everything we can do today with the PSTN) and to send facsimiles over IP-based data networks with a suitable quality of service (QoS) and a much superior cost/benefit. " It is also known as Internet Telephony. However, the latter term is often used in reference to calls made over the public Internet, and VoIP is often used to refer to calls made on a private network.

The traditional voice network, or POTS (plain old telephone system), uses circuit switching techniques. This means that a particular communication uses a dedicated path for the duration of the call. Although this provides a very reliable connection for voice transmissions, it makes very inefficient use of bandwidth. On the other hand, data networks generally use packet or cell switching technologies. These use Statistical Time Division Multiplexing (STDM) in order to dynamically allot bandwidth to a particular stream of data, based on its requirements and the requirements and demands of other data on the network. This provides for much more efficient use of available bandwidth but can create problems for voice traffic, which is very sensitive to delay. Because each packet is individually routed across the network, this makes packet switching networks inherently less efficient in dealing with voice traffic and poses a number of challenges to a quality voice transmission. These include: packet loss, delay (echo), jitter (variable delay) and unreliable and out of order packet delivery due to the connectionless nature of packet networks. So, then, how does VoIP work, and how does it overcome these obstacles in order to provide reliable, quality telephone conversations?

3. How Does It Work?

In order to deal with these issues and provide a voice service with a reasonable measure of quality, there are many techniques that are employed in order to deal with network congestion and delay by making better use of bandwidth. These bandwidth saving schemes include prioritization, fragmentation, jitter buffering, voice compression, silence suppression and echo cancellation. This is where the various protocols, such as H. 323 come in, as standards are being set to control the quality of voice transmissions on a data network.

Prioritization techniques are related to QoS (quality of service), which is a method of guaranteeing throughput for certain traffic on the network. This can ensure that voice traffic on a data network is given high priority. This prioritization can be based on location, protocol or application type.

Protocols used to ensure this QoS are RTP (Real Time Protocol) and RSVP (Resource Reservation Protocol).

Fragmentation divides packets into smaller fragments so that their priority can be ensured. This can help reduce the overall delay of voice delivery. However, on IP-based networks, this can create extra overhead because of the large size of IP headers (20 bytes). So although necessary, fragmentation alone cannot ensure the reliable delivery of real time voice applications.

This is why compression is also necessary. Various codecs (coder/decoder) standards have been implemented. ITU G. 723, which provides for 3. 1 kbps bandwidth over 5. 3 and 6. 3 kbps channels, has been adopted for use with VoIP. The ITU G. 729 standard has been adopted for VoFR (Voice Data Convergence Glossary).

In IP-based networks, packets that belong to the same transmission (whether voice or data) do not always arrive with the same amount of delay. For example, packets 1-5 of a given data stream may all arrive with a consistent amount of delay between each packet, but the delay between packet 5 and 6 may be twice as long. This variation in delay is referred to as "jitter". As a result, voice transmissions will sound unnatural. When the next packet in a voice stream does not arrive in time, the previous packet is usually replayed. However, this can create conversations that lack a natural quality. In order to handle this delay variability, a jitter buffer is established. This allows packets to be collected into a buffer and held there long enough for the slower packets to arrive so that they can all be played in proper sequence and in a natural voice flow. Although this can remove packet delay, this creates additional overall delay. According to Gil Biran, Vice President of Research and Development for RAD Data Communications, "The jitter buffer should fit the network's differential delay." This will provide for the necessary balance between packet delay and overall delay, allowing for voice quality transmissions.

In human telephone conversations, generally only about 50% of the full duplex bandwidth is used at any given time. This is because one person is generally listening while the other is talking. When you couple this with the fact that there are natural pauses, pauses for breath and between words, the total required bandwidth for a conversation is reduced an additional 10%. This means that there is between 50% −60% of the available bandwidth that is not being used. Silence suppression techniques take advantage of this by detecting when there is a gap and then suppresses the transmission of these silences. This can result in more bandwidth being available for other transmissions. However, because these silences are necessary for the conversation to sound natural, the receiving device must interpret the lack of packets and re-insert the silent spots into the output.

When the total end to end delay of a voice transmission is greater than 50 milliseconds, echo becomes a problem that can detract from the quality of the conversation. An echo cancellation unit solves this problem by performing echo cancellation on the signals. ITU G. 165 or G. 168 provides the standards and requirements for echo cancellation.

When dealing with data transmission on IP networks, TCP (Transmission Control Protocol) handles any packets that may be lost due to congestion or link failures by issuing acknowledgements and requesting retransmittal of lost packets. Although this works well for data, this method is not efficient for time sensitive information such as voice. In order to help ensure a quality voice conversation, packet losses greater than 10% are not tolerable. For any packet losses under 10%, interpolation (playback of the last packet) can help maintain a continuous flow of voice with minimal distraction to the quality.

In order for different manufacturers to implement these various techniques and maintain interoperability, various standards have been recommended and approved. There are a few VOIP protocol stacks which are derived from various standard bodies and vendors, namely H. 323, SIP, MEGACO and MGCP.

H. 323 is the ITU-T's standard, which was originally developed for multimedia conferencing on LANs, but was later extended to cover Voice over IP. The standard encompasses both point to point communications and multipoint conferences. H. 323 defines four logical components: Terminals, Gateways, Gatekeepers and Multipoint Control Units (MCUs). Terminals, gateways and MCUs are known as endpoints.

Session Initiation Protocol (SIP) is the IETF's standard for establishing VOIP connections. SIP is an application layer control protocol for creating, modifying and terminating sessions with one or more participants. The architecture of SIP is similar to that of HTTP (client-server protocol). Requests are generated by the client and sent to the server. The server processes the requests and then sends a response to the client. A request and the responses for that request make a transaction.

Media Gateway Control Protocol (MGCP) is a Cisco and Telcordia proposed VOIP protocol that defines communication between call control elements (Call Agents or Media Gateway) and telephony gateways. MGCP is a control protocol, allowing a central coordinator to monitor events in IP phones and gateways and instructs them to send media to specific addresses. In the MGCP architecture, the call control intelligence is located outside the gateways and is handled by the call control elements (the Call Agent). Also the call control elements (Call Agents) will synchronize with each other to send coherent commands to the gateways under their control.

The Media Gateway Control Protocol (Megaco) is a result of joint efforts of the IETF and the ITU-T (ITU-T Recommendation H. 248). Megaco/H. 248 is for control of elements in a physically decomposed multimedia gateway, which enables separation of call control from media conversion. Megaco/H. 248 addresses the relationship between the Media Gateway (MG), which converts circuit-switched voice to packet-based traffic, and the Media Gateway Controller, which dictates the service logic of that traffic. Megaco/H. 248 instructs an MG to connect streams coming from outside a packet or cell data network onto a packet or cell stream such as the Real-Time Transport Protocol (RTP). Megaco/H. 248 is essentially quite similar to MGCP from an architectural standpoint and the controller-to-gateway relationship, but Megaco/H. 248 supports a broader range of networks, such as ATM.

Obviously, enhancements to equipment and standards for VoIP are constantly being improved. You may have heard about VoIP but may have wondered whether or not it is a good solution for your company. So, then, what are the benefits of implementing VoIP?

4. Benefits of VoIP

Many companies are seeing the value of implementing VoIP in their data networks for many reasons. These include:

- Cost reduction—low cost phone calls
- Convergence of data/voice networks—unification
- Simplification and consolidation—centralized management

As data networks continue to grow, implementing VoIP can be a very appealing option that can allow for reduced costs and provide for greater flexibility. In addition to replacing internal voice networks at large corporate offices, VoIP can be used to connect various branch offices through existing WAN links. This gives companies an alternative to the PSTN that can continue to grow and be scaled to fit their needs.

5. Key Issues

- Quality of voice—As IP was designed for carrying data, so it does not provide real time guarantees but only provides best effort service. For voice communications over IP to become acceptable to the users, the packet delay and getter needs to be less than a threshold value.
- Interoperability—In a public network environment, products from different vendors need to operate with each other for voice over IP is to become common among users.
- Security—Encryption (such as SSL) and tunneling (L2TP) technologies are developed to protect VoIP signaling and bear traffic.
- Integration with Public Switched Telephone Network (PSTN) —While Internet telephony is being introduced, it will need to work in conjunction with PSTN in the foreseeable future. Gateway technologies are developed to bridge the two networks.
- Scalability—VoIP systems needs to be flexible enough to grow to large user market for both private and public services. Many network management, user management technologies and products are developed to address the issue.

6. Conclusion

As data traffic continues to increase and surpass that of voice traffic, the convergence and integration of these technologies will not only continue to improve, but also will pave the way for a truly unified and seamless means of communication.

Exercises

I. Fill in the following blanks with proper words or phrases:

1. IDS stand for _____.
2. In addition to automation, the automated intrusion response system needs two further desira-

ble characteristics, which are _____ and _____.

3. Based on the concept of a coordinating host handling the monitoring of a number of net-worked client systems, the authors' research has proposed the conceptual framework for a _____.

4. Among the core elements of FAIR, _____ is used for monitoring alerts and considering them in conjunction with incident context to take appropriate actions where necessary.

5. The data that change so frequently that definitive schemas are often not possible is call _____ data.

6. The fundamental unit of storage in a native XML database is a/an _____.

7. The architectures of native XML databases fall into two broad categories: _____ and _____.

8. The most popular of query languages for native XML databases are _____ and _____.

9. All native XML databases support _____ as a way to increase query speed.

Ⅱ. Answer the following questions:

1. Why people need an automated intrusion response system even if they have the IDS?

2. List some possible response actions in the intrusion response process.

3. List several various factors related to the incident.

4. List several various factors related to the IDS.

5. List all the core elements of FAIR.

6. What's difference between Native XML databases and other general databases?

7. Why Native XML databases are most commonly used to store document-centric documents?

8. Give the definition of Native XML databases.

9. List some features of Native XML databases.

10. Briefly describe two somewhat standard languages for updating XML documents.

Reference

[1] Ruud van der Pas. Memory hierarchy in cache-based systems. Sun Microsystems, Inc.

[2] The I^2C-bus specification. Philips semiconductors, 2000.

[3] Sudip Misra, B. John Oommen. New algorithms for maintaining all-pairs shortest paths. IEEE Symposium on Computers and Communications, 2005.

[4] Harry Li. Porting Windows CE operating system to broadband enabled STB devices, IECON 02 [Industrial Electronics Society].

[5] Andrew S Tanenbaum. Modern operating system [M]. Prentice Hall, 2001.

[6] C J Date. An introduction to database systems [M]. Addison Wesley, 2003.

[7] Raghu Ramakrishnan. Database management systems [M]. McGraw-Hill, 2002.

[8] Mark Lutz. Programming python [M]. O'Reilly, 2006.

[9] Christian Huitema. IPv6: The new Internet protocol [M]. Prentice Hall PTR, 1998.

[10] Bradley Mitchell. Network topologies, About Inc. www. about. com.

[11] Tim O'Reilly. What is Web 2. 0 [M]. O'Reilly, 2005.

[12] Douglas E Comer. Internetworking with TCP/IP [M]. Prentice Hall, 2005.

[13] United States Computer emergency readiness team. The National Strategy to Secure Cyberspace, 2003.

[14] Richard Stallman. Can you trust your computer, Free Software Foundation, 2002.

[15] Avi Kak. Classical encryption techniques [M]. Purdue University, 2006.

[16] William Stallings. Cryptography and network security: principles and practice [M]. Prentice Hall, 2003.

[17] Refik Molva. Internet security architecture [J]. Computer Networks and ISDN Systems Journal, 1999.

[18] Oracle Data Mining. Know more, do more, spend less. Oracle, 2005.

[19] Oracle Database Data Mining Option, Oracle, 2006.

[20] Harold Reynolds. An introduction to geographical information systems, 2002.

[21] Michael Haustein. An efficient infrastructure for native transactional XML processing [J]. Elseiver Science, 2007.

[22] Hrri Holma. WCDMA for UMTS radio access for third generation mobile communication [M]. Wiley Technology Publishing, 2000.

[23] Jason Morris. What is VoIP and how does it work [J]. Ezine Articles, 2005.

[24] Jeremy Meyers. A short history of the computer (b. c. -1993a. d.) . http: //www. softlord. com/comp/.

[25] Laura Cohen. A basic guide to the Internet. http: //www. internettutorials. net/internet. html.

[26] Annie Y W Chan. Application of GIS techniques in Hong Kong's population census. 22nd Population Census Conference, March, 2005.

[27] Sharon L Qi. Quality assessment program—South Platte River basin study. ESRI User Conference Proceedings, 1995.

[28] Mu Cheng-po, Huang Hou-kuan, Tian Sheng-feng, Fuzzy cognitive maps for decision support in automatic intrusion response mechanism，北京交通大学学报（英文版），2005（2）.

[29] Benson Yeung. Introduction to firewall. http：//www. tns. com/firewalls. asp.

[30] Baya Pavliashvili. Steps involved in building a data warehouse. Sams, 2002.

[31] Nick Weynand, TradeMark Media President. Taking payments online：The 5 elements of e-commerce trademarkmedia, 2006.

[32] Drs Steven Furnell and Maria Papadaki. Automated intrusion response [J]. Data management, storage & security review, 2005.

[33] K R Castleman. Digital image processing [M]. Prentice Hall and Publishing House of Electronics Industry, 1999.